WITHDRAWN

THE POEMS OF
Richard
LOVELACE

Colonel Richard Lovelace

From the portrait in the Dulwich Gallery

THE POEMS OF Richard LOVELACE

1618–1658

Edited by

C. H. WILKINSON

PR
3542
L2
1930

OXFORD
AT THE CLARENDON PRESS

Oxford University Press, Amen House, London E.C.4

GLASGOW NEW YORK TORONTO MELBOURNE WELLINGTON
BOMBAY CALCUTTA MADRAS KARACHI LAHORE DACCA
CAPE TOWN SALISBURY NAIROBI IBADAN ACCRA
KUALA LUMPUR HONG KONG

First edition 1930
Reprinted lithographically in Great Britain
at the University Press Oxford 1953
from corrected sheets of the first edition
Reprinted lithographically by Latimer Trend & Co. Ltd. Whitstable
1963

THIS edition is based on *The Poems of Richard Lovelace*, published in two volumes in 1925. The reproductions given in those volumes of seventeenth-century musical settings of various songs, of the portraits of Lovelace and Lucasta (with one exception), of the title-pages and engravings in the volumes of 1649 and 1659–60, the notes relating to these and to some other matters both textual and bibliographical, as well as appendices containing the accounts of Lovelace given by John Aubrey and Anthony a Wood and the history and text of the Kentish Petition are omitted here. Some additional notes are printed on p. 344.

A mistake in the two-volume edition, 1925, may be corrected here. On p. lxxxiv it is said that the Hollar engraving of the portrait bust of Lovelace designed by his brother Francis exists in three states. The differences between them are correctly given, but the issue described by Parthey, dated 1660, is in fact the first. The engraving reproduced from the copy then in the possession of Mr. John Drinkwater, of which a print is inserted in the Douce copy of *Lucasta*, 1649, in the Bodleian, probably by Douce himself, is taken from a copper plate of William Richardson's 1795 engraving. All mention of Richardson and of the date has been erased from the copper plate, now in my possession, leaving the words 'In memoriam fratris desideratissimi delin: Fran: Lovelace'. The paper and general appearance of the engraving in the Douce copy suggest an intention to deceive. Whether intended or not, it has done so.

TO record obligations is both a duty and a pleasure. When an editor has the privilege of being able to mention the names of Mr. G. Thorn-Drury, K.C., and of Mr. Percy Simpson, it is also to some extent a guarantee, for with two such names 'in the forehead of the book' any edition must contain matter of value, whatever the shortcomings of the editor. Mr. Simpson has made a number of helpful suggestions, particularly with regard to the text. It is impossible fully to acknowledge the extent of my obligations to Mr. Thorn-Drury. He has lent me his own annotated copy of Lovelace, from which I have borrowed freely; he has patiently answered every question, and there were many, which I have asked him; he has looked through my proofs and saved me from numerous blunders. I have made particular mention only of what seem the more important of his contributions. I should wish to add my gratitude to the late Sir Walter Raleigh, who suggested to me that I should undertake this edition.

C. H. W.

NOTE

The sign † indicates additional notes, pp. 345 ff.

CONTENTS

CONTENTS.

ILLUSTRATIONS

INTRODUCTION

RICHARD LOVELACE

RICHARD LOVELACE, the eldest son of Sir William Lovelace 'of Woollidg in *Kent* Knight' and of his wife Anne (Barne), was born in 1618, possibly at Woolwich, but more probably in Holland. His name has not been found in any church register—the Woolwich register does not begin till 1663—and his mother certainly spent some time in Holland, a fact she herself mentions in her will where she bequeaths to Richard 'my sonne . . . my best suite of diaper, which I made in the Low Countries'.[1] The verses contributed by John Harmar to *Lucasta* also tend to cast doubt on the theory that Lovelace was born in Kent, for, though he refers to the poet's Kentish ancestors—'Cujus honoratos Cantia vidit Avos'—Harmar makes no reference to Lovelace's own connexion with the county.

The Lovelaces were an old Kentish family—a William Lovelace of Bethersden[2] was among the gentlemen concerned in the rising of the 'Commons of Kent' in 1450 under Cade

[1] She also leaves him 'my furniture for a bedde of blacke velvet with cushions, chaires, and carpetts, as the same is wrought in colours by his grandmother the Lady Lovelace, . . . and a pair of fine holland sheets and a black gilded Cabonett which was his father's, and all those goods and implements of household which are standing and remaining in his chief house at Bethersden, and the pictures of his father and myself and his grandfather, and my wedding ring which was his father's'. Provision is made in the will for the younger children. (*Archæologia Cantiana*, x, p. 209.)

[2] '*Bethersden*, written anciently *Beatrixden*, that is, *Beatrix's* Valley.' (Philipott, *Villare Cantianum*, 1659, p. 395.)

Cade—and owned property at Bethersden from 1368 until the middle of the seventeenth century, when Richard Lovelace sold Lovelace Place to Richard Hulse. Philipott relates in picturesque language the history of the place:

Bethersden in the Hundred of *Chart* and *Longbridge*, contains several places in it considerable, the first that summons our Notice is *Bethersden-Lovelace*, which celebrates the Memory of a Family called *Grensted*, now vulgarly styled *Greenstreet*, who were its elder proprietaries, the last of whom was *Henry de Grensted*, a man of eminent Repute, as the Records of this county testifie, in the reign of *Edward* the second, and *Edward* the third, but fell under some Umbrage and Obscurity, when he passed away his Estate here to *Kinet*, in whom the possession was very volatile, for *William Kinet* in the forty first year of *Edward* the third, conveyed it by Sale to *John Lovelace*, who here erected that Structure that for so many Descents hath born the Name of this Family, and was the Seminary or Seedplot from whence a Race of Gentlemen issued forth, who have in Military Affairs atchieved Reputation and Honour, with a prodigal Losse and Expence both of Blood and Life, and by their deep Judgement in the municipal Laws have deserved well of the Common-Wealth; and as by their Extraction they are descended from noble Families, so from hence have sprung those of *Bayford* in *Sedingbourn* and *Kingsdown*, with the right Honourable the Lord *Lovelace* of *Hurley*, and other Gentlemen of that Stem in *Barkeshire*; but alas! this Mansion is now like a Dial when the Sun is gone, that then onely is of use to declare that there hath been a Sun, for not many years since Colonel *Richard Lovelace* eldest son to Sir *William Lovelace* the last of this Name at this place, passed away his right in *Bethersden Lovelace* to Mr. *Richard Hulse* descended from the ancient Family of *Hulse* of *Norbury* and *Astly* in *Cheshire*.[1]

Richard

[1] *Villare Cantianum*, 1659, p. 72. A full account of the Kentish families

Richard Lovelace had four brothers, Thomas, Francis, William, and Dudley Posthumus,[1] and three sisters, Anne, Elizabeth, and Johanna.[2] His father, who had been knighted at Theobald's by James I in 1609, was killed at the siege of Groll in 1627 at the age of forty-four.[3] His will, made on July 15, 1622, was proved on July 23, 1628. The poet's grandfather, also Sir William Lovelace, who was knighted at Dublin by the Earl of Essex in 1599, died two years after his son on Oct. 6, 1629, and was buried on the 12th 'in the South Chappell of the Parish Church of Bethersden in the County of Kent near unto the south wall therein',[4] as

of Lovelace, with genealogies of different branches of the family, is given in the articles by the Rev. A. J. Pearman in vols. x and xx of *Archæologia Cantiana*.

[1] For Thomas and Francis Lovelace see note to p. 2. William was killed at Carmarthen in 1645, probably when serving under the command of Francis. See Richard's poem, p. 86. For Dudley see note to p. 13.

[2] Anne married John Gorsage, Rector of Walkern, Herts.; Elizabeth, Daniel Hayne of Kintbury Eaton, Berks.; and Johanna, Robert Caesar, son of Sir Julius Caesar. See p. 179.

[3] Eight days before the surrender of the town to the Prince of Orange, after the first summons to capitulate. 'Cela estant rapporte à Dulquen, respondit hardiment, comme s'il eust este beaucoup esloigne du peril, qu'il ne vouloit entendre à aucune composition. C'est pourquoy, sur l'heure de midy, du dix-huictiesme du mois d'Aoust, ayant mis le feu aux mines que les Anglois auoient faites, les éuenta, & toutefois les assiegeans ne tindrẽt les choses qui estoient offertes, par des Herauts enuoyez, furent par trois diuerses fois chassez, par vn inconuenient qui leur arriua, de ce que le passage du dessus des vignes, n'estoit pas encores assez parfaict: en ce combat Guillaume de Louelac Capitaine des Anglois doüe de grand courage, fut tue d'vn coup de mousquet.' (*Histoire Generale de la Gverre de Flandre*, Gabriel Chappvys, ed. 1633, ii, p. 674.) Contrast the Latin verses on p. 14, where it is said that he was blown up.

[4] Quoted in *Archæologia Cantiana*. In his will he confirms the indenture he had already made of his 'cattell, plate, utensils, money, and money's worth whatsoever' to Richard, Thomas, and William Lovelace, with the addition that a moiety of the property so conveyed should belong to Elizabeth Lovelace on her attaining the age of eighteen.

as he had desired. The elder Sir William Lovelace owned a considerable amount of property at Bethersden, Halden, Woolwich—which his wife Elizabeth, daughter of Sir Edward Aucher of Bishopsbourne, brought to him—Canterbury—where 'Grey Friars', in which he used to live, is still standing in part—and other places. Most of this property was sold by his grandson when he fell on evil days towards the end of his life.[1]

We have no record of any of the events of the poet's boyhood before he went to school. His mother had been granted the wardship of her son Richard, and in 1629 she petitioned the King for a nomination to Sutton's Foundation at Charterhouse on behalf of one of her sons.[2] The following document, a copy of the original, is preserved in the British Museum (Eg. 2553, f. 50 b).

ffrom his Matie to ye Couns^el^ of Suttons Hospitall.

Whereas wee are given to understand that Sr William Lovelace K^t^ after hee had served about thirty yeares in ye warres and was slayne at ye last Seige of Grolle and his fortune most depending upon ye warre left his Lady ritch only in great store of Children And shee most humbly beseeching us, to bestow one of the places in Suttons Hospitall upon one of hir Sonnes. Wee are well pleased to grant hir request. Wherefore our Royall pleasure is y^t^ the Lord Arch Bishopp of Canterbury and other ye Governors of ye said Hospitall doe take

[1] The question of the possessions of Richard Lovelace is fully treated of by Mr. A. E. Waite in his article on Lovelace in *The Gentleman's Magazine*, November, 1884. He concludes that the poet was a country gentleman possessed of a sufficient, but moderate competence.

[2] Lady Lovelace married, on Jan. 20, 1630, a second husband, Jonathan Brown or Browne of London, Doctor of Laws, whom with her brother Miles Barne, M.A., she constitutes trustee of Richard Lovelace in her will. Browne died in 1644. See *Athenae Oxonienses*, 1691, vol. i, p. 868.

take order that Thomas Lovelace hir sonne may bee admitted into y[e] said house in our prime place at y[e] next eleccon. Given under our hand this day In ye fourth year of our raigne etc.

Mr. A. E. Waite in his memoir on Lovelace in *The Gentleman's Magazine*, November, 1884, concluded that this was a mistake for Richard Lovelace. Charterhouse had not been founded 20 years and so the rules would probably be in full force. One of these, signed by Charles I as late as 1627, directs the schoolmaster to 'admit none under the age of ten years and above fourteen, else he should answer to the contrary'. This, Mr. Waite points out, supports his theory, as in 1629 Richard Lovelace would be eleven while his brother Thomas would not be more than six years old. It may also be noticed that on the corner of the King's order is written, 'for one of S[r] William Lovelace sonnes', and it seems probable that the order was intended for Richard. It is certain, however, that he did not profit by it as his name is not in the list of Foundation Scholars. The first admission register begins in 1680, though it is probable that there was an earlier one which has since been lost. Before that date the record of Scholars is to be found in the 'Assembly Books' and 'Committee Books' of the Governors—usually it consists of lists of Scholars as nominated by the Governors for admission—and lists of Scholars 'elected out' either to the University or as apprentices. The surname of Lovelace does not occur at all, though these 'Committee Books' are very full, there being more than 600 names for the years 1614–80. There is, further, no mention of Lovelace either receiving an Exhibition, going to Oxford without one, or leaving the University while still an Exhibitioner. From this

this it seems certain that he was not on Sutton's Foundation at Charterhouse, but that he must have been a 'Boarder'.[1] Such boys were usually the sons of people in a higher social position than the parents of the scholars, and it is probable that Lovelace would have been at Charterhouse on this footing. It is possible that though Lady Lovelace found herself 'ritch only in great store of Children' at the time she made her request, the death of her father-in-law in the same year and Richard's inheritance of the property placed them beyond the need of any assistance.

The Headmaster of Charterhouse during Lovelace's time at school was Robert Brooke, a staunch Royalist who was removed from his post by Parliament in 1643. No record of the poet's school-days is known to exist, but it may be noted that he must have been nearly three years at Charterhouse with Richard Crashaw. On leaving school Lovelace went to Oxford, becoming a Gentleman Commoner at Gloucester Hall, now Worcester College and formerly Gloucester College, the Benedictine settlement in Oxford from the thirteenth century until the dissolution of the monasteries. The College possesses no record of him to-day, but it may be presumed that he was sent to Gloucester Hall by his stepfather, Dr. Jonathan Browne, a Prebendary of Westminster, Minister of St. Faiths in London ('from which he was sequestred by the Presbyterians in the time of the rebellion',

[1] It was not at all unusual for Royal nominees to be refused as the number was restricted to two at each election, i.e. in general one a year, and the Royal promises and warrants were practically unrestricted, most of the boys who received them becoming too old before their turn arrived. Several of the Scholars, entered in the Committee Books, even when receiving Royal Warrants, were never admitted. I am indebted to Mr. Bower Marsh for the above information.

rebellion ', Wood), Rector of Hertingfordbury and later Dean of Hereford, who was himself a member of the Hall, and presented £5 towards the restoration of the Chapel when he took his Doctor's degree in 1630, making a second gift of the same amount in the same year.[1]

The entry of Lovelace's matriculation is preserved among the University Archives for the year 1634:

Jun: 27° Richũs Louelace: Kant: fil: j^us^ Gul: Louelace de Woolwich in Cõm p'd Arm: an: nat—16.

His signature in the Book of Subscriptions to the articles of Religion, an oath then required of every undergraduate, is here reproduced.

Richard Lovelace.

Another specimen of his signature is to be found on the document containing his petition to be released from the Gatehouse in 1642. There is a third example in the British Museum on a document connected with the sale of land at Halden[2] and another signature at Cambridge. Mr. W. C. Hazlitt stated that his name, with the date March 5, 1630, is written in a small school book, Clenardus' *Institutiones Graecae Linguae*, 1626.

When he went to Oxford Lovelace was 'accounted the most amiable and beautiful person that ever eye beheld', and the poet, whom Wood described as wearing 'Cloth of gold and silver' when he was in his glory, was no doubt one of the fashionable young gentlemen to whom the same writer referred when, comparing the condition of Gloucester Hall

[1] MS. recording degrees, gifts, etc., now in the Library of Worcester College.

[2] This signature is reproduced in *Archæologia Cantiana*, vol. xxiii, p. 337.

Hall in 1678 with its former prosperity, he said, 'I have been credibly enformed that before the warr, in Degory Whear's time, (there) hath been an hundred students (and some being persons of qualitie, 10 or 12 went in their doublets of cloth of silver and gold) : but since the King's restauration to this yeare, I never knew above 14 in number.'[1]

During his first year at the University he wrote a comedy called *The Scholar* or *The Schollars.* This play, which may have first been acted by the undergraduates of Gloucester Hall,[2] was later 'presented at the White-Fryers' and 'acted with applause'. It was never printed, and only the Prologue and Epilogue, written for its presentation in London, were included in *Lucasta.*

Lovelace took his degree in his second or at the beginning of his third year. 'In 1636,' writes Wood, 'when the King and Queen were for some days entertained at *Oxon*, he was, at the request of a great Lady belonging to the Queen, made to the Archb of *Cant.* then Chancellor of the University, actually created, among other persons of quality, Master of Arts, tho but of about two years standing.' Wood in the first volume of *Athenae Oxonienses*[3] gives a list of the 'Creation in several faculties' which it was his Majesty's pleasure

[1] A. Clark, *The Life and Times of Anthony Wood* (Oxford Historical Society), 1892, vol. ii, p. 398.

[2] In his Autobiography Wood, recording the death in 1660 of John Glendall, a Fellow of Brasenose who 'had been a witty *Terrae filius* of the University in 1655', states: 'He was a great Mimick, and acted well in several Playes, which the Scholars before acted by stealth, either in the Stone house behind and Southward from Pembroke Coll. or in Kettle hall, or at Holywell Mill, or in the Refectory at Glocester hall.' (Hearne's *Thomæ Caii . . . Vindiciæ Antiquitatis Academiæ Oxoniensis* . . . 1730. ii, p. 533.) The period indicated by 'before' is not clear, but was presumably in Commonwealth times.

[3] pp. 386–9, ed. 1691.

pleasure there should be, the twelfth in the list of the Masters of Arts being '*Rich. Lovelace* a Gentleman Commoner of *Gloc.* Hall. . . . Afterwards eminent for his valour and poetry, as I shall tell you either in the next Vol. or elsewhere.' Wood does not give the complete list, but the full account of the King's visit and reception by the University, and the list of all those who were given degrees may be found in the University Archives for 1636. (Register R. 24.)

Lovelace was given his Honorary Degree on Aug. 31, 1636. His name, 'Rich. Lovelas Aul. Glos.', is given in the Archives in the list of forty-five 'Magistri in artibus tempore Adventus Regis'. Many of his companions were men of importance. The first was 'Rupertus Princeps Palatinus' the King's nephew. Others were the Duke of Lennox, afterwards Duke of Richmond, the Earl of Hertford, later Duke of Somerset, the Earl of Essex, 'who in the year 1605 had been created M. of A. was now actually created again', the Earl of Berkshire, the Earl of Elgin, George Lord Digby, and William Lord Craven. In the following year Lovelace was incorporated at Cambridge. His entry in the Book of Subscriptions is '4 Oct 1637 Richardus Lovelace Aul: Gloucestrensis Oxon. Art. mag.' It seems likely that he stayed a few months in Cambridge, at any rate long enough to make friends with a group of Cambridge men then in residence, who twelve years later contributed commendatory verses to *Lucasta*, Norreys Jephson, Villiers Harington, and Andrew Marvell. Thomas Hammersley and John Needler wrote some lines for *Lucasta* and were Cambridge men, but Lovelace presumably met them when they were at Gray's Inn, to which they were admitted in 1629 and 1634 respectively. Wood does not mention this stay at Cambridge, but, as will be seen

later

later, his account of Lovelace is neither exhaustive nor altogether reliable. He says that after leaving the University [Oxford] Lovelace 'retired in great splendour' to the Court, where, owing to his 'innate modesty, virtue and courtly deportment',[1] he was 'much admired and adored by the female sex', while he was endeared to his own by the discovery of his 'ingenuity and generous soul'.

At Court he was 'taken into the favour of *George*, Lord Goring, afterwards Earl of Norwich, was by him adopted a Soldier, and sent in the quality of Ensign in the *Scotch* Expedition *an.* 1639'. Among the names of the officers under the Earl of Northumberland in 1640, 'Taken according to the Muster Roll after the Armies Retreat into Yorkshire', Richard Lovellis appears as senior Ensign in George Goring's regiment.[2] He must soon have been promoted, as Wood says he was 'commissionated a Captain in the same Regiment' in the second expedition.

The first of these inglorious expeditions was ended by the treaty of June 18, 1639, the second by the cessation of arms agreed on at Ripon on Oct. 26, 1640, though it was long before the armies were disbanded.[3]

During

[1] Thomas Jordan in *Wit in a Wildernesse of Promiscuous Poesie*, which is undated, but printed after 1649, wrote 'An Apologie for Danceing, Dedicate to all the active Proficients, but more peculiarly unto Mr. R. L.'† The lines, which are too long to quote, may be addressed to Lovelace, though it seems probable that Jordan would have called him 'Colonel'. Howell, however, calls him 'Mr.' in 1660. See p. 225.

[2] See *The Army Lists of the Roundheads and Cavaliers Containing the Names of the Officers in the Royal and Parliamentary Armies of 1642.* Edited by Edward Peacock, 2nd ed., 1874.

Wood has mixed the two Gorings. It was the son of the Earl of Norwich in whose regiment Lovelace served and to whom he addressed his poem, though the elder Goring raised a body of horse for this expedition.

[3] See Clarendon's *History of the Rebellion*, ii. 80–93, 107–30.

During the second expedition Lovelace 'wrot a Tragedy called *The Soldier*, but never acted, because the stage was soon after suppress'd'.[1] The spirited drinking song *To Generall Goring, after the pacification of Berwicke*, is the only poem by Lovelace which contains a direct reference to the Scottish expeditions. There are two copies of verses, however, which he wrote before going to the North, one prefixed to Anthony Hodges' translation of *The Loves of Clitophon and Levcippe*, the other contributed to *Musarum Oxoniensium Charisteria*, both belonging to the year 1638. The fact that Lovelace should, at the age of twenty, write commendatory verses, one set of which was given the place of honour and the other included after *Charisteria* had already been published,[2] shows that he must even at that age have been known as a 'fair pretender to the Title of Poet'.

On the Scottish expeditions Lovelace would have had the company of Suckling, who is supposed to have addressed him in the first line of his *Ballade Upon a Wedding*, 'I tell thee *Dick* where I have been'. The ballad was written for the occasion of the marriage of a member of Lovelace's family if *An Antidote against Melancholy: Made up in Pills*... 1661, which contains 'Suckling's Ballad on the Ld. L. Wedding', and Harleian MS. 6917, which describes it as 'Upon the Marriage of the Lord Lovelace', are correct. As this wedding took place in London in July, 1638, at a time when Suckling was absent from Court in temporary disgrace, Lovelace must have met him in 1636 or 1637. Some critics, however, state that the 'Ballade' was written for the marriage of Roger Boyle, Lord Broghill, and Lady Margaret Howard in 1641. It is far more probable that it was not written for any wedding and

[1] September 2, 1642.

[2] See note to p. 29.

and that its connexion with Richard Lovelace is merely based on an inaccurate guess. *Wits Recreations* has a woodcut which represents 'two Countrey-men', not Suckling and Lovelace, 'Dick' being merely a rustic, just as Robert Baron, a faithful imitator of many poets, in his *Ballade Vpon the Wedding* makes one of his 'honest Swaines' address the other, 'I tell the *Jack* as I sought out . . .'[1]

After his return from the North Lovelace retired to Kent, and a gentleman of his position would become a Justice of the Peace in the ordinary course of events. It was, no doubt, in the exercise of his duties that he was present in the Session House at Maidstone, where he tore in pieces a disloyal petition in the presence of its makers shortly before he delivered the Kentish Petition to the House of Commons in 1642.

Wood describes the latter event briefly: . . . 'he was made choice of by the whole body of the County of *Kent* at an Assize, to deliver the *Kentish Petition* to the H. of Commons, for the restoring the King to his Rights and for setling the Government, etc. For which piece of service he was committed to the *Gatehouse* at *Westminster*, where he made that celebrated song called *Stone walls do not a prison make*,[2] *etc.* After

[1] *Pocula Castalia*, 1650, p. 66. Compare also 'A Dialogue betwixt TOM and DICK: the former a Country-man, the other a Citizen.' (*Rump Songs*, ed. 1662, ii, p. 189.)

[2] This is not the only well-known poem which has come from the prison at Westminster, if it is true that the lines attributed to Sir Walter Raleigh,

> Even such is *time* that takes on trust
> Our *youth*, our *Joyes*, our all we have,
> And payes us but with *Age* and *dust*, . . .

were really written by him on Oct. 28, 1618, and found in his Bible in the Gatehouse. (*Reliquiæ Wottonianæ*, 1651, p. 538.) If they were so found, Raleigh probably wrote down and added two lines to the last stanza of an earlier poem of his own, 'Nature that wash'd her hands in milk', which was

After 3 or 4 months prisonment, he had his liberty upon bayle of 40000 *l* not to stir out of the Lines of Communication, without a pass from the Speaker.'

Clarendon gives a fuller account:

About the same time, at the general assizes in Kent the justices of the peace and principal gentlemen of that county prepared a petition to be presented to the two Houses, with a desire 'that the militia might not be otherwise exercised in that county than the known law permitted, and that the Book of Common Prayer established by law might be observed.' This petition was communicated by many to their friends, and copies thereof sent abroad, before the subscription was ready; whereupon the House of Peers took notice of it as tending to some commotion in Kent; and in the debate the earl of Bristol taking note that he had seen a copy of it, and had had some conference about it with Judge Mallet, who was then judge of assize in Kent, and newly returned out of his circuit, both the earl and judge, for having but seen the petition, were presently committed to the Tower;[1] and a declaration published that 'none should presume to deliver that or the like petition to either House'. Notwithstanding which, some gentlemen of Kent, with a great number of the substantial inhabitants of that county, came to the city; which upon the alarum was put in arms, strong guards placed at London Bridge, where the petitioners were disarmed, and only some few suffered to passwith their petition to Westminster, the rest forced to return to their country [*sic*]. And upon the delivery thereof (though the same was very modest, and in a more dutiful dialect than most petitions delivered to them) to the House of Commons, the bringers of the petition were sharply reprehended, two or three of them committed to several prisons, the principal gentlemen of the country who

first printed in full by A. H. Bullen from *Harl. MS.* 6917. (*Speculum Amantis*, ed. 1902, pp. 76–7.)

[1] See Clarendon's *History*, v. 426.

who had subscribed and advised it sent for as delinquents, and charges and articles of impeachment drawn up against them; and a declaration published, 'that whosoever should henceforth advise or contrive the like petitions should be proceeded against as enemies to the commonwealth'. So unlike and different were their tempers, and reception of those modest addresses which were for duty and obedience to the laws established, and those which pressed and brought on alterations and innovations.[1]

Clarendon shows how members of the Long Parliament encouraged petitions so long as they were favourable to themselves, 'most counties in England, or rather, the factious and seditious persons in most counties, having been induced to frame and subscribe petitions to the Parliament against the established government of the Church, with other clauses scandalous to the government of the State too';[2] while they strongly discouraged any others, 'receiving and cherishing all mutinous and seditious petitions, and discountenancing such as besought the continuance and vindication of the so long celebrated and happy government in Church and State; the prime leaders of that faction not blushing in public debates in the House to aver, "that no man ought to petition for the government established by law, because he had already his wish; but they that desired an alteration could not otherwise have their desires known, and therefore were to be countenanced"'.[3] Consequently Lovelace was not favourably received when he arrived with the same petition as that 'contrived by Sir Edward Dering and others' only the month before, which had already been 'burnt by order of both

[1] *History of the Rebellion*, v. 52 ed. Macray, 1888, ii. 28–89.
[2] *Ibid.* iii. 169. [3] *Ibid.* iv. 340.

both Houses by the Hands of the Common Hangman' and had for some weeks occupied the attention of their Committees.

Lovelace and Sir William Boteler or Butler presented the Kentish Petition on April 30, 1642.† Butler had just returned from York, where the King was engaged with the question of the garrison and magazine at Hull and 'Sir John Hotham's Treasonable insolencie', and 'by the earnest solicitation of the Gentry of *Kent*, ingaged to joyne with them in presenting the most honest and famous Petition of theirs to the House of Commons'.[1] A large meeting was to assemble at Blackheath at 9 o'clock on the 29th to accompany the petition to Parliament, a fact of which the Commons acquainted the Lords on the 28th.

The entry in the *Lords Journals* runs:

28th April. A Message was brought from the House of Commons, by *Oliver Cromwell*, Esquire and others:

To desire that their Lordships would please to sit a while, because they shall have some important Business concerning *Kent* to impart to their Lordships.

The Answer returned to this Message was:

That their Lordships will sit a while, as desired.

A message was brought from the House of Commons, by Sir *Henry Vane*, Junior, and others:

To desire a Conference, by a Committee of both Houses, presently, if it may stand with their Lordships Conveniency, touching some Informations they have received concerning some Proceedings in the *Kentish* Petition, much importing the Safety of the Kingdom.

The Answer returned to this Message was:

That their Lordships will give a Conference presently, in the Painted Chamber.

Then this House was adjourned during Pleasure, and the Lords

[1] Bruno Ryves, *Angliae Ruina, or Englands Ruine*, 1647, p. 7.

Lords went to the Conference; which being ended, the House was resumed.

The Lord Keeper reported the Effect of this Conference: 'That the House of Commons have received Information of a Meeting to be To-morrow at *Blackeheath*, whither divers People intend to come in Numbers, with their rejected Petition of *Kente*; and there are Reports given out that they threaten to shed Blood. The House of Commons, taking this into Consideration, for preventing of Mischief as may happen, desires their Lordships to join with them, that Directions from both Houses may be given to those that have charge of the Militia of *London*, that none be suffered to come in Numbers into the City of *London* To-morrow, with Arms or Weapons.'[1]

ORDERED, That this House agrees with the House of Commons in the Matter of this last Conference.

Two days earlier, when presenting to the Lords the articles of impeachment by the Commons against Dering,[2] the Lord Keeper mentioned that Dering 'sticks not to affirm, that he can have Forty Thousand Persons to attend the Petition, proclaims a Meeting at *Blackheath* (a fatal and ominous Place for Actions of this Nature); and all this under Colour of a Petition, being in Truth a Challenge, an Objurgation, a Scandal upon the Parliament, and purporting nothing

[1] The same facts may be gathered from the *Commons Journals* (pp. 545–6) which add that Pym and Holles managed the conference for the Commons. 'And to desire, that an Order of both Houses may be sent to Serjeant-major Skippon, and the Committee for the Militia of London, requiring them to have an Eye, and a Care, to prevent all Inconveniences that may ensue, by the tumultuous and disorderly gathering together of any Multitudes, to the Disturbance of the publick Peace.'

[2] Resolved on April 18th, voted on 19th and sent to the Lords on the 21st. On the 21st the Lords desired a conference concerning the Kentish Petition. 'That it is yet, by the malignant and ill-affected Party, with great, though secret Industry, carried on; and not only in that County, but in some others of this Kingdom: . . . ' (p. 536.)

nothing else but a desperate Design, to put not only *Kent*, but for aught is known, all Christendom into Combustion; carrying the Sails full swoln with Spight, Arrogancy, and Sedition; . . .'

A contemporary pamphlet of four leaves purports to describe the meeting at Blackheath. The full title is *Strange Newes from Kent. Concerning The Passages of the Kentish men which came to Westminster*, *April 29. about some great and weighty Affairs*, *concerning their own County*, *and the whole Kingdome. With many other Matters of great Note, and high Consequence, which this following Treatise makes mention of. Also the Names of two Kentish Men, who were committed*, April *30. 1642. Likewise the Names of the Committee, who are appointed for the Irish affairs, and the places where they live. Whereunto is annexed more sad News from* Hul, *concerning a great Disturbance which hapned there*, April *28. MDCXLII. Printed for* Richard Cooper, *1642.*

The
Names of two of the Kentish Petitioners
who were committed to custody, *April* 30.
Sir *William Lovelace*, and Captain
Butler.

It was observed by divers at the Royall Exchange, that as Captain *Butler* and the rest passed by, his horse stumbled in a very fair plain place, so that he fell over his horse neck, And divers of the spectators by, one of them said to the rest, take notice of this man, this is an omnious thing; mark what will betide him.

And on the 29. of Aprell. 1642. a Cording to ther apointment thay Came from Blakeheath a bout the number of 14 score marching 2 in a ranke and when thay came in the Boro the Chane was dran our whart the Bredg and Captene

Captene Bunch. with his Cumpnie, at the Bredg fot and demanded of them ther intent, and the 2 foremast told them that thay came to delivre ther petsiou to the Parlemeut and there petsione was red and Captene Bunch asked them why thay came armed and thay told him thay had no harmes but the armes of Gentlmen and deliured there Sordes there.[1] . . .

Strange News from Black-Heath.

Vpon the 29 of April 1642. two men of great estimation in the County of Kent, about 5 of the clock in themorning met at the said place, one of them by name Mr. *Samuel Gray*; the other Mr. *Nicholas Robinson*: And falling into Discourse of the Affairs of the said County of KENT, amongst other passages, they spake of some great Mutituds that were to meet at the said Black-Heath in the County of Kent, on that present day about 9 of the clock. But to what intent this meeting should be, is now brought to light.[2]

They

[1] The difference in spelling between this part of the pamphlet and the remainder is curious. It would seem to have been set up by a different compositor and it is interesting to notice, as Mr. C. T. Onions has pointed out to me, that two words at least show by the spelling traces of the East Anglian dialect which has features in common with Kent; 'Bredg' for 'Bridg(e)'—a pronunciation still common in Suffolk—and 'our whart'= 'overthwart'. The compositor must himself have been a Kentishman or have set up from dictation the pronunciation of a native of that county. Spellings like 'petsiou' and 'petsione' seem to be attempts to cope with an unfamiliar word. Mr. Waite first drew attention to the pamphlet.

[2] This part of the pamphlet is clearly borrowed from another, of which there is a copy in the British Museum [E. 144 (13)]: *Newes from Black-Heath Concerning The meeting of the Kentish men upon the nine and twentieth of Aprill, about some great and weighty Affairs, now in Agitation. With many other Passages worthy of Note and Observation. . . . London: Printed for Henrie Andrews.* 1642.

Newes from Black-Heath.

Upon *Munday* last, being the 18. day of *April*, 1642. two men of great estimation, in the County of *Kent*, one of them by Name, Mr. *Samuel Gray*; the other M. *Nicholas Robinson*: meeting at *Black-Heath*, falling into Discourse of the affairs of the said County of KENT, amongst other passages, they spake of some great Multitudes that were to meet at the

They had divers others such like consultationss concerning some Particular matters of high consepuence. in the said petition. And concerning a speedy remedy, that might be taken, for the further reliefe of our distressed brethren in Ireland, and for all other such like necessities, as may be for the good and benefit of the whole Kingdom.

According to a communication from Secretary Nicholas to Sir Thomas Roe, Parliament avoided receiving the petition on the 29th by rising.

Also the Petition of Kent was on the 29th past brought to London by about 500 gentlemen of that county, as we hear, but the House, having showed former dislike against it, rose; and so they were frustrate till the following day, when, having delivered it, they returned to their homes, leaving Sir William Boteler and Captain Lovelace behind, whom the House restrained.[1]

The actual proceedings in the House itself when Lovelace and Boteler arrived with the petition may be gathered from the entries in the *Commons Journals.*

Sabbati, ultimo Aprilis, 1642.

The House being informed, That divers Gentlemen of the County of *Kent* were at the Door, that desired to present a Petition to the House;

They were called in; presented their Petition;

And then withdrew.

And their Petition was read, and appeared to be that the same

said *Black-Heath* in the County of *Kent*, on the 29. Day of *April*, about 9. of the clock in the morning, next ensuing, about 9 of the clock at the furthest.

But to what intent this meeting should be is not as yet known. It was supposed by them, concerning a Petition of theirs, which is to be accompanied by them to the honourable House of Parliament, there to be delivered. . . . (Sig. A2.)

[1] *Calendar of State Papers* (*Domestic*), Charles I, 1641–3, p. 316.

same that was formerly burnt by order of both Houses by the Hands of the Common Hangman.

Captain *Leigh* reports, That being at the Quarter Sessions held at *Maidston*, he observed certain Passages, which he delivered in Writing.

Captain *Lovelace*, who preferred the Petition, was called in: And Mr Speaker was commanded to ask him, From whose Hand he had this Petition; and who gave him Warrant to present it.

'Mr *Geo Chute*[1] delivered him the Petition the next day after the Assizes.'——

'The Gentlemen, that were assembled at *Black-heath*, commanded him to deliver it'——

Whether he knew that the like was burnt by Order of this House; and that some Gentlemen were here questioned for the Business.

'He understood a general Rumour, That some Gentlemen were questioned.'——

'He had heard a Fortnight since, that the like Petition was burnt by the Hand of the Common Hangman.'——

'He knew nothing of the Bundle of Printed Petitions.'——

He likewise said, 'That there was a Petition at the Quarter Sessions, disavowed by all the Justices there, which he tore.'

Sir *Wm Boteler* was likewise called in; asked, When he was at *Yorke*.

Answered, 'On *Wednesday* last was Sevennight he came from *Yorke*, and came to his House in *London*'——

'He heard of a Petition, that was never delivered'——

'He never heard of any Censure of the Parliament.'——

'He heard that a Paper was burnt for being irregularly burnt'—— (? presented)

'He has heard that the Petition that went under the Name of the *Kentish* Petition, was burnt by the Hands of the Common Hangman.'

'He

[1] Dudley Lovelace was later an officer under George Chute. See note to p. 13.

'He never heard of any Order of either, of both, the Houses concerning * *'

'He was at *Hull* on *Thursday* or *Friday* was a Seven-night: As he came from *Yorke*, he took *Hull* in the Way. He has heard, That Sir *Roger Twisden* was questioned for the like Petition.'

'He was yesterday at *Blackheath*.'

Resolved, upon * * That Captain *Lovelace* shall be presently committed Prisoner to the *Gatehouse*.

Resolved, upon the Question, That Sir *Wm Boteler*, shall be presently committed Prisoner to the *Fleet*.

Ordered, That the Serjeant shall apprehend them, and carry them in safe Custody, and deliver them as Prisoners to the several Prisons aforesaid.

. . . .

The Serjeant was commanded to require the Gentlemen that preferred the *Kentish* Petition, to attend, till the House came down from the Conference.

. . . .

The Gentlemen of *Kent* that presented the Petition, were called in: And Mr Speaker, by the Command of the House, told them, 'That the House has considered of the Petition that you presented. And they know you cannot be ignorant, what Opinion both Houses have formerly expressed of the same Petition: Yet, considering that you are young Gentlemen, misled by the Sollicitation of some not affected to the Peace of the Kingdom; and that, however they intend to proceed against the chief Agents and prime Actors in this Business; yet they are willing, that you should be dismissed; hoping that you may hereafter prove good Members of the Commonwealth.'

The *Lords Journals* continue on the same day:

A message was brought from the House of Commons, by Sir *John Evelyn*, Knight, and others:

To inform their Lordships, that, notwithstanding the Dislike

Dislike both Houses took to the Petition of *Kent*, yet this day some have presumed to exhibit that Petition to the House of Commons, for which the House of Commons have committed Sir *William Butler* to *The Fleet*, and Captain *Lovelace* to *The Gatehouse*; and the House of Commons desires their Lordships, that the former select Committee for the Petition of *Kent* may be appointed to meet, and receive further Information herein, and examine the said Sir *William Butler* and Captain *Lovelace*, and such Witnesses as shall be produced, concerning that Business. . . .

ORDERED, That this House agrees with the House of Commons, for the Examination of Sir *William Butler* and Captain *Lovelace* as they have desired.

Sir Symons D'Ewes in his MS. Diary, Saturday, April 30, gives another account of the two Petitioners being sent to prison, as well as a fuller history of the 'certain Passages' at the Quarter Sessions at Maidstone, and the petition which Lovelace acknowledged he tore. (Harl. MS. 163, fo. 99.)

Notice being given that divers of the Kentish gentlemen were at the doore with their petition although we knewe it to bee the same for which Sr Edward Deering had been questioned yet wee admitted them in one Captaine Louelace delivered it and they being withdrawne it was read after which there ensued much debate what answer should bee given them during the debate one Captaine Lee a member of the howse and a Justice of peace for Kent showed that at the late quarter Sessions at Maidstone halfe of the whole bench of Justices there had openly disclaimed the former Kentish petition contrived by Sr Edward Deering and others and had prepared another petition for the Parliament the said Captaine Louelace and some others came into the said place and after the said Justices and all the rest of the company who were mett there excepting but one man had given their [mark for votes] for the disclaiming of the said former petition, and

and in a furious manner cried Noe Noe Noe and then with great contempt of the Court clapped on their hatts and said they heard that there was a new petition intended to be preferred to the Parliament of which they had a copy and found many falsities therein and so lifting it over his head rent it in peeces and said they were ashamed of it and committed also diuers others insolencyes there which the said Captaine Lee read out of a paper and then delivered it to the Clarke. After divers had spoken the said Captaine Louelace was called in and the Speaker asked him diuers questions and particularly touching the said former Kentish petition and his carriage at the late Sessions in both which hee did acknowledge enough against himselfe. then was one Sr William Boteler called in being a gentleman pensioner to his Mat:ie and lately come from Yorke who was supposed to haue gone to blacke heath and to have encouraged the said Kentish men to the delivery of the said petition who was likewise examined and did confes his late coming from Yorke that hee had been at Hull on friday last soe hee being withdrawn it was resolved upon the Question first that Captaine Louelace should bee sent to the Gatehowse and next that Sr William Butler should be sent prisoner to the Fleete wch was done accordinglie.

The *Commons Journals* continue:

Die Mercurii, 4° *Maii*, 1642.

Ordered, that Mr *Whittlock*, Mr *Prideaux*, Mr *Crue*, and Mr *Nichollas*, do prepare a Charge, with all Expedition, against Mr *Lovelace* and Sir *Wm Butler*; and that they be added to the former Committee.

Die Jovis, 12° *Maii*, 1642.

The humble Petition of Sir *Wm Boteler* Knight, a Prisoner in the *Fleete*, upon Order of this House, was this Day read.

And the Question being put for his Bail;

It passed with the Negative.

Ordered

Ordered, that the Charge against Mr *Lovelace* and Sir *Wm Boteler*, Prisoners in the *Fleete* and the *Gatehouse*, be brought in on *Monday* Morning next: And that Mr *Peard* do take particular Care of these Charges.

Die Veneris, 17° *Junii*, 1642.

The humble Petition of Sir *William Boteler*, Prisoner in the *Fleete*, desiring that he may be at Liberty upon Bail, was this Day read: And it is

Resolved, upon the Question, That Sir *Wm Boteler*, be forthwith bailed, upon the Security of Sir *Jo. Mounson*, and Sir *Peter Richaut*, the Principal in the Sum of Ten thousand Pounds, the Security, in Five thousand Pounds apiece.[1]

Ordered, That the Impeachment against Sir *Wm Boteler* be brought on *Monday* Morning.

. . . .

The humble petition of *Richard Lovelace* Esquire, a Prisoner in the *Gatehouse*, by a former Order of this House, was this Day read: And

It is *Ordered*, upon the Question, That he be forthwith bailed, upon good Security.

Die Sabbati, 18° *Junii*, 1642.

Resolved, &c. That this House doth approve of M^r^ *Jo. Bedle*, to be Bail for Sir *Wm. Boteler*, instead of Sir *Peter Riccautt*.

Die Martis, 21° *Junii*, 1642.

Resolved, &c. That this House doth approve of *William Clarke*, Esquire, of *Rootham* in *Kent*, and *Tho. Flood*[2] Esquire of *Otton* in *Kent*, to be bail for Captain *Lovelace*; Ten thousand

[1] The same sum was fixed in the case of Sir Roger Twisden and Richard Spencer, two of those who originally contrived the Kentish Petition at Maidstone. (*Commons Journals*, vol. ii, p. 520.)

[2] Thomas Flood or Fludd was of Gore Court in Otham; William Clarke, afterwards knighted, was of Ford in Wrotham, and fell in the skirmish at Cropredy Bridge. See *Archæologia Cantiana*, vol. xx.

thousand Pounds the Principal; Five thousand Pounds apiece the Sureties.

Sir Symons D'Ewes also refers to these events.[1] He records under June 17 that, 'Mr Bainton [M P for Devizes] deliuered in the petition of Captaine Lovelace in wch hee desir'd to be bailed having formerlie deliuered in the dangerous Kentish petition, wch saied petition being full of submission hee was bailed accordinglie without anie debate.' He records on the same day (fo. 187 b), 'Mr Bainton deliuered in the names of the baile offered by Captaine Louelace in wch the first was allowed, on Sr Denner Strut (of Little Worley Hall in Essex Esquire created March 5. 1641·2) the latter being latelie created a baronet, was disallowed because none in the house knew him.' On June 21 he writes, '3 of the clocke in the afternoon. . . . Upon Mr Bainton's motion Captaine Lovelace baile accepted.'

These extracts from the *Commons Journals* dispose of the difficulty of believing the enormous figure, £40,000, which Wood states to have been Lovelace's bail. Lovelace and Butler were to be released on finding security for £40,000 between them. Whether either of them paid, or was ever called on to pay anything, is another question. As Lovelace's income, according to Aubrey and Wood, was about £500 a year mostly derived from land, he probably did not. There is one other brief account of the presentation of the Kentish Petition which may be quoted from the *Verney Papers*.[2]

Satterday,

[1] Harl. MS. 163, fo. 183 b. Printed in *Notes and Queries* by Mr. John Eglington Bailey in 1876. D'Ewes records that Edmund Waller, 'one of those who came vpp wth the Kentish petition wch Captaine Lovelace deliuered in', presented Butler's petition to the House.

[2] Camden Society, 1845 (R. Ac. 8113/31), p. 175.

Satterday, 30th Aprill, 1642.
The Kentish Petition.

Sir Edward Deering, and some other magistrates of Kent, procured a petition to be signed in which the validity of the ordinance respecting the militia was called in question. For this offence Sir Edward, sir George Strode, and Mr Spencer were impeached. The persons named in the following note had the folly to present the petition after the house had determined to impeach its framers, and had ordered the petition to be burnt by the hangman. (Journ. ii. 549.)

Captaine Lovelace comitted to the gatehouse [a] } concerning Deer-
Sir William Butler committed to the Fleete } ings petition.

[a] Captain Lovelace was released on bail the 21st June, 1642. (Journ. ii. 635.)

Lovelace's petition to the House of Commons is preserved to-day among the Historical Manuscripts in the House of Lords in his own handwriting.[1]

To the Honourable the House of Commons.
The humble petition of Richard Louelace Esqr.

Sheweth

That your petitioner beeinge verie sensible of the displeasure of this Great Assemblie, the sadde effect whereof he hath allreadie felt allmost these seu'n-weekes by his inprisonment within the Gate-house, expectinge patientlie yr farther purpose; in all humilitie doth offer to your wise considerations, that your petitioner beeinge confined here in this Springe-tide of Action, when open Rebellion treads on the late peacefull bosome of his Maiesties Kingdome of Ireland, is to his farther Greefe disabled from discharginge parte of that duetie, which he owes unto his Kinge and Countrie by his service there; to

[1] This petition was printed in *Notes and Queries* by Mr. John Eglington Bailey in August, 1876, and again in *The Gentleman's Magazine*, 1884, pp. 468–9.

to which he longe since had a resolution not onelie to devote himselfe, but to imploy such summes of monie as latelie he sett out and destin'd to the same intent. Hee therefore humblie prayes that in your wonted Clemencie you would be pleas'd to make a favourable, milde construction of his actions, from whence he may receiue your gentle thoughts, and by your gratious Order be admitted to his former Libertie, or if your well-knowne Wisdomes shall conceiue this Course more fitt; to be allow'd but a conditionall freedome, & for the certaintie of his attendance on your future pleasures he will humblie offer the ingagement of some able friends as a sufficient bayle, and hee shall euer pray that a moste happie ende may close up all your labours and Indeuours.

Rich: Lovelace.

An interesting comparison might be made between this document and John Cleveland's petition *To His Hignesse The Lord Protector*, written a few years later. Cleveland laboured under the disadvantage of not having any fortune which he could offer as security for bail, for, as he said, 'none stand committed whose estate can bail them'. His petition is remarkable for its manly and sensible appeal to his old enemy Cromwell.

For the service of his *Majesty* (if it be objected) I am so far from excusing it, that I am ready to alledge it in my vindication: I cannot conceive that my fidelity to my Prince should taint me in your opinion; I should rather expect it should recommend me to your favour; Had not we been faithfull to our *King*, we could not have given our selves to be so to your *Highness*; you had then trusted us *gratis*, whereas now we have our former Loyalty to vouch us.[1]

Parliament granted the second part of Lovelace's petition. His

[1] *Poems by J. C.*, 1657.

His desire of serving where 'open Rebellion treads on the late peacefull bosome of his Maiesties Kingdome of Ireland' would be sufficient to ensure a refusal of the first part. The Civil War was on the point of breaking out and the King had recently offered to go to Ireland in person. Clarendon states that neither before nor after did Parliament ever receive any message from the King which more discomposed them than this. Parliament, no less than the King, wished to control the army serving against the Irish rebels. Though Butler first petitioned some weeks before Lovelace did so, they were finally released within a few days of each other. Butler was killed two years later at Cropredy Bridge, after experiencing considerable ill-treatment and a second imprisonment in the Gatehouse from which he escaped.[1]

Lovelace was released in June, 1642, and possibly stayed a few months in London. 'During this time of confinement to *London*', says Wood, 'he lived beyond the income of his Estate, either to keep up the credit and reputation of the Kings Cause by furnishing men with Horse and Arms, or by relieving ingenious men in want, whether Scholars, Musitians, Soldiers *etc.* Also by furnishing his two brothers Colonel *Franc. Lovelace* and Capt. *Will. Lovelace* (afterwards slain at *Caermarthen*) with men and money for the Kings Cause, and his other brother called *Dudley Posthumus Lovelace* with moneys for his maintenance in *Holland* to study Tacticks and Fortification in that school of War.' Wood probably knew nothing at all about Lovelace himself, his information being derived from Aubrey and other untrustworthy sources. He

[1] See the *Commons Journals*; Clarendon's *History*, viii. 66; Sandyes' *A perfect Diurnall of the severall passages in our late journey into Kent*, and Bruno Ryves, *Angliae Ruina*, 1647, pp. 6–14.

He makes no mention of Lovelace having been abroad at any date before 1646; indeed he conveys the impression that he stayed in London till after the 'rendition of the *Oxford* Garrison', that he then formed a Regiment for the Service of the French King, became Colonel of this regiment, was wounded at Dunkirk, and returned again to England. This is inaccurate. Lovelace certainly spent a part and probably the greater part of the years 1643–6 in Holland and France. He may have assisted the King and supported his brothers while he was abroad, but he did not stay long enough in London to exercise the universal philanthropy attributed to him by Wood. One 'ingenious man', however, Henry Glapthorne† the poet and dramatist, had already received assistance from Lovelace as he acknowledges in the Dedication to *White-Hall. A Poem. Written 1642. With Elegies . . . 1643.*

To my noble Friend and Gossip, Captaine *Richard Lovelace.*

Sir,

I have so long beene in your debt, that I was almost desperate in my selfe of making you paiment, till this fancy by ravishing from you a new Courtesie in its patronage, promised me it would satisfie part of my former engagements to you. Wonder not to see it invade you thus, on the sudden: Gratitude is aeriall, and like that Element nimble in its motion and performance; though I would not have this of mine of a French disposition, to charge hotly and retreat unfortunately: there may appeare something in this, that may maintain the field courageously against Envy, nay come off with honour; if you, Sir, please to rest satisfied, that it marches under your Ensignes, which are the desires of

Your true honourer

Hen. Glapthorne.

His

His exact movements are uncertain, but Lovelace probably went to Holland in September, 1642, in the train of his old commander Goring, who visited the Low Countries after the surrender of Portsmouth to recruit among the English troops in the Dutch service.[1] It was probably on this occasion that he wrote *To Lucasta, Going beyond the Seas.* From the fact that his signature occurs on a legal document,[2] a delivery of seisin to Richard Hulse of land in Halden and a wood in Bethersden, to which he set his hand and seal on the 20th of March in the nineteenth year of the reign of Charles I, i. e. March 1643/4, and that he signed another document relating to the purchase of some property at Smarden on August 4, 1645,[3] it would seem that Lovelace returned at least twice to England, but there is no doubt that he spent some time in Holland, and that he was in that country before 1646.

> Holland and France have known his nobler parts,
> And found him excellent in Arms, and Arts.

wrote Samuel Holland in his elegy on Lovelace. Lovelace's own poems in *Lucasta* also bear evidence to the fact that he met Princess Luisa of Bohemia, a friend of Goring, probably at the Hague,[4] and that he was at Rotterdam,[5] before his second imprisonment in 1648. The poem *Peinture. A*

Panegyrick

[1] That Lovelace was not himself in the Dutch military service at any time seems certain from the fact that his name is not mentioned in the Registers of officers and subaltern officers from 1642 to 1657 in the Dutch Archives at The Hague. His father's name, however, is found in 1621. I am indebted to the Chief of the First Section for this information.

[2] Now in the British Museum. Add. Ch. 47354. See p. lvi. The appointment of a certain Isaac Hunte as attorney in Lovelace's absence is significant.

[3] *Archæologia Cantiana*, x, p. 211.

[4] See p. 27.

[5] See p. 80.

Panegyrick to the best Picture of Friendship Mr. Pet. Lilly, printed in 1659, suggests further that Lovelace stayed long enough in Holland to acquire the language, as he not only refers to Karel Van Mander but also quotes an anecdote from that writer's account of Holbein.[1] It is certain that he was there before September, 1645, as the first stanza of the following poem by John Tatham was set to music by William Lawes who was killed at the siege of Chester in that month.[2]

Vpon my Noble friend, Richard Lovelace
Esquire, his being in Holland.
An Invitation.
A Song.

Come A*donis*, come again,
what distast could drive thee hence,
Where so much *delight* did reign,
sateing ev'n the *soul* of *sense*?
And though thou *unkind* hast prov'd,
never *Youth was* more belov'd.
Then lov'd A*donis* come away,
For *Venus* brooks not thy delay.

Wert thou sated with the S*poil*
of so many *Virgins* H*earts*,
And therefore didst *change* thy Soil,
to seek *fresh* in other parts:
D*angers* wait on *forreigne Game*,
we have Deer more *sound* and *tame*.
Then lov'd A*donis*, &c.

Phillis,

[1] See p. 182. It is possible, however, that Lovelace was again in Holland between 1649 and 1656.

[2] *Ostella: Or the Faction of Love and Beauty Reconcil'd.* . . . 1650, pp. 82–3. The stanza was set to music by William Lawes under the title of 'Venus *to her* Adonis', and was printed in *Select Ayres and Dialogues For One, Two, and Three Voyces; To the Theorbo-Lute or Basse-Viol.* . . . 1659, p. 37.

Phillis, fed with thy *delights*,
in thy *absence pines* away;
And Love too hath lost his Rites:
not one Lasse keeps Holi-day.
They have chang'd their *Mirth* for *Cares*,
and do onely *sigh* thy Airs.
Then lov'd *Adonis*, &c.

Elpine, in whose Sager Looks
thou wert wont to *take* Delight,
Hath forsook his Drink and *Books*,
'cause he cann't enjoy thy sight.
He hath laid his Learning by,
'cause his *Wit* wants *Company*.
Then lov'd Adonis come away,
For Friendship brooks not thy Delay.

All the Swains that one did use
to converse with *Love* and *thee*,
In the *language* of thy *Muse*,
have forgot Loves Deity·
They deny to *write* a line,
and do onely talk of *thine*.
Then lov'd Adonis come away,
For Friendship brooks not thy Delay.

By thy sweet Althea's voice
we conjure thee to return;
Orwe'l rob thee of that *choice*
in whose *Flames* each Heart would *burn*:
That inspir'd by *her* and *sack*,
such Company we will not lack.
That Poets in the Age to come,
Shall write of our *Elizium*.

These lines are particularly interesting as showing that about 1644 Lovelace was known as the poet of 'Althea' and not of 'Lucasta'. The poem *To Althea, From Prison* is, so far as we know,

know, the only one he addressed to 'Althea', consequently these verses by Tatham give some evidence of the popularity of this fine song before it was printed in 1649. It is clear then that Lovelace was in Holland before September, 1645. According to Wood he was present at the siege of Dunkirk in the following year, but before discussing that and Wood's story of his relations with Lucasta, it must be noticed that a Colonel Lovelace was in command at Carmarthen in 1644.

Mercurius Aulicus, 29th week, writes under the date Thursday, July 18, 1644:

This done, he [i. e. 'that valiant brave Gentleman Colonell Charles Gerard, Generall of His Majesties Forces in those parts';] advanced into Carmarthenshire, and tooke Kidwellye, a strong Haven towne, where he left a good Garrison; and then fell on the Towne and Castle of Carmarthen, which he presently mastered, and there he placed another good Garrison under Colonel Lovelace, and left a Garrison also at Abermalas . . . .

This passage is quoted in J. R. Phillips's *Civil War in Wales*, 1874 (vol. i, p. 232), which also shows that Colonel Lovelace was still at Carmarthen when the town was taken in Oct. 1645, by the Parliamentary forces under Laugharne or Langhorne.[1]

Major-General Stradling and Colonel Lovelace, the Governor, were dismissed, and that night they departed the town with their soldiers . . .

On the 2nd of November Public Thanksgiving was given for the capture of Camarthen. The few horse under Lovelace and Stradling went to Newcastle-Emlyn, which remained in the hands of the Royalists, and strengthened the garrison there (p. 337).

It

[1] Phillips (vol. ii, p. 273) quotes the whole of a letter from Laugharne to Lenthall dated from Carmarthen, Oct. 12, 1645. Another letter from Langhorne to the Speaker is quoted in the note to p. 2.

It is probable that this Colonel Lovelace was Francis, the poet's brother, and that William Lovelace was killed or died when under his command.[1] Mr. Seccombe, in his article on Lovelace in the *Dictionary of National Biography*, calls attention to the fact that a certain 'Thomas Willys, a clerk of the crown in chancery, was taken prisoner by a Captain Lovelace, presumably the poet', in 1645. *The Historical MSS. Commission, 6th Report, App.*, p. 107, under March 21, 1646, prints the following:

Petition of Thomas Willys. For two years and a half petitioner attended the House as Clerk of the Crown in Chancery, losing all profits for a year because of the carrying away of the Great Seal. In August last, having sold his plate, and having no further means of subsistence, he obtained leave to go to his house in Hampshire to see if he could raise means to support himself and his family, but he was made prisoner by Captain Lovelace, and many of his horses and goods taken: for redress of this, and to save the rest of his goods, he was constrained to go to Oxford, and when there was forbidden to depart without leave; in his absence Mr. Bolls, a clerk, left by petitioner as his deputy, has been sworn in his place, in favour of petitioner as he conceives, till he should return to execute it himself; petitioner having got out of Oxford has voluntarily come in, and in his absence has been ready to do all service for the friends of Parliament. Prays to be restored to his office. (*L. J.*, viii. 225.)[2]

It is possible that Richard Lovelace was in England in August, 1645, but he would probably by then have been promoted to the rank of Colonel, and this Captain Lovelace is more

[1] See the poem 'To his Deare Brother Colonel F. L. immoderately mourning my Brothers untimely Death at Carmarthen', p. 86.

[2] The Lords appointed a Committee to consider the matter and report.

more likely to have been his youngest brother Dudley. The Latin lines contributed by Harmar to *Lucasta*, 1649, seem to point to the fact that Lovelace was about this time serving in the French army against the Spaniards, before he served under d'Enghien at Dunkirk.

> Gnaviter Hesperios compressit Marte cachinnos,
> Devictasque dedit Cantaber ipse manus.
> Non evitavit validos Dunkerka lacertos,
> Non intercludens alta Lacuna vias.

Dunkirk fell on Oct. 11, 1646, the siege having begun on Sept. 29, and during that winter or in the following year Lovelace returned to England. Wood mentions his being wounded during the siege of Dunkirk, and goes on to tell of his second imprisonment and the publication of *Lucasta.* 'The reason', says Wood, 'why he gave that title was, because, some time before, he had made his amours to a Gentlewoman of great beauty and fortune named *Lucy Sacheverel*, whom he usually called *Lux casta*; but she upon a strong report that *Lovelace* was dead of his wound received at Dunkirk, soon after married.'

Much conjecture has been expended on the identity of Lucasta, but no satisfactory explanation has yet been given.

'Many of the Writers I have consulted', wrote Joseph Hunter in *Chorus Vatum Anglicanorum. Collections concerning the Poets and Verse-Writers of the English Nation*, 1843,[1] 'inform us who the Lucy Sacheverel was who is the Lu-casta of Lovelace. But I seem to recollect having read in that immense depository, The Gentleman's Magazine, a disquisition on the subject, issuing in a very satisfactory determination.—I suppose she was issue of the marriage of Ferdinando Sacheverel with Lucy daughter of Sir Henry Hastings of Newark near Leicester. This Ferdinando was aged 20, in 1619, and was an

[1] Add. MS. 24,488, vol. ii, p. 201.

an illegitimate son of Henry Sacheverel of Morley in Derbyshire and of Newhall in Warwickshire. This Henry died in 1620 and by his wife a daughter of Sir Humphrey Bradborn had Jacinth Sacheverel aged 40 in 1619 who carried on the line. (See his Mon. Ins. Le Neve 1656. p. 47.)[1] The mother of Ferdinando is described as "Mrs Keigs", or "Kayes", "Concubine" to Henry. There was another son named Valence, who was 15 in 1619. This I have from Harl. 1167. f. 160b.

'As Ferdinando married so well the probability is that he was well provided for: and no doubt some account of his residence and issue is somewhere to be found without having recourse to the troublesome search of Wills. One would like to know who was the happy man that became master of so much beauty sense and affection.'

This theory as to the identity of Lucasta cannot be accepted. Francis Lovelace's verses contributed to the 1649 volume are in themselves sufficient to cast doubts on it, Richard's own lines *To Lucasta. Ode Lyrick* (p. 55) confirm these doubts, and Lucasta, who was acquainted with the family of Lovelace's mother,[2] certainly came from the North, 'Lucasta that bright Northerne star', as Lovelace himself calls her in *Amyntor from beyond the Sea to Alexis*.

Wood's account of Lovelace is very inaccurate, as has already been noticed, and no particular reliance need be placed on his identification of Lucasta with Lucy Sacheverel. It is quite as likely that she was a member of the family of Lucas, and that the poet addressed her in the same way as Walton

[1] The date 1656 in Hunter's marginal note refers to the monument, not to the book. The reference is to p. 47 of John Le Neve's *Monumenta Anglicana* (1650–1679), 1718.

[2] See *Lucasta paying her Obsequies to the Chast memory of my dearest Cosin Mrs. Bowes Barne.*

Walton did his second wife, Anne Ken, whom, in the song 'The Angler's Wish', he calls 'my Kenna'.[1] Further, the song 'Come my *Lucasta*', which is set to music in Henry Lawes' *Ayres and Dialogues*, 1653, is said in the Table to be by Sir Charles Lucas, a point which may have some bearing on this question.[2]

If Wood's identification of Lucasta may be wrong, his story of her marrying another on a report that Lovelace had been killed at Dunkirk is demonstrably inaccurate. The poem *To Lucasta. From Prison* obviously cannot have been written during the poet's imprisonment in the Gatehouse in 1642, and there is absolutely no evidence or hint that he was again in prison before 1648 when the lines must have been written. The existence of this poem alone disposes of Wood's story,[3] and it is also unlikely that Lovelace would have collected and published his poems to Lucasta, or that his brother would have included other poems addressed to her in his collection of Lovelace's *Posthume Poems*, without some mention or reference to the circumstances had they been such as are described by Wood.

The evidence which proves that Lovelace returned to England in 1647 or late in 1646 is furnished by the fact that he contributed some verses in 1647 to the first folio edition of Beaumont and Fletcher. The book was probably published early in the year as Moseley's note 'The Stationer to the Readers' is dated Feb. 14, 1646, i.e. 1646/7.

Probably

[1] 'Here hear my Kenna sing a song.'

[2] I am indebted to Mr. G. Thorn-Drury, K.C., for the suggestion. It may, however, be noted that Charles Cotton's wife Isabella Hutchinson was distantly connected with the Nottinghamshire Sacheverells, among whom was Lucy, wife of Henry Sacheverell of Ratcliffe and Lucy daughter of Ralph Sacheverell (he died in 1605).

[3] See also the *Dialogue* on p. 101 and note.

Probably Lovelace was now living in London. W. C. Hazlitt was the first to note that on Oct. 26, 1647, he was one of four persons admitted to the Freedom of the Painters' Company. The minute-book of the Company states 'Dr George Wild, Colonel Richard Lovelace, Thomas Rawlins, Esq., graver of seals to his Majesty, and Mr. Peter Lilly were all made free.'[1] That he should be accorded this unusual honour shows that Lovelace was a gentleman of some note as well as a critic of taste and, obviously, that he was well known to the painters of the day. There is no evidence that he was himself an amateur painter, but it is not impossible. His brother Francis was sufficiently skilled to draw the portrait bust of the poet which was engraved for *Lucasta. Posthume Poems.* The King had introduced a love of painting into the Court but, outside his own immediate following, anything like an intelligent appreciation of art was very rare in England. Lovelace had the advantage of staying in Holland at a time when Dutch painting was almost at its best and many of the earlier masters were at the height of their power. Rembrandt himself was nearing his fortieth year before Lovelace left Holland. That he brought from the Low Countries a true and delicate appreciation of painting is abundantly proved by his poem on Lely's portrait of

[1] Quoted by Mrs. Poole in her article on Edward Pierce the Sculptor in the Walpole Society's eleventh volume, 1923. Rawlins, who contributed verses to *Lucasta*, and Lely were friends of Lovelace, and he may well have known Wild, who was afterwards Bishop of Derry. Elected a scholar of St. John's College, Oxford, in 1628, at the age of nineteen, Wild became a chaplain to Laud and later was appointed preacher to the King and Parliament in Oxford. Being turned out of his Fellowship by the Parliamentarian Visitors in 1648, he kept up a religious meeting for Loyalists in Fleet Street. 'In his younger years he was accounted a Person of great ingenuity.' (Wood's *Athenae*, 1691, vol. ii, p. 252.)

of the King and the Duke of York and also by his lines called *Peinture. A Panegyrick to the best Picture of Friendship Mr. Pet. Lilly*, in which he smiles at 'this un-understanding land' and those who

their own dull counterfeits adore,
Their Rainbow-cloaths admire, and no more.

Nothing more which is definite, however, is known concerning him till the following year, when he was committed prisoner to Peterhouse. The reason for this movement is not known, but it was probably a precautionary step which the state of affairs in Kent at that time would fully warrant. Wood only says that 'in 1648, returning into *England*, he, with *Dud. Posthumus* before mention'd, then a Captain under him, were both committed prisoners to *Peterhouse* in *London*, where he fram'd his Poems for the Press, intit., *Lucasta*: Epodes, Odes, Sonnets, Songs, &c., *Lond.* 1649, etc.'†

That Dudley Lovelace was imprisoned with his brother rests entirely on Wood's authority. *The Calendar of State Papers* (Domestic Series) contains the following entries:

June 9. 1648. That a warrant of commitment be made to send Captain Lovelace to the prison of Peterhouse.

Oct. 3. 1648. Proceedings at the Committee of both Houses at Derby House. Present: Earls of Kent and Mulgrave, Sir Wm. Armyne, Sir J. Evelyn, Col. Fiennes, and Mr Knightley. Ordered,

1. That Col. Moore be desired to be here on Thursday, as also Col. Richd. Lovelace that his petition may be cleared.

Oct. 17. 1648. Proceedings at the Committee of both Houses at Derby House. Present: Earl of Mulgrave, Lords Howard and Lisle, Sir H. Vane, Sir W. Armyne, Sir J. Danvers,

Danvers, Sir J. Evelyn, Sir Wm. Masham, Mr Solicitor St. John, and Messrs. Knightley and Rous. Ordered,

. . . .

4. That Col. Moore be desired to be here to-morrow touching the business of Col. Lovelace.

April 10. 1649. Warrant from the Council of State to the Keeper of Peterhouse, To discharge Rich. Lovelace.

The 'Captain Lovelace' in the first of these entries may refer to Dudley, but is almost certainly a clerical error for 'Colonel Lovelace'. The poet's second imprisonment, therefore, lasted for ten months. Nothing is known of his movements during the next few years.†

'After the Murther of K. *Ch.* 1,' continues Wood, '*Lovelace* was set at liberty, and having by this time consumed all his Estate, grew very melancholy, (which brought him at length into a Consumption) became very poor in body and purse, was the object of charity, went in ragged Cloaths (whereas when he was in his glory he wore Cloth of gold and silver) and mostly lodged in obscure and dirty places, more befitting the worst of Beggars, than poorest of Servants, &c. . . . He died in a very mean Lodging in *Gun-powder Alley* near Shoe-lane, and was buried at the west end of the Church of S. *Bride* alias *Bridget* in *London*, near to the body of his Kinsman *Will. Lovelace* of *Greys Inn* Esq. in sixteen hundred fifty and eight, . . .'

There is no record of Lovelace at the church, which was utterly destroyed during the Great Fire, though he must have been buried 'close to the spot where a little more than a hundred years later Chatterton was given a pauper's funeral'.[1]

Wood's

[1] *D. N. B.* 'Lovelace's connexion with St. Bride's suggested to Richardson the name of the hero of "Clarissa" and thus, by an ironical destiny, "Lovelace" passed through the agency of Clarissa into common use in the

Wood's story of Lovelace's miserable end and death is probably totally inaccurate and was no doubt largely derived from Aubrey's account which he had read.

Obiit in a Cellar, in Long-acre a little before the Restoration of his Mat^ie^ Mr Edm: Wyld etc haue made collections for him & givn him money: . . .
Geo. Petty Haberdasher in Fleet-street carryed xx^s^ to him every monday morning from S^r^ . . . Many & Charles Cotton Esq for . . . moneths: but was never repayd.

He may have had other information, but, from whatever source he derived his story, Wood himself knew nothing about the manner or place of Lovelace's death. On Nov. 2, 1686, he was writing to Mr. Thomas Creech for information about Lovelace; on Dec. 15, 1687, to Sir Edward Sherburne for the 'obit' of R. Lovelace; on Feb. 7, $168\frac{7}{8}$, to Sherburne again about a College lease of 300*li.* per annum and obit and place of buriall of poet Lovelace from his sister Caesar wife of Robert Caesar.[1] In 1674 he wrote in the *Historia et Antiquitates* that he had been told that Lovelace died in the Strand *about* the year 1658, having wasted his substance in dissipations not unusual among poets. It would seem that he had learnt little more in the seventeen years that intervened before the publication of the *Athenae* as to the real facts about Lovelace's last days. Sir Edward Sherburne might have known Lovelace. He was a relative of Thomas Stanley and was in London, in custody of the usher of the Black Rod, from August to October, 1642, at a time when

eighteenth century as a synonym for a libertine. Though now supplanted by the older Lothario, it still survives in France.' *Ibid.*

[1] *The Life and Times of Anthony Wood, antiquary, of Oxford, 1632–1695, described by Himself.* (Oxford Historical Society, 1894, vol. iii.)

when Lovelace was also there. He was again in London after the surrender of Oxford in 1646, living in straitened circumstances with Thomas Povey, a near relation. Lovelace's sister would naturally have been able to give Wood accurate information about her brother's death, but he probably did not obtain any information from this source. Had he done so he would have known the correct date, for the poet died, not in 1658, but in 1656 or 1657. This is conclusively proved by the fact that Revett's elegy on Lovelace was printed in 1657. His book of *Poems* is dated 1657 on both title-pages and the Dedication is dated Oct. 19, 1647, which is clearly a misprint for 1657.[1]

This proves that Lovelace was dead in Oct. 1657. He was alive in the summer of 1656 as he wrote *The Triumphs of Philamore and Amoret* for the marriage of Charles Cotton, which took place then. Lovelace died, therefore, between the summer of 1656 and the autumn of 1657, probably in 1657, as he contributed some lines to Hall's *Hierocles upon the Golden Verse of Pythagoras*, and to a translation of Voiture's *Letters*, both of which were published in that year.[2] It may also be noticed that the phrase in Samuel Holland's unsigned

[1] Mr. G. Thorn-Drury, K.C., who first discovered this conclusive evidence, has kindly sent me details of his exceedingly rare copy of Revett. I have only heard of one other copy, which was sold from the Library of Britwell Court. The full title is as follows:

POEMS, | BY | ELDRED REVETT. | Horat. Ep. lib. 2. | *Ad August.* | —*Quia nil rectum, nisi quod placuit* | *sibi ducunt:* | *Vel quia turpe putant parere* minori-|bus *&* *quæ* | Imberbes *didicere, Senes perdenda* | *fateri.* | LONDON, | Printed by *E. T.* for the Authour. | *Anno Dom.* 1657.

The second title is: POEMS | DIVINE. | By | *ELDRED REVET* | *Gent.* | *Qui recto Cælum vultu petis, Exerisque* | *Frontem,* | *In sublime feras animum quoque.* | Boëth. de con. Ph. li. 5. | LONDON, | *Anno Dom.* 1657.

[2] Hall's book was, however, received by Thomason on Dec. 8, 1656. John Davies's translation of Voiture is marked by him June 1, 1657.

unsigned elegy 'Lovelace hath long been dead' is better suited to 1657 than to 1658.[1]

Wood's account of the miseries of Lovelace's last days and his death in 'a very mean Lodging' is also, in all probability, misleading.

Till Death with slow and easie pace,
Snatcht the bright Jewell from the Case

is hardly the language one would expect Dudley Lovelace to have used had his brother died in the circumstances mentioned by Wood and by Aubrey.[2]

That Lovelace was at one time in difficulty, and possibly in poverty, cannot be doubted. He sold Lovelace Place at Bethersden to Richard Hulse in 1649, having let it to him since 1644.[3] In 1643 he had already sold 'All that his Messuage or te'nt Barne and Outhouses thereunto belonginge And also all his landes meadowes pastures and arrable lyeing in Halden in the said Countie of Kent, conteyninge Threescore acres more or lesse Togeather wth a p'cell of Woodland called Bottenden Wood al's Barr Bottenden conteynninge Twentie ffive acres more or lesse situat in Bethersden aforesaid

[1] Holland's elegy was published in 1660 with the others edited by Dudley Lovelace and also in broadside form without date. See note to p. 229.

[2] In vol. iv of *The Retrospective Review*, 1821, pp. 118–19, a suggestion was made that Wood had 'somewhat exaggerated the miseries of our unfortunate author, or been in some measure misinformed'. Though the argument—first used by Hasted and followed by *Biographica Dramatica*, Campbell and others—based on the inheritance of Lovelace's daughters is worthless, the suggestion that the poet's brothers would not have permitted him to fall into such an abject state and that the elegies 'are not in the strain which might have been expected, had Lovelace died in the friendless and wretched state described by Wood and Aubrey', does not seem to have been followed up by subsequent editors and biographers. Mr. Waite, however, thought that the story was probably exaggerated. (*Gentleman's Magazine*, Nov. 1884.)

[3] See *Archæologia Cantiana*.

said in the said Countie of Kent.'[1] He also sold some property at Rucking.[2] Lovelace may often have been in need of ready money if he lived the life described by Wood, but there is no reason to believe that he was ever in a desperate condition of penury and misery. Charles Cotton speaks of him as,

> In Fortune humble, constant in mis-chance,
> Expert in both, and both serv'd to advance
> Thy Name by various Trialls of thy Spirit,
> And give the Testimony of thy merit;

and it is most unlikely that Cotton would have limited himself to the statement that Lovelace was neither unduly exalted by good, nor depressed by bad fortune, had Aubrey's story been correct.

Cotton must have known the truth. He was one of the two gentlemen from whom, according to Aubrey, twenty shillings was conveyed to Lovelace every Monday morning for months. It is this assistance given by him which is probably the origin of the whole story. Lovelace himself in

[1] From an article, signed by Richard Lovelace and endorsed Bethersden, 1643, now in the British Museum (Add. Ch. 47354). It appoints 'Isaac Hunte of Bethersden aforesaid yeoman his true and lawfull Attorney' and empowers him to take 'full and peacable possession state & seizen of the same to deliver to the said Richard Hulse according to the tenoe purporte intent and true meaning of the said recited Indenture Ratifyeinge and confirminge all & whatsoever the said Isaac Hunte shall doe or cause to be done touchinge or concerninge the premisses as fully whollie and effectuallie as if the said Richard Lovelace were then and there p'rsonallie p'nte and did the same In Witnes whereof the said Richard Lovelace hath hereunto sett his hand and seale this Twentieth daie of March In the Nyneteenth yeare of the Raigne of or sov'ainge Lord Charles by the grace of god kinge of England Scotland ffrance Ireland defender of the ffaith. Annoqr d'm 1643.' The document is reprinted in *Archæologia Cantiana*, vol. xxiii, p. 337, and a reproduction of the signature is also given.

[2] See article by Mr. A. E. Waite in *The Gentleman's Magazine*, 1884.

in *The Triumphs of Philamore and Amoret* acknowledges generous help from Cotton at some crisis:

> What fate was mine when in mine obscure Cave
> (Shut up almost close Prisoner in a Grave)
> Your Beams could reach me through this Vault of Night,
> And Canton the dark Dungeon with Light!
> Whence me (as gen'rous *Spahy's*) you unbound,
> Whilst now I know myself both *Free* and Crown'd.

These lines contain the key to the difficulty. Aubrey must have heard, no doubt from Wyld, some account of this assistance rendered by Cotton to Lovelace at a time of need, remembered it vaguely, and produced the chatty, inaccurate story given above which is so characteristic of him. Wood, for want of any more reliable information, followed Aubrey's account.[1] What this assistance was and why it was needed remains unknown, though it is possible to form a conjecture. Possibly Cotton was in some way instrumental in procuring Lovelace's release after his second imprisonment, or, which is more probable, at some time between 1649 and 1656 Lovelace was again in trouble with the Parliament and was in hiding. A possible date is August, 1655, shortly before his death. Harassed by fear of rebellion and in constant peril of assassination, Cromwell had put England under the rule of the Major-Generals. For a time a severe policy was adopted towards the Cavaliers, many were arrested and a close watch kept on all prominent men. A well-known Royalist like Lovelace would not be forgotten, and it is, at any rate, a tenable theory that he was forced into hiding in the autumn of this year. Such a theory would account to some extent for

[1] It should be noted, however, that 'George Petty, haberdasher', was a distant connexion of Anthony Wood (Clark's *Wood's Life and Times*, i. 35), and, which is more important, that Wyld was intimate with Aubrey. (*Brief Lives*, ed. A. Clark, 1898, i, pp. 4, 41, &c.)

for Aubrey's story which, demonstrably inaccurate though it is, cannot be altogether ignored as it probably had some origin in truth. But had Lovelace died miserably in rags in one of the meanest quarters of London, some of the elegies would have referred to the fact.[1] Not one of them gives so much as the smallest hint that his death took place in circumstances in the least out of the ordinary, and his brother's lines are direct evidence to the contrary.

Before his death Lovelace was contemplating, and may actually have begun to prepare for publication, a second volume of his poems. He did not live to see the book through the press. The work of editing *Lucasta. Posthume Poems* was carried out by his youngest brother, Dudley Posthumus, assisted by Eldred Revett. The following copy of a letter from Revett is preserved in the Cambridge University Library, in Revett's commonplace-book. (D. D. IV. SS. c.)

To Capt: Dudley Louelace into y^e^
Low Countryes.

Sir,

ye noe desire I had to put you to an vnnecessary charge hath bin ye Occasion of my (perhaps ill constru'd) silence, I haue not bin Idle in ye executing those commands you entrusted mee w^th^, but haue found soe little satisfactory Returns that I thought it not Convenient to discourage you wth ye slow proceedings, when my Lrẽs could not Countervayl ye expences to ye poast this might haue had ye same excuse & haue waited for a more considerable season, but y^t^ a too long forbearance may endanger ye suspicion y^t^ I am slack in duty, & y^t^ y^t^ though it bring noe essentiall Comfort, may yet entitle you

[1] Gunpowder Alley, near Shoe Lane, was, as Mr. Seccombe points out in the *Dictionary of National Biography*, 'a well-known haunt of indigent refugees, lurking papists, and delinquents'. It is quite possible that Lovelace hid there for some time.

you to a fayr hopes, Mr Cæsar (whom I haue solicited by lrẽ) hath informed M^{r}. Davis that by the next opportunity hee will doe somthing Concerning y^{e} [*sic* ? y^{r}] desires, the Collonell Poems are not yet in ye press, if they haue birth in Michaelmas Term it will bee ye soonest, ye Taylor still pretends ye want of a Chapman & how long he may I know not, howeuer I shall not bee wanting to Imiportune [*sic*] him, words once Words once [*sic*] Committed to paper are more y^{n} winde, and many may bee preiudiciall to a Lrẽ y^{t} as I ame here informd must bee payd for by weight I shall therefore ye sooner embrace ye honour to subscribe my selfe y^{r}

Ready freind & servant

Junii 20 Eld: Reuett.[1]

That Richard Lovelace himself was intending to edit the book seems probable from the second of the two following sets of verses addressed to him by Revett and published in the latter's *Poems* in 1657.

To

[1] There is a copy of another letter from Revett, in the same common-place-book, which seems to refer to the above. This latter is without name or address.

S^{r}

It was a custome not disingenious in our young Archery, y^{t} w^{hn} wee had shot an arrow to som place less Commodious for discouerye, wee directed, ye same way another but wth an aime more assurd and by ye stratagem not vnfrequently Recoverd both, thus hauing let fly my first missiue through ye hands of an ill Conveyance, I haue designd this (but wth a charge more particular) to my first proposall, y^{t} it may lay open a way to ye pursuance of my former thoughts wch I shall beleiue enough found if you haue receiued them, at leest if I loos both I shall have ye satisfaction y^{t} they were sacrificd to you, since I lost ye happiness of yours I begin to disrellish all Company, & finde a less gusto in theyr entertayning mee, ye less excellent we but impt more to diuersion and ye best but obliging troubles, you must therfor expect but an ill Return of thos cōmands you engaged mee in, I am like him in new Rome a stranger in ye midst of ye Citty, I convers not wth ye Publick Lyre, & sequester my selfe from ye Cups & Garlands, & liue wthin it, though a stranger to my Studdy. This paper howeuer shall haue its business, if it may inform you how much I endeavour

To bee y^{r}.

To his Honoured Friend, Col. R.L. *upon his second failing.*

One Fault to you is Death agen
A super-errogating sin,
And I thus fall'n from all Repaire,
Set Raving down by wild despaire;
And as the damn'd already do,
Repent my sins by adding to.

Poems, p. 6.

To my honoured Friend, Coll.

Richard Lovelace,

On his second Poems.

As in the presence of some Prince, not one,
But rates his bliss, as he is next the throne,
To which he adds not but himself applies
To boast the Kings to him indulgencies:
Thus Sir (as one you suffer) I appear
Not to give to your fame, but to be near.
How must I then approach? how my self shew,
So just, as that I can be, just to you!
Thou great dispenser of that all we be
Who giv'st us else enough, but to thanke thee
Thou hast our cheaper gratitude out-went
And mak'st us sin in being excellent.
How from thy first chaste flames thou didst inspire
That earth we fashion'd with *Promethean* fire?
And thine rise no less bright for what they lent
From the Communicative Element:
But the insinuating Rayes derive
Something from us that was not primitive:
Though pure in their own essences they dwell
Not to be mixt with our corruptible;
And should we in our courser matter die
Would rise to their own immortalitie.

But

But at a kingdomes second birth though ne'r
So much devout to the already heire,[1]
A Nation throngs, and doth (suspended) pay
Duty howe're unto the newer day,
Thus from ador'd *Lucasta* we come on
But to bring hither our devotion:
And though we crowd with a tumultuous pace,
We have like *Ianus* a respective face:
Thou that immortal wer't enough before,
Dost now but ever live, and all this ore;
And art above the Eagle that assumes
(By casting the now aged off) new plumes,
Who dost thy first as vigorous not shed,
But when thou would'st renew thy pomp dost spread.
Vast *Heroe* that will not alone not die,
But lay'st steps to thine immortalitie,
Who dost in thy applausive, Giant-wars
From thine own blest ascent invade the Stars;
Thou hast throughout divided the cleft mount,
And to thine aid with its own spire dost crown't,
Though as thou grow'st near heav'n it hangs the while
As in a dear expectance of the pile,
That swells no sacrilegious hight to gain
But doth the weighty machine there sustain.
There then advance thy glory till our sight
Conceive thee some new disputable light;
That we cannot define from whence it streams
Although we find thee by thy warmth and beams.

Ibid., pp. 34–5.

Lucasta. Posthume Poems, though dated 1659, did not appear till 1660, when it was issued with the *Elegies Sacred To the Memory of the Author: By several of his Friends*, also edited by

[1] Corrected in Errata. The text reads 'hire'.

by Dudley Lovelace.[1] The contents of this second volume add little to Lovelace's reputation, for no one of the poems in it ranks among his best work. There is nothing which can be set beside the opening songs of *Lucasta*. The spontaneity and freshness which are characteristic of so much of the first volume are more rarely met with, 'the sound is forced, the notes are few'. The style is more harsh and crabbed, though a genuine fancy and the knack of paying a graceful compliment are still to be found. The satire *On Sanazar's being honoured* shows some power, and had he done more in this way, Lovelace might have rivalled even John Cleveland, the keenest of contemporary satirists who published anything of importance during his lifetime.

With the exception of *To Althea, From Prison*,[2] Lovelace's poems do not seem to have achieved any great popularity in his own day; he certainly did not enjoy a reputation equal to that of Suckling or Randolph or Cartwright or Cleveland. One of his songs and four stanzas of another were included in the principal mid-seventeenth-century anthology, Cotgrave's *Wits Interpreter*, 1655, though these were reprinted from the song-books and not from *Lucasta*, and a discerning criticism, all the more interesting because it may have met with Milton's approval, was written by Edward Phillips in his *Theatrum Poetarum, or a Compleat Collection of the Poets*, 1675.[3]

Richard Lovelace, an approv'd both Souldier, Gentleman &

[1] See below under *Text of the Poems*. If Wood's story of Dudley Lovelace's imprisonment in 1648 is correct, he may have helped his brother prepare *Lucasta*, 1649, for the press.

[2] See note to p. 78.

[3] ii, p. 160. In Joshua Poole's *The English Parnassus*, 1657, p. 41, *Lovelace's Pastorals* is mentioned as one of 'The Books principally made use of in the compiling of this Work'.

& Lover, and a fair pretender to the Title of Poet; a Souldier, having Commanded a Regiment in the late King's Army; a Gentleman of a Vicounts[1] Name and Family; a Lover Militant under the Bannor of *Lucasta*, the Lady Regent under a Poetical Name of his Poetical endeavours; and as to the last of his Qualifications, besides the acute and not unpleasant stile of his Verses, a Man may discern therein sometimes those sparks of a Poetic fire, which had they been the main design, and not Parergon, in some work of Heroic argument, might happily have blaz'd out into the perfection of sublime Poesy.

As was his habit, William Winstanley borrowed much of Phillips' summary for his own account of Lovelace whom he thought not unworthy to be compared to the idol of a past generation when he wrote:[2]

I can compare no Man so like this Colonel *Lovelace* as Sir *Philip Sidney*, of which latter it is said by one in an Epitaph made of him,

Nor is it fit that more I should acquaint,
Lest Men adore in one
A Scholar, Souldier, Lover, and a Saint.[3]

As

[1] The Lord Lovelace of Hurley was a Baron, not a Viscount.

[2] *The Lives Of the most Famous English Poets, or the Honour of Parnassus*, 1687, p. 170. Both Oldys and Malone left annotated copies of Winstanley, but neither has any note on Lovelace.

[3] *In Recreation for Ingenious Head-peeces*, 1654 (Sig. O 8 verso), the lines are printed:

Reader: within this ground Sir *Philip Sidney* lyes,
Nor is it fit, that more
I should acquaint;
Lest superstition rise,
And men adore
A Lover, Scholler, Souldier, and a Saint.

Another version is given in *Occasional Verses of Edward Lord Herbert, Baron of Cherbery and Castle-Island*, 1665, p. 53.

Epitaph on Sir Philip Sidney lying in St. Pauls's without a Monument, to be fastned upon the Church door.

As for their parallel, they were both of noble Parentage, Sir *Philip's* Father being Lord Deputy of *Ireland*, and President of *Wales*; our Colonel of a Vicount's name and Family; Scholars none can deny them both: The one Celebrated his Mistress under the bright name of *Stella*, the other the Lady Regent of his Affections, under the Banner of *Lucasta*, both of them endued with transcendent Sparks of Poetick Fire, and both of them exposing their Lives to the extreamest hazard of doubtful War; both of them such Soldiers as is expressed by the Poet.

> Undaunted Spirits, that encounter those
> Sad dangers, we to Fancy scarce propose.

To conclude, Mr *Lovelace's* Poems, did, do, and still will live in good Esteem with all knowing true Lovers of Ingenuity.

It is possible that Sedley may have intended Eugenio in *The Mullbery-Garden*, 1668, as a portrait of Lovelace. Eugenio is a Cavalier imprisoned and in danger of losing his life for his loyalty; he is the lover of Althea and he is made to say (Act III, Sc. i.)

> The strictest Prison, I have freedom thought,
> And been on Scaffolds without terror brought.
> But these few words (*Althea* is a Bride)
> More wound my Soul, than can the world beside

Althea, however, is no one's bride but Eugenio's in the play. He also says, 'Though Love possess, Honour must rule my heart', and Diana says to Althea (i, IV.):

On

Reader,
> Within this Church Sir *Philip Sidney* lies,
> Nor is it fit that I should more acquaint,
> Lest superstition rise,
> And Men adore,
> Souldiers, their Martyr; Lovers, their Saint.

On thee *Eugenio* did his Life bestow,
To me *Philander* did his Service vow;
Yet both for Honour have those ties despis'd,
And now are fled, or must be sacrific'd. . . .

This possible portrait does not seem to have been noticed before.[1]

In the earlier part of the eighteenth century Lovelace seems to have been almost entirely forgotten. He is not mentioned by Pope, and in the middle of the century even such a comprehensive work at Cibber's *The Lives of the Poets*, 1753, ignores him altogether. His popularity may be said to date from 1765, when Percy reprinted 'To Althea' and 'To Lucasta, Going to the Warres' in his *Reliques of Ancient English Poetry*. In 1792 Sir Egerton Brydges complained in one of a series of articles on Lovelace which he contributed to *The Gentleman's Magazine*, that the subject of his criticism had been excluded from the first edition of *Biographia Britannica*, but by that date Lovelace was beginning to find his way into the anthologies and dictionaries. Accounts of his life, selections from his poems and criticisms appeared in Ellis's *Specimens of Early English Poets*, 1790;[2] Headley's *Select Beauties of Ancient English Poetry*, 1787;[3] *The Gentleman's Magazine*, 1791-2;[4] Lyson's *Environs of London*, 1792;[5] Ritson's *The English Anthology*,

[1] The suggestion was made to me by Mr. Thorn-Drury.

[2] pp. 186-90. [3] i. lvii-lviii, ii. 39-40.

[4] Vol. lxi, 2nd part, pp. 1094-5; vol. lxii, 1st part, pp. 99, 135, 166-7, 320-1; vol. lxii, 2nd part, pp. 604-5, 971-2.

[5] Vol. i, pp. 109, 273. The statement made here on the authority of *Occurences from Forreigne Parts*, Number 17, August 23 to August 30, 1659, that the poet was imprisoned in that year in Lambeth house is, of course, worthless. The Colonel Lovelate (*sic*) whose name is given in the list of 'Prisoners who are in custody taken in the late war, or upon suspicion of promotin[g] the same', was Francis Lovelace. See note to p. 2.

Anthology, 1793;[1] *The Biographical Mirrour*, 1795; the *British Critic*, 1802 (a review of Ellis);[2] Brydges, *Censura Literaria*, 1809;[3] Baker's *Biographia Dramatica*, 1812;[4] Chalmers' *The General Biographical Dictionary*;[5] Campbell's *Specimens of the British Poets*, 1819;[6] *The Retrospective Review*, 1821.[7]

In 1817–18 the second editions of both *Lucasta* and *Lucasta. Posthume Poems* were published by Singer.†

It is unnecessary now to praise Lovelace's well-known songs, but it may be urged that though two or three of his poems—reprinted in every anthology and universally allowed a high place among the lyrics of an age supreme in the art of song—have made his name one of the best known of the seventeenth century, they have also prevented full justice ever being done to the bulk of his work. Overshadowed by his famous songs, his other poems have received less attention than is properly their due. Like the majority of the 'mob of gentlemen who wrote with ease', or wished to be thought to write with ease, Lovelace had his happy moments and, as they were happier than those of most of his contemporaries, critics have been irritated to find that he did not always write equally well, and, from Sir Egerton Brydges onwards, have urged this against him with wearisome iteration, as though it was a fault peculiarly his own. A certain amount of his work does not reach a very high level of merit, but he wrote a larger amount of respectable verse than is generally allowed. Had

[1] Vol. i, 72–3. [2] Vol. xix, pp. 621–2.
[3] Vol. ix, pp. 337–8, 353–7. [4] Vol. ii, pp. 462–3; ed. 1782, i. p. 288.
[5] ed. 1812–17; vol. 20 (1815), pp. 425–6. Lovelace's poems were not included in Chalmers' *The Works of the English Poets From Chaucer to Cowper*, 1810, 'a work professing to be a Body of the Standard English Poets'.
[6] Vol. iii, pp. 399–404. [7] Vol. iv, pp. 116–30.

Had he never written *To Althea, from Prison*, or *To Lucasta, Going to the Warres*, Lovelace must still have been accorded a reputable, if not a prominent position among the lesser poets of the seventeenth century. These poets affected wit and with 'their slender conceits and laboured particularities' imitated to the best of their ability the tricks of a style which Donne had made fashionable. Lovelace was a minor poet who was generally content to follow the fashion so far as the form of his verse was concerned. Occasionally he wrote satirical lines against his lady such as 'When I by thy faire shape did sweare' or *Courante Monsieur*, but his poems in this vein are few and Lovelace generally adopts an attitude of chivalrous devotion, couching his compliments to Lucasta in extravagant conceits. In his best poems he does not depend for effect on the methods and peculiarities of the 'metaphysical' school, and, though he will occasionally carry off a conceit with the best, as in *The Scrutinie*, *Gratiana dancing and singing* or even *The Apostacy of one, and but one Lady*, he is neither sufficiently profound nor sufficiently clever to take quite naturally to this form of poetry. His faults are obvious; he is often careless and obscure because of his carelessness, not as Donne, because of the complexity or subtlety of his thought. His elliptical style is difficult and his 'wit' tends to be laboured and artificial. Lovelace is essentially an amateur, the 'idle singer of an empty day', the courtier and soldier to whom verse writing was a fashionable hobby, and he has the faults as well as the virtues of his kind. At his best he displays an ease and grace, a delicate chivalry and spontaneity in which Wyatt, perhaps, approaches him as closely as any other English poet; at his worst he sinks to a level from which mere craftsmanship would have saved a more experienced author, but, as

 Swinburne

Swinburne said of Nabbes, 'there is no great matter to be looked for in the minor poems of a minor poet'. None the less, with Lovelace as with many others in that age of song writers, these minor poems would have been the better without a continual striving after an unnecessary and often false effect. What Pope said of Crashaw is peculiarly appropriate to Lovelace, and the following extract is not an unfair judgement on his work:

'I take this Poet to have writ like a Gentleman, that is, at leisure hours, and more to keep out of idleness, than to establish a reputation; so that nothing regular or just can be expected from him. All that regards Design, Form, Fable, (which is the Soul of Poetry) all that concerns exactness, or consent of parts, (which is the Body) will probably be wanting; only pretty conceptions, fine metaphors, glitt'ring expressions, and something of a neat cast of Verse, (which are properly the dress, gems, or loose ornaments of Poetry) may be found in these verses. This is indeed the case of most other Poetical Writers of *Miscellanies*; nor can it well be otherwise, since no man can be a true Poet, who writes for diversion only. These Authors shou'd be considered as *Versifiers* and *witty Men*, rather than as *Poets*; and under this head will only fall the Thoughts, the Expression, and the Numbers. These are only the pleasing parts of Poetry, which may be judg'd of at a view, and comprehended all at once. And (to express myself like a Painter) their *Colouring* entertains the sight, but the *Lines* and *Life* of the Picture are not to be inspected too narrowly. . . .

His thoughts one may observe, in the main, are pretty; but oftentimes far fetched, and too often strain'd and stiffned to make them appear the greater.' His poetry is 'a mixture of tender gentle thoughts and suitable expressions, of forc'd and inextricable conceits, and of needless fillers-up to the rest. From all which it is plain, this Author writ fast, and set down what came uppermost. A reader may skim off the

froth,

froth, and use the clear underneath; but if he goes too deep, will meet with a mouthful of dregs'.[1]

This, it may be added, is the rather patronizing judgement of a professed man of letters on the amateur who only 'writ like a gentleman'. But to write in this way was the aim of the Cavalier poets, and Lovelace, had the same criticism been passed on him in his lifetime, would not have felt hurt. If it is impossible for one who writes for 'diversion only' to be a true poet, he would not have aspired to a title which carried with it some implication of professionalism. The ideal which he shared with his contemporaries, and with predecessors like Philip Sidney, was different to that of the eighteenth century, or that of Samuel Butler, who held that 'there is no excuse for amateur work being bad'.[2]

The compliment which Lovelace would have appreciated was paid him by Francis Lenton, when that rather indifferent poet, after praising his verse, asked:

> Thus if thy careles draughts are cal'd the best,
> What would thy lines have beene, had'st thou profest
> That faculty (infus'd) of Poetry,
> Which adds such honour unto thy Chivalry?

The Cavalier poets still held the broad and sane view of the Italian Renaissance which despised specialization and would have a gentleman seek to educate himself in all possible ways, and be good at many things rather than excel in one. The complete gentleman was a man of many parts, a statesman, a soldier well versed in the arts of war, a courtier no less well versed in those of peace, exercising his body in all proper

sports

[1] Letter to Cromwell, dated Dec. 17th, 1710. *Mr. Pope's Literary Correspondence*, 1735, I, ii, pp. 302–4; *Letters of Mr. Pope*, 1735, i, pp. 153–5.
[2] *Note Books*, ed. 1918, p. 145.

sports and his mind in the study and practice of music, of painting, and of literature. All accomplishments were desirable, but each was a means to the end and not an end in itself. Above all things it was necessary that the gentleman should do whatever he undertook, whether it was the writing of a set of verses or the playing of a game of tennis, with an apparently effortless and rather disdainful grace and ease—'sprezzatura' as the Italians called it.[1] The ideal is that which Baldassare Castiglione set forth at length in his *Book of the Courtier* and to which a feebler expression was given by Henry Peacham, whose *Compleat Gentleman* was highly popular among the Royalists. One of 'the chiefe conditions and qualities in a Courtier' is that he should 'do his feates with a slight, as though they were rather naturally in him, then earned with studye: and use a Reckelesness to couer art, without minding greatly what he hath in hand, to a mans seeminge'.[2] The sentence may stand as a description of the method of the Cavalier poets. Lovelace, who seems to have been a man of many accomplishments—'inur'd to Arms and exercis'd in Arts', a scholar, a musician and a wit—largely fulfilled the requirements of Castiglione, and this has led to the often quoted comparison with Sidney. He certainly wrote with this 'recklessness', nor was it always 'to a mans seeminge' only.

[1] Florio translates the word, which Hoby gives as 'recklessness', as 'a despising or contemning'; other dictionaries add 'disdain'.

[2] *The Courtyer of Count Baldessar Castilio . . . done into Englyshe by Thomas Hoby*, 1561, Sig. Yy 4. Compare Johnson on Congreve; 'There seems to be a strange affectation in authors of appearing to have done every thing by chance' (*Lives of the . . . Poets*, 1781, iii, p. 48), and Moseley's statement prefixed to Heath's *Clarastella*, 1650, '. . . the gallantness and Ingenuity of the Gentleman is so Eminent in every thing, that I could not imagine, but that the meanest of his Recreations, (for such was this) might carry much in it, worthy of the publick view: . . .'

only. Such a course has obvious dangers, and like other of his contemporaries he often succumbed to them. Haste, want of practice, and consequent lack of mastery over technique, inevitably tend to render the Caroline poet incoherent and his verse laboured; he does not always attain that ease which he seeks. The 'recklessness' is too often in evidence, the 'art' is sometimes altogether forgotten.

So much may fairly be urged against the Carolines in general and Lovelace in particular, but it is clearly not the conclusion of the whole matter. Even if these seventeenth-century poets favoured a way of writing which could not win them very high places in the hierarchy of literature, if they did not try to write any poetry which could rank among the greatest—for gay and gallant and graceful, and even sincere though their songs may be, they are seldom more than songs—their method was none the less attended by a measure of success which was its justification then, as it has been at other times in the history of our literature. It is not that they had any particular diffidence, or that they necessarily recognized their own limitations and preferred to write minor poetry, which was often good and occasionally excellent, to indifferent verse of a more ambitious nature. Besides the writing of verse they had other things to do which they considered of more importance. Whatever they thought about it, however, the result is the same, and their method is responsible for the freshest and most delicate lyrics and all the most passionate love songs of the seventeenth century. Lovelace is typical of his times; he shares the faults of his contemporaries, and they are not a few, he shares their success and that to a degree which makes him a worthy representative of his class—the amateur poets. 'He writes very well for a gentleman.'

TEXT

TEXT OF THE POEMS

With the exception of some lines engraved under the portrait of Voiture in J. Davies's translation of *Letters of Affaires*, 1657, the whole of Lovelace's poetry which we possess to-day is contained in the two little volumes of *Lucasta* and *Lucasta. Posthume Poems* of 1649 and 1659 respectively.

These two volumes are the sole authority for the text. The second edition did not appear for over 150 years. A few verses were written in commendation of various books, and are to be found prefixed to them, but these were sometimes corrected, and one copy was rewritten, before they were included in *Lucasta*. Some contemporary MSS. of the song *To Althea, From Prison* are still in existence, but they do not challenge the authority of the 1649 text, though they are interesting as showing that some alterations were made from the song as it was actually written.[1] Otherwise there is nothing of any importance.

Lucasta, 1649.

According to the Stationers' Registers, *Lucasta* was licensed on Feb. 4, 164$\frac{7}{8}$, and entered on May 14, 1649.[2] The text of this volume is good. A few corrections, mostly towards the end, were made while the book was in the press. The following is a list of those that I have noticed:

Page 88	line 13	Daere	to	Dare
,, 95	,, 16	chrusht	,,	crusht
,, 105	,, 5	Heovenly	,,	Heavenly
,, 105	,, 9	colme	,,	calme
,, 106	,, 4	now *omitted in some copies*		
,, 108	,, 12	loook	,,	looke

Page 108

[1] See Note to p. 78.

[2] See Note to title-page, 1649.

Page 108	line 33	And her	to	And as her
,, 108	,, 34	loayall	,,	loyall
,, 109	,, 1	sight.	,,	sight,
,, 109	,, 32	stop	,,	strip
,, 111	,, 30	blest.	,,	blest;
,, 112	,, 12	cracking squirrells	,,	squirrells cracking
,, 112	,, 13	The	,,	She
,, 114	,, 2	tempting	,,	temp'ring
,, 114	,, 15	my breaths	,,	thy breaths
,, 114	,, 21	bth,	,,	both,
,, 116	,, 12	th' Rage	,,	Rage
,, 116	,, 14	sends	,,	finds
,, 116	,, 15	exposing	,,	expiring

Apart from this there are some points of bibliographical interest connected with the book. It is to be found, certainly in two, and perhaps in three different states. Sheet B (pp. 1–16)[1] was entirely reprinted and in some copies Sheet A, containing part of the Commendatory Verses, is missing. So there are the three states:

1. Without A. B in the first state (Bodleian, Douce L. 524).[2]
2. With A. B in the first state (British Museum, E. 1373).
3. With A. B in the second state (Bodleian copy, Ash: B. 14).

The two main questions which arise are whether Sheet A was or was not included in the book as it was originally published, and the reason why Sheet B was reprinted. The collation of the book is, the engraved title, of which the reverse is blank; *a* eight leaves, the first being the printed

[1] These contain the poems from 'If to be absent were to be' to the end of 'Gratiana dancing and singing'.

[2] A copy of the engraving by Hollar after Francis Lovelace, which belongs to *Lucasta, Posthume Poems*, has been inserted before the engraved title in this copy.

printed title, the verso of which is blank; A four leaves, A 4 blank; B–L in eights; M 4 leaves, M 4 blank. *a* and A, 22 pp. with the title-page, contain the Commendatory Verses, and M 3 the 'Table of the Contents'. There is a second engraving representing 'Lucasta' or 'Aramantha', of which the reverse is blank. This is generally found between Sheets K and L, the engraving facing p. 145 on which the poem 'Aramantha. A Pastorall' begins; in some copies the engraving is found between Sheets A and B, facing p. 1. The total is 96 leaves not including the two engravings. The text of Lovelace's poems occupies pp. 1–164.

I have seen or have some account of thirty-one copies of *Lucasta*. The evidence which suggests that A is supplementary to the book as at first issued is furnished in the main by three of these. The first is the Douce copy in the Bodleian from which this edition is reprinted.[1] This is a very nice copy, and there is no sign that any one has tampered with it. It is certainly an early issue, as it has only the first five of the corrections noted above. It has, however, been rebound. Secondly, there is the copy which once belonged to Lovelace's sister and has 'Johanna Caesar her book' written over the 'Dedication'. This copy is, perhaps, stronger evidence that A is an addition to the book as it was first issued because it contains the Sheet, not in its proper place, but bound in at the end.[2] This seems even more significant than its complete omission. If added by a recent owner, the sheet would in all probability have been put into its proper place after *a*, with

[1] The verses in A are taken from the Ashmole copy in the same Library, and the text throughout has been checked with two other copies, one in my own possession, the other in the Worcester College Library.

[2] This copy was kindly shown to me some years ago by Messrs. Pickering and Chatto.

with the object of perfecting the book. The original owner, on the contrary, while wishing to have leaves which would make her copy complete, might not wish to break it up. It is unfortunate that this copy is not in its original binding. It has also some corrected readings as 'finds' and 'expiring'. The third copy which I have seen is very imperfect, lacking many pages. By itself it would furnish no evidence of any value, but it would seem to have been issued without the four leaves of A. Lastly, it must be added that the copy which Singer used lacked this sheet, and the poems included in it are omitted in his edition, though he may, of course, have used the Douce copy, and that 'a very indifferent copy' bought by Hunter on Sept. 30, 1853, also wanted it,[1] but this again may have been the imperfect copy just mentioned. The evidence afforded by these three, or possibly five copies, though it is certainly not conclusive, is too important to be altogether ignored.

Against it, however, must be put the very important fact that the copy in the British Museum (E. 1373) which once belonged to Thomason, and has the date June 21 marked by him on the title-page is complete. Thomason was a bookseller who made a vast collection of tracts and pamphlets between 1641 and 1660, each piece being dated by him on the day he purchased it. Though he sometimes allowed books to accumulate for a short time, his dates are nearly always the days of publication and are generally accepted as such. It may be noted that this copy has the corrected reading 'crusht' on p. 95, while what would seem to be later copies, with the reprinted B and other corrections, still have

[1] See *Chorus Vatum* where Hunter gives a list of the Commendatory Verses in his copy.

have the uncorrected reading 'chrusht', but evidence afforded by these readings is of very little value. If they prove anything it is that the printer made up no complete copies until he had reprinted Sheet B, as will be seen below.

Taking into consideration the evidence on both sides, the most that can safely be said is that it may originally have been intended to issue *Lucasta* without A, and some copies got into the market without this Sheet. It was not unusual for verses which arrived late to be included in a book, some copies of which had already been issued, printed on a special sheet or half sheet. This was done with Lovelace's own lines written for *Musarum Oxoniensium Charisteria*, 1638.[1] But even if some copies of *Lucasta* were made up without A, there is no ground for assuming that they were issued before the complete book was ready, and we may accept Thomason's date, June 21, as the approximate day of publication.

There is one other point connected with the Commendatory Verses which may be mentioned. In one of the British Museum copies (238 b. 52) the order of the preliminary matter is altered; the verses by Marvell, Hall, Lenton, Rawlins, and Dudley Lovelace are placed immediately after the Dedication and before the verses by Francis Lovelace; *i.e.* Sigs. a 7, a 8, A 1 and A 2 are put between a 2 and a 3. The signatures and the catchword 'De' on A 2 prove that it is no more than a mere alteration of the order. Possibly the purpose of this was to give Marvell the place of honour, a supposition which is supported by the fact that two other copies, now in America, also have the Commendatory Verses 'improperly arranged', presumably in the same order as the British

[1] See note to p. 29.

British Museum copy.[1] This same copy differs from any other that I have seen in that there is an ornamental initial on p. 1 and also a head ornament to the same page.

There remains the question with regard to Sheet B. That this was entirely reprinted can be seen at a glance from the position of the signatures. The reprint is genuine and not a later fake. This is certain both from the number of copies in which it is found and from the paper which, though it is inferior and though the watermarks are different, is not substantially of a later date than the earlier issue. Old paper might well have been used for a single or even a few forgeries, but it is hardly conceivable that over a dozen copies should want this particular sheet, or that a forger would not have kept closer to the original. There are many differences of spelling and a few of punctuation between the two versions. These are referred to below as B (1) and B (2). The following is a complete list:

				Original Sheet.	*Reprint.*
Page	17	line	10	foaming	foming
,,	17	,,	17	wee	we
,,	17	,,	18	Unseene,	Unseen,
,,	17	,,	18	unknowne,	unknown,
,,	18	,,	1	doe	do
,,	18	Title		*Warres.*	*Wars.*
,,	18	line	8	Nunnerie	Nunnery
,,	18	,,	10	Warre	War
,,	19	,,	1	Starre	Star
,,	19	,,	9	face	face,
,,	19	,,	10	Ayre,	Ayre
,,	19	,,	11	knowne	known
,,	19	,,	15	Sunne,	Sun,
,,	19	,,	17	runne	run
,,	20	,,	1	keepes	keeps

Page 20

[1] Nothing was known of Marvell in 1649, but the change could have been made a number of years later.

Page	20	line	3	poore	poor
,,	20	,,	3	sleepes	sleeps
,,	20	,,	6	stole,	stole
,,	20	,,	7.	Beare,	Bear,
,,	20	Title		To Amarantha,	To Amarantha.
,,	20	line	8	*AMarantha*	*AMarantha*,
,,	20	,,	12	unconfin'd	inconfin'd
,,	21	,,	1	Ev'ry	Eve'ry
Catchword after Stanza III				Doe	Do
Page	21	line	5	Doe	Do
,,	21	,,	11	downe	down
,,	21	,,	12	fanne	fan
,,	21	,,	12	breast.	brest.
,,	21	,,	13	Heere	Heer
,,	21	,,	13	strippe	strip
,,	21	,,	14	Creame	Cream
,,	21	,,	15	drawne	drawn
,,	21	,,	16	teare	tear
,,	21	,,	19	sorrowes	sorrows [*some copies*]
,,	21	,,	19	weepe.	weep,
,,	21	,,	20	*keepe.*	*keep.*
,,	22	,,	1	bowe,	bow,
,,	22	,,	2	possest,	possesse,
,,	22	,,	7	Our	our
,,	22	,,	14	Pearles	Pearls
,,	22	,,	14	shells	shels
,,	22	,,	18	more;	more:
,,	22	,,	21	afresh	a fresh
,,	23	,,	2	Crowne	Crown
,,	23	,,	2	awhile	a while
,,	23	,,	9	faire	fair
,,	23	,,	12	blackest,	Blackest,
,,	23	,,	13	skye-like	sky-like
,,	23	,,	15	clowdy	cloudy
,,	23	,,	16	damaske	damask
,,	24	,,	1	New-startled	New startled
,,	24	,,	4	strowe	strow
Catchword after Stanza II				Vermi-	Vermilion
Page	24	line	9	Offpring	Ofspring
,,	24	,,	10	*Silenus*;	*Silenus*:
,,	24	,,	11	decke	deck
,,	24	,,	15	nest	Nest
,,	24	,,	17	dresses,	dresses;

Page 24

Page 24	line 19	feare;	fear;
,, 24	,, 20	neere.	near.
,, 25	Title	*dauncing*	*dancing*
,, 25	line 8	Starre	Star
,, 25	,, 10	swells	swels
,, 25	,, 13	thought	thought,
,, 25	,, 14	Ambitious	ambitious
,, 26	,, 7	sweare	swear
,, 26	,, 14	must	Must
,, 26	,, 14	wrong,	wrong.
,, 27	,, 1	browne	brown
,, 27	,, 1	haire,	hair,
,, 27	,, 5	un-plow'd-up	un-plow'd up

Of thirty-one copies about which I have information, eighteen have B (1) and thirteen B (2). It is possible that part of the original issue was in some way destroyed. This is not very likely, however, and the printer certainly had in stock sheets of B (1) after he had printed B (2), and he went on using them as well as the newer and worse printed sheets when making up the complete book. This is clearly proved by the corrections, noted above, which were made when *Lucasta* was in the press.

As a rule these corrections are quite easy to follow, e. g. the readings 'sends' and 'exposing' in lines 14 and 15 of p. 116 were corrected to 'finds' and 'expiring'. Of fifteen copies with B (1), five have the uncorrected and ten the corrected readings. No copy with B (2) has the uncorrected readings, while eleven have the words 'finds' and 'expiring'.

Again, in line 32 of p. 109, 'stop' was corrected to 'strip'. I find that of twenty-two copies, about which I have this information, three with B (1) have the uncorrected and ten the corrected reading; the remaining nine copies with (B 2) all have the corrected reading.

These are both instances of a correction made before many copies of the sheet had been printed. It is different with

with two misprints, in lines 5 and 9 of p. 105, which were obviously not corrected till later. Eleven copies with B (1) and seven copies with B (2) have the uncorrected readings 'Heovenly' and 'colme'; five copies with B (1) and five with B (2) have the corrected readings 'Heavenly' and 'calme'.

Again the word 'Chrusht' in line 16 of p. 95 was corrected to 'Crusht'. I have information on this point about twelve copies only, but the evidence is sufficient. Five copies with B (1) and one copy with B (2) read 'Chrusht'; two copies with B (1) and four with B (2) read 'Crusht'.

These figures prove that the printer still had in his hands many, if not all, copies of the first issue of Sheet B after he had reprinted it. The fact that there is so large a proportion of copies with B (2) might seem to lend weight to the theory that some of the original sheets must have been spoilt or destroyed, but it is quite possible that the sheet had to be re-set simply because the printer made a bad miscalculation of the numbers he would require, and distributed his type after printing an entirely insufficient quantity.[1] It was not an uncommon practice in Elizabethan times for a printer to distribute his type as he went along so that he could use it again,[2] and though by the middle of the seventeenth century printers may have had more type, it is not improbable that Harper was forced to use the same economy. Originally he followed copy and kept Lovelace's spelling. Reprinting, he saved time—it would also be more economical—by spelling as he chose and this would account for the shorter spellings,

[1] Judging from the scarcity of *Lucasta* now, no large number can ever have been printed.

[2] See *Notes on Bibliographical Evidence*, R. B. McKerrow, reprinted from the *Transactions of the Bibliographical Society*, vol. xii, 1914, p. 46.

spellings, then beginning to come into use, which form the majority of differences between the reprint of the sheet and the original. Mr. Percy Simpson has pointed out to me a parallel instance in the case of Jonson's *The Divell is an Asse*, Folio 2, 1640. The sheets of the original issue of the play, which was printed in 1630, for some reason gave out and had to be made good in 1641. The printer reset the sheets with innumerable alterations and blunders. It was, of course, a common practice in the seventeenth century for printers to make corrections in the text of a book while they were actually engaged in printing it, and to collect the sheets afterwards quite indiscriminately, so that in one book there are often countless combinations of sheets in different states. A well-known example of this is the first edition of *Paradise Lost*. In the case of *Lucasta* it would seem that the sheets were kept roughly in the order in which they were printed, and though, as is proved by the figures quoted above, this did not always happen, sheets containing a misprint which was afterwards corrected are generally bound with B (1). In the present edition the spelling of B (1) is kept. This is clearly the form in which Lovelace intended his poems to appear and it is in harmony with the rest of the book.

The 1649 *Lucasta* is a rare volume. I have seen or heard of twenty-seven copies of it in England; of these the British Museum and the Bodleian have each three copies and there are two in the Dyce Collection. The others are in private hands.[1] I traced two copies in America and the late Mr. Beverley Chew kindly told me of eight others. One of

[1] One or two which I have seen at Messrs. Sotheby's may have since gone to America, though one at least of the ten copies mentioned as being in America has since returned to England.

of these contains the reputed signature of Anne Lovelace to whom *Lucasta* was dedicated. Hazlitt mentioned it in his edition of Lovelace and stated that the autograph 'was taken from a copy of Massinger's *Bondman* (edit. 1638, 4to) which her Ladyship once owned'.[1] Mr. Chew told me that the signature is pasted on the back of the title. A hundred years ago Sir Egerton Brydges spoke of *Lucasta* as still procurable, though by no means common. To-day perfect copies with both the engravings are very scarce. At the date of publication the book sold for a few pence; the copy which once belonged to John Aubrey, now in the Bodleian, has the prices 8*d.* and 4*d.* marked in it. In 1914 the Huth copy was bought by Messrs. Quaritch for £145.[2]

Lucasta. Posthume Poems and *Elegies Sacred to the Memory of the Author.*

The second volume of Lovelace's poems was published two years after his death by his youngest brother, Dudley Posthumus Lovelace, assisted by Eldred Revett, who seems to have been a kind of literary agent to Lovelace.[3] The collation of the book is four leaves without signature; B–I 6 in eights, irregularly marked. There is an engraved title to the *Elegies* on H 6 verso; the printed title to them is on H 7, the verso of which is blank. Lovelace's poems and translations

[1] This fact Hazlitt took without acknowledgement from *Bibliotheca Anglo-Poetica*, 1815, p. 194.

[2] Messrs. Quaritch kindly sent me details of this copy. Another interesting copy, bought by Messrs. Quaritch in 1906, was that presented by Charles Cotton to Lord Chesterfield. According to *Book Prices Current*, 1906, p. 642, there is an inscription on the fly-leaf, 'Charles Cotton ex dono Authoris', and the arms of Philip Stanhope, second Earl of Chesterfield, are stamped in gold on the side. This inscription is in Cotton's hand, not Lovelace's.

[3] See above and note to p. 184. There was a delay in the publication.

tions occupy pp. 1–107. The *Elegies* are paged afresh, beginning on H 8, 14 pages;[1] the signatures are continuous. The question of the half sheet or two quarter sheets which make up the first four leaves is complicated. Without entering into details, it may be said that the two leaves with the title-page and the Dedication by Dudley Lovelace are the same in all copies. The differences occur in the two other leaves. These may be a blank and the Faithorne engraving of 'Lucasta' in any one of three states, a blank and the Hollar engraving in any one of three states,[2] generally the second or third, or they may contain both the Faithorne and the Hollar engravings. The blank may appear only as a stub. The Hollar engraving may be added to a copy which already contained the other, in which case it forms an extra leaf. When the Hollar engraving occurs in the third state, and probably when it is found in the second, it was printed at a later date than the rest of the book. This is possibly true of the Faithorne engraving in the third state.[3]

Lucasta. Posthume Poems was not published till 1660, the date on the title-page of the *Elegies*. The book could not have been issued before the very end of 1659, as it is entered on the Stationers' Registers under Nov. 14.[4] The copy used for this edition is that in the Bodleian (Malone 372). I have also used my own copy and one in the Worcester College Library. This little volume is now very rare, much more

[1] The first page of the *Elegies* was numbered 101. If the title was counted and the pagination otherwise continuous, it would have been 111. From this it seems possible that the printer at first intended to make the pagination continuous.

[2] The first is undated; the second is dated *1660*, the third *1662*.

[3] I have, of course, not seen copies in all these states, or perfect copies in more than one or two of them.

[4] See note to title-page [*1659*] and Revett's letter quoted above (p. lviii).

more so than *Lucasta*, 1649. I have only been able to see nine copies of it. The sale of nineteen copies of *Lucasta* is recorded in *Book Prices Current* between 1887 and 1920. In the same period only four copies of *Lucasta. Posthume Poems* were sold. One of these, a perfect copy with three engravings, was bought by Messrs. Quaritch in 1912. It was then stated to be the only perfect copy in that condition sold for twenty-five years. The Britwell copy, a presentation copy from the editor, also with three engravings, was bought by the same firm in 1924.

As is mentioned above, the second editions of the two volumes of Lovelace's poems appeared in 1817 and 1818, when they were separately reprinted by S. W. Singer at Chiswick, from the Press of C. Whittingham.[1] This edition, which was limited, cut out all passages which were thought to be obscene or improper. The Commendatory Verses comprised in Sheet A of the 1649 volume are omitted. One new poem was included, *A Dialogue betwixt Cordanus and Amoret on a Lost Heart*, which, says the editor in his Preface to the second volume, 'is to be met with, set to music, in Lawes's "First Book of Ayres"'. W. C. Hazlitt also included this poem in his edition. The *Dialogue* is not by Richard Lovelace, but by his brother Colonel Francis Lovelace, to whom it is attributed in the table of *Ayres and Dialogues, For One, Two, and Three Voyces. By Henry Lawes . . . the First Booke London 1653*. The poem was reprinted in Cotgrave's *Wits Interpreter*, 1655.

The next edition of Lovelace was that by Mr. W. Carew Hazlitt in the *Library of Old Authors*, published in 1864 and reprinted in 1897. Mr. Hazlitt gave Anthony Wood's life, and

[1] Volumes i and iv of *Select Early English Poets*.

and added notes to it and to the poems, the order of which he altered.

In 1906 the two *Lucastas* were included in the 'Unit Library'; the edition was afterwards sold in 'Hutchinson's Popular Classics'. This book is nearly a reprint of the original volumes, has a few notes, and gives Wood's 'Life'. It follows the British Museum copy (238. b. 52) in the order of the Commendatory Verses.

An edition in two volumes, 8vo, was privately printed for the members of the Caxton Club, Chicago, in 1921. This is a reprint of Hazlitt's edition of Lovelace rather than of Lovelace. It faithfully reproduces every impossible reading invented by that editor, and prints the poems in the order devised by him.

The lines by Lovelace already mentioned as not having been included in *Lucasta* or *Lucasta. Posthume Poems* were contributed to *Letters of Affaires Love and Courtship. Written To several persons of Honour and Quality; By the Exquisite Pen of Monsieur de Voiture, A member of the Famous French Academy established at Paris by Cardinall de Richelieu. Englished by J. D. London, Printed for T. Dring and J. Starkey, and are to be sold at their shops, at the George in Fleet street near Cliffords Inne, and the Miter at the West end of St Pauls Church, 1657.* The lines are under the portrait to which there is no inscription, the whole being on copper. In this edition they are placed after the 1659 volume.[1]

W. C. Hazlitt quoted some lines, which were prefixed to John Quarles' *Fons Lachrymarum*, 1648, and signed R. L., with the suggestion that they might be by Lovelace. He added,

[1] See note to p. 236.

added, however, that if so it was strange that they were not admitted into either of the volumes of his poetry. It is almost certain that they.are not by Lovelace, but by Richard Love of Corpus Christi College, Cambridge, who also wrote verses before Quarles' *Emblems* and was, with Quarles, a contributor to the Cambridge collection *Carmen Natalitium*, 1635.

The following lines by Alexander Brome were first noticed by a writer, signing himself F. W., in the *Gentleman's Magazine*, 1792, i. 166. They were not included among the Commendatory Verses prefixed to *Lucasta* and have not been printed in any of the subsequent editions.

To Colonel Lovelace *on his Poems.*

So through the *Chaos* crept the first born ray,
That was not yet grown up to be a day,
And form'd the *World*; as do your powerful rythmes
[rhymes?]
Through the thick darkness of these verseless times,
These *antigenius* dayes, this boystrous age,
Where there dwells nought of Poetry but rage:
Just so crept learning forth the rav'nous fire
Of the Schismatick *Goths*, and *Vandals* ire:
As do in these more barbarous dayes our times,
VVhen what was meant for ruine, but refines.
Why mayn't we hope for *Restauration*, when
As ancient *Poets* Townes, the new rais'd men,
The tale of *Orpheus* and *Amphion* be
Both solid truths with this *Mythology*?
For though you make not stones & trees to move,
Yet men more senceless you provoke to love.
I can't but think, spite of the filth that's hurl'd
Over this small *Ench'ridion of the World*,
A *day* will break, when we again may see

Wits

Wits like themselves, club in an harmony.
Though *Pulpiteers* can't do it, yet 'tis fit
Poets have more *success*, because more *wit.*
Their *Prose* unhing'd the State; why mayn't your verse
Polish those souls, that were fil'd rough by theirs?
Go on, and prosper; though I want your skill,
In weighty matters tis enough to will.
And novv the *Reader* looks I should help rear
Your glories *Trophy*, else what make I here?
'Tis not to praise you; for one may as well
Go tell *Committees* that there is an hell,
Or tell the World there is a *Sun*, as praise
Your amorous fancy, which it self cant raise
'Bove *Envies* reach or flatteries; Ladies love
To kiss those accents; who dares disapprove
What they stile good? our lines, our lives, and all;
[By their *opinions* either rise or fall:]
Therefore the cause why these are fixed here,
Is livery-like to shew some great man 's near;
Let them stand bare, and usher, not commend;
They are not for *Encomiums*, but t'*attend.*[1]

In the present edition the text of 1649 and 1659 is closely followed; the only departures from it are in the case of more or less obvious mistakes. The chief difficulty, the question of the titles to the poems on pp. 95 and 96, is discussed in the notes. The punctuation has only been altered when it seems wrong by seventeenth-century standards or when there is a second authoritative text, as in the case of verses contributed to other publications, the punctuation of which has sometimes been preferred. All changes are recorded in the textual notes.

[1] See *Songs and other Poems. By Alex. Brome, Gent. . . . London, Printed for Henry Brome, at the Gun in Ivy-Lane, 1661*, pp. 138–9.

The line in brackets is not found in this edition, but is taken from the second and third editions of 1664 and 1668. In line 27 the first edition reads 'help near'.

LUCASTA:

EPODES, ODES, SONNETS, SONGS, &c.

TO WHICH IS ADDED ARAMANTHA,

A

PASTORALL.

BY

RICHARD LOVELACE, Esq.

LONDON,

Printed by THO. HARPER, and are to be sold by THO. EVVSTER, at the GUN, in Ivie Lane. 1649.

THE DEDICATION.

To the Right Honourable, my Lady

ANNE LOVELACE.

TO the Richest TREASURY
That e're fill'd Ambitious Eye;
'To the faire bright MAGAZIN
Hath impoverisht Loves Queen;
'To th' EXCHEQUER of all Honour,
(All take Pensions but from her)
'To the TAPER of the Thore
Which the God himselfe but bore;
'To the SEA of Chast Delight
Let me cast the DROP I write.
And as at LORETTO's shrine
CÆSAR shovels in his Mine,
Th' Empres spreads her Carkanets,
The Lords submit their Coronets,
Knights their Chased Armes hang by,
Maids Diamond-Ruby Fancies tye;
Whilst from the PILGRIM she wears
One poore false Pearl, but ten true tears:
So among the Orient Prize,
(Saphyr-Onyx Eulogies)
Offer'd up unto your Fame:
Take my GARNET-DUBLET Name,
And vouchsafe 'midst those Rich Joyes
(With Devotion) these TOYES.

RICHARD LOVELACE.

To my best Brother on his Poems, called LUCASTA.

NOw y'have oblieg'd the age, thy wel known Worth
Is to our joy auspiciously brought forth.
Good morrow to thy Son, thy first borne flame,
Which as thou gav'st it birth, stamps it a name;
That Fate, and a discerning age shall set
The chiefest jewell in her Coronet.

Why then needs all this paines, those season'd pens,
That standing lifeguard to a booke, (kinde friends)
That with officious care thus guard thy gate,
As if thy Child *were illegitimate?*
Forgive their freedome, since unto their praise
They write to give, not to dispute thy Bayes.

As when some glorious Queen, *whose pregnant wombe*
Brings forth a Kingdome, with her first borne Sonne;
Marke but the Subjects joyfull hearts, and eyes,
Some offer Gold, and others Sacrifice;
This *slayes a Lambe,* That *not so rich as hee,*
Brings but a Dove, This *but a bended knee;*
And though their gifts be various, yet their sence
Speaks only this one thought, Long live the Prince.

So, my best Brother, if unto your name
I offer up a thin blew burning flame;
Pardon my love, since none can make thee shine;
Vnlesse they kindle first their Torch *at thine:*
Then as inspir'd, they boldly write, nay that,
Which their amazed Lights but twinkl'd at,
And their illustrate thoughts doe voice this right,
Lucasta *held their* Torch, *thou gav'st it Light.*

Francis Lovelace *Col.*

AD

AD EUNDEM.

EN puer Idalius *tremulis circumvolat alis,*
Quem propè ſidentem castior uret amor.
Lampada ſic videas circum volitare Pyrauſtā,
Cui contingenti eſt flamma futura rogus.
Ergo procul fugias, Lector, cui nulla placebunt
Carmina, ni fuerint turpia, ſpurca, nigra.
Sacrificus Romæ *luſtralem venditat undam:*
Caſtior eſt illâ Caſtalis *unda mihi:*
Limpida, & εἰλικρινὴς, *nullâ putredine ſpiſſa,*
Scilicet ex puro defluit illa Iugo.
Ex pura veniunt tam dîa poemata mente,
Cui ſcelus eſt Veneris, *vel tetigiſſe fores.*
Thomas Hamerſley *Eques Auratus.*

On the POEMS.

HOw humble is thy Muſe (*Deare*) *that can daign*
Such ſervants as my pen to entertaine?
When all the ſonnes of wit glory to be
Clad in thy Muſes gallant livery?
I ſhall diſgrace my maſter, prove a ſtaine,
And no addition to his honour'd traine.
Though all that read me will preſume to ſwear
I neer read thee: yet if it may appear
I love the Writer and admire the writ,
I my owne want betray, not wrong thy wit.
Did thy worke want a prayſe, my barren brain
Could not afford it: my attempt were vaine.
It needs no foyle: All that ere writ before
Are foyles to thy faire Poems and no more.
Then to be lodg'd in the ſame ſheets with thine,
May prove diſgrace to yours, but grace to mine.
Norris Jephſon *Col.*

To my much loved friend, *Richard Lovelace* Esq.

Carmen Eroticum.

D*Eare* Lovelace, *I am now about to prove*
I cannot write a verse, but can write Love.
On such a subject as thy Booke, I cou'd
Write Books much greater, but not half so good.
But as the humble tenant that does bring
A chicke or egges for's offering,
Is tane into the buttry, and does fox
Equall with him that gave a stalled oxe:
So, (since the heart of ev'ry cheerfull giver
Makes pounds no more accepted then a stiver,)
Though som thy praysse in rich stiles sing, I may
In stiver stile write Love as well as they.
I write so well that I no Criticks feare;
For who'le read mine, when as thy booke's so neer,
Vnlesse thy selfe? then you shall secure mine
From those, and Ile engage my selfe for thine;
They'd do't themselves, thẽ this allay you'l take,
I love thy book, and yet not for thy sake.

John Jephson *Col.*

To my Noble and most ingenious Friend, Col. *Richard Lovelace,* upon his LUCASTA.

S*O from the pregnant braine of* Jove *did rise*
Pallas, *the Queene of wit, and beautious eyes:*
As faire LUCASTA *from thy temples flowes,*
Temples no lesse ingenious then Joves.
Alike in birth, so shall she be in Fame,
And be immortall to preserve thy Name.

Another,

Another, upon the POEMS.

NOw when the wars augment our woes and fears
And the ſhrill noiſe of drums oppreſſe our ears,
Now peace and ſafety from our ſhores are fled
To holes and cavernes to ſecure their head:
Now all the graces from the Land are ſent,
And the nine Muſes ſuffer baniſhment,
Whence ſpring theſe raptures? whence this heavenly rime?
So calme and even in ſo harſh a time:
Well might that charmer his faire Cælia *crowne,*
And that more poliſh't Tyterus *renowne*
His Sacariſſa, *when in groves and bowres*
They could repoſe their limbs on beds of flowrs:
When wit had prayſe, and merit had reward,
And every noble ſpirit did accord
To love the Muſes, and their Prieſts to raiſe,
And interpale their browes with flouriſhing bayes;
But in a time diſtracted ſo to ſing,
When peace is hurried hence on rages wing,
When the freſh bayes is from the Temple torne,
And every Art and Science made a ſcorne,
Then to raiſe up by muſicke of thy Arts
Our drooping ſpirits and our grieved hearts,
Then to delight our ſouls, and to inſpire
Our breaſt with pleaſure, from thy charming Lyre,
Then to divert our ſorrowes by thy ſtraines,
Making us quite forget our ſeven yeers paines
In the paſt wars, unleſſe that Orpheus *be*
A ſharer in thy glory: for when he
Deſcended downe for his Euridice,
He ſtroke his Lute with like-admired Art,
And made the damned to forget their ſmart.

John Pinchbacke *Col.*

ΕΞΑΣΤΙΧΟΝ.

ΕΞΑΣΤΙΧΟΝ.

Ψεύδεται ὅττις ἔφη· δολιχὸς χρόνος οἶδεν ἀμείβειν
  Οὔνομα, καὶ πάντων μνημοσύνην ὀλέσαι.
Ὠιδὴν γὰρ ποιεῖν ἀγαθὴν πόνος ἄφθονός ἐστι,
  Ὃν μηδεὶς αἰὼν οἶδεν ὀδοῦσι φαγεῖν.
Ὠιδὴν σοί, φίλε, δῶκε μέγ' ἄφθιτον, ὠγαθέ, μοῦσα,
  Ὡς εἰς αἰῶνας οὔνομα ᾗε τέον.

Villiers Harington *L. C.*

To his much honoured Friend Mr. *Richard Lovelace,* on his Poems.

HE *that doth paint the beauties of your verse*
  Must use your pensil, be polite, soft, terse;
Forgive that man whose best of Art is love,
If he no equall Master to you prove;
My heart is all my Eloquence, and that
Speaks sharp affection, when my words fall flat.
I reade you like my Mistresse, and discry
In every line the quicknesse of her eye,
Her smoothnesse in each syllable, her grace
To marshall ev'ry word in the right place:
It is the excellence, and soule of wit
When ev'ry thing is free, as well as fit,
For Metaphors packt up and crowded close,
Swath ẏ minds sweetnes, & display the throws,
And like those chickens hatcht in furnaces,
Produce or one limbe more, or one limbe lesse
Then nature bids: survey such when they write,
No clause but's justl'd with an Epithite;

So powerfully you draw when you perſwade,
Paßions in you, in us are Vertues made;
Such is the Magick of that lawfull ſhell
That where it doth but talke, it doth compell:
For no Apelles *'till this Time e're drew*
A Venus *to the waſte ſo well as you.*

W. RUDYERD.

THe world ſhall now no longer mourne, nor vex
For th' obliquity of a croſſ-grain'd ſex;
Nor beauty ſwell above her Bankes, (and made
For Ornament) the univerſe invade
So fiercely, that 'tis queſtion'd in our Bookes,
Whether kils moſt, the Amazon's ſword, or Lookes.
Lucaſta *in loves game diſcreetly makes*
Women, and men joyntly to ſhare the ſtakes,
And lets us know, when women ſcorne, it is
Mens hot Love, makes the Antiperistasis.
And a Lay Lover here ſuch comfort finds,
As Holy Writ gives to affected minds.
The wilder Nymphs Lov's power could not comand
Are by thy Almighty Numbers brought to hand,
And flying Daphne's *caught, amazed vow*
They never heard Apollo *court till now.*
Tis not by force of Armes this feat is done,
For that would puzzle even the Knight o' th' Sun,
But 'tis by pow'r of Art, and ſuch a way
As Orpheus *us'd, when he made fiends obay.*

J. NEEDLER, *Hoſp. Grayenſis.*

To

To his Noble Friend Mr. *Richard Lovelace,* upon his POEMS.

SIR,

OVr *times are much degenerate from those*
Which your sweet Muse, which your fair Fortune chose,
And as complexions alter with the Climes,
Our wits have drawne th' infection of our times.
That candid Age no other way could tell
To be ingenious, but by speaking well.
Who best could prayse, had then the greatest prayse,
Twas more esteemd to give, then weare the Bayes:
Modest ambition studi'd only then,
To honour not her selfe, but worthy men.
These vertues now are banisht out of Towne,
Our Civill Wars have lost the Civicke crowne.
He highest builds, who with most Art destroys,
And against others Fame his owne employs.
I see the envious Caterpillar sit
On the faire blossome of each growing wit.
The Ayre's already tainted with the swarms
Of Insects which against you rise in arms.
Word-peckers, Paper-rats, Book-scorpions,
Of wit corrupted, the unfashion'd Sons.
The barbed Censurers begin to looke
Like the grim consistory on thy Booke;
And on each line cast a reforming eye,
Severer then the yong Presbytery.
Till when in vaine they have thee all perus'd,
You shall for being faultlesse be accus'd.
Some reading your Lucasta, *will alledge*
You wrong'd in her the Houses Priviledge.

Some

Some that you under ſequeſtration are,
Becauſe you write when going to the Warre,
And one the Book prohibits, becauſe Kent
Their firſt Petition by the Authour ſent.
But when the beauteous Ladies came to know
That their deare Lovelace *was endanger'd ſo:*
Lovelace *that thaw'd the moſt congealed breſt,*
He who lov'd beſt, and them defended beſt,
Whoſe hand ſo rudely graſps the ſteely brand,
Whoſe hand ſo gently melts the Ladies hand,
They all in mutiny though yet undreſt
Sally'd, and would in his defence conteſt.
And one the lovelieſt that was yet e're ſeen,
Thinking that I too of the rout had been,
Mine eyes invaded with a female ſpight,
(She knew what pain 't would be to loſe that ſight.)
O no, miſtake not, I reply'd, for I
In your defence, or in his cauſe would dy.
But he ſecure of glory and of time
Above their envy, or mine aid doth clime.
Him, valianſt men, and faireſt Nymphs approve,
His Booke in them finds Judgement, with you Love.

Andr. Marvell.

To Colonel *RICHARD LOVELACE,*
on the publishing of his ingenious Poems.

I*F the deſire of Glory ſpeak a mind*
More nobly operative, & more refin'd,
What vaſt ſoule moves thee? Or what Hero's ſpirit
(Kept in'ts traduction pure) doſt thou inherit,
That not contented with one ſingle Fame,
Doſt to a double glory ſpread thy Name?

And

And on thy happy temples ſafely ſet
Both th' Delphick *wreath and* Civic *Coronet?*
Waſt not enough for us to know how far
Thou couldſt in ſeaſon ſuffer, act, and dare?
But we muſt alſo witneſſe with what height
And what Ionick *ſweetneſſe thou canſt write?*
And melt thoſe eager paſſions that are
Stubborn enough t'enrage the God of war,
Into a noble Love, which may aſpire
In an illuſtrious Pyramid of Fire,
Which having gained his due ſtation may
Fix there, and everlaſting flames diſplay.
This is the braver path, time ſoone can ſmother
The dear-bought ſpoils & tropheis of the other.
How many fiery Heroes have there been,
Whoſe triumphs were as ſoone forgot, as ſeen?
Becauſe they wanted ſome diviner one
To reſcue thẽ from night and make thẽ known.
Such art thou to thy ſelfe: while others dream
Strong flatt'ries on a fain'd or borrow'd theam,
Thou ſhalt remaine in thine owne luſtre bright,
And adde unto't LVCASTA'S chaſter light.
For none ſo fit to ſing great things as He
That can act o're all lights of Poetry.
Thus had Achilles *his owne Geſts deſign'd,*
He had his Genius Homer *far outſhin'd.*

JO. HALL.†

To the Honorable, Valiant, and Ingenious Colonel RICHARD LOVELACE, *on his Exquisite POEMS.*

Poets, and Painters have ſome near relation,
Compar'd with Fancy and Imagination;
The one paints ſhadowed perſons (in pure kind,)
The other points the Pictures of the Mind
In purer Verſe. And as rare Zeuxes *fame*
Shin'd till Apelles *Art eclips'd the ſame*
By a more exquiſite, and curious line
Than Zeuxeſes *(with penſill far more fine,)*
So have our modern Poets, late done well
Till thine appear'd (which ſcarce have paralel.)
They like to Zeuxes *Grapes beguile the ſenſe,*
But thine do raviſh the Intelligence;
Like the rare banquet of Apelles, *drawn,*
And covered over with moſt curious Lawn.
Thus if thy careles draughts are cal'd the beſt,
What would thy lines have beene, had'ſt thou profeſt
That faculty (infus'd) of Poetry,
Which adds ſuch honour unto thy Chivalry?
Doubtles thy verſe had all as far tranſcended
As Sydneyes *Proſe, who Poets once defended.*
For when I read thy much renowned Pen,
My Fancy there finds out another Ben
In thy brave language, judgement, wit, & art,
Of every piece of thine, in every part:

Where

Where thy ſeraphique Sydneyan *fire is raiſed high,*
In Valour, Vertue, Love, and Loyalty:
Virgil *was ſtyl'd the loftieſt of All,*
Ovid *the ſmootheſt, and moſt naturall,*
Martiall *conciſe, and witty, quaint, and pure,*
Iuvenall *grave and learned, (though obſcure:)*
But all theſe rare ones, which I heere reherſe,
Do live againe in Thee, and in thy Verſe:
Although not in the language of their time,
Yet in a ſpeech as copious and ſublime:
The rare Apelles, *in thy picture wee*
Perceive, and in thy ſoule Apollo *ſee.*

Wel may each grace, & muſe then crown thy praiſe
With Mars *his Banner, and* Minerva's *Bayes.*

FRA. LENTON.

To his Honoured and Ingenious Friend Col. RICHARD LOVELACE, on his LUCASTA.

CHaſt *as Creation meant us, and more bright*
Then the firſt day in's uneclipſed light,
Is thy Lucaſta, *and thou offereſt heere*
Lines *to her* Name *as undefil'd and cleere:*
Such as the firſt indeed more happy dayes,
(When Vertue, Wit, and Learning, wore the bayes;
Now Vice aſſumes) would to her memory *give*
A Veſtall Flame, *that ſhould for ever live*

Plac't

Plac't in a Christal Temple, rear'd to be
The Embleme of her thoughts integrity;
And on the Porch thy Name *insculpt, my* Friend,
Whose Love like to the flame can know no end:
The Marble steps that to the Alter brings
The hallowed Priests *with their cleane Offerings*
Shall hold their Names, *that humbly crave to be*
Votaries *to' th' shrine, and grateful* Friends *to thee:*
So shal we live (although our Offrings prove
Meane to the World) for ever by thy Love.

THO. RAWLINS.

To my Deare Brother, Colonel RICHARD LOVELACE.

I*LE doe my nothing too; and try*
To dabble to thy memory:
Not that I offer to thy Name,
Encomiums, *of thy lasting Fame.*
Those, by the Landed have been writ,
Mine's but a Yonger-Brother-Wit;
A Wit thats hudled up in scarres,
Borne like my rough selfe in the Warres;
And as a Squire in the fight,
Serves only to attend the Knight:
So 'tis my glory in this Field,
Where others act, to beare thy Shield.

Dudley Lovelace, *Capt.*

De

De Domino *Richardo Lovelacio*, Armigero & Chiliarcha, viro incomparabili.

ECce Tibi Herôem claris natalibus ortum;
Cujus honoratos Cantia vidit Avos.
Cujus adhuc memorat rediviva Batavia Patrem,
Inter & Herculeos enumerare solet.
Qui Tua, Grolla ferox, laceratus vulnere multo,
Fulmineis vidit mœnia fracta globis.
Et cum, sæva, Tuas fudisset, Iberia, Turmas,
e Afflatu pyrii pulveris ictus obit.
Hæc sint Magna; tamen major majoribus hic est,
Nititur & pennis altiùs ire novis.
Sermonem patrium callentem, & murmura Celtæ,
Non piguit Linguas edidicisse Duas.
Quicquid Roma vetus, vel quicquid Græcia jactat,
Musarum nutrix alma Calena dedit.
Gnaviter Hesperios compressit Marte cachinnos,
Devictasq; dedit Cantaber ipse manus.
Non evitavit validos Dunkerka lacertos,
Non intercludens alta Lacuna *vias.*
Et scribenda gerens vivaci marmore digna,
Scribere, Cæsareo more, vel ipse potest.
Cui gladium Bellona dedit, Calamumq; Minerva,
Et geminæ Laurus circuit umbra Comam,
Cujus si Faciem spectes, vultusq; decorem,
Vix puer Idalius gratior ore fuit.

AD

AD EUNDEM.

HERRICO *succede meo: dedit Ille priora*
Carmina, carminibus non meliora Tuis.

ΠΕΡΙ ΤΟΥ ΑΥΤΟΥ.

Λουλάκιες πολλαπλασίως φίλος ἐστὶν ἐμεῖο.
Τοὔνομά τ' ἐστι φίλος, καὶ το νόημα φίλος.
Καὶ φίλον ἀντιφιλῶ μεγάλοισιν ἀγακλυτὸν ἔργοις
Τῆς ἀρετῆς· Χειρὸς, καὶ Φρενὸς ἀγχινόου.
Ὃς νέος ἐν τυτθαῖς πινυτῶς σελίδεσσιν ἔθηκε
Ποιητῶν ἑκατὸν χρώματ' ἐπαγρόμενος.
Φροῦρον Μουσάων, πυκινῶν ἑσσῆνα Μελισσῶν,
Ἐν Χαρίτεσσι Χάριν, καὶ Μελέεσσι μέλι.

Scripsit JO. HARMARUS *Oxoniensis*

C. W. M.

Song.

Set by Mr. *Henry Lawes.*

TO LUCASTA,

Going beyond the Seas.

I.

IF to be abſent were to be
Away from thee;
Or that when I am gone,
You or I were alone;
Then my *Lucaſta* might I crave
Pity from bluſtring winde, or ſwallowing wave.

II.

But I'le not ſigh one blaſt or gale
To ſwell my ſaile,
Or pay a teare to ſwage
The foaming blew-Gods rage;
For whether he will let me paſſe
Or no, I'm ſtill as happy as I was.

III.

Though Seas and Land betwixt us both,
Our Faith and Troth,
Like ſeparated ſoules,
All time and ſpace controules:
Above the higheſt ſphere wee meet
Unſeene, unknowne, and greet as Angels greet.

IV.

So then we doe anticipate
Our after-fate,
And are alive i' th' skies,
If thus our lips and eyes
Can ſpeake like ſpirits unconfin'd
In Heav'n, their earthy bodies left behind.

Song.

Set by Mr. *John Laniere.*

To Lucasta,

Going to the Warres.

I.

TELL me not (Sweet) I am unkinde,
That from the Nunnerie
Of thy chaſte breaſt, and quiet minde,
To Warre and Armes I flie.

II.

True; a new Miſtreſſe now I chaſe,
The firſt Foe in the Field;
And with a ſtronger Faith imbrace
A Sword, a Horſe, a Shield.

III.

Yet this Inconſtancy is ſuch,
As you too ſhall adore;
I could not love thee (Deare) ſo much,
Lov'd I not Honour more.

A PARADOX.

I.

TIS true the beauteous Starre
To which I firſt did bow
Burnt quicker, brighter far
Then that which leads me now;
Which ſhines with more delight;
For gazing on that light
So long, neere loſt my ſight.

II.

Through foule, we follow faire,
For had the World one face
And Earth been bright as Ayre,
We had knowne neither place;
Indians ſmell not their Neaſt;
A *Swiſſe* or *Finne* taſtes beſt,
The Spices of the Eaſt.

III.

So from the glorious Sunne,
Who to his height hath got,
With what delight we runne
To ſome black Cave, or Grot?
And Heav'nly *Sydney* you
Twice read, had rather view
Some odde *Romance*, ſo new.

IV.

The God that conſtant keepes
Unto his Dieties,
Is poore in Joyes, and ſleepes
Impriſon'd in the skies:
This knew the wiſeſt, who
From *Juno* ſtole, below
To love a Beare, or Cow.

Song.

Set by Mr. *Henry Lawes.*

TO AMARANTHA,

That ſhe would diſhevell her haire.

I.

AMarantha ſweet and faire,
Ah brade no more that ſhining haire!
As my curious hand or eye,
Hovering round thee let it flye.

II.

Let it flye as unconfin'd
As it's calme Raviſher, the winde;
Who hath left his darling th' Eaſt,
To wanton o're that ſpicie Neaſt.

Ev'ry

III.

Ev'ry Tresse must be confest
But neatly tangled at the best;
Like a Clue of golden thread,
Most excellently ravelled.

IV.

Doe not then winde up that light
In Ribands, and o're-cloud in Night;
Like the Sun in's early ray,
But shake your head and scatter day.

V.

See 'tis broke! Within this Grove
The Bower, and the walkes of Love,
Weary lye we downe and rest,
And fanne each others panting breast.

VI.

Heere wee'l strippe and coole our fire
In Creame below, in milke-baths higher:
And when all Well's are drawne dry,
I'le drink a teare out of thine eye.

VII.

Which our very Joyes shall leave
That sorrowes thus we can deceive;
Or our very sorrowes weepe,
That joyes so ripe, so little keepe.

To

TO CHLOE,
Courting her for his Friend.

I.

CHloe behold! againe I bowe,
Againe posseſt, againe I woe;
From my heat hath taken fire,
Damas, noble youth, and fries:
Gazing with one of mine eyes
Damas, halfe of me expires:
Chloe behold! Our Fate's the ſame,
Or make me Cinders too, or quench his Flame.

II.

I'd not be King, unleſſe there ſate
Leſſe Lords that ſhar'd with me in State;
Who by their cheaper Coronets know
What glories from my Diadem flow:
It's uſe and rate values the Gem,
Pearles in their ſhells have no eſteem;
And I being Sun within thy Sphere,
'Tis my chiefe beauty thinner lights ſhine there.

III.

The Us'rer heaps unto his ſtore,
By ſeeing others praiſe it more;
Who not for gaine, or want doth covet,
But 'cauſe another loves, doth love it:
Thus gluttons cloy'd afreſh invite
Their Guſts, from ſome new appetite;
And after cloth remov'd, and meate,
Fall too againe by ſeeing others eate.

Sonnet.

Sonnet.

Set by Mr. *Hudſon.*

I.

DEpoſe your finger of that Ring,
And Crowne mine with't awhile;
Now I reſtor't—Pray do's it bring
Back with it more of ſoile?
Or ſhines it not as innocent,
As honeſt, as before 'twas lent?

II.

So then inrich me with that Treaſure,
Will but increaſe your ſtore,
And pleaſe me (faire one) with that pleaſure
Muſt pleaſe you ſtill the more:
Not to ſave others is a curſe
The blackeſt, when y'are ne're the worſe.

Ode.

Set by Dr. *John Wilſon.*

TO LUCASTA.

The Roſe.

I.

SWeet ſerene skye-like Flower,
Haſte to adorn her Bower:
From thy long clowdy bed,
Shoot forth thy damaske head.

New-

II.

New-ſtartled bluſh of *Flora*!
The griefe of pale *Aurora*,
Who will conteſt no more;
Haſte, haſte, to ſtrowe her floore.

III.

Vermilion Ball that's given
From lip to lip in Heaven;
Loves Couches cover-led:
Haſte, haſte, to make her bed.

IV.

Deare Offſpring of pleas'd *Venus*,
And Jollie, plumpe *Silenus*;
Haſte, haſte, to decke the Haire
Of th' only, ſweetly Faire.

V.

See! Roſie is her Bower,
Her floore is all this Flower;
Her Bed a Roſie neſt
By a Bed of Roſes preſt.

VI.

But early as ſhe dreſſes,
Why fly you her bright Treſſes?
Ah! I have found I feare;
Becauſe her Cheekes are neere.

Gratiana

Gratiana *dauncing and ſinging.*

I.

SEE! with what conſtant Motion
Even, and glorious, as the Sunne,
Gratiana ſteeres that Noble Frame,
Soft as her breaſt, ſweet as her voyce
That gave each winding Law and poyze,
And ſwifter then the wings of Fame.

II.

She beat the happy Pavement
By ſuch a Starre made Firmament,
Which now no more the Roofe envies;
But ſwells up high with *Atlas* ev'n,
Bearing the brighter, nobler Heav'n,
And in her, all the Dieties.

III.

Each ſtep trod out a Lovers thought
And the Ambitious hopes he brought,
Chain'd to her brave feet with ſuch arts,
Such ſweet command, and gentle awe,
As when ſhe ceas'd, we ſighing ſaw
The floore lay pav'd with broken hearts.

So

IV.

So did ſhe move; ſo did ſhe ſing
Like the Harmonious ſpheres that bring
Unto their Rounds their muſick's ayd;
Which ſhe performed ſuch a way,
As all th' inamour'd world will ſay
The *Graces* daunced, and *Apollo* play'd.

THE SCRUTINIE.†

Song.

Set by Mr. *Thomas Charles*.

I.

WHY ſhould you ſweare I am forſworn,
Since thine I vow'd to be?
Lady it is already Morn,
And 'twas laſt night I ſwore to thee
That fond impoſſibility.

II.

Have I not lov'd thee much and long,
A tedious twelve houres ſpace?
I muſt all other Beauties wrong,
And rob thee of a new imbrace;
Could I ſtill dote upon thy Face.

Not,

III.

Not, but all joy in thy browne haire,
By others may be found;
But I muſt ſearch the black and faire
Like skilfull Minerallist's that ſound
For Treaſure in un-plow'd-up ground.

IV.

Then, if when I have lov'd my round,
Thou prov'ſt the pleaſant ſhe;
With ſpoyles of meaner Beauties crown'd,
I laden will returne to thee,
Ev'n ſated with Varietie.

Princeſſe LÖYSA *drawing*

I Saw a little Diety,
Minerva in Epitomy,
Whom *Venus* at firſt bluſh, ſurpris'd,
Tooke for her winged wagge diſguis'd;
But viewing then whereas ſhe made
Not a diſtreſt, but lively ſhade
Of *Eccho*, whom he had betrayd,
Now wanton, and ith' coole oth' Sunne
With her delight a hunting gone;
And thouſands more, whom he had ſlaine,
To live, and love, belov'd againe:
Ah this is true Divinity!
I will un-God that Toye! cri'd ſhe;

Then

Then markt ſhe *Syrinx* running faſt
To *Pans* imbraces, with the haſte
Shee fled him once, whoſe reede-pipe rent,
He finds now a *new Inſtrument.*
Theſeus return'd, invokes the Ayre
And windes, then wafts his faire;
Whilſt *Ariadne* raviſh't ſtood
Halfe in his armes, halfe in the flood.

Proud *Anaxerete* doth fall
At *Iphis* feete, who ſmiles of all:
And he (whilſt ſhe his curles doth deck)
Hangs no where now, but on her neck.

Heere *Phœbus* with a beame untombes
Long-hid *Leucothoë*, and dombes
Her Father there; D*aphne* the faire
Knowes now no bayes but round her haire;
And to *Apollo* and his Sons
Who pay him their due Oriſons,
Bequeaths her Lawrell-robe, that flame
Contemnes, Thunder and evill Fame.

There kneel'd *Adonis* freſh as ſpring,
Gaye as his youth, now offering
Her ſelfe thoſe joyes with voice and hand,
Which firſt he could not underſtand.

Transfixed *Venus* ſtood amas'd,
Full of the Boye and Love, ſhe gaz'd;
And in imbraces ſeemed more
Senceleſſe and cold, then he before.
Uſeleſſe Childe! In vaine (ſaid ſhe)
You beare that fond Artillerie:
See heere a Pow'r above the ſlow
Weake execution of thy bow.

So

So ſaid, ſhe riv'd the Wood in two,
Unedged all his Arrowes too,
And with the ſtring their feathers bound
To that part whence we have our wound.

See, ſee! the darts by which we burn'd
Are bright *Löyſa's* pencills turn'd;
With which ſhe now enliveth more
Beauties, then they deſtroy'd before.

An Elegie.

Princeſſe KATHERINE *borne, chri-ſtened, buried in one day.*

YOu that can aptly mixe your joyes with cries,
And weave white Iös with black Elegies,
Can Caroll out a Dirge, and in one breath
Sing to the Tune, either of life, or death;
You that can weepe the gladneſſe of the ſpheres,
And pen a Hymne in ſtead of Inke with teares,
Here, here, your unproportion'd wit let fall
To celebrate this new-borne Funerall, (wombe
And greete that little Greatneſſe, which from th'
Dropt both a load to th' Cradle, and the Tombe.

Bright ſoule! teach us to warble, with what feet
Thy ſwathing linnen, and thy winding ſheet,
Mourne or ſhout forth that Fonts ſolemnitie,
Which at once buried, and chriſt'ned thee,
And change our ſhriller paſſions with that ſound,
Firſt told thee into th' ayre, then the ground.

Ah

Ah wert thou borne for this, only to call
The *King* and *Queen* guests to your buriall?
To bid good night, your day not yet begun,
And showe's a setting, ere a rising Sun?

Or wouldst thou have thy life a Martyrdom?
Dye in the Act of thy Religion;
Fit, excellently, innocently good,
First sealing it with water, then thy blood?
As when on blazing wings a blest man sores,
And having past to God through fiery dores
Straight's roab'd wth flames, whẽ the same Elemẽt
Which was his shame, proves now his Ornament;

Oh how he hast'ned death, burn't to be fryed,
Kill'd twice with each delay, 'till deified:
So swift hath been thy race, so full of flight,
Like him condemn'd, ev'n aged with a night,
Cutting all lets with clouds, as if th' hadst been
Like Angels plum'd, and borne a *Cherubin.*

Or in your journey towards Heav'n, say,
Tooke you the World a little in your way?
Saw'st and dislik'st its vaine pompe, then didst flye
Up for eternall glories to the skye?
Like a Religious Ambitious one
Aspiredst for the everlasting Crowne?

Ah holy Traytour to your brother Prince,
Rob'd of his birth-right, and preheminence:
Could you ascend yon' Chaire of State e're him,
And snatch from th' heire the Starry Diadem?
Making your honours now as much uneven
As Gods on earth, are lesse then Saints in Heav'n.

Triumph!

Triumph! ſing triumphs then! Oh put on all
Your richeſt lookes dreſt for this Feſtivall;
Thoughts full of raviſht reverence, with eyes
So fixt as when a Saint we canonize;
Clap wings with *Seraphins* before the Throne,
At this eternall Coronation,
And teach your ſoules new mirth, ſuch as may be
Worthy this Birth-day to Divinity.

But ah! theſe blaſt your feaſts, the Jubilies
We ſend you up are ſad, as were our cries,
And of true joy, we can expreſſe no more
Thus crown'd, then when we buried thee before.

Princeſſe in heav'n forgivenes! whilſt we
Reſigne our office to the *Hierarchy.*

Love Conquer'd.†

A Song.

Set by Mr. *Henry Lawes.*

I.

THE childiſh God of Love did ſweare
Thus; by my awfull Bow and Quiver,
Yon' weeping, kiſſing, ſmiling pair,
I'le ſcatter all their vowes ith' Ayr,
And their knit imbraces ſhiver.

Up

II.

Up then to th' head with his beſt Art,
  Full of ſpite and envy blowne,
At her conſtant Marble Heart,
  He drawes his ſwifteſt ſureſt Dart,
Which bounded back, and hit his owne.

III.

  Now the Prince of fires burnes!
Flames in the luſter of her eyes;
Triumphant ſhe, refuſes, ſcornes;
  He ſubmits, adores, and mournes,
And is his Votreſſe Sacrifice.

IV.

  Fooliſh Boye! Reſolve me now
What 'tis to ſigh and not be heard?
He weeping, kneel'd, and made a vow,
  The world ſhall love as yon' faſt two,
So on his ſing'd wings up he ſteer'd.

A looſe SARABAND.

Set by Mr. *Henry Lawes.*†

I.

AH me! the little Tyrant Theefe!
  As once my heart was playing,
He ſnatcht it up and flew away,
  Laughing at all my praying.

Proud

II.

Proud of his purchaſe he ſurveyes,
And curiouſly ſounds it,
And though he ſees it full of wounds,
Cruell ſtill on he wounds it.

III.

And now this heart is all his ſport,
Which as a Ball he boundeth
From hand to breaſt, from breaſt to lip,
And all it's reſt confoundeth.

IV.

Then as a Top he ſets it up,
And pitifully whips it;
Sometimes he cloathes it gay and fine,
Then ſtraight againe he ſtrips it.

V.

He cover'd it with *falſe beliefe*,
Which glorioully ſhow'd it;
And for a morning-Cuſhionet,
On's Mother he beſtow'd it.

VI.

Each day with her ſmall brazen ſtings,
A thouſand times ſhe rac'd it;
But then at night, bright with her Gemmes,
Once neere her breaſt ſhe plac'd it.

VII.

There warme it gan to throb and bleed;
She knew that ſmart and grieved;
At length this poore condemned Heart
With theſe rich drugges repreeved.

VIII.

She waſht the wound with a freſh teare,
Which my *Lucaſta* dropped,
And in the ſleave-ſilke of her haire,
'Twas hard bound up and wrapped.

IX.

She proab'd it with her conſtancie,
And found no Rancor nigh it;
Only the anger of her eye,
Had wrought ſome proud fleſh by it.

X.

Then preſt ſhe *Narde* in ev'ry veine
Which from her kiſſes trilled;
And with the balme heald all it's paine
That from her hand diſtilled.

XI.

But yet this heart avoyds me ſtill,
Will not by me be owned;
But's fled to it's *Phyſitians* breaſt,
There proudly ſits inthroned.

A

A forsaken Lady to her false Servant that is disdained by his new Mistris.

WEre it that you so shun me 'cause you wish
(Cruel'est) a fellow in your wretchednesse,
Or that you take some small ease in your owne
Torments, to heare another sadly groane,
I were most happy in my paines, to be
So truely blest, to be so curst by thee:
But Oh! my cries to that doe rather adde,
Of which too much already thou hast had,
And thou art gladly sad to heare my moane;
Yet sadly hearst me with derision.

Thou most unjust, that really dost know,
And feelst thy selfe the flames I burne in, Oh!
How can you beg to be set loose from that
Consuming stake, you binde another at?

Uncharitablest both wayes, to denie
That pity me, for which your selfe must dye,
To love not her loves you, yet know the paine
What 'tis to love, and not be lov'd againe.

Flye on, flye on swift Racer, untill she
Whom thou of all ador'st shall learne of thee,
The pace t' outfly thee, and shall teach thee groan,
What terrour 'tis t' outgo, and be outgon.

Not yet looke back, nor yet, muſt we
Run then like ſpoakes in wheeles eternally
And never overtake? Be dragg'd on ſtill
By the weake Cordage of your untwin'd will,
Round without hope of reſt? No, I will turne
And with my goodnes boldly meete your ſcorne;
My goodneſſe which Heav'n pardon, and that fate
Made you hate love, and fall in love with hate.

But I am chang'd! bright reaſon that did give
My ſoule a noble quicknes, made me live
One breath yet longer, and to will, and ſee,
Hath reacht me pow'r to ſcorne as well as thee:
That thou which proudly trampleſt on my grave,
Thy ſelfe mightſt fall, conquer'd my double ſlave,
That thou mightſt ſinking in thy triumphs moan,
And I triumph in my deſtruction.

Hayle holy cold! chaſte temper hayle! the fire
Rav'd o're my purer thoughts I feele t' expire,
And I am candied Ice; yee pow'rs! If e're
I ſhall be forc't unto my Sepulcher;
Or violently hurl'd into my Urne,
Oh make me chooſe rather to freeze, then burne.

ORPHEUS *to* BEASTS.

Song.

Set by Mr. *Curtes.*

I.

HEre, here, oh here *Euridice*,
Here was ſhe ſlaine;
Her ſoule 'ſtill'd through a veine:
The Gods knew leſſe
That time Divinitie,
Then ev'n, ev'n theſe
Of brutiſhneſſe.

II.

Oh could you view the Melodie
Of ev'ry grace,
And Muſick of her face,
You'd drop a teare,
Seeing more Harmonie
In her bright eye,
Then now you heare.

ORPHEUS

ORPHEUS *to* WOODS.

Song.

Set by Mr. *Curtes.*

HEark! Oh heark! you guilty Trees,
In whoſe gloomy Galleries
Was the cruell'ſt murder done,
That e're yet eclipſt the Sunne;
Be then henceforth in your twigges
Blaſted e're you ſprout to ſprigges;
Feele no ſeaſon of the yeere,
But what ſhaves off all your haire,
Nor carve any from your wombes
Ought but Coffins, and their Tombes.

The Graſſe-hopper.

To my Noble Friend, Mr. CHARLES COTTON.

Ode.

I.

OH thou that ſwing'ſt upon the waving haire
Of ſome well-filled Oaten Beard,
Drunke ev'ry night with a Delicious teare
Dropt thee from Heav'n, where now th' art (reard.

The

II.

The Joyes of Earth and Ayre are thine intire,
That with thy feet and wings doſt hop and flye;
And when thy Poppy workes thou doſt retire
To thy Carv'd Acron-bed to lye.

III.

Up with the Day, the Sun thou welcomſt then,
Sportſt in the guilt-plats of his Beames,
And all theſe merry dayes mak'ſt merry men,
Thy ſelfe, and Melancholy ſtreames.

IV.

But ah the Sickle! Golden Eares are Cropt;
Ceres and *Bacchus* bid good night;
Sharpe froſty fingers all your Flowr's have topt,
And what ſithes ſpar'd, Winds ſhave off quite.

V.

Poore verdant foole! and now green Ice! thy Joys
Large and as laſting, as thy Peirch of Graſſe,
Bid us lay in 'gainſt Winter, Raine, and poize
Their floods, with an o'reflowing glaſſe.

VI.

Thou beſt of *Men* and *Friends*! we will create
A Genuine Summer in each others breaſt;
And ſpite of this cold Time and froſen Fate
Thaw us a warme ſeate to our reſt.

Our

VII.

Our ſacred harthes ſhall burne eternally
As Veſtall Flames, the North-wind, he (flye
Shall ſtrike his froſt-ſtretch'd Winges, diſſolve and
This *Ætna* in Epitome.

VIII.

Dropping *December* ſhall come weeping in,
Bewayle th' uſurping of his Raigne;
But when in ſhow'rs of old Greeke we beginne,
Shall crie, he hath his Crowne againe!

IX.

Night as cleare *Heſper* ſhall our Tapers whip
From the light Caſements where we play,
And the darke Hagge from her black mantle ſtrip,
And ſticke there everlaſting Day.

X.

Thus richer then untempted Kings are we,
That asking nothing, nothing need:
Though Lord of all what Seas imbrace; yet he
That wants himſelfe, is poore indeed.

Dialogue.

LUCASTA, ALEXIS.

Set by Mr. *John Gamble.*

I.

Lucasta.

TEll me *Alexis* what this parting is,
That ſo like dying is, but is not it?

Alexis.

It is a *ſwounding* for a while from bliſſe,
'Till kind *how doe you* call's us from the fit.
If then the ſpirits only ſtray, let mine
Fly to thy boſome.

Lucasta.

And my Soule to thine.

Chorus.

Thus in our native ſeate we gladly give
Our right, for one where we can better live.

II.

Lucaſta.

But Ah this ling'ring murdring Farewel!
Death quickly wounds, & wounding cures the ill.

Alexis.

Alexis.

It is the glory of a valiant Lover,
Still to be dying, ſtill for to recover.

Chorus.

Souldiers ſuſpected of their courage goe,
That Enſignes, and their Breaſts untorne ſhow:
Love neere his Standard when his Hoſte he ſets,
Creates alone freſh-bleeding *Bannerets.*

III.

Alexis.

But part we when thy Figure I retaine
Still in my Heart, ſtill ſtrongly in mine Eye?

Lucaſta.

Shadowes no longer then the Sun remaine,
But whē his beams that made 'em fly, they fly.

Chorus.

Vaine dreames of Love! that only ſo much bliſſe
Allow us, as to know our wretchedneſſe;
And deale a larger meaſure in our Paine
By ſhowing Joy, then hiding it againe.

IV.

Alexis.

No, whilſt light raigns, *Lucaſta* ſtil rules here,
And all the night ſhines wholy in this ſphere.

Lucaſta.

I know no Morne but my *Alexis* Ray,
To my dark thoughts the breaking of the day.

Chorus.

Alexis.

Alexis.

So in each other if the pitying Sun
Thus keep us fixt; nere may his Courſe be run!

Lucaſta.

And Oh! if Night us undivided make;
Let us ſleepe ſtill, and ſleeping never wake!

The Cloſe.

Cruell *Adiev's* may well adjourne awhile
The Seſſions of a Looke, a Kiſſe, or Smile,
And leave behinde an angry grieving Bluſh;
But time nor Fate can part us joyned thus.

TO ELLINDA,
That lately I have not written.

I.

IF in me Anger, or diſdaine
In you, or both, made me refraine
From th' Noble intercourſe of Verſe,
That only Vertuous thoughts rehearſe;
  Then Chaſte *Ellinda* might you feare
  The ſacred Vowes that I did ſweare.

II.

But if alone ſome pious thought
Me to an inward ſadneſſe brought;
Thinking to breath your Soule too well,
My tongue was charmed with that ſpell,
  And left it (ſince there was no roome
  To Voyce your worth enough) ſtrooke dumbe.

So

III.

So then this *Silence* doth reveale
No thought of Negligence, but Zeale:
For as in Adoration,
This is Loves true Devotion:
Children and Fooles the words repeate,
But *Anch'rites* pray in teares and ſweate.

Sonnet.

Set by Mr. *William Lawes*.†

I.

WHen I by thy faire ſhape did ſweare,
And mingled with each Vowe a teare,
I lov'd, I lov'd thee beſt,
I ſwore as I profeſt;
For all the while you laſted warme and pure,
My Oathes too did endure;
But once turn'd faithleſſe to thy ſelfe, and Old,
They then with thee inceſſantly grew Cold.

II.

I ſwore my ſelfe thy Sacrifice
By th' *Ebon* Bowes that guard thine eyes,
Which now are alter'd White,
And by the glorious Light
Of both thoſe Stars, of which (their Spheres bereft)
Only the Gellie's left:
Then changed thus, no more I'm bound to you
Then ſwearing to a Saint that proves untrue.

LUCASTA

LUCASTA *Weeping*.

Song.

Set by Mr. *John Laneere.*

I.

L*Ucasta* wept, and ſtill the bright
Inamour'd God of Day,
With his ſoft Handkercher of Light,
Kiſt the wet Pearles away.

II.

But when her Teares his heate or'e came,
In Cloudes he quenſht his Beames,
And griev'd, wept out his Eye of Flame,
So drowned her ſad Streames.

III.

At this ſhe ſmil'd, when ſtraight the Sun
Cleer'd, with her kinde deſires;
And by her eyes Reflection,
Kindled againe his Fires.

The

The Vintage *to the* Dungeon.

A Song.

Set by Mr. *William Lawes.*

I.

SIng out pent Soules, ſing cheerefully!
Care Shackles you in Liberty,
Mirth frees you in Captivity:
Would you double fetters adde?
Elſe why ſo ſadde?

Chorus.

Beſides your pinion'd armes you'l finde
Griefe too can manakell the minde.

II.

Live then Pris'ners uncontrol'd;
Drinke oth' ſtrong, the Rich, the Old,
Till Wine too hath your Wits in hold;
Then if ſtill your Jollitie,
And Throats are free;

Chorus.

Tryumph in your Bonds and Paines,
And daunce to th' Muſick of your Chaines.

On

On the Death of Mrs. ELIZABETH FILMER.

An Elegiacall Epitaph.

YOU that ſhall live awhile before
Old Time tyr's, and is no more;
When that this Ambitious Stone
Stoopes low as what it tramples on;
Know that in that Age when Sinne
Gave the World Law, and governd Queene,
A Virgin liv'd, that ſtill put on
White Thoughts, though out of faſhion;
That trac't the Stars 'ſpite of report,
And durſt be good, though chidden for't:
Of Such a Soule that Infant Heav'n
Repented what it thus had giv'n;
For finding equall happy man,
Th' impatient Pow'rs ſnatcht it agen:
Thus Chaſte as th' Ayre whither ſhee's fled,
She making her Celeſtiall bed
In her warme Alablaſter lay
As cold as in this houſe of Clay;
Nor were the Rooms unfit to feaſt
Or Circumſcribe This Angel-gueſt;
The Radiant Gemme was brightly ſet
In as Divine a Carkanet;
For which the clearer was not knowne,
Her Minde, or her Complexion:

Such

Such an everlasting Grace,
Such a beatifick Face
Incloysters here this narrow floore
That possest all hearts before.
Blest and bewayl'd in Death and Birth!
The smiles and teares of Heav'n and Earth!
Virgins at each step are afeard,
FILMER is shot by which they steer'd,
Their Star extinct, their beauty dead
That the yong world to honour led;
But see! the rapid Spheres stand still,
And tune themselves unto her will.
Thus, although this Marble must,
As all things crumble into dust,
And though you finde this faire-built Tombe
Ashes, as what lyes in it's Wombe;
Yet her Saint-like name shall shine
A living Glory to this Shrine,
And her eternall Fame be read,
When all, but *very Vertue's dead.*

TO LUCASTA.

From Prison.

An Epode.

I.

LOng in thy Shackels, liberty,
I ask not from these walls, but thee;
Left for a while anothers Bride
To fancy all the world beside.

Yet

II.

Yet e're I doe begin to love,
See! How I all my objects prove;
Then my free Soule to that confine,
'Twere possible I might call mine.

III.

First I would be in love with *Peace*,
And her rich swelling breasts increase;
But how alas! how may that be,
Despising Earth, will she love me?

IV.

Faine would I be in love with *War*,
As my deare Just avenging star;
But War is lov'd so ev'ry where,
Ev'n He disdaines a Lodging here.

V.

Thee and thy wounds I would bemoane
Faire thorough-shot *Religion*;
But he lives only that kills thee,
And who so bindes thy hands, is free.

VI.

I would love a *Parliament*
As a maine Prop from Heav'n sent;
But ah! Who's he that would be wedded
To th' fairest body that's beheaded?

VII.

Next would I couirt my *Liberty*,
And then my Birth-right, *Property*;
But can that be, when it is knowne
There's nothing you can call your owne?

VIII.

A *Reformation* I would have,
As for our griefes a *Sov'raigne* ſalve;
That is, a cleanſing of each wheele
Of State, that yet ſome ruſt doth feele:

IX.

But not a Reformation ſo,
As to reforme were to ore'throw;
Like Watches by unskilfull men
Disjoynted, and ſet ill againe.

X.

The *Publick Faith* I would adore,
But ſhe is banke-rupt of her ſtore;
Nor how to truſt her can I ſee,
For ſhe that couzens all, muſt me.

XI.

Since then none of theſe can be
Fit objects for my Love and me;
What then remaines, but th' only ſpring
Of all our loves and joyes? The KING.

He

XII.

He who being the whole Ball
Of Day on Earth, lends it to all;
When ſeeking to ecclipſe his right,
Blinded, we ſtand in our owne light.

XIII.

And now an univerſall miſt
Of Error is ſpread or'e each breaſt,
With ſuch a fury edg'd, as is
Not found in th' inwards of th' Abyſſe.

XIV.

Oh from thy glorious Starry Waine
Diſpenſe on me one ſacred Beame
To light me where I ſoone may ſee
How to ſerve you, and you truſt me.

LUCASTA'S FANNE,

With a Looking glaſſe in it.

I.

EAſtrich! Thou featherd Foole, and eaſie prey,
That larger ſailes to thy broad Veſſell needſt;
Snakes through thy guttur-neck hiſſe all the day,
Then on thy I'ron Meſſe at ſupper feedſt.

II.

Oh what a glorious tranſmigration
 From this, to ſo divine an edifice
Haſt thou ſtraight made! neere from a winged ſtone
 Transform'd into a Bird of Paradice!

III.

Now doe thy Plumes for hiew and Luſter vie
 With th' Arch of heav'n that triumphs o're paſt wet,
And in a rich enamel'd pinion lye
 With Saphyres, Amethiſts, and Opalls ſet.

IV.

Somtime they wing her ſide, thẽ ſtrive to drown
 The Day's eyes piercing beames, whoſe am'rous heat
Sollicites ſtill, 'till with this ſhield of down
 From her brave face, his glowing fires are beat.

V.

But whilſt a plumy curtaine ſhe doth draw,
 A Chryſtall Mirror ſparkles in thy breaſt,
In which her freſh aſpect when as ſhe ſaw,
 And then her Foe retired to the Weſt,

VI.

Deare *Engine* that oth' Sun got'ſt me the day,
 'Spite of his hot aſſaults mad'ſt him retreat!
No wind (ſaid ſhe) dare with thee henceforth play
 But mine own breath to coole the Tyrants heat.

My

VII.

My lively ſhade thou ever ſhalt retaine
In thy incloſed feather-framed glaſſe,
And but unto our ſelves to all remaine
Inviſible, thou feature of this face!

VIII.

So ſaid, her ſad Swaine over-heard, and cried
Yee Gods! for faith unſtaind this a reward!
Feathers and glaſſe t'outweigh my vertue tryed?
Ah ſhow their empty ſtrength! the Gods accord.

IX.

Now fall'n the brittle Favourite lyes, and burſt!
Amas'd *Lucaſta* weepes, repents, and flies
To her *Alexis*, vowes her ſelf acurſt
If hence ſhe dreſſe her ſelfe, but in his eyes.

LUCASTA, *taking the waters at Tunbridge.*

Ode.

I.

YEE happy floods! that now muſt paſſe
The ſacred conduicts of her Wombe,
Smooth, and tranſparent as your face,
When you are deafe, and windes are dumbe.

Be

II.

Be proud! and if your Waters be
  Foul'd with a counterfeyted teare,
Or ſome falſe ſigh hath ſtained yee,
  Haſte, and be purified there.

III.

And when her Roſie gates y' have trac'd,
  Continue yet ſome Orient wet,
'Till turn'd into a Gemme, y' are plac'd
  Like Diamonds with Rubies ſet.

IV.

Yee drops that dew th' *Arabian* bowers,
  Tell me did you e're ſmell or view
On any leafe of all your flowers
  Soe ſweet a ſent, ſo rich a hiew?

V.

But as through th' Organs of her breath,
  You trickle wantonly, beware;
Ambitious Seas in their juſt death
  As well as Lovers muſt have ſhare.

VI.

And ſee! you boyle as well as I,
  You that to coole her did aſpire,
Now troubled, and neglected lye,
  Nor can your ſelves quench your owne fire.

Yet

VII.

Yet ſtill be happy in the thought,
That in ſo ſmall a time as this,
Through all the *Heavens* you were brought
Of *Vertue*, *Honour*, *Love* and *Bliſſe*.

TO LUCASTA.
Ode *Lyrick*.

I.

AH *Lucaſta*, why ſo Bright!
Spread with early ſtreaked light!
If ſtill vailed from our ſight,
What is't but eternall night?

II.

Ah *Lucaſta*, why ſo Chaſte!
With that vigour, ripenes grac't!
Not to be by Man imbrac't
Makes that Royall coyne imbace't,
And this golden Orchard waſte.

III.

Ah *Lucaſta*, why ſo Great!
That thy crammed coffers ſweat;
Yet not owner of a ſeat
May ſhelter you from Natures heat,
And your earthly joyes compleat.

Ah

IV.

Ah *Lucaſta*, why ſo Good!
Bleſt with an unſtained flood
Flowing both through ſoule and blood;
If it be not underſtood,
'Tis a Diamond in mud.

V.

Lucaſta! ſtay! why doſt thou flye?
Thou art not Bright, but to the eye,
Nor Chaſte, but in the Mariage-tye,
Nor Great, but in this Treaſurie,
Nor Good, but in that ſanctitie.

VI.

Harder then the Orient ſtone,
Like an Apparition,
Or as a pale ſhadow gone
Dumbe and deafe ſhe hence is flowne.

VII.

Then receive this equall dombe,
Virgins ſtrow no teare or bloome,
No one dig the *Parian* wombe;
Raiſe her marble heart ith' roome,
And tis both her Coarſe and Tombe.

To

To my Worthy Friend Mr. Peter Lilly: *on that excellent Picture of his Majesty, and the Duke of Yorke, drawne by him at* Hampton-Court.

SEE! what a *clouded Majesty*! and eyes (rise!
Whose glory through their mist doth brighter
See! what an humble bravery doth shine,
And griefe triumphant breaking through each line;
How it commands the face! so sweet a scorne
Never did *happy misery* adorne!
So sacred a contempt! that others show
To this, (oth' height of all the wheele) below;
That mightiest Monarchs by this shaded booke
May coppy out their proudest, richest looke.

Whilst the true *Eaglet* this quick luster spies,
And by his *Sun's* enlightens his owne eyes;
He cares his cares, his burthen feeles, then streight
Joyes that so lightly he can beare such weight;
Whilst either eithers passion doth borrow,
And both doe grieve the same victorious sorrow.

These my best *Lilly* with so bold a spirit
And soft a grace, as if thou didst inherit
For that time all their greatnesse, and didst draw
With those brave eyes your *Royall Sitters* saw.

Not

Not as of old, when a rough hand did ſpeake
A ſtrong Aſpect, and a faire face, a weake;
When only a black beard cried Villaine, and
By *Hieroglyphicks* we could understand;
When Chryſtall typified in a white ſpot,
And the bright Ruby was but one red blot;
Thou doſt the things *Orientally* the ſame,
Not only paintſt its colour, but its *Flame*:
Thou ſorrow canſt deſigne without a teare,
And with the Man his very *Hope* or *Feare*;
So that th' amazed world ſhall henceforth finde
None but my *Lilly* ever drew a *Minde*.†

ELINDA'S GLOVE.

Sonnet.

I.

THou ſnowy Farme with thy five Tenements!
Tell thy white Miſtris here was one
That call'd to pay his dayly Rents:
But ſhe a gathering Flowr's and Hearts is gone,
And thou left voyd to rude Poſſeſſion.

II.

But grieve not pretty *Ermin* Cabinet,
Thy Alablaſter Lady will come home;
If not, what Tenant can there fit
The ſlender turnings of thy narrow Roome,
But muſt ejected be by his owne dombe?

Then

III.

Then give me leave to leave my Rent with thee;
 Five kiſſes, one unto a place:
 For though the *Lute's* too high for me;
Yet Servants knowing Minikin nor Baſe,
Are ſtill allow'd to fiddle with the Caſe.

To FLETCHER *reviv'd.*

HOw have I bin Religious? what ſtrange good
Ha's ſcap't me that I never underſtood?
Have I Hel-guarded *Hæreſie* o'rthrowne?
Heald wounded States? made Kings & Kingdoms one?
That *Fate* ſhould be ſo merciful to me,
To let me live t' have ſaid I have read thee.

Fair Star aſcend! the Joy! the Life! the Light
Of this tempeſtuous Age, this darke worlds ſight!
Oh from thy Crowne of Glory dart one flame
May ſtrike a ſacred Reverence, whileſt thy Name
(Like holy *Flamens* to their God of Day)
We bowing, ſing; and whilſt we praiſe, we pray.

Bright Spirit! whoſe Æternal motion
Of Wit, like *Time*, ſtil in it ſelfe did run,
Binding all others in it, and did give
Commiſſion, how far this or that ſhal live;
Like *Deſtiny* of Poems, who, as ſhe
Signes death to all, her ſelfe can never dye.

And

And now thy purple-robed *Tragœdy*,
In her imbroider'd Buskins, cals mine eye,
Where brave *Aëtius* we ſee betray'd,
T' obey his Death, whom thouſand lives obey'd;
Whilſt that the *Mighty Foole* his Scepter breakes,
And through his *Gen'rals* wounds his own doome
Weaving thus richly *Valentinian* (ſpeakes,
The coſtlieſt Monarch with the cheapeſt man.

Souldiers may here to their old glories adde,
The *Lover* love, and be with reaſon *mad*:
Not as of old, *Alcides* furious,
Who wilder then his Bull did teare the houſe,
(Hurling his Language with the Canvas ſtone)
Twas thought the Monſter ror'd the ſob'rer Tone.

But ah! when thou thy ſorrow didſt inſpire
With Paſſions, Blacke as is her darke attire,
Virgins as *Sufferers* have wept to ſee
So white a Soule, ſo red a Crueltie;
That thou haſt griev'd, and with unthought redreſſe,
Dri'd their wet eyes who now thy mercy bleſſe;
Yet loth to loſe thy watry jewell, when
Joy wip't it off, Laughter ſtraight ſprung't agen.

Now ruddy cheeked *Mirth* with Roſie wings,
Fans ev'ry brow with gladneſſe, whilſt ſhe ſings
Delight to all, and the whole Theatre
A Feſtivall in Heaven doth appeare:
Nothing but Pleaſure, Love, and (like the Morne)
Each face a gen'ral ſmiling doth adorne.

Heare

Heare ye foul Speakers, that pronounce the Aire
Of Stewes and Shores, I will informe you where
And how to cloath aright your wanton wit,
Without her nasty Bawd attending it:
View here a loose thought sayd with such a grace,
Minerva might have spoke in *Venus* face;
So well disguis'd, that t'was conceiv'd by none
But *Cupid* had *Diana's* linnen on;

And all his naked parts so vail'd, th' expresse
The shape with clowding the uncomlinesse;
That if this *Reformation* which we
Receiv'd, had not been buried with thee,
The Stage (as this worke) might have liv'd and lov'd
Her Lines, the austere *Skarlet* had approv'd;
And th' *Actors* wisely been from that offence
As cleare, as they are now from *Audience.*

Thus with thy *Genius* did the *Scæne* expire,
Wanting thy Active and correcting fire,
That now (to spread a darknesse over all,)
Nothing remaines but *Poesie* to fall:
And though from these thy *Embers* we receive
Some warmth, so much as may be said, we live,
That we dare praise thee, blushlesse, in the head
Of the best piece *Hermes* to *Love* e're read,
That We rejoyce and glory in thy Wit,
And feast each other with remembring it,
That we dare speak thy thought, thy Acts recite;
Yet all men henceforth be afraid to write.

The

The Lady *A. L.*

My Asylum *in a great extremity.*

WIth that delight the Royal Captiv's brought
Before the Throne, to breath his farewell
To tel his last tale, and so end with it; (thought,
Which gladly he esteemes a Benefit;
When the brave Victor at his great Soule dumbe
Findes something there, Fate cannot overcome,
Cals the chain'd Prince, and by his glory led,
First reaches him his Crowne, and then his Head;
Who ne're 'til now thinks himself slave and poor;
For though nought else, he had himselfe before;
He weepes at this faire chance, nor wil allow,
But that the Diadem doth brand his brow,
And under-rates himselfe below mankinde,
Who first had lost his Body, now his Minde.

With such a Joy came I to heare my Dombe,
And haste the preparation of my Tombe,
When like good Angels who have heav'nly charge
To steere and guide mans sudden giddy barge,
She snatcht me from the Rock I was upon,
And landed me at lifes Pavillion:
Where I thus wound out of th' immense Abysse,
Was straight set on a Pinacle of Blisse.

Let

Let me leape in againe! and by that Fall
Bring me to my firſt woe, ſo cancel all:
Ah's this a quitting of the debt you owe,
To Cruſh her and her goodneſſe at one blow?
Defend me from ſo foule Impiety,
Would make Fiends grieve, & Furies weep to ſee.

Now ye Sage Spirits which infuſe in Men
That are oblidg'd, twice to oblige agen;
Informe my tongue in Labour, what to ſay,
And in what Coyne or Language to repay;
But you are ſilent as the Ev'nings Ayre,
When windes unto their hollow Grots repaire:
Oh then accept the all that left me is,
Devout Oblations of a ſacred Wiſh!

When ſhe walks forth, ye perfum'd wings oth' Eaſt
Fan her, 'til with the Sun ſhe haſtes to th' Weſt,
And when her heav'nly courſe calles up the day,
And breakes as bright, deſcend ſome gliſtering ray
To Circle her, and her as gliſtering Haire,
That all may ſay a living Saint ſhines there;
Slow Time with woollen feet make thy ſoft pace,
And leave no tracks ith' ſnow of her pure face:
But when this Vertue muſt needs fall, to riſe,
The brighteſt conſtellation in the Skies,
When we in Characters of Fire ſhall reade
How Cleere ſhe was alive, how ſpotles Dead;
All you that are a kinne to Piety,
For onely you can her cloſe mourners be,
Draw neer, and make of hallowed teares a Dearth,
Goodnes and Juſtice both, are fled the Earth.

If

If this be to be thankful, I'v a Heart
Broaken with Vowes, eaten with grateful ſmart,
And beſide this, the Vild World nothing hath
Worth any thing, but her provoked Wrath:
So then who thinkes to ſatisfie in time,
Muſt give a ſatisfaction for that Crime:
Since ſhe alone knowes the Gifts value, She
Can onely to her ſelfe requitall be,
And worthyly to th' Life paynt her owne Story
In it's true Colours and full native Glory;
Which when perhaps ſhe ſhal be heard to tell,
Buffoones and Theeves ceaſing to do ill,
Shal bluſh into a Virgin-Innocence,
And then woo others from the ſame offence;
The Robber and the Murderer in 'ſpite
Of his red ſpots ſhal ſtartle into White:
All good (Rewards layd by) ſhal ſtil increaſe
For Love of her, and Villany deceaſe;
Naught be ignote, not ſo much out of Feare
Of being puniſht, as offending Her:

So that when as my future daring Bayes
Shall bow it ſelfe in Lawrels to her praiſe,
To Crown her Conqu'ring Goodnes & proclaime
The due renowne, and Glories of her Name;
My Wit ſhal be ſo wretched, and ſo poore,
That 'ſtead of prayſing, I ſhal ſcandal her,
And leave when with my pureſt Art I'v done,
Scarce the Deſigne of what ſhe is begunne;
Yet men ſhal ſend me home, admir'd, exact,
Proud that I could from Her ſo wel detract.

Where then thou bold Inſtinct ſhal I begin
My endleſſe taske? To thanke her were a ſin

Great

Great as not ſpeake, and not to ſpeake a blame
Beyond what's worſt, ſuch as doth want a Name;
So thou my All, poore Gratitude, ev'n thou
In this, wilt an unthankful Office do:
Or wilt I fling all at her feet I have?
My Life, my Love, my very Soule a Slave?
Tye my free Spirit onely unto her,
And yeeld up my Affection Priſoner?
Fond Thought in this thou teacheſt me to give
What firſt was hers, ſince by her breath I live;
And haſt but ſhow'd me how I may reſigne
Poſſeſſion of thoſe things are none of mine.

A *Prologue* to the Scholars.

A Comædy *preſented at the White Fryers.*

A Gentleman to give us ſomewhat new,
Hath brought up *Oxford* with him to ſhow you;
Pray be not frighted – Tho the Scæne and Gown's
The *Univerſities*, the Wit's the Town's;
The Lines, each honeſt *Engliſhman* may ſpeake;
Yet not miſtake his Mother-tongue for *Greeke*,
For ſtil 'twas part of his vow'd Liturgie,
From learned Comedies *deliver me*!
Wiſhing all thoſe that lov'd 'em here aſleepe,
Promiſing *Scholars*, but no *Scholarſhip*.

You'd ſmile to ſee, how he do's vex and ſhake,
Speakes naught, but if the *Prologue* do's but take,
Or the firſt Act were paſt the Pikes once, then—
Then hopes and Joys, then frowns and fears agen,
Then bluſhes like a Virgin now to be
Rob'd of his Comicall Virginity
In preſence of you all; in ſhort you'd ſay
More hopes of Mirth are in his looks then Play.

Theſe feares are for the Noble and the Wiſe;
But if 'mongſt you there are ſuch fowle dead eyes
As can Damne unaraign'd, cal Law their Pow'rs,
Judging it ſin enough that it is *Ours*,
And with the Houſe ſhift their decreed Deſires,
Faire ſtill to th' *Blacke*, *Blacke* ſtill to the *White-Fryers*;
He dos proteſt he wil ſit down and weep
Caſtles and Pyramids ——— ——— ———
——— ——— ——— ——— No, he wil on,
Proud to be rais'd by ſuch *Deſtruction*,
So far from quarr'lling with himſelfe and Wit,
That he wil thank them for the *Benefit*,
Since finding nothing worthy of their *Hate*,
They reach him that themſelves muſt *Envy* at.

The Epilogue.

THE ſtubborne Author of the trifle, Crime,
That juſt now cheated you of 2 hour's time,†
Preſumptuous, it lik't him, began to grow
Careleſſe, whether it pleaſed you or no.

But

But we who ground th' excellence of a Play
On what the women at the dores wil ſay,
Who judge it by the Benches, and afford
To take your money ere his Oath or word
His *Schollars* ſchool'd, ſayd if he had been wiſe
He ſhould have wove in one, two *Comedies*;
The firſt for th' Gallery, in which the Throne
To their amazement ſhould deſcend alone,
The roſin-lightning flaſh, and Monſter ſpire
Squibs, and words hotter then his fire.

Th' other for the Gentlemen oth' Pit,
Like to themſelves, all Spirit, Fancy, Wit,
In which plots ſhould be ſubtile as a Flame,
Diſguiſes would make *Proteus* ſtil the ſame:
Humours ſo rarely humour'd, and expreſt,
That ev'n they ſhould thinke 'em ſo, not dreſt;
Vices acted and applauded too, Times
Tickled, and th' Actors acted, not their Crimes,
So he might equally applauſe have gain'd
Of th' hardned, ſooty, and the ſnowy hand.

Where now one *ſo ſo* ſpatters, t'other, no;
Tis his firſt Play, twere Soleciſme 'tſhould goe;
The next, 't ſhew'd pritily, but ſearcht within
It appeares bare and bald, as is his Chin;
The Towne-wit Sentences; a Scholars Play!
Piſh! I know not why-but-th'ave not the way.

We, whoſe gaine is all our pleaſure, ev'n theſe
Are bound by Iuſtice and Religion to pleaſe;
Which he whoſe Pleaſure's all his gaine, goes by
As ſlightly, as they doe his Comædy.

 Cull's

Cull's out the few, the worthy, at whose feet
He sacrifices both himselfe, and it
His Fancies first fruits: Profit he knowes none
Unles that of your Approbation,
Which if your thoughts at going out will pay,
Hee'l not looke farther for a *Second Day*.

CLITOPHON *and* LUCIPPE *translated.*

To the Ladies.

PRay Ladies breath, awhile lay by
Cælestial *Sydney's Arcady*;
Heere's a Story that doth Claime
A little respite from his Flame:
Then with a quick dissolving looke
Unfold the smoothnes of this book,
To which no Art (except your sight)
Can reach a worthy Epithite;
'Tis an Abstract of all Volumes,
A Pillaster of all Columnes
Fancy e're rear'd to *Wit*, to be
The smallest Gods Epitome,
And so compactedly expresse
All Lovers pleasing Wretchednes.

Gallant

Gallant *Pamela's* Majesty,
And her sweet Sisters Modesty
Are fixt in each of you; you are
Distinct, what these together were:
Divinest that are really
What *Cariclea's* feign'd to be;
That are ev'ry *one* the *Nine*,
And brighter here *Astrea's* shine;
View our *Lucippe*, and remaine
In her, these Beauties o're againe.

Amazement! Noble *Clitophon*,
Ev'n now lookt somewhat colder on
His cooler Mistresse, and she too
Smil'd not as she us'd to do;
See! the Individuall Payre
Are at sad Oddes, and parted are;
They quarrell, æmulate, and stand
At strife, who first shal kisse your hand.

A new Dispute there lately rose
Betwixt the *Greekes* and *Latines*, whose
Temple's should be bound with Glory
In best languaging this Story;
Yee Heyres of Love, that with one *Smile*
A ten-yeeres *War* can reconcile;
Peacefull *Hellens*! Vertuous! See!
The jarring Languages agree,
And here all Armes layd by, they doe
In English meet, to wayt on you.

To

To my truely valiant, learned Friend, who in his booke resolv'd the Art Gladiatory into the Mathematick's.

I.

HEarke Reader! wilt be learn'd ith' warres?
  A Gen'rall in a gowne?
Strike a league with Arts and Scarres,
  And snatch from each a Crowne?

II.

Wouldst be a wonder? Such a one,
  As should win with a Looke?
A Bishop in a Garison,
  And Conquer by the Booke?

III.

Take then this Mathematick shield,
  And henceforth by it's rules,
Be able to dispute ith' field,
  And Combate in the Schooles.

IV.

Whilst peaceful Learning once againe,
  And the Souldier so concord,
As that he fights now with her Penne,
  And she writes with his Sword.

AMYNTOR'S

AMYNTOR'S GROVE, *His* CHLORIS, ARIGO, *and* GRATIANA.

An Elogie.

IT was *Amyntor's* Grove, that *Chloris*
For ever Ecchoes and her Glories;
Chloris, the gentleſt Sheapherdeſſe,
That ever Lawnes and Lambes did bleſſe;
Her Breath like to the whiſpering winde,
Was calme as thought, ſweet as her Minde;
Her Lips like coral-gates kept in
The perfume and the pearle within;
Her eyes a double-flaming torch
That alwayes ſhine, and never ſcorch:
Her ſelfe the Heav'n in which did meet
The *All* of bright, of faire and ſweet.

Here was I brought with that delight
That ſeperated Soules take flight;
And when my Reaſon call'd my ſence
Back ſomewhat from this excellence,
That I could ſee; I did begin
T' obſerve the curious ordering
Of every Roome, where 'ts hard to know
Which moſt excels in *ſent* or *ſhow*:
Arabian gummes do breath here forth,
And th' *Eaſt's* come over to the *North*;

The

The Windes have brought their hyre of ſweet
To ſee *Amyntor Chloris* greet;
Balme and Nard, and each perfume
To bleſſe this payre chafe and conſume;
And th' *Phœnix*, ſee! already fries!
Her Neaſt a fire in *Chloris* eyes!

Next the great and powerful hand
Beckens my thoughts unto a ſtand
Of *Titian*, *Raphael*, *Georgone*
Whoſe *Art* ev'n *Nature* hath out-done;
For if weake *Nature* only can
Intend, not perfect what is man,
Theſe certainely we must prefer,
Who mended what *She* wrought, and *Her*;
And ſure the ſhadowes of thoſe rare
And kind incomparable fayre
Are livelier, nobler Company,
Then if they could or ſpeake, or ſee:
For theſe I aske without a tuſh,
Can kiſſe or touch, without a bluſh,
And we are taught that *Subſtance* is,
If uninjoy'd, but th' ſhade of bliſſe.

Now every Saint Cleerly divine,
Is clos'd ſo in her ſeverall ſhrine;
The Gems ſo rarely, richly ſet,
For them wee love the Cabinet;
So intricately plac't withall,
As if th' imbrodered the Wall,
So that the Pictures ſeem'd to be
But one continued Tapiſtrie.

After

After this travell of mine eyes
We ſate, and pitied Dieties;
Wee bound our looſe hayre with the Vine,
The Poppy, and the Eglantine;
One ſwell'd an Oriental bowle
Full, as a grateful, Loyal Soule
To *Chloris! Chloris!* heare, Oh heare!
'Tis pledg'd above in ev'ry Sphere.

Now ſtreight the *Indians* richeſt prize
Is kindled a glad Sacrifice;
Cloudes are ſent up on wings of Thyme,
Amber, Pomgranates, Jeſſemine,
And through our Earthen Conduicts ſore
Higher then Altars fum'd before.

So drencht we our oppreſſing cares,
And choakt the wide Jawes of our feares,
Whilſt raviſht thus we did deviſe,
If this were not a Paradice
In all, except theſe harmeleſſe ſins;
Behold! flew in two *Cherubins*
Cleare as the skye from whence they came,
And brighter then the ſacred Flame:
The Boy adorn'd with Modeſty,
Yet armed ſo with Majeſty;
That if the *Thunderer* againe
His Eagle ſends, ſhe ſtoopes in vaine;
Beſides his *Innocence* he tooke
A Sword and Casket, and did looke
Like *Love* in *Armes*; he wrote but five,
Yet ſpake eighteene, each *Grace* did ſtrive,
And twenty *Cupids* thronged forth,
Who firſt ſhould ſhow his prettier worth.

But

But Oh the *Nymph*! did you ere know
Carnation mingled with *Snow*?
Or have you ſeene the Lightning ſhrowd,
And ſtraight breake through th' oppoſing cloud?
So ran her blood, ſuch was it's hue;
So through her vayle her bright Haire flew,
And yet its Glory did appeare
But thinne, becauſe her *eyes* were neere.

Blooming Boy, and bloſſoming Mayd,
May your faire Sprigges be neere betrayd
To eating worme, or fouler ſtorme;
No Serpent lurke to do them harme;
No ſharpe froſt cut, no North-winde teare,
The Verdure of that fragrant hayre;
But may the Sun and gentle weather,
When you are both growne ripe together,
Load you with fruit, ſuch as your Father
From you with all the joyes doth gather:
And may you when one branch is dead
Graft ſuch another in it's ſtead,
Laſting thus ever in your prime
'Til 'th' Sithe is ſnatcht away from *Time*.

Againſt the Love of Great Ones.

VNhappy youth betrayd by Fate
To ſuch a Love hath *Sainted Hate*,
And *damned* thoſe *Cæleſtiall* bands
Are onely knit with equal hands;
The Love of Great Ones? 'Tis a Love
Gods are incapable to prove;

For

For where there is a Joy uneven,
There never, never can be Heav'n:
'Tis ſuch a Love as is not ſent
To Fiends as yet for puniſhment;
Ixion willingly doth feele
The Gyre of his eternal wheele,
Nor would he now exchange his paine
For Cloudes and Goddeſſes againe.

Wouldſt thou with tempeſts lye? Then bow
To th' rougher furrows of her brow;
Or make a Thunder-bolt thy Choyce?
Then catch at her more fatal Voyce;
Or 'gender with the Lightning? trye
The ſubtler Flaſhes of her eye:
Poore *Semele* wel knew the ſame,
Who both imbrac't her God and Flame;
And not alone in Soule did burne,
But in this Love did Aſhes turne.

How il doth Majeſty injoy
The Bow and Gaity oth' Boy,
As if the *Purple-roabe* ſhould ſit,
And ſentence give ith' Chayr of *Wit.*

Say ever-dying wretch to whom
Each anſwer is a certaine dombe,
What is it that you would poſſeſſe,
The *Countes,* or the naked *Beſſe?*
Would you her *Gowne,* or *Title* do?
Her *Box,* or *Gem,* her *Thing* or *ſhow?*
If you meane *Her,* the very *Her*
Abſtracted from her caracter;

Unhappy

Unhappy Boy! you may as ſoone
With fawning wanton with the Moone,
Or with an amorous Complaint
Get proſtitute your very Saint;
Not that we are not mortal, or
Fly *Venus* Altars, or abhor
The ſelfeſame Knack for which you pine;
But we (defend us!) are divine,
Female, but Madam borne, and come
From a right-honourable Wombe:
Shal we then mingle with the baſe,
And bring a ſilver-tinſell race?
Whilſt th' iſſue Noble wil not paſſe,
The Gold allayd (almoſt halfe braſſe)
And th' blood in each veine doth appeare,
Part thick *Booreinn*, part *Lady* Cleare:
Like to the ſordid Inſects ſprung
From Father *Sun*, and Mother *Dung*;
Yet loſe we not the hold we have,
But faſter graſpe the trembling ſlave;
Play at Baloon with's heart, and winde
The ſtrings like ſcaines, ſteale into his minde
Ten thouſand *Hells*, and *feigned Joyes*
Far worſe then they, whilſt like whipt Boys,
After this ſcourge hee's huſh with Toys.

This heard Sir, play ſtil in her eyes,
And be a dying Lives, like Flyes
Caught by their Angle-legs, and whom
The Torch laughs peece-meale to conſume.

LUCASTA

LUCASTA *paying her Obſequies to the Chaſt memory of my deareſt Coſin Mrs.* Bowes Barne.

I.

SEE! what an undiſturbed teare
She weepes for her laſt ſleepe;
But viewing her ſtraight wak'd a *Star*,
She weepes that ſhe did weepe.

II.

Griefe ne're before did Tyranize
On th' Honour of that brow,
And at the wheeles of her brave Eyes
Was Captive led til now.

III.

Thus for a Saints Apoſtacy,
The unimagin'd Woes,
And ſorrowes of the *Hierarchy*,
None but an Angel knowes.

IV.

Thus for loſt ſoules Recovery,
The Clapping of all Wings,
And Triumphs of this Victory,
None but an Angel ſings.

V.

So none but *She* know's to bemone
This equal Virgins Fate,
None but *Lucaſta* can her Crowne
Of Glory celebrate.

Then

VI.

Then dart on me (*Chast Light*) one ray
By which I may discry
Thy Joy cleare through this cloudy Day
To dresse my sorrow by.

TO ALTHEA, *From Prison.*†

Song.

Set by Dr. *John Wilson.*

I.

VVHen Love with unconfined wings
Hovers within my Gates;
And my divine *Althea* brings
To whisper at the Grates:
When I lye tangled in her haire,
And fetterd to her eye;
The *Gods* that wanton in the Aire,
Know no such Liberty.

II.

When flowing Cups run swiftly round
With no allaying *Thames*,
Our carelesse heads with Roses bound,
Our hearts with Loyall Flames;
When thirsty griefe in Wine we steepe,
When Healths and draughts go free,
Fishes that tipple in the Deepe,
Know no such Libertie.

When

III.

When (like committed Linnets) I†
  With shriller throat shall sing
The sweetnes, Mercy, Majesty,
  And glories of my KING;
When I shall voyce aloud, how Good
  He is, how Great should be;
    Inlarged Winds that curle the Flood,
    Know no such Liberty.

IV.

Stone Walls doe not a Prison make,
  Nor I'ron bars a Cage;
Mindes innocent and quiet take
  That for an Hermitage;
If I have freedome in my Love,
  And in my soule am free;
Angels alone that sore above,
  Injoy such Liberty.

Being treated
TO ELLINDA.

FOR Cherries plenty, and for Coran's
  Enough for fifty, were there more 'on's;
For Elles of Beere, Flutes of Canary
That well did wash downe pasties-mary;
For Peason, Chickens, sawces high,
Pig, and the Widdow-Venson-pye;
With certaine promise (to your Brother)
Of the Virginity of another,

Where

Where it is thought I too may peepe in
With Knuckles far as any deepe in;
For glaſſes, heads, hands, bellies full
Of Wine, and Loyne right-worſhipfull;
Whether all of, or more behind-a
Thankes freeſt, freſheſt, Faire *Ellinda*:
Thankes for my Viſit not diſdaining,
Or at the leaſt thankes for your feigning;
For if your mercy doore were lockt-well,
I ſhould be juſtly ſoundly knockt-well;
Cauſe that in dogrell I did mutter
Not one Rhime to you from *dam-Rotter*.

Next beg I to preſent my duty
To pregnant Siſter in prime Beauty,
Whom well I deeme (e're few month's elder)
Will take out *Hans* from pretty *Kelder*,
And to the ſweetly fayre *Mabella*,
A match that vies with *Arabella*;
In each reſpect but the misfortune,
Fortune, Fate, I thee importune.

Nor muſt I paſſe the lovely *Alice*,
Whoſe health I'd quaffe in golden Chalice;
But ſince that Fate hath made me neuter,
I only can in Beaker Pewter:
But who'd forget, or yet left un-ſung
The doughty Acts of *George* the yong-Son?
Who yeſterday to ſave his Siſter
Had ſlaine the Snake, had he not miſt her:
But I ſhall leave him 'till a Nag on
He gets to proſecute the Dragon;

And

And then with helpe of Sun and Taper,
Fill with his deeds twelve Reames of paper,
That *Amadis*, Sir *Guy* and *Topaz*
With his fleet Neigher ſhall keep no-pace.
But now to cloſe all I muſt ſwitch-hard,
Servant ever;

Lovelace Richard.

Sonnet.

To Generall Goring, *after the pacification at* Berwicke.

A la Chabot.

I.

NOw the *Peace* is made at the Foes rate,
Whilſt men of Armes 'to Kettles their old
(Helmes tranſlate,
And drinke in Caskes of Honourable Plate;
In ev'ry hand a Cup be found,
That from all Hearts a health may ſound
To *Goring!* to *Goring!* ſee't goe round.

II.

He whoſe Glories ſhine ſo brave and high,
That Captive they in Triumph leade each eare and eye,
Claiming uncombated the Victorie,
And from the Earth to Heav'n rebound
Fixt there eternall as this Round,
To *Goring!* to *Goring!* ſee him Crown'd.

III.

To his lovely Bride in love with ſcars,
(ſword in wars;
Whoſe eyes wound deepe in Peace, as doth his
They ſhortly muſt depoſe the Queen of Stars:
Her cheekes the Morning bluſhes give,
And the benighted World repreeve,
To *Lettice!* to *Lettice!* let her live.

IV.

Give me ſcorching heat, thy heat dry *Sun*,
That to this payre I may drinke off an Ocean,
Yet leave my grateful thirſt unquenſht, undone;
Or a full Bowle of heav'nly wine,
In which diſſolved Stars ſhould ſhine,
To the Couple! to the Couple! th' are Divine.

Sir THOMAS WORTLEY'S Sonnet Anſwered.

The Sonnet.

I.

NO more
Thou little winged Archer, now no more
As heretofore,
Thou maiſt pretend within my breaſt to bide,
No more,
Since Cruell Death of deareſt *Lyndamore*
Hath me depriv'd,
I bid adieu to Love, and all the world beſide.

Go,

II.

Go, go;
Lay by thy quiver and unbend thy Bow
Poore ſillie Foe,
Thou ſpend'ſt thy ſhafts but at my breaſt in Vain,
Since Death
My heart hath with a fatall Icie Deart
Already ſlain,
Thou canſt not ever hope to warme her wound,
Or wound it o're againe.

The Anſwer.

I.

AGaine,
Thou witty Cruell Wanton now againe,
Through ev'ry Veine,
Hurle all your lightning, and ſtrike ev'ry Dart,
Againe,
Before I feele this pleaſing, pleaſing paine,
I have no Heart,
Nor can I live but ſweetly murder'd with
So deare, ſo deare a ſmart.

II.

Then flye,
And kindle all your Torches at her Eye,
To make me Dye
Her Martyr, and put on my Roabe of Flame:
So I
Advanced on my blazing Wings on high,
In Death became
Inthroan'd a Starre, and Ornament unto
Her glorious glorious name.

A Guiltlesse Lady imprisoned; after penanced.†

Song.

Set by Mr. *William Lawes.*

I.

HEark Faire one how what e're here is
  Doth laugh and sing at thy distresse;
Not out of hate to thy reliefe,
  But Joy t'enjoy thee, though in griefe.

II.

See! that which chaynes you, you chaine here;
  The Prison is thy Prisoner;
How much thy Jaylors Keeper art,
  He bindes your hands, but you his Heart.

III.

The Gyves to Rase so smooth a skin,
Are so unto themselves within,
  But blest to kisse so fayre an Arme
Haste to be happy with that harme.

IV.

And play about thy wanton wrist
  As if in them thou so wert drest;
But if too rough, too hard they presse,
  Oh they but Closely, closely kisse.

And

V.

And as thy bare feet blesse the Way
The people doe not mock, but pray,
And call thee as amas'd they run
Instead of prostitute, a Nun.

VI.

The merry Torch burnes with desire
To kindle the eternall Fire,
And lightly daunces in thine eyes
To tunes of *Epithalamies.*

VII.

The sheet's ty'd ever to thy Wast,
How thankfull to be so imbrac't!
And see! thy very very bands
Are bound to thee, to binde such Hands.

Upon the Curtaine of LUCASTA'S *Picture, it was thus wrought.*

OH stay that Covetous hand—first turn all Eye,
All Depth, and minde; then Mystically spye
Her Soul's faire Picture, her faire Soul's, in all
So truely Copied from th' Originall;
That you will sweare her Body by this Law,
Is but it's shadow, as this it's, — now draw.

To

To his Deare Brother Colonel F. L. *immoderately mourning my Brothers untimely Death at* Carmarthen.

I.

IF Teares could waſh the Ill away,
A Pearle for each wet bead I'd pay;
But as dew'd Corne the fuller growes,
So water'd eyes but ſwell our Woes.

II.

One drop another cals, which ſtill
(Griefe adding Fuell) doth diſtill;
Too fruitfull of her ſelfe is Anguiſh,
We need no cheriſhing to Languiſh.

III.

Coward *Fate* degen'rate Man
Like little Children uſes, when
He whips us firſt untill we weepe,
Then 'cauſe we ſtill a weeping keepe.

IV.

Then from thy firme ſelfe never ſwerve;
Teares fat the Griefe that they ſhould ſterve;
I'ron decrees of Deſtinie
Are ner'e wipe't out with a wet Eye.

V.

But this way you may gaine the field,
Oppoſe but ſorrow and 'twill yield;
One gallant thorough-made Reſolve
Doth *Starry Influence* diſſolve.

An

An Elegie.

On the Death of Mrs. Caſſandra Cotton, *only Siſter to Mr.* C. Cotton.

HIther with hallowed ſteps as is the Ground
That muſt enſhrine this Saint, with lookes pro-
And ſad aſpects as the dark vails you weare (found,
Virgins oppreſt draw gently, gently neare;
Enter the diſmall chancell of this roome,
Where each pale gueſt ſtands fixt a living Tombe,
With trembling hands helpe to remove this Earth
To its laſt death, and firſt victorious birth:
Let Gums and incenſe fume who are at ſtrife
To enter th' Hearſe and breath in it new life;
Mingle your ſteppes with flowers as you goe,
Which as they haſte to fade will ſpeake your woe.

And when y' have plac't your Tapers on her Urn,
How poor a tribute 'tis to weep & mourn!
That flood the channell of your Eye-lids fils,
When you loſe trifles, or what's leſſe, your Wills.
If you'l be worthy of these Obſequies,
Be blind unto the World, and drop your Eyes;
Waſte and conſume, burn downward as this fire
That's fed no more, ſo willingly expire;
Paſſe through the cold and obſcure narrow way,
Then light your torches at the ſpring of Day,
There with her triumph in your Victory,
Such Joy alone and ſuch Solemnity
Becomes this Funerall of Virginity.

Or,

Or, if you faint to be ſo bleſt: Oh heare!
If not to dye, dare but to live like her:
Dare to live Virgins till the honour'd Age
Of thrice fifteen cal's Matrons on the ſtage,
Whilſt not a blemiſh or leaſt ſtaine is ſeene
On your white roabe 'twixt fifty and fifteene;
But as it in your ſwathing-bands was given,
Bring't in your winding ſheet unſoyl'd to Heav'n.
Dare to do purely, without Compact good,
Or Herald, by no one underſtood
But him, who now in thanks bows either knee,
For th' early benefit and ſecreſie.

Dare to affect a ſerious holy ſorrow,
To which Delights of Pallaces are narrow,
And laſting as their ſmiles, dig you a roome
Where practiſe the probation of your tombe;
With ever-bended knees & piercing Pray'r (Ay'r;
Smooth the rough paſſe through craggy Earth to
Flame there as Lights that ſhipwrackt Mariners
May put in ſafely, and ſecure their feares,
Who adding to your Joyes, now owe you theirs.

Virgins, if thus you dare but Courage take
To follow her in Life, elſe through this Lake
Of Nature wade, and breake her earthly bars,
Y' are fixt with her upon a Throne of ſtars
Arched with a pure Heav'n Chryſtaline,
Where round you Love and Joy for ever ſhine.

But you are dumbe, as what you do lament,
More ſenſeles then her very monument (teare!
Which at your weaknes weeps— Spare that vaine
Enough to burſt the rev'rend Sepulcher:

Riſe

Riſe and walk home; there groaning proſtrate fall
And celebrate your owne ſad Funerall;
For howſoe're you move, may heare or ſee,
You are more dead and buried then ſhee.

LUCASTA'S *World.*

Epode.

I.

COld as the breath of winds that blow
To ſilver ſhot deſcending ſnow

LUCASTA ſight; when ſhe did cloſe
The World in froſty chaines!
And then a frowne to Rubies froſe
The blood boyl'd in our veines:

Yet cooled not the heat her Sphere
Of Beauties, firſt had kindled there.

II.

Then mov'd, and with a ſuddaine Flame
Impatient to melt all againe,

Straight from her eyes ſhe lightning hurl'd,
And Earth in aſhes mournes;
The Sun his blaze denies the world,
And in her luſter burnes:

Yet warmed not the hearts, her nice
Diſdaine had firſt congeal'd to Ice.

And

III.

And now her teares nor griev'd desire
Can quench this raging, pleasing fire;

Fate but one way allowes; behold
Her smiles Divinity!
They fann'd this heat, and thaw'd that cold,
So fram'd up a new sky.

Thus Earth from flames and Ice repreev'd,
E're since hath in her Sun-shine liv'd.

To a Lady that desired me I would beare my part with her in a Song. *Madam* A. L.

THis is the Prittiest Motion:
Madam, th' Alarums of a Drumme
That cals your Lord, set to your Cries,
To mine are sacred *Symphonies.*

What, though 'tis said I have a Voice;
I know 'tis but that hollow noise
Which (as it through my pipe doth speed)
Bitterns do Carol through a Reed;
In the same Key with Monkeys Jiggs,
Or Dirges of Proscribed Piggs,
Or the soft SERENADES above
In calme of Night, when Cats make Love.

Was

Was ever ſuch a Conſort ſeen!
Fourſcore and fourteen with forteen?
Yet ſooner they'l agree, One Paire,
Then we in our Spring-Winter Aire;
They may Imbrace, Sigh, Kiſſe the reſt:
Our Breath knows nought but Eaſt and Weſt.
Thus have I heard to Childrens Cries,
The faire Nurſe 'ſtill ſuch Lullabies
That well all ſayd (for what there lay)
The Pleaſure did the ſorrow pay.

Sure ther's another way to ſave
Your Phanſie Madam, that's to have
('Tis but petitioning kinde Fate)
The Organs ſent to Bilingſgate;
Where they to that ſoft murm'ring Quire
Shall reach you All you can admire!

Or do but heare how Love-bang KATE
In Pantry darke for freage of Mate
With edge of ſteele the ſquare wood ſhapes,
And DIDO to it chaunts or ſcrapes.
The merry PHAETON oth' Carre,
You'l vow makes a melodious Jarre;
Sweeter and ſweeter whiſleth He
To un-anointed Axel-tree;
Such ſwift notes he and 's wheels do run;
For me, I yeeld him PHŒBUS Son.

Say faire COMANDRES, can it be
You ſhould Ordaine a Mutinie?
For where I howle, all Accents fall
As Kings Harangues to *One and All.*

ULYSSES

ULYSSES Art is now withstood,
You ravish both with Sweet and Good;
Saint SYREN sing, for I dare heare,
But when I Ope', Oh stop your Eare.

Far lesse be't ÆMULATION
To passe me, or in trill or Tone
Like the thin throat of PHILOMEL,
And the smart Lute who should excell,
As if her soft Chords should begin
And strive for sweetnes with the Pin.

Yet can I Musick too; but such,
As is beyond all Voice or Touch;
My minde can in faire Order Chime,
Whilst my true Heart still beats the Time:
My Soule so full of Harmonie,
That it with all parts can agree:
If you winde up to the highest Fret
It shall descend an Eight from it,
And when you shall vouchsafe to fall
Sixteene above you it shall call,
And yet so dis-assenting One,
They both shall meet an Unison.

Come then bright Cherubin begin!
My loudest Musick is within:
Take all notes with your skillfull Eyes,
Hearke if mine do not sympathise!
Sound all my thoughts, and see exprest
The *Tablature* of my large Brest,
Then you'l admit that I too can
Musick above dead sounds of Man;
Such as alone doth blesse the Spheres,
Not to be Reacht with humane Eares.

Valiant

Valiant Love.

I.

NOw fie upon that everlaſting Life, I Dye!
She hates! Ah me! It makes me mad;
As if Love fir'd his Torch at a moiſt Eye,
Or with his Joyes e're Crown'd the ſad?
Oh let me live and ſhout when I fall on!
Let me ev'n Triumph in the firſt attempt!
Loves Duelliſt from Conqueſt's not exempt
When his fair Murdreſſe ſhall not gain one groan,
And He expire ev'n in Ovation.

II.

Let me make my approach when I lye downe
With counter-wrought and Travers Eyes;
With Peals of Confidence Batter the Towne:
Had ever Beggar yet the Keyes?
No, I will vary ſtormes with Sun and Winde;
Be rough, and offer Calme Condition,
March in (and pray't) or ſtarve the Garriſon.
Let her make ſallies hourely, yet I'le find
(Though all beat of) ſhee's to be undermin'd.

III.

Then may it pleaſe your *Little Excellence*
Of Hearts, t' ordaine by ſound of Lips,
That henceforth none in Tears dare Love comence
(Her thoughts ith' full, his in th' Eclipſe)
On paine of having's Launce broke on her Bed,
That he be branded all Free Beauties ſlave,
And his own hollow eyes be domb'd his grave:
Since in your Hoaſt that Coward nere was fed
Who to his Proſtrate ere was Proſtrated.

The

The Apostacy of one, and but one Lady.

I.

THat Frantick Errour I Adore,
And am confirm'd the Earth turns Round;
Now satisfied O're and o're,
As rowling Waves so flowes the Ground,
And as her Neighbour reels the shore:
Finde such a Woman says she loves,
She's that fixt Heav'n which never moves.

II.

In Marble, Steele, or Porphyrie,
Who carves or stampes his Armes or Face,
Lookes it by Rust or Storme must dye:
This Womans Love no Time can raze,
Hardned like Ice in the Sun's Eye,
Or Your Reflection in a Glasse,
Which keepes possession though you passe.

III.

We not behold a Watches hand
To stir, nor Plants or Flowers to grow:
Must we infer that this doth stand,
And therefore that those do not blow?
This she acts Calmer, like Heav'ns Brand
The stedfast Lightning, slow Loves Dart,
She kils but ere we feele the smart.

Oh

IV.

Oh ſhe is Conſtant as the Winde
  That Revels in an Ev'nings Aire!
Certaine, as Wayes unto the Blinde,
  More reall then her Flatt'ries are;
Gentle, as Chaines that Honour binde,
  More faithfull then an Hebrew Jew,
  But as the Divel not halfe ſo true.

To my Lady H.

Ode.

I.

TEll me, ye ſubtill Judges in Loves Treaſury,
  Inform me which hath moſt inricht mine eye,
This Diamonds greatnes, or its Clarity?

II.

Ye cloudy ſpark-lights, whoſe vaſt multitude
Of Fires, are harder to be found then view'd;
Waite on this Star in her *firſt Magnitude.*

III.

Calmely or Roughly! Ah ſhe ſhines too much!
That now I lye, (her influence is ſuch)
Cruſht with too ſtrong a hand, or ſoft a touch.

IV.

Lovers beware! a certaine, double harme
Waits your proud hopes, her lookes al killing charm
Guarded by her as true Victorious Arme.

Thus

V.

Thus with her Eyes brave TAMYRIS ſpake dread,
Which when the Kings dull Breaſt not entered,
Finding ſhe could not looke, ſhe ſtrook him dead.

La Bella Bona Roba.

I.

I Cannot tell who loves the Skeleton
Of a poor Marmoſet, nought but boan, boan.
Give me a nakedneſſe with her cloath's on.

II.

Such whoſe white-ſattin upper coat of skin,
Cut upon Velvet rich Incarnadin,
Ha's yet a Body (and of Fleſh) within.

III.

Sure it is meant good Husbandry in men,
Who do incorporate with Aëry leane,
T' repair their ſides, and get their Ribb agen.

IV.

Hard hap unto that Huntſman that Decrees
Fat joys for all his ſwet, when as he ſees,
After his 'Say, nought but his Keepers Fees.†

V.

Then Love I beg, when next thou tak'ſt thy Bow,
Thy angry ſhafts, and doſt Heart-chaſing go,
Paſſe *Raſcall Deare*, ſtrike me the largeſt Doe.

A

A LA BOURBON.

Done moy plus de pitiè ou plus de Cre-aultè, car ſans ce Ie ne puis pas Viure, ne morir.

I.

DIvine Deſtroyer pitty me no more,
Or elſe more pitty me;
Give me more Love, Ah quickly give me more,
Or elſe more Cruelty!
For left thus as I am,
My Heart is Ice and Flame;
And languiſhing thus I
Can neither Live nor Dye!

II.

Your Glories are Eclipſt, and hidden in the Grave
Of this indifferency;
And CÆLIA you can neither Altars have,
Nor I a Diety:
They are Aſpects Divine
That ſtill, or smile, or ſhine,
Or like th' Offended Sky
Frowne Death Immediately.

The faire Begger.†

I.

COmanding Asker, if it be
  Pity that you faine would have,
Then I turne Begger unto thee,
  And aske the thing that thou doſt crave;
I will ſuffice thy hungry need
So thou wilt but my Fancy feed.

II.

In all ill yeares, wa'ſt ever knowne
  On ſo much beauty ſuch a dearth?
Which in that thrice-bequeathed gowne
  Lookes like the Sun Eclipſt with Earth,
Like Gold in Canvas, or with dirt
Unſoyled Ermins cloſe begirt.

III.

Yet happy he that can but taſt
  This whiter skin who thirſty is,
Fooles dote on ſattin motions lac'd,
  The Gods go naked in their bliſſe,
At th' Barrell's head there ſhines the Vine,
There only reliſhes the Wine.

IV.

There quench my heat, and thou ſhalt ſup
  Worthy the lips that it muſt touch:
NECTAR from out the ſtarry Cup,
  I beg thy breath not halfe ſo much;
So both our wants ſupplied ſhall be,
You'l give for Love, I Charity.

Cheape

V.

Cheape then are pearle-imbroderies
That not adorne, but clouds thy waſt;
Thou ſhalt be cloath'd above all priſe,
If thou wilt promiſe me imbrac't;
Wee'l ranſack neither Cheſt or Shelfe,
I'll cover thee with mine owne ſelfe.

VI.

But Cruel, if thou doſt deny
This neceſſary almes to me;
What ſoft-ſoul'd man but with his Eye
And hand will hence be shut to thee?
Since all muſt judge you more unkinde;
I ſtarve your Body, you my minde.

TO ELLINDA.
Upon his late recovery.
A Paradox.

I.

HOw I grieve that I am well!
All my Health was in my ſicknes,
Go then Deſtiny and tell
Very Death is in this quicknes.

II.

Such a Fate rules over me
That I glory when I languiſh,
And do bleſſe the remedy
That doth feed, not quench my anguiſh.

III.

'Twas a gentle warmth that ceas'd
  In the Vizard of a feavor;
But I feare now I am eas'd
  All the flames ſince I muſt leave her.

IV.

Joyes though witherd, circled me,
  When unto her voice inured,
Like thoſe who by Harmony
  Only can be throughly Cured.

V.

Sweet ſure was that Malady,
  Whilſt the pleaſant Angel hover'd,
Which ceaſing they are all as I,
  Angry that they are recover'd.

VI.

And as men in Hoſpitals
  That are maim'd, are lodg'd and dined;
But when once their danger fals,
  Ah, th' are healed to be pined!

VII.

Fainting ſo I might before
  Sometime have the leave to hand her,
But luſty, am beat out of dore,
  And for Love compell'd to wander.

AMYNTOR

AMYNTOR *from beyond the Sea to* ALEXIS.

A Dialogue.

AMYNTOR.

ALEXIS! ah ALEXIS! can it be
Though ſo much wet and drie
Doth drowne our Eye,
Thou keep'ſt thy winged voice from me?

ALEXIS.

AMYNTOR a profounder ſea I feare
Hath ſwallow'd me, where now
My armes do row,
I floate i' th' Ocean of a Teare.

LUCASTA weepes leſt I look back and tread
Your watry Land againe.
AMYNT. I'd through the raine,
Such ſhowrs are quickly over-ſpread.

IV.

Conceive how Joy after this ſhort divorce
Will circle her with beames,
When like your ſtreames
You ſhall rowle back with kinder force

And

V.

And call the helping winds to vent your thought.
ALEX. AMYNTOR! CHLORIS where,
Or in what Sphere
Say may that glorious faire be ſought?

AMYNTOR.

She's now the center of theſe armes e're bleſt
Whence may ſhe never move
Till Time and Love
Haſte to their everlaſting reſt.

ALEXIS.

Ah ſubtile ſwaine! doth not my flame riſe high
As yours, and burne as hot?
Am not I ſhot
With the ſelfe ſame Artillery?

VIII.

And can I breath without her ai'r? AMYN. Why
From thy tempeſtuous Earth (then
Where blood and dearth
Raigne 'ſtead of Kings, agen

Wafte thy ſelfe over, and leſt ſtormes from far
Ariſe, bring in our ſight
The Seas delight,
LUCASTA that bright Northerne ſtar.

ALEXIS.

But as we cut the rugged deepe, I feare
The green-God ſtops his fell
Chariot of ſhell
And ſmooths the maine to raviſh her.

AMYNTOR.

AMYNTOR.

Oh no, the Prince of waters fires are done,
He as his Empire Old
And Rivers Cold,
His Queen now runs a bed to th' Sun;

XII.

But all his treasure he shall ope' that day:
TRITONS shall sound, his fleete
In silver meete,
And to her their rich offrings pay.

ALEXIS.

We flye AMYNTOR, not amaz'd how sent
By Water, Earth, or Aire:
Or if with her
By Fire, ev'n there
I move in mine owne Element.

A Lady with a Falcon on her fist.

To the Honourable my Cousin A. L.

I.

THis Queen of Prey (now Prey to you)
Fast to that Pirch of Ivory
In silver Chaines and silken Clue
Hath now made full thy Victory:

The

II.

The ſwelling Admirall of the dread
Cold Deepe, burnt in thy Flames, Oh Faire!
Waſt not enough, but thou muſt lead
Bound too the Princeſſe of the Aire?

III.

Unarm'd of Wings and Scaly Oare,
Unhappy Crawler on the Land,
To what Heav'n fly'ſt? div'ſt to what Shoare
That her brave Eyes do not Command?

IV.

Aſcend the Chariot of the Sun
From her bright pow'r to ſhelter thee:
Her Captive (Foole) outgaſes him;
Ah what loſt wretches then are we!

V.

Now proud Uſurpers on the Right
Of ſacred Beauty heare your dombe;
Recant your SEX, your MASTRY, MIGHT;
Lower you cannot be or'ecome:

VI.

Repent, ye er'e nam'd HE or HEAD,
For y' are in Falcons Monarchy,
And in that juſt Dominion bred
In which the NOBLER is the SHEE.

Calling

Calling LUCASTA *from her Retirement.*

Ode.

I.

FRom the dire Monument of thy black roome
Wher now that veſtal flame thou doſt intombe
As in the inmoſt Cell of all Earths Wombe,

II.

Sacred LUCASTA like the pow'rfull ray
Of Heavenly Truth paſſe this Cimmerian way,
Whilſt all the Standards of your beames diſplay.

III.

Ariſe and climbe our whiteſt higheſt Hill,
There your ſad thoughts with joy and wonder fill,
And ſee Seas calme as Earth, Earth as your Will.

IV.

Behold how lightning like a Taper flyes
And guilds your Chari't, but aſhamed dyes
Seeing it ſelfe out-gloried by your Eyes.

V.

Threatning and boyſtrous tempeſts gently bow,
And to your ſteps part in ſoft paths, when now
There no where hangs a Cloud, but on your brow.

No

VI.

No ſhowrs but 'twixt your lids, nor gelid ſnow,
But what your whiter chaſter breſt doth ow,
Whilſt winds in Chains colder your ſorrow blow.

VII.

Shrill Trumpets now doe only ſound to Eate,
Artillery hath loaden ev'ry diſh with meate,
And Drums at ev'ry Health Alarmes beate.

VIII.

All Things LUCASTA, but LUCASTA call,
Trees borrow Tongues, Waters in accents fall,
The Aire doth ſing, and Fire's Muſicall.

IX.

Awake from the dead Vault in which you dwell,
All's Loyall here, except your thoughts rebell,
Which ſo let looſe, often their Gen'rall quell.

X.

See! She obeys! by all obeyed thus;
No ſtorms, heats, Colds, no ſoules contentious,
Nor Civill War is found —— I meane, to us.

XI.

Lovers and Angels, though in Heav'n they ſhow
And ſee the Woes and Diſcords here below,
What they not feele, muſt not be ſaid to know.

The end of LUCASTA: *Odes, &c.*

Aramantha.

A

PASTORALL.

VP with the jolly Bird of Light
Who ſounds his third Retreat to Night;
Faire *Aramantha* from her bed
Aſhamed ſtarts, and riſes Red
As the Carnation-mantled Morne,
Who now the bluſhing Robe doth ſpurne,
And puts on angry Gray, whilſt ſhe
The *Envy of a Deity*
Arayes her limbes, too rich indeed
To be inſhrin'd in ſuch a Weed;
Yet lovely 'twas and ſtrait, but fit;
Not made for her, but ſhe to it:
By Nature it ſate cloſe and free,
As the juſt bark unto the Tree:
Unlike Loves Martyrs of the Towne,
All day impriſon'd in a Gown,
Who Rackt in Silke 'ſtead of a Dreſſe,
Are cloathed in a Frame or Preſſe,
And with that liberty and room,
The dead expatiate in a Tombe.
No Cabinets with curious Waſhes,
Bladders, and perfumed Plaſhes;

No

No venome-temper'd water's here,
Mercury is banished this Sphere:
Her Payle's all this, in which wet Glasse,
She both doth cleanse and view her Face.
  Far hence all *Iberian* smells,
Hot Amulets, Pomander spells;
Fragrant Gales, cool Ay'r, the fresh,
And naturall Odour of her Flesh,
Proclaim her sweet from th' Wombe as Morne.
Those colour'd things were made not borne,
Which fixt within their narrow straits,
Do looke like their own counterfeyts.
So like the Provance Rose she walkt,
Flowerd with Blush, with Verdure stalkt;
Th' Officious Wind her loose Hayre Curles,
The Dewe her happy linnen purles,
But wets a Tresse, which instantly
Sol with a Crisping Beame doth dry.
  Into the Garden is she come,
Love and Delights *Elisium*;
If ever Earth show'd all her store,
View her discolourd budding Floore;
Here her glad Eye she largely feedes,
And stands 'mongst them, as they 'mong weeds;
The flowers in their best aray,
As to their Queen their Tribute pay,
And freely to her Lap proscribe
A Daughter out of ev'ry Tribe:
Thus as she moves, they all bequeath
At once the Incense of their Breath.
  The noble *Heliotropian*
Now turnes to her, and knowes no Sun;
  And as her glorious face doth vary,
So opens loyall golden *Mary*;

Who

Who if but glanced from her ſight,
Straight ſhuts again as it were Night.
  The *Violet* (elſe loſt ith' heap)
Doth ſpread freſh purple for each ſtep;
With whoſe Humility poſſeſt,
Sh' inthrones the *poore Girle* in her breaſt:
The *July-flow'r* that hereto thriv'd,
Knowing her ſelf no longer liv'd,
But for one look of her, upheaves,
Then 'ſtead of teares ſtraight ſheds her leaves.
  Now the rich robed *Tulip*, who
Clad all in Tiſſue cloſe doth woe,
Her (ſweet to th' eye but ſmelling ſower)
She gathers to adorn her Bower.
  But the proud *Hony-ſuckle* ſpreads
Like a Pavilion her Heads,
Contemnes the wanting Commonalty,
That but to two ends uſefull be,
And to her lips thus aptly plac't,
With *ſmell* and *Hue* preſents her *Taſt*.
  So all their due Obedience pay,
Each thronging to be in her Way:
Faire *Aramantha* with her Eye
Thanks thoſe that live, which elſe would dye:
The reſt in ſilken fetters bound,
By *Crowning* her are *Crown* and *Crown'd*.
  And now the Sun doth higher riſe,
Our *Flora* to the meadow hies:
The poore diſtreſſed Heifers low,
And as ſh' approacheth gently bow,
Begging her charitable leaſure
To strip them of their milkie Treaſure.
  Out of the Yeomanry oth' Heard,
With grave aſpect, and feet prepar'd,

A

A rev'rend Lady Cow drawes neare,
Bids *Aramantha* welcome here;
And from her privy purſe lets fall
A Pearle or two, which ſeeme to call
This adorn'd adored Fayry
To the banquet of her Dayry.
  Soft *Aramantha* weeps to ſee
'Mongſt men ſuch inhumanitie,
That thoſe who do receive in Hay,
And pay in ſilver twice a Day,
Should by their cruell barb'rous theft,
Be both of that, and life bereft.
  But 'tis decreed when ere this dies,
That ſhe ſhall fall a Sacrifice
Unto the Gods, ſince thoſe that trace
Her ſtemme, ſhow 'tis a God-like race;
Deſcending in an even line
From Heifers, and from Steeres divine,
Making the honour'd extract full
In *Ió* and *Europa's* Bull.
She was the largeſt goodlieſt Beaſt,
That ever Mead or Altar bleſt;
Round as her Udder, and more white
Then is the *milkie way* in Night:
Her full broad Eye did ſparkle fire,
Her breath was ſweet as kind deſire,
And in her beauteous creſcent ſhone,
Bright as the Argent-horned Moone.
  But ſee! this whitenesſe is obſcure,
Cynthia ſpotted, ſhe impure;
Her body writheld, and her eyes
Departing lights at obſequies:
Her lowing hot, to the freſh Gale,
Her breath perfumes the field withall;

To

To thoſe two Suns that ever ſhine,
To those plump parts ſhe doth inſhrine,
To th' hovering Snow of either hand,
That *Love* and *Cruelty* command.
After the breakfaſt on her Teat,
She takes her leave oth' mournfull Neat,
Who by her toucht now prize their life,
Worthy alone the *hallowed knife*.
Into the neighbring Wood ſhe's gone,
Whoſe roofe defies the tell-tale Sunne,
And locks out ev'ry prying beame;
Cloſe by the Lips of a cleare ſtreame
She ſits and entertaines her Eye
With the moiſt Chryſtall, and the frye
With burniſht-ſilver mal'd, whoſe Oares
Amazed ſtill make to the ſhoares;
What need ſhe other bait or charm
But look? or Angle, but her arm?
The happy Captive gladly ta'n,
Sues ever to be ſlave in vaine,
Who inſtantly (confirm'd in's feares)
Haſts to his Element of teares.
From hence her various windings roave
To a well orderd ſtately grove;
This is the Pallace of the Wood,
And Court oth' Royall Oake, where ſtood
The whole Nobility, the Pine,
Strait Aſh, tall Firre, and wanton Vine;
The proper Cedar, and the reſt;
Here ſhe her deeper ſenſes bleſt;
Admires great Nature in this Pile
Floor'd with greene-velvet Camomile,
Garniſht with Gems of unſet fruit,
Supply'd ſtill with a ſelf recruit;

Her

Her boſom wrought with pretty Eyes
Of never-planted Strawberries;
Where th' winged Muſick of the ayre
Do richly feaſt and for their fare
Each Evening in a ſilent ſhade,
Beſtow a gratefull *Serenade.*
  Thus ev'n tyerd with delight,
Sated in Soul and Appetite;
Full of the purple plumme and Peare,
The golden Apple with the faire
Grape, that mirth fain would have taught her,
And nuts which Squirrells cracking brought her;
She ſoftly layes her weary limbs,
Whilſt gentle ſlumber now beginnes
To draw the Curtaines of her Eye;
When ſtraight awakend with a Crie
And bitter groan, again repoſes,
Again a deep ſigh interpoſes.
And now ſhe heares a trembling Voyce;
Ah can there ought on earth rejoyce!
Why weares ſhe this gay Livery
Not black as her dark entrails be?
Can trees be green, and to the Ay'r
Thus proſtitute their flowing Hayr?
Why do they ſprout, not witherd dy?
Muſt each thing live ſave wretched I?
Can dayes triumph in *blew* and *red*,
When both their *light*, and *life* is fled?
Fly Joy on wings of *Popinjayes*
To Courts of fools, there as your playes
Dye, laught at and forgot; whilſt all
That's good, mourns at this Funerall.
Weep all ye *Graces*, and you ſweet
Quire, that at the Hill inſpir'd meet:

Love

Love put thy tapers out that we
And th' World may ſeem as blind as thee:
And be, ſince ſhe is loſt (ah wound!)
Not *Heav'n* it ſelf by any found.
  Now as a Priſoner new caſt,
Who ſleeps in chaines that night his laſt,
Next morn is wak't with a repreeve,
And from his trance not dream bid Live;
Wonders (his ſence not having ſcope)
Who ſpeaks, his friend, or his falſe Hope.
  So *Aramantha* heard, but feare
Dares not yet truſt her tempting Eare:
And as againe her armes oth' ground
Spread pillows for her Head, a ſound
More diſmall makes a ſwift divorce,
And ſtarts her thus —— Rage, Rapine, Force!
Ye blew-flam'd daughters oth' Abyſſe,
Bring all your Snakes, here let them hiſſe;
Let not a leaf its freſhneſſe keep;
Blaſt all their roots, and as you creepe
And leave behind your deadly ſlime,
Poyſon the budding branch in's prime:
Waſt the proud Bowers of this Grove,
That Fiends may dwell in it, and move
As in their proper Hell, whilſt ſhe
Above, laments this Tragedy;
Yet pities not our Fate; Oh faire
Vow-breaker, now betroth'd to th' Ay'r;
Why by thoſe Lawes did we not die,
As live but one, *Lucaſta*! why———
As he *Lucaſta* nam'd, a groan
Strangles the fainting paſſing tone;
But as ſhe heard *Lucaſta* ſmiles,
Poſſes her round, ſhe's ſlipt mean whiles

Behind the blind of a thick Bush,
When each word temp'ring with a blush,
She gently thus bespake: Sad swaine,
If mates in woe do ease our pain,
Here's one full of that antick grief,
Which stifled would for ever live,
But told expires; pray then reveale
(To show our wound is half to heale)
What Mortall Nymph or Deity
Bewail you thus? Who ere you be
The Shepheard sight, my woes I crave
Smotherd in me, I in my Grave;
Yet be in show or truth a Saint,
Or fiend breath *Anthemes*, heare my plaint
For her and her breaths symphony,
Which now makes full the Harmony
Above, and to whose voice the Spheres
Listen, and call her Musick theirs;
This was I blest on earth with, so
As *Druids* amorous did grow
Jealous of both, for as one day
This *Star* as yet but set in *clay*
By an imbracing River lay,
They steept her in the hollowed brooke
Which from her humane nature tooke,
And straight to heaven with winged feare,
Thus *ravisht* with her, *ravish* her.
The Nymph reply'd, this holy rape
Became the Gods, whose obscure shape
They cloth'd with light, whilst ill you grieve
Your better life should ever live,
And weep that she to whom you wish
What Heav'n could give, ha's all its blisse;

Calling

Calling her Angell here, yet be
Sad at this true Divinity:
She's for the *Altar* not the *skies*,.
Whom firſt you *crowne*, then *ſacrifice*.
  Fond man thus to a precipice
Aſpires, till at the top his eyes
Have loſt the ſafety of the plain,
Then begs of Fate the vales againe.
  The now confounded Shepheard cries
Ye all confounding Deſtinies!
How did you make that voice ſo ſweet
Without that glorious form to it?
Thou ſacred ſpirit of my Deare
Where e're thou hoverſt o're us hear!
Imbark thee in the Lawrell tree,
And a new Phebus follows thee,
Who 'ſtead of all his burning rayes
Will ſtrive to catch thee with his layes;
Or if within the Orient Vine,
Thou art both Deity and Wine;
But if thou takeſt the mirtle grove
That *Paphos* is, thou *Queene of Love*
And I thy ſwaine who (elſe) muſt die
By no Beaſts, but thy cruelty:
But you are rougher then the Winde;
Are Souls on *Earth* then *Heav'n* more kind?
Impriſoned in Mortality,
Lucaſta would have anſwered me.
Lucaſta! Aramantha ſaid,
Is ſhe that Virgin-ſtar a Maid
Except her prouder Livery,
In beauty poore, and cheap as I?

Whoſe

Whoſe glory like a Meteor ſhone,
Or aëry Apparition
Admir'd a while but ſlighted known.
Fierce, as the chafed Lyon hies,
He rowſes him, and to her flies,
Thinking to anſwer with his Speare ——
Now as in warre inteſtine, where
Ith' miſt of a black Battell, each
Layes at his next, then makes a breach
Through th' entrayles of another whom
He ſees nor knows when he did come
Guided alone by Rage and th' Drumme,
But ſtripping and impatient wild,
He finds too ſoon his onely child.
So our expiring deſp'rate Lover
Far'd, when amaz'd he did diſcover
Lucaſta in this Nymph, his ſinne
Darts the accurſed Javelin
'Gainſt his own breaſt, which ſhe puts by
With a ſoft Lip and gentle Eye,
Then cloſes with him on the ground
And now her ſmiles have heal'd his wound,
Alexis too again is found:
But not untill thoſe heavy Crimes
She hath kis'd off a thouſand times,
Who not contented with this pain
Doth threaten to offend again.
And now they gaze, and ſigh, and weep,
Whilſt each cheek doth the others ſteep,
Whilſt tongues as exorcis'd are calm;
Onely the Rhet'rick of the Palm
Prevailing pleads, untill at laſt
They chain'd in one another faſt:

LUCASTA to him doth relate
Her various chance and diffring Fate:
How chac'd by HYDRAPHIL, and tract,
The num'rous foe to PHILANACT,
Who whilst they for the same things fight,
As BARDS Decrees, and DRUIDS rite,
For safeguard of their proper joyes,
And Shepheards freedome, each destroyes
The glory of this Sicilie;
Since seeking thus the remedie,
They fancy (building on false ground)
The means must them and it confound,
Yet are resolv'd to stand or fall,
And win a little or lose all.
  From this sad storm of fire and blood
She fled to this yet living Wood;
Where she 'mongst savage beasts doth find
Her self more safe then humane kind.
  Then She relates how CÆLIA
The Lady here strippes her array,
And girdles her in home spunne bayes,
Then makes her conversant in Layes
Of birds, and swaines more innocent
That kenne not guile or courtshipment.
  Now walks she to her bow'r to dine
Under a shade of Eglantine,
Upon a dish of Natures cheere
Which both grew drest, and serv'd up there:
That done, she feasts her smell with Po'ses
Pluckt from the Damask cloath of Roses,
Which there continually doth stay,
And onely frost can take away;

Then

Then wagers which hath moſt content,
Her eye, eare, hand, her guſt or ſent.
  Intranc'd ALEXIS ſees and heares,
As walking above all the ſpheres:
Knows and adores this, and is wilde
Untill with her he live thus milde.
So that which to his thoughts he meant
For loſſe of her a puniſhment,
His armes hung up and his Sword broke,
His Enſignes folded, he betook
Himſelf unto the humble Crook:
And for a full reward of all,
She now doth him her ſhepheard call,
And in a SEE of flow'rs inſtall:
Then gives her faith immediately,
Which he returnes religiouſly;
Both vowing in her peacefull Cave
To make their Bridall-bed and grave.
  But the true joy this pair conceiv'd
Each from the other firſt bereav'd;
And then found after ſuch alarmes
Faſt pinion'd in each others armes:
Ye panting Virgins that do meet
Your Loves within their winding-ſheet,
Breathing and conſtant ſtill ev'n there;
Or ſouls their bodies in yon' ſphere,
Or Angels men return'd from Hell,
And ſeparated mindes can tell.

FINIS.

LUCASTA.

Posthume

POEMS

OF

Richard Lovelace Esq;

Those Honours come too late,
That on our Ashes waite.

Mart. lib. 1. Epig. 26.

LONDON.

Printed by *William Godbid* for
Clement Darby.
1659.

THE DEDICATION.

To the Right Honorable

John Lovelace

Esquire.

SIR,

Lucasta (*fair, but hapless Maid!*)
Once flourisht underneath the shade
Of your Illustrious Mother; *Now,*
An Orphan grown, she bows to you!
To YOU, Her *vertues noble Heir,*
Oh may she find protection there;
Nor let her welcome be the less
'Cause a rough hand makes her Addresse,
One (to whom Foes the Muses are)
Born and Bred up in Rugged War;
For, Conscious how unfit I am,
I only have pronounc'd her Name,
To waken pity in your Brest,
And leave Her Tears to plead the Rest.

SIR,

Your most obedient

Servant and Kinsman

Dudley Posthumus-Lovelace.

P O E M S.

To *LUCASTA*:

Her Reſerved looks.

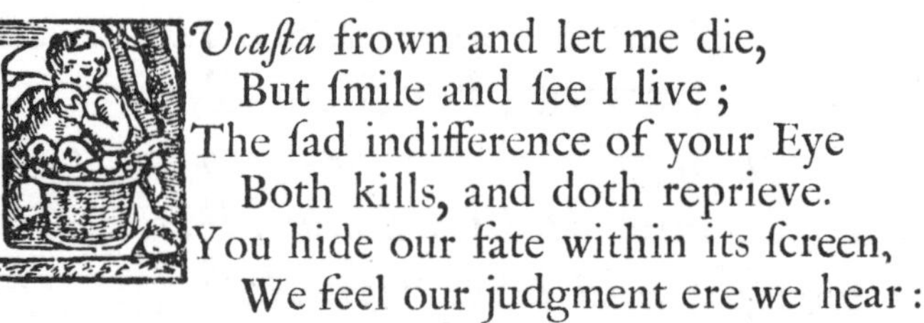

L*Ucaſta* frown and let me die,
But ſmile and ſee I live;
The ſad indifference of your Eye
Both kills, and doth reprieve.
You hide our fate within its ſcreen,
We feel our judgment ere we hear:
So in one Picture I have ſeen
An Angel here, the Divel there.

Lucaſta laughing.

HEark how ſhe laughs aloud,
Although the world put on its ſhrowd;
Wept at by the fantaſtick Crowd,
Who cry, One drop let fall
From her, might ſave the Univerſal Ball.
She laughs again
At our ridiculous pain;
And at our merry miſery
She laughs until ſhe cry;
Sages, forbear
That ill-contrived tear,
Although your fear,

Doth

Doth barricadoe Hope from your ſoft Ear.
That which ſtill makes her mirth to flow,
Is our ſiniſter-handed woe,
Which downwards on its head doth go;
And ere that it is ſown, doth grow.
This makes her ſpleen contract,
And her juſt pleaſure feaſt;
For the unjuſteſt act
Is ſtill the pleaſant'ſt jeſt.

SONG.

1

Strive not, vain Lover, to be fine,
Thy ſilk 's the Silk-worms, and not thine;
You leſſen to a Fly your Miſtris Thought,
To think it may be in a Cobweb caught.
What though her thin tranſparent lawn
Thy heart in a ſtrong Net hath drawn?
Not all the Arms the God of Fire ere made,
Can the ſoft Bulwarks of nak'd Love invade.

2.

Be truly fine then, and your ſelf dreſs
In her fair Souls immac'late glaſs:
Then by reflection you may have the bliſs
Perhaps to ſee what a True fineneſs is;
When all your Gawderies will fit
Thoſe only that are poor in wit:
She that a *clinquant* outſide doth adore,
Dotes on a gilded *Statue*, and no more.

In

In allusion to the *French-Song.*

N' entendez vous pas ce language.

Cho. *THen underſtand you not (Fair choice)*
This Language without tongue or voice?

1.

How often have my Tears
Invaded your ſoft Ears,
And dropt their ſilent Chimes
A thouſand thouſand times,
Whilſt Echo did your eyes,
And ſweetly Sympathize;
But that the wary Lid
Their Sluces did forbid?
Cho. *Then underſtand you not (Fair choice)*
This Language without tongue or voice?

2.

My Arms did plead my wound,.
Each in the other bound;
Volleys of Sighs did crowd,
And ring my griefs alowd;
Grones, like a Canon Ball,
Batter'd the Marble Wall,
That the kind Neighb'ring Grove,
Did mutiny for Love.
Cho. *Then underſtand you not (Fair Choice)*
This Language without tongue or voice?

3. The

3.

The Rheth'rick of my Hand
Woo'd you to underſtand;
Nay, in our ſilent walk
My very Feet would talk,
My Knees were eloquent,
And ſpake the Love I meant;
But deaf unto that Ayr,
They bent, would fall in Prayer.
Cho. *Yet underſtand you not (Fair Choice)*
This Language without tongue or voice?

4.

No? Know then I would melt,
On every Limb I felt,
And on each naked part
Spread my expanded Heart,
That not a Vein of thee,
But ſhould be fill'd with mee.
Whil'ſt on thine own Down, I
Would tumble, pant, and dye.
Cho. *You underſtand not this (Fair Choice;)*
This Language wants both tongue and voice.

Night. *To* Lucaſta.

NIght! loathed Jaylor of the lock'd up Sun,
And Tyrant-turnkey on committed day;
Bright Eyes lye fettered in thy Dungeon,
And Heaven it ſelf doth thy dark Wards obey:
Thou doſt ariſe our living Hell,
With thee grones, terrors, furies dwell,
Untill *Lucaſta* doth awake,
And with her Beams theſe heavy chains off ſhake.

Behold, with opening her Almighty Lid
Bright eyes break rowling, and with luſtre ſpread,
And captive Day his chariot mounted is;
Night to her proper Hell is beat,
And ſcrued to her Ebon Seat;
Till th' Earth with play oppreſſed lies,
And drawes again the Curtains of her Eyes.

But Bondſlave, I, know neither Day nor Night;
Whether ſhe murth'ring ſleep or ſaving wake;
Now broyl'd ith' Zone of her reflected light,
Then froſe my Iſicles, not Sinews ſhake:
Smile then new Nature, your ſoft blaſt
Doth melt our Ice, and Fires waſt:
Whil'ſt the ſcorch'd ſhiv'ring world new born
Now feels it all the day one riſing morn.

Love

Love Inthron'd.

Ode.

1.

IN troth, I do my ſelf perſwade,
That the wilde Boy is grown a Man;
And all his Childiſhneſſe off laid,
E're ſince *Lucaſta* did his fires Fan;
H' has left his apiſh Jigs,
And whipping Hearts like Gigs;
For t'other day I heard him ſwear
That Beauty ſhould be crown'd in Honours Chair.

2.

With what a true and heavenly State
He doth his glorious Darts diſpence,
Now cleans'd from Falſhood, Blood, and Hate,
And newly tipt with Innocence;
Love Juſtice is become,
And doth the Cruel doome:
Reverſed is the old Decree;
Behold! he ſits Inthron'd with Majeſtie.

3.

Inthroned in *Lucaſta's* Eye
He doth our Faith and Hearts Survey;
Then meaſures them by Sympathy,
And each to th' others Breaſt convey;
Whilſt to his Altars Now
The frozen Veſtals Bow,
And ſtrickt *Diana* too doth go,
A hunting with his fear'd, exchanged Bow.

Th'

4.

Th' Imbracing Seas, and Ambient Air,
  Now in his holy fires burn;
Fish couple, Birds and Beasts in pair,
  Do their own Sacrifices turn:
    This is a Miracle,
    That might Religion swell:
  But she that these and their God awes,
Her crowned Self submits to her own Laws.

Her Muffe.

1.

'TWas not for some calm blessing to receive,
Thou didst thy polish'd hands in shagg'd furs weave;
  It were no blessing thus obtain'd,
  Thou rather would'st a curse have gain'd,
Then let thy warm driven snow be ever stain'd.

2.

Not that you feared the discolo'ring cold,
Might alchymize their Silver into Gold;
  Nor could your ten white Nuns so sin,
  That you should thus pennance them in
Each in her course hair smock of Discipline.

3.

Nor *Hero*-like, who on their crest still wore
A Lyon, Panther, Leopard or a Bore,
  To look their Enemies in their Herse;
  Thou would'st thy hand should deeper pierce,
And, in its softness rough, appear more fierce.

No,

4.

No, no, *Lucasta*, destiny Decreed
That Beasts to thee a sacrifice should bleed,
And strip themselves to make you gay;
For ne'r yet Herald did display,
A Coat, where *Sables* upon *Ermin* lay.

5.

This for Lay-Lovers, that must stand at dore,
Salute the threshold, and admire no more:
But I, in my Invention tough,
Rate not this outward bliss enough,
But still contemplate must the hidden Muffe.

A Black patch on Lucasta's *Face.*

DUll as I was, to think that a Court Fly,
Presum'd so neer her Eye;
When 'twas th'industrious Bee
Mistook her glorious Face for Paradise,
To summe up all his Chymistry of Spice;
With a brave pride and honour led,
Neer both her Suns he makes his bed;
And though a Spark struggles to rise as red:
Then Æmulates the gay
Daughter of Day,
Acts the *Romantick Phœnix* fate:
When now with all his Sweets lay'd out in state,
Lucasta scatters but one Heat,
And all the Aromatick pills do sweat,
And Gums calcin'd, themselves to powder beat;

Which a fresh gale of Air
Conveys into her Hair;
Then chaft he's set on fire,
And in these holy flames doth glad expire;
And that black marble Tablet there
So neer her either Sphere,
Was plac'd; nor foyl, nor Ornament,
But the sweet little Bees large Monument.

Another.

I.

AS I beheld a Winters Evening Air,
Curl'd in her court false locks of living hair,
Butter'd with Jessamine the Sun left there,

2.

Galliard and clinquant she appear'd to give,
A Serenade or Ball to us that grieve,
And teach us *A la mode* more gently live.

3.

But as a *Moor*, who to her Cheeks prefers
White Spots t'allure her black Idolaters,
Me thought she look'd all ore bepatch'd with Stars;

4.

Like the dark front of some *Ethiopian* Queen,
Vailed all ore with Gems of Red, Blew, Green;
Whose ugly Night seem'd masked with days Skreen;

5. Whilst

5.

Whilſt the fond people offer'd Sacrifice
To Saphyrs 'ſtead of Veins and Arteries,
And bow'd unto the Diamonds, not her Eyes.

6.

Behold *Lucaſta*'s Face, how't glows like Noon!
A Sun intire is her complexion,
And form'd of one whole Conſtellation.

7.

So gently ſhining, ſo ſerene, ſo cleer,
Her look doth Univerſal Nature cheer;
Only a cloud or two hangs here and there.

To Lucaſta.

1.

I Laugh and ſing, but cannot tell
Whether the folly on't ſounds well;
But then I groan
Methinks in Tune,
Whilſt Grief, Deſpair, and Fear, dance to the Air
Of my deſpiſed Prayer.

2.

A pretty Antick Love does this,
Then ſtrikes a Galliard with a Kiſs;
As in the end
The Chords they rend;
So you but with a touch from your fair Hand,
Turn all to Saraband

To Lucasta.

1.

LIke to the Sent'nel Stars,†I watch all Night;
For still the grand round of your Light,
And glorious Breast
Awakes in me an East,
Nor will my rolling Eyes ere know a West.

2.

Now on my Down I'm toss'd as on a Wave,
And my repose is made my Grave;
Fluttering I lye,
Do beat my Self and dye,
But for a Resurrection from your eye.

3.

Ah my fair Murdresse! dost thou cruelly heal,
With Various pains to make me well?
Then let me be
Thy cut Anatomie,
And in each mangled part my heart you'l see.

Lucasta *at the Bath.*

1.

I'th' Autumn of a Summers day,
When all the Winds got leave to play;
Lucasta, that fair Ship, is lanch'd,
And from its crust this Almond blanch'd.

2. Blow

2.

Blow then, unruly Northwind, blow,
'Till in their holds your Eyes you ſtow;
And ſwell your Cheeks, bequeath chill Death:
See! ſhe hath ſmil'd thee out of Breath.

3.

Court gentle *Zephyr*, court and fan
Her ſofter breaſt's carnation'd Wan;
Your charming Rhethorick of Down
Flyes ſcatter'd from before her frown.

4.

Say, my white Water-Lilly, ſay,
How is't thoſe warm ſtreams break away?
Cut by thy chaſt cold breaſt which dwells
Amidſt them arm'd in Iſicles.

5.

And the hot floods more raging grown
In flames of Thee, then in their own;
In their diſtempers wildly glow,
And kiſſe thy Pillar of fix'd Snow.

6.

No Sulphur, through whoſe each blew Vein
The thick and lazy Currents ſtrein,
Can cure the Smarting, nor the fell
Bliſters of Love wherewith they ſwell.

7.

Theſe great Phyſicians of the Blind,
The Lame, and fatal Blains of *Inde*,
In every drop themſelves now ſee
Speckled with a new Leproſie.

8. As

8.

As Sick drinks are with old Wine dash'd,
Foul Waters too with Spirits wash'd;
Thou greiv'd, perchance, one tear let'st fall,
Which straight did purifie them all.

9.

And now is cleans'd enough the flood,
Which since runs cleare, as doth thy blood;
Of the wet Pearls uncrown thy hair,
And mantle thee with *Ermin* Air.

10.

Lucasta, hail! fair Conqueresse
Of Fire, Air, Earth, and Seas;
Thou whom all kneel to, yet even thou
Wilt unto Love, thy captive, bow.

The Ant.

1.

FOrbear thou great good Husband, little Ant;
A little respite from thy flood of sweat;
Thou, thine own Horse and Cart, under this Plant
Thy spacious tent, fan thy prodigious heat;
Down with thy double load of that one grain;
It is a Granarie for all thy Train.

2.

Cease large example of wise thrift a while,
(For thy example is become our Law)
And teach thy frowns a seasonable smile:
So *Cato* sometimes the nak'd Florals saw.
And thou almighty foe, lay by thy sting,
Whilst thy unpay'd Musicians, Crickets, sing.

3. *Lucasta,*

3.

Lucaſta, She that holy makes the Day,
And 'ſtills new Life in fields of Fueillemort:
Hath back reſtor'd their Verdure with one Ray,
And with her Eye bid all to play and ſport.
Ant to work ſtill; Age will Thee Truant call;
And to ſave now, th' art worſe than prodigal.

4.

Auſtere and *Cynick*! not one hour t'allow,
To loſe with pleaſure what thou gotſt with pain:
But drive on ſacred Feſtivals, thy Plow;
Tearing high-ways with thy ore charged Wain.
Not all thy life time one poor Minute live,
And thy o're labour'd Bulk with mirth relieve?

5.

Look up then miſerable Ant, and ſpie
Thy fatal foes, for breaking of her Law,
Hov'ring above thee, Madam, *Margaret Pie*,
And her fierce Servant, Meagre, Sir *John Daw*:
Thy Self and Storehouſe now they do ſtore up,
And thy whole Harveſt too within their Crop.

6.

Thus we unthrifty thrive within Earths Tomb,
For ſome more rav'nous and ambitious Jaw:
The *Grain* in th' *Ants*, the *Ants* in the *Pies* womb,
The *Pie* in th' *Hawks*, the *Hawks* ith' *Eagles* maw:
So ſcattering to hord 'gainſt a long Day,
Thinking to ſave all, we caſt all away.

The

The Snayl.

WIſe Emblem of our Politick World,
Sage Snayl, within thine own ſelf curl'd;
Inſtruct me ſoftly to make haſt,
Whilſt theſe my Feet go ſlowly faſt.
Compendious Snayl! thou ſeem'ſt to me,
Large *Euclids* ſtrickt Epitome;
And in each Diagram, doſt Fling
Thee from the point unto the Ring.
A Figure now Triangulare,
An Oval now, and now a Square;
And then a Serpentine doſt crawl
Now a ſtraight Line, now crook'd, now all.
Preventing Rival of the Day,
Th'art up and openeſt thy Ray,
And ere the Morn cradles the Moon,
Th' art broke into a Beauteous Noon.
Then when the Sun ſups in the Deep,
Thy Silver Horns e're *Cinthia's* peep;
And thou from thine own liquid Bed
New *Phœbus* heav'ſt thy pleaſant Head.
Who ſhall a Name for thee create,
Deep Riddle of Myſterious State?
Bold Nature that gives common Birth
To all products of Seas and Earth,
Of thee, as Earth-quakes, is affraid,
Nor will thy dire Deliv'ry aid.
Thou thine own daughter then, and Sire,
That Son and Mother art intire,
That big ſtill with thy ſelf doſt go,
And liv'ſt an aged Embrio;
That like the Cubbs of *India*,
Thou from thy ſelf a while doſt play:

But

But frighted with a Dog or Gun,
In thine own Belly thou doſt run,
And as thy Houſe was thine own womb,
So thine own womb, concludes thy tomb.
But now I muſt (analys'd King)
Thy Oeconomick Virtues ſing;
Thou great ſtay'd Husband ſtill within,
Thou, thee, that's thine doſt Diſcipline;
And when thou art to progreſs bent,
Thou mov'ſt thy ſelf and tenement,
As Warlike *Scythians* travayl'd, you
Remove your Men and City too;
Then after a ſad Dearth and Rain,
Thou ſcattereſt thy Silver Train;
And when the Trees grow nak'd and old,
Thou cloatheſt them with Cloth of Gold,
Which from thy Bowels thou doſt ſpin,
And draw from the rich Mines within.
Now haſt thou chang'd thee Saint; and made
Thy ſelf a Fane that's cupula'd;
And in thy wreathed Cloiſter thou
Walkeſt thine own Gray fryer too;
Strickt, and lock'd up, th'art Hood all ore
And ne'r Eliminat'ſt thy Dore.
On Sallads thou doſt feed ſevere,
And 'ſtead of Beads thou drop'ſt a tear,
And when to reſt, each calls the Bell,
Thou ſleep'ſt within thy Marble Cell;
Where in dark contemplation plac'd,
The ſweets of Nature thou doſt taſt;
Who now with Time thy days reſolve,
And in a Jelly thee diſſolve.
Like a ſhot Star, which doth repair
Upward, and Rarifie the Air.

Another.

Another.

THe Centaur, Syren, I foregoe,
Thoſe have been ſung, and lowdly too;
Nor of the mixed Sphynx Ile write,
Nor the renown'd Hermaphrodite:
Behold, this Huddle doth appear
Of Horſes, Coach, and Charioteer;
That moveth him by traverſe Law,
And doth himſelf both drive and draw;
Then when the Sun the South doth winne,
He baits him hot in his own Inne;
I heard a grave and auſtere Clark,
Reſolv'd him Pilot both and Barque;
That like the fam'd Ship of *Trevere*,
Did on the Shore himſelf Lavere:
Yet the Authentick do beleeve,
Who keep their Judgement in their Sleeve,
That he is his own Double man,
And ſick, ſtill carries his Sedan:
Or that like Dames i' th' Land of Luyck,
He wears his everlaſting Huyck:
But baniſht, I admire his fate
Since neither Oſtraciſme of State,
Nor a perpetual exile,
Can force this Virtue change his Soyl;
For whereſoever he doth go,
He wanders with his Country too.

Courante Monſieur.

THat frown, *Aminta* now hath drown'd
Thy bright fronts power, and crown'd
Me that was bound.
No, no, deceived Cruel no,
Loves fiery darts
Till tipt with kiſſes, never kindle Hearts.

Adieu weak beauteous Tyrant, ſee!
Thy angry flames meant me,
Retort on thee:
For know, it is decreed, proud fair,
I ne'r muſt dye
By any ſcorching, but a melting Eye.

A looſe Saraband.

1.

NAy, prethee Dear, draw nigher,
Yet cloſer, nigher yet;
Here is a double Fire,
A dry one and a wet:
True laſting Heavenly Fuel
Puts out the Veſtal jewel,
When once we twining marry
Mad Love with wilde Canary.

2. Off

2.

Off with that crowned Venice
'Till all the Houſe doth flame,
Wee'l quench it ſtraight in Rheniſh,
Or what we muſt not name:
Milk lightning ſtill aſſwageth,
So when our fury rageth,
As th' only means to croſs it,
Wee'l drown it in Love's poſſet.

3.

Love never was Well-willer,
Unto my Nag or mee,
Ne'r watter'd us ith' Cellar,
But the cheap Buttery:
At th' head of his own Barrells,
Where broach'd are all his Quarrels,
Should a true noble Maſter
Still make his Gueſt his Taſter.

4.

See all the World how't ſtaggers,
More ugly drunk then we,
As if far gone in daggers,
And blood it ſeem'd to be:
We drink our glaſs of Roſes,
Which nought but ſweets diſcloſes,
Then in our Loyal Chamber,
Refreſh us with Loves Amber.

5. Now

5.

Now tell me, thou fair Cripple,
  That dumb canst scarcely see
Th' almightinesse of Tipple,
  And th' ods 'twixt thee and thee:
What of Elizium's missing?
Still Drinking and still Kissing;
Adoring plump *October*;
Lord! what is Man and Sober?

6.

Now, is there such a Trifle
  As Honour, the fools Gyant?
VVhat is there left to rifle,
  When Wine makes all parts plyant?
Let others Glory follow,
In their false riches wallow,
And with their grief be merry;
Leave me but Love and Sherry.

The Falcon.

FAir Princesse of the spacious Air,
  That hast vouchsaf'd acquaintance here,
With us are quarter'd below stairs,
That can reach Heav'n with nought but Pray'rs;
Who when our activ'st wings we try,
Advance a foot into the Sky.

Bright

Bright Heir t' th' Bird Imperial,
From whoſe avenging penons fall
Thunder and Lightning twiſted Spun;
Brave Couſin-german to the Sun,
That didſt forſake thy Throne and Sphere,
To be an humble Pris'ner here;
And for a pirch of her ſoft hand,
Reſign the Royal Woods command.

How often would'ſt thou ſhoot Heav'ns Ark,
Then mount thy ſelf into a Lark;
And after our ſhort faint eyes call,
When now a Fly, now nought at all;
Then ſtoop ſo ſwift unto our Sence,
As thou wert ſent Intelligence.

Free beauteous Slave, thy happy feet
In ſilver Fetters vervails meet,
And trample on that noble Wriſt
The Gods have kneel'd in vain t' have kiſt:
But gaze not, bold deceived Spye,
Too much oth' luſtre of her Eye;
The Sun, thou doſt out-ſtare, alas!
VVinks at the glory of her Face.

Be ſafe then in thy Velvet helm,
Her looks are calms that do orewhelm,
Then the *Arabian* bird more bleſt,
Chafe in the ſpicery of her breaſt,
And looſe you in her Breath, a wind
Sow'rs the delicious gales of *Inde*.

But

But now a quill from thine own Wing
I pluck, thy lofty ſate to ſing;
Whilſt we behold the various fight,
With mingled pleaſure and affright,
The humbler Hinds do fall to pray'r,
As when an Army's ſeen i' th' Air
And the prophetick Spannels run,
And howle thy *Epicedium*.

The *Heron* mounted doth appear
On his own Peg'ſus a Lanceer,
And ſeems on earth, when he doth hut,
A proper Halberdier on foot;
Secure i' th' Moore, about to ſup,
The Dogs have beat his Quarters up.

And now he takes the open air,
Drawes up his Wings with Tactick care;
Whilſt th' expert *Falcon* ſwift doth climbe,
In ſubtle Mazes ſerpentine;
And to advantage cloſely twin'd
She gets the upper Sky and Wind,
Where ſhe diſſembles to invade,
And lies a pol'tick Ambuſcade.

The hedg'd-in *Heron*, whom the Foe
Awaits above, and Dogs below,
In his fortification lies,
And makes him ready for ſurprize;
When rouſed with a ſhrill alarm,
Was ſhouted from beneath, they arm.

The

The *Falcon* charges at firſt view
With her brigade of Talons; through
Whoſe Shoots, the wary *Heron* beat,
VVith a well counterwheel'd retreat.
But the bold Gen'ral never loſt,
Hath won again her airy Poſt;
VVho wild in this affront, now fryes,
Then gives a Volley of her Eyes.

The deſp'rate *Heron* now contracts,
In one deſign all former facts;
Noble he is reſolv'd to fall
His, and his En'mies funerall,
And (to be rid of her) to dy
A publick Martyr of the Skv.

VVhen now he turns his laſt to wreak
The palizadoes of his Beak;
The raging foe impatient
Wrack'd with revenge, and fury rent,
Swift as the Thunderbolt he ſtrikes,
Too ſure upon the ſtand of Pikes,
There ſhe his naked breaſt doth hit
And on the caſe of Rapiers 's ſplit.†

But ev'n in her expiring pangs
The *Heron*'s pounc'd within her Phangs,
And ſo above ſhe ſtoops to riſe
A Trophee and a Sacrifice;
VVhilſt her own Bells in the ſad fall
Ring out the double Funerall.

Ah

Ah Victory, unhap'ly wonne!
VVeeping and Red is ſet the Sun,
VVhilſt the whole Field floats in one tear,
And all the Air doth mourning wear:
Cloſe hooded all thy kindred come
To pay their Vows upon thy Tombe;
The *Hobby* and the *Musket* too,
Do march to take their laſt adieu.

The *Lanner* and the *Lanneret*,
Thy Colours bear as Banneret;
The *Goſhawk* and her *Tercel* rows'd,
VVith Tears attend thee as new bows'd,
All theſe are in their dark array
Led by the various *Herald-Jay*.

But thy eternal name ſhall live
VVhilſt Quills from Aſhes fame reprieve,
VVhilſt open ſtands Renown's wide dore,
And VVings are left on which to ſoar;
Doctor *Robbin*, the Prelate *Pye*,
And the poetick *Swan* ſhall dye,
Only to ſing thy Elegie.

Love made in the first Age: *To* Chloris.

1.

IN the Nativity of time,
Chloris! it was not thought a Crime
In direct *Hebrew* for to woe.
Now wee make Love, as all on fire,
Ring Retrograde our lowd Desire,
And Court in *English* Backward too.

2.

Thrice happy was that golden Age,
When Complement was constru'd Rage,
And fine words in the Center hid;
When cursed *No* stain'd no Maids Blisse,
And all discourse was summ'd in *Yes*,
And Nought forbad, but to forbid.

3.

Love then unstinted, Love did sip,
And Cherries pluck'd fresh from the Lip,
On Cheeks and Roses free he fed;
Lasses like *Autumne* Plums did drop,
And Lads, indifferently did crop
A Flower, and a Maiden-head.

4.

Then unconfined each did Tipple
Wine from the Bunch, Milk from the Nipple,
Paps tractable as Udders were;
Then equally the wholsome Jellies,
Were squeez'd from Olive-Trees, and Bellies,
Nor Suits of Trespasse did they fear.

5. A

5.

A fragrant Bank of Straw-berries,
Diaper'd with Violets Eyes,
Was Table, Table-cloth, and Fare;
No Pallace to the Clouds did ſwell,
Each humble Princeſſe then did dwell
In the *Piazza* of her Hair.

6.

Both broken Faith, and th' cauſe of it,
All damning Gold was damm'd to th' Pit;
Their Troth ſeal'd with a Claſp and Kiſſe,
Laſted untill that extreem day,
In which they ſmil'd their Souls away,
And in each other breath'd new bliſſe.

7.

Becauſe no fault, there was no tear;
No grone did grate the granting Ear;
No falſe foul breath their Del'cat ſmell:
No Serpent kiſs poyſon'd the Taſt,
Each touch was naturally Chaſt,
And their mere Senſe a Miracle.

8.

Naked as their own innocence,
And unimbroyder'd from Offence
They went, above poor Riches, gay;
On ſofter than the Cignets Down,
In beds they tumbled of their own;
For each within the other lay.

9.

Thus did they live: Thus did they love,
Repeating only joyes Above;
  And Angels were, but with Cloaths on,
Which they would put off cheerfully,
To bathe them in the *Galaxie*,
  Then gird them with the Heavenly Zone.

10.

Now, *CHLORIS*! miſerably crave,
The offer'd bliſſe you would not have;
  Which evermore I muſt deny,
Whilſt raviſh'd with theſe Noble Dreams,
And crowned with mine own ſoft Beams,
  Injoying of my ſelf I lye.

To a Lady with child that ask'd an Old Shirt.

AND why an honour'd ragged Shirt, that ſhows,
Like tatter'd Enſigns, all its Bodies blows?
Should it be ſwathed in a veſt ſo dire,
It were enough to ſet the Child on fire;
Diſhevell'd Queens ſhould ſtrip them of their hair,
And in it mantle the new riſing Heir:
Nor do I know ought worth to wrap it in,
Except my parchment upper-coat of Skin:
And then expect no end of its chaſt Tears,
That firſt was rowl'd in Down, now Furs of Bears.

But

But ſince to Ladies 't hath a Cuſtome been
Linnen to ſend, that travail and lye in;
To the nine Sempſtreſſes, my former friends,
I ſu'd, but they had nought but ſhreds and ends.
At laſt, the jolli'ſt of the three times three,
Rent th' apron from her ſmock, and gave it me,
'Twas ſoft and gentle, ſubt'ly ſpun no doubt;
Pardon my boldneſs, Madam; *Here's the clout.*

SONG.

1.

IN mine one Monument I lye,
And in my Self am buried;
Sure the quick Lightning of her Eye
Melted my Soul ith' Scabberd, dead;
And now like ſome pale ghoſt I walk,
And with anothers Spirit talk.

2.

Nor can her beams a heat convey
That may my frozen boſome warm,
Unleſs her Smiles have pow'r, as they
That a croſs charm can countercharm;
But this is ſuch a pleaſing pain,
I'm loth to be alive again.

Another.

Another.

I Did believe I was in Heav'n
When firſt the Heav'n her ſelf was giv'n,
That in my heart her beams did paſſe
As ſome the Sun keep in a glaſſe,
So that her Beauties thorow me
Did hurt my Rival-Enemy.
But fate alaſs! decreed it ſo,
That I was Engine to my woe;
For as a corner'd Chriſtal Spot
My heart Diaphanous was not,
But ſolid Stuffe, where her Eye flings
Quick fire upon the catching ſtrings:
Yet as at Triumphs in the Night,
You ſee the Princes Arms in Light;
So when I once was ſet on flame,
I burnt all ore the Letters of her Name.

ODE.

1.

YOu are deceiv'd; I ſooner may dull fair,
Seat a dark *Moor* in *Caſſiopea*'s chair,
Or on the Glow-worms uſeleſſe Light
Beſtow the watching flames of Night,
Or give the Roſes breath
To executed Death,
Ere the bright hiew
Of Verſe to you;
It is juſt Heaven on Beauty ſtamps a fame,
And we alaſs! its Triumphs but proclaim.

2. What

2.

What chains but are too light for me, ſhould I
Say that *Lucaſta*, in ſtrange Arms could lie;
  Or, that *Caſtara* were impure,
  Or *Saccariſa*'s faith unſure;
    That *Chloris* Love as hair,
    Embrac'd each En'mies air:
      That all their good
      Ran in their blood;
'Tis the ſame wrong th'unworthy to inthrone,
As from her proper ſphere t' have vertue thrown.

3.

That ſtrange force on the ignoble hath renown,
As *Aurum Fulminans*, it blows Vice down;
  'Twere better (heavy one) to crawl
  Forgot, then raiſed, trod on fall;
    All your defections now
    Are not writ on your brow.
      Odes to faults give
      A ſhame, muſt live.
When a fat miſt we view, we coughing run;
But that once Meteor drawn, all cry, undone.

4.

How bright the fair *Paulina* did appear,
When hid in Jewels ſhe did ſeem a Star:
  But who could ſoberly behold
  A wicked Owl in Cloath of Gold?
    Or the ridiculous *Ape*,
    In ſacred *Veſta*'s Shape?
      So doth agree
      Juſt Praiſe with thee;
For ſince thy birth gave thee no beauty, know
No Poets pencil muſt or can do ſo.

The

The Duell.

1.

LOve drunk the other day, knockt at my breſt,
But I, alas! was not within:
My man, my Ear, told me he came t' atteſt,
That without cauſe h' had boxed him,
And battered the Windows of mine eyes,
And took my heart for one of 's Nunneries.

2.

I wondred at the outrage ſafe return'd,
And ſtormed at the baſe affront;
And by a friend of mine, bold Faith, that burn'd,
I call'd him to a ſtrict Accompt.
He ſaid, that by the Law, the challeng'd might
Take the advantage both of Arms, and Fight.

3.

Two darts of equal length and points he ſent,
And nobly gave the choyce to me;
Which I not weigh'd, young and indifferent;
Now full of nought but Victorie.
So we both met in one of 's Mothers Groves,
The time, at the firſt murm'ring of her Doves.

4.

I ſtript my ſelf naked all o're, as he,
For ſo I was beſt arm'd, when bare;
His firſt paſſe did my Liver raſe, yet I
Made home a falſify too neer;
For when my Arm to it's true diſtance came
I nothing touch'd but a fantaſtick flame.

5. This,

5.

This, this is Love we daily quarrel ſo,
An idle *Don-Quichoterie*:
We whip ourſelves with our own twiſted wo,
And wound the Ayre for a Fly.
The only way t'undo this Enemy,
Is to laugh at the Boy, and he will cry.

CUPID *far gone.*

1.

WHat ſo beyond all madneſſe is the Elf,
Now he hath got out of himſelf!
His fatal Enemy the *Bee*,
Nor his deceiv'd Artillerie;
His Shackles, nor the Roſes bough
Ne'r half ſo netled him as he is now.

2.

See! at's own Mother he is offering,
His Finger now fits any Ring;
Old *Cybele* he would enjoy,
And now the Girl, and now the Boy.
He proffers *Jove* a back Careſſe,
And all his Love in the *Antipodes*.

3.

Jealous of his chaſt *Pſyche*, raging he,
Quarrels the Student *Mercurie*;
And with a proud ſubmiſſive Breath
Offers to change his Darts with Death.
He ſtrikes at the bright Eye of Day,
And *Juno* tumbles in her milky way.

4. The

4.

The dear Sweet Secrets of the Gods he tells,
And with loath'd hate lov'd heaven he ſwells;
Now like a fury he belies
Myriads of pure Virginities;
And ſwears, with this falſe frenzy hurl'd,
There's not a vertuous She in all the World.

5.

Olympus he renownces, then deſcends,
And makes a friendſhip with the Fiends;
Bids *Charon* be no more a ſlave,
He *Argos* rigg'd with Stars ſhall have;
And triple *Cerberus* from below
Muſt leaſh'd t' himſelf with him a hunting go.

A Mock-Song.†

1.

NOw *Whitehalls* in the grave,
And our *Head* is our ſlave,
The bright pearl in his cloſe ſhell of Oyſter;
Now the *Miter* is loſt,
The proud *Prælates*, too, croſt,
And all *Rome*'s confin'd to a Cloyſter:
He that *Tarquin* was ſtyl'd,
Our white Land's exil'd,
Yea undefil'd,
Not a Court *Ape*'s left to confute us:
Then let your Voyces riſe high,
As your Colours did fly,
And flour'ſhing cry,
Long live the brave *Oliver-Brutus*.

2. Now

2.

Now the *Sun* is unarm'd,
And the *Moon* by us charm'd,
All the *Stars* dissolv'd to a Jelly;
Now the *Thighs* of the Crown,
And the *Arms* are lopp'd down,
And the *Body* is all but a Belly:
Let the *Commons* go on,
The Town is our own,
We'l rule alone;
For the *Knights* have yielded their Spent-gorge;
And an order is tane,
With *HONY SOIT* profane,
Shout forth amain,
For our Dragon hath vanquish'd the St. *George*.

A Fly caught in a Cobweb.

SMall type of great ones, that do hum,
Within this whole World's narrow Room,
That with a busie hollow Noise
Catch at the people's vainer Voice,
And with spread Sails play with their breath,
Whose very Hails new christen Death.
Poor Fly caught in an airy net,
Thy Wings have fetter'd now thy feet;
Where like a *Lyon* in a Toyl,
Howere, thou keep'st a noble Coyl,
And beat'st thy gen'rous breast, that ore
The plains thy fatal buzzes rore,
Till thy all-belly'd foe (round Elf)
Hath quarter'd thee within himself.

Was

Was it not better once to play
I' th' light of a Majestick Ray?
Where though too neer and bold, the fire
Might ſindge thy upper down attire,
And thou ith' ſtorm to looſe an Eye,
A Wing, or a ſelf-trapping Thigh;
Yet hadſt thou faln like him, whoſe Coil
Made Fiſhes in the Sea to broyl;
When now th' aſt ſcap'd the noble Flame,
Trapp'd baſely in a ſlimy frame;
And free of Air, thou art become
Slave to the ſpawn of Mud and Lome.
Nor is't enough thy ſelf do'ſt dreſſe
To thy ſwoln Lord a num'rous meſſe,
And by degrees thy thin Veins bleed,
And piece-meal doſt his poyſon feed;
But now devour'd, art like to be
A Net ſpun for thy Familie,
And ſtraight expanded in the Air
Hang'ſt for thy iſſue too a ſnare.
Strange witty Death, and cruel ill,
That killing thee, thou thine doſt kill!
Like Pies in whoſe intombed ark,
All Fowl crowd downward to a Lark;
Thou art thine En'mies Sepulcher,
And in thee burieſt too thine heir.
Yet Fates a glory have reſerv'd
For one ſo highly hath deſerv'd;
As the *Rhinoceros* doth dy
Under his Caſtle-Enemy,
As through the *Cranes* trunk Throat doth ſpeed,
The *Aſpe* doth on his feeder feed;
Fall yet triumphant in thy woe,
Bound with the entrails of thy foe.

A

A Fly about a Glaſſe of Burnt Claret.

1.

FOrbear this liquid Fire, *Fly*,
It is more fatal then the dry,
That ſingly, but embracing, wounds,
And this at once, both burns and drowns.

2.

The Salamander that in heat
And flames doth cool his monſtrous ſweat;
Whoſe fan a glowing cake, 'tis ſaid,
Of this red furnace is afraid.

3.

Viewing the Ruby-chriſtal ſhine,
Thou tak'ſt it for Heaven-Chriſtalline;
Anon thou wilt be taught to groan,
'Tis an aſcended *Acheron*.

4.

A Snowball-heart in it let fall,
And take it out a Fire-ball:
An Icy breaſt in it betray'd,
Breaks a deſtructive wild Granade.

5.

'Tis this makes *Venus* Altars ſhine,
This kindles froſty *Hymen*'s Pine;
When the Boy grows old in his deſires,
This *Flambeau* doth new light his fires.

6. 'Though

6.

'Though the cold *Hermit* ever wail,
Whoſe ſighs do freeze, and tears drop hail,
Once having paſſed this, will ne'r
Another flaming purging fear.

7.

The *Veſtal* drinking this doth burn,
Now more than in her fun'ral Urn;
Her fires, that with the Sun kept race,
Are now extinguiſh'd by her Face.

8.

The *Chymiſt*, that himſelf doth ſtill,
Let him but taſt this *Limbecks* bill,
And prove this ſublimated Bowl,
He'l ſwear it will calcine a Soul.

9.

Noble and brave! now thou doſt know,
The falſe prepared decks below,
Doſt thou the fatal liquor ſup,
One drop alas! thy Barque blowes up.

10.

What airy Country haſt to ſave,
Whoſe plagues thou'lt bury in thy grave?
For even now thou ſeemſt to us
On this Gulphs brink a *Curtius*.

11.

And now th' art faln (magnanimous *Fly*)
In, where thine Ocean doth fry,
Like the Sun's ſon who bluſh'd the flood,
To a complexion of blood.

12.

Yet ſee! my glad Auricular
Redeems thee (though diſſolv'd) a Star,
Flaggy thy Wings, and ſcorch'd thy Thighs,
Thou ly'ſt a double Sacrifice.

13.

And now my warming, cooling, breath
Shall a new life afford in Death;
See! in the Hoſpital of my hand
Already cur'd, thou fierce do'ſt ſtand.

14.

Burnt Inſect! doſt thou reaſpire
The moiſt-hot-glaſſe, and liquid fire?
I ſee! 'tis ſuch a pleaſing pain,
Thou would'ſt be ſcorch'd, and drown'd again.

Female Glory.

'M*Ongſt the worlds wonders, there doth yet remain*
One greater than the reſt, that's all thoſe o're again
And her own ſelf beſide; A Lady *whoſe ſoft Breaſt,*
Is with vaſt Honours Soul, and Virtues Life poſſeſt.
Fair, *as Original Light, firſt from the* Chaos *ſhot,*
When day in Virgin-beams triumph'd, and Night was not.
And as that Breath infus'd, in the New-breather Good,
When Ill unknown was dumb, and Bad not underſtood;
Chearful, *as that Aſpect at this world's finiſhing,*
When Cherubims clapp'd wings, and th' Sons of Heav'n did
(ſing.
Chaſt *as th'* Arabian *bird, who all the Ayr denyes,*
And ev'n in Flames expires, when with her ſelf ſhe lyes.
Oh!

Oh! ſhe's as kind *as drops of new faln* April *Showers,*
That on each gentle breaſt, ſpring freſh perfuming flowers;
She's Conſtant, Gen'rous, Fixt, *ſhe's* Calm, *ſhe is the* All
We can of Vertue, Honour, Faith, *or* Glory *Call,*
And ſhe is (whom I thus tranſmit to endleſs fame)
Miſtreſſe *oth' World, and me, &* LAURA *is her Name.*

A Dialogue.

Lute *and* Voice.

L. SIng *Laura*, ſing, whilſt ſilent are the Sphears,
And all the eyes of Heaven are turn'd to Ears.

V. Touch thy dead Wood, and make each living tree,
Unchain its feet, take arms, and follow thee.

Chorus.

L. Sing. *V.* Touch. O Touch. *L.* O Sing,
Both. It is the Souls, Souls, Sole offering.

V. Touch the Divinity of thy Chords, and make
Each Heart ſtring tremble, and each Sinew ſhake.

L. Whilſt with your Voyce you Rarifie the Air,
None but an hoſt of Angels hover here.

Chorus. Sing. Touch, &c.

V. Touch thy ſoft Lute, and in each gentle thread,
The *Lyon* and the *Panther* Captive lead.

L. Sing, and in Heav'n Inthrone depoſed Love,
Whilſt Angels dance and Fiends in order move.

Double

Double Chorus.

What ſacred Charm may this then be
In Harmonie,
That thus can make the Angels wild,
The Devils mild,
And teach low Hell to Heav'n to ſwell,
And the High Heav'n to ſtoop to Hell.

A Mock Charon.

DIALOGUE.

Cha. W.

W. CHaron! Thou Slave! Thou Fool! Thou Cava-(leer!
Cha. A Slave, a Fool, What Traitors voice I Hear?
W. Come bring thy Boat. *Ch.* No Sir. *W.* No ſirrah why?
Cha. The Bleſt will diſagree, and Fiends will mutiny
At thy, at thy, unnumbred Treachery.
W. Villain, I have a Paſs, which who diſdains,
I will ſequeſter the *Elizian* plains.
Cha. Woes me! Ye gentle ſhades! where ſhall I dwell?
He's come! It is not ſafe to be in Hell.

Chorus.

Thus man, his Honor loſt, falls on theſe Shelves;
Furies and Fiends are ſtill true to themſelves.

Cha. You muſt loſt Fool come in. *W.* Oh let me in!
But now I fear thy Boat will ſink with my ore-weighty (ſin.
Where courteous *Charon* am I now? *Cha.* Vile Rant!
At th' Gates of thy ſupreme Judge *Rhadamant.*

Double Chorus of Divels.

Welcome to Rape, to Theft, to Perjurie,
To all the ills thou wert, we cannot hope to be;
Oh pitty us condemn'd! Oh ceaſe to wooe,
And ſoftly, ſoftly breath, leaſt you infect us too.

The Toad *and* Spyder.

A *Duell.*

UPon a Day when the Dog-ſtar
Unto the World proclaim'd a War,
And poyſon bark'd from his black Throat,
And from his jaws Infection ſhot,
Under a deadly Hen-bane ſhade
With ſlime infernal Miſts are made;
Met the two dreaded Enemies,
Having their Weapons in their Eyes.
First from his Den rolls forth that Load
Of Spite and Hate the ſpeckl'd Toad,
And from his Chaps a foam doth ſpawn,
Such as the loathed three Heads yawn;
Defies his foe with a fell Spet,
To wade through Death to meet with it;
Then in his Self the *Lymbeck* turns,
And his Elixir'd poyſon Urns.
Arachne once the fear 'oth Maid
Cœleſtial, thus unto her pray'd:
Heaven's blew-ey'd Daughter, thine own Mother!
The *Python*-killing Sun's thy Brother.
Oh! thou from gods that did'ſt deſcend,
With a poor Virgin to contend,

Shall

Shall ſeed of Earth and Hell ere be
A Rival in thy Victorie?
Pallas aſſents: for now long time
And pity, had clean rins'd her crime;
When ſtraight ſhe doth with active fire,
Her many legged foe inſpire.
Have you not ſeen a Charact lye
A great Cathedral in the Sea,
Under whoſe *Babylonian* Walls,
A ſmall thin frigot-Alms-houſe ſtalls;
So in his ſlime the Toad doth float,
And th' Spyder by, but ſeems his Boat;
And now the Naumachie Begins
Cloſe to the Surface, her ſelf ſpins
Arachne, when her foe lets flye
A broad-ſide of his Breath, too high,
That's over-ſhot, the wiſely ſtout
Adviſed Maid doth tack about,
And now her pitchy barque doth ſweat,
Chaf'd in her own black fury wet;
Laſie and cold before, ſhe brings
New fires to her contracted Stings,
And with diſcolour'd Spumes doth blaſt
The Herbs that to their Center haſt.
Now to the Neighb'ring Henbane top
Arachne hath her ſelf wound up,
And thence, from its dilated Leaves,
By her own cordage downwards weaves;
And doth her Town of Foe Attack,
And ſtorms the Rampiers of his Back;
Which taken in her Colours ſpread,
March to th' Citadel of's Head.

Now as in witty torturing *Spain*,
The Brain is vext, to vex the Brain;
Where *Hereticks* bare Heads are arm'd
In a cloſe Helm, and in it charm'd
An overgrown and Meagre Rat,
That Peece-meal nibbles himſelf fat;
So on the *Toads* blew-checquer'd Scull
The *Spider* gluttons her ſelf full,
And Vomiting her *Stygian* Seeds,
Her poyſon, on his poyſon, feeds:
Thus the invenom'd Toad, now grown
Big, with more poyſon than his own,
Doth gather all his pow'rs, and ſhakes
His Stormer in's Diſgorged Lakes;
And wounded now, apace crawls on
To his next Plantane Surgeon;
With whoſe rich Balm no ſooner dreſt,
But purged, is his ſick ſwoln Breaſt;
And as a glorious Combatant,
That only reſts a while to pant;
Then with repeated ſtrength, and Scars,
That ſmarting, fire him to new Wars,
Deals Blows that thick themſelves prevent,
As they would gain the time he ſpent.
So the diſdaining angry Toad,
That, calls but a thin uſeleſs Load;
His fatal feared ſelf comes back
With unknown Venome fill'd to crack.
Th' amaſed *Spider* now untwin'd,
Hath crept up, and her ſelf new lin'd
With freſh ſalt foams, and Miſts that blaſt
The Ambient Air as they paſt.

And

And now me thinks a *Sphynx*'s wing
I pluck, and do not write but ſting;
With their black blood, my pale inks blent,
Gall's but a faint Ingredient.
The Pol'tick *Toad* doth now withdraw,
Warn'd, higher in *Campania.*
There wiſely doth intrenched deep,
His Body, in a Body keep,
And leaves a wide and open paſs
T' invite the foe up to his jaws;
Which there within a foggy blind
With fourſcore fire-arms were lin'd;
The gen'rous active *Spider* doubts
More Ambuſcadoes, then Redoubts;
So within ſhot ſhe doth pickear,
Now gall 's the Flank, and now the Rear;
As that the *Toad* in's own diſpite
Muſt change the manner of his fight,
Who like a glorious General,
With one home Charge, lets fly at All.
Chaf'd with a fourfold ven'mous Foam
Of Scorn, Revenge, His Foes and 's Own;
He ſeats him in his loathed Chair,
New-made him by each Mornings Air;
With glowing Eyes, he doth ſurvey
Th' undaunted hoaſt, he calls his prey;
Then his dark Spume he gred'ly laps,
And ſhows the foe his Grave, his Chaps.
Whilſt the quick wary Amazon
Of 'vantage takes occaſion,
And with her troop of Leggs Carreers.
In a full ſpeed with all her Speers;

Down

Down (as ſome mountain on a Mouſe)
On her ſmall Cot he flings his houſe;
Without the poyſon of the Elf,
The *Toad* had like t' have burſt himſelf,
For ſage *Arachne* with good heed,
Had ſtopt herſelf upon full ſpeed;
And 's body now diſorder'd, on
She falls to Execution.
The paſſive *Toad* now only can
Contemn, and ſuffer: Here began
The wronged Maids ingenious Rage,
Which his heart venome muſt Aſſwage;
One Eye ſhe hath ſpet out, ſtrange Smother!
When one flame doth put out Another,
And one Eye wittily ſpar'd, that he
Might but behold his miſerie;
She on each ſpot a wound doth print,
And each ſpeck hath a ſting within't;
Till he but one new Bliſter is,
And ſwells his own Periphraſis;
Then fainting, ſick, and yellow, pale,
She baths him with her ſulph'rous Stale;
Thus ſlacked is her *Stygian* fire,
And ſhe vouchſafes now to retire;
Anon the *Toad* begins to pant,
Bethinks him of th' Almighty plant,
And leſt he peece-meal ſhould be ſped,
Wiſely doth finiſh himſelf dead.
Whilſt the gay Girl, as was her fate,
Doth wanton and luxuriate,
And crowns her conqu'ring head all ore
With fatall Leaves of *Hellebore*,

Not

Not guessing at the pretious Aid
Was lent her by the Heavenly Maid.
The neer Expiring *Toad* now rowls
Himself in lazy bloody Scrowls,
To th' sov'raign Salve of all his ills,
That only life and health distills.
But loe! a Terror above all
That ever yet did him befall!
  Pallas still mindful of her foe,
(Whilst they did with each fires glow)
Had to the place the *Spiders Lar*,
Dispatch'd before the Ev'nings Star;
He learned was in Natures Laws,
Of all her foliage knew the cause,
And 'mongst the rest in his choice want
Unplanted had this Plantane plant.
  The all-confounded *Toad* doth see
His life fled with his Remedie,
And in a glorious Despair
First burst himself, and next the Air;
Then with a Dismal Horred yell,
Beats down his loathsome Breath to Hell.
  But what inestimable bliss
This to the sated Virgin is,
Who as before of her fiend foe,
Now full is of her Goddess too;
She from her fertile womb hath spun
Her stateliest Pavillion,
Whilst all her silken Flags display,
And her triumphant Banners play;
Where *Pallas* she ith' midst doth praise,
And counterfeits her Brothers Rayes;

Nor

Nor will ſhe her dear *Lar* forget,
Victorious by his Benefit;
Whoſe Roof inchanted ſhe doth free,
From haunting Gnat, and goblin Bee,
Who trapp'd in her prepared Toyle,
To their deſtruction keep a coyle.
Then ſhe unlocks the *Toad's* dire Head,
Within whoſe cell is treaſured
That pretious ſtone, which ſhe doth call
A noble recompence for all,
And to her *Lar* doth it preſent,
Of his fair Aid a Monument.

The *Triumphs* OF PHILAMORE and AMORET.

To the Noblest of our Youth And Best of Friends, *CHARLES COTTON* Esquire.

Being at *Berisford*, at his house in *Staffordshire*.

From *LONDON*.

A *POEM*.

SIR your sad absence I complain, as Earth (birth,
Her long hid Spring, that gave her verdures
Who now her cheerful Aromatick Head
Shrinks in her *cold* and *dismal* widow'd *bed*;
Whilst the false Sun her Lover doth him move
Below, and to th' *Antipodes* make Love.
What Fate was mine, when in mine obscure Cave
(Shut up almost close Prisoner in a Grave) (Night,
Your Beams could reach me through this Vault of
And Canton the dark Dungeon with Light!
Whence me (as gen'rous *Spahy's*) you unbound,
Whilst I now know my self both *Free* and Crown'd.

But

But as at *Mœcha's* tombe, the Devout blind
Pilgrim (great Husband of his Sight and Mind)
Pays to no other Object this chast prise,
Then with hot Earth anoynts out both his Eyes:
So having seen your dazling Glories store;
Is it enough, and sin for to see more?
Or, do you thus those pretious Rayes withdraw
To whet my dull Beams, keep my Bold in aw?
Or, are you gentle and compassionate,
You will not reach me *Regulus* his Fate?
Brave Prince who Eagle-ey'd of Eagle kind,
Wert blindly damn'd to look thine own self blind!
But oh return those Fires, too Cruel Nice!
For whilst you fear me Cindars, See! I'm Ice;
A nummed speaking clod, and mine own show,
My Self congeal'd, a Man cut out in Snow:
Return those living Fires, Thou who that vast
Double advantage from one ey'd Heav'n hast;
Look with one *Sun*, though't but Obliquely be,
And if not shine, vouchsafe to wink on me.
Percieve you not a gentle, gliding heat,
And quickning warmth that makes the *Statua* sweat;
As rev'rend *Ducaleon*'s back-flung stone,
Whose rough out-side softens to Skin, anon
Each crusty Vein with wet red is suppli'd,
Whilst nought of Stone but in its heart doth 'bide.
So from the rugged North, where your soft stay
Hath stampt them a *Meridian*, and kind day;
Where now each *a la Mode* Inhabitant,
Himself and's Manners both do pay you rent,
And 'bout your house (your Pallace) doth resort
And 'spite of Fate and War creates a Court.

So

So from the taught North, when you ſhall return
To glad thoſe Looks that ever ſince did mourn,
When men uncloathed of themſelves you'l ſee,
Then ſtart new made, fit, what they ought to be;
Haſt! haſt! you that your Eyes on rare Sights feed,
For thus the golden *Triumph* is decreed.

The twice-born God, ſtill gay and ever young,
With Ivie crown'd, firſt leads the glorious Throng:
He *Ariadnes* ſtarry Coronet
Deſigns for th' brighter Beams of *Amoret*;
Then doth he broach his Throne, and ſinging quaff
Unto her Health his pipe of God-head off.

Him follow the recanting, vexing Nine,
Who, wiſe, now ſing thy laſting Fame in Wine;
Whilſt *Phœbus* not from th' Eaſt, your Feaſt t'adorn,
But from th' inſpir'd *Canaries* roſe this morn.

Now you are come, Winds in their Caverns ſit,
And nothing breaths, but new inlarged Wit;
Hark! One proclaims it *Piacle* to be ſad,
And th' people call't *Religion* to be Mad.

But now, as at a Coronation
VVhen noyſe, the guard, and trumpets are oreblown,
The ſilent Commons mark their Princes way,
And with ſtill Reverence both look, and pray;
So they amaz'd, expecting do adore,
And count the reſt but *Pageantry* before.

Behold! an Hoaſt of Virgins, pure as th' Air,
In her firſt face, ere Miſts durſt vayl her hair;
Their ſnowy Veſts, VVhite as their whiter Skin,
Or their far chaſter whiter Thoughts within:
Roſes they breath'd and ſtrew'd, as if the fine
Heaven, did to Earth his Wreath of ſweets reſigne;

They

They ſang aloud! *Thrice, Oh Thrice happy They*
That can like theſe in Love both yield and ſway.
Next Herald Fame (a Purple Clowd her bears)
In an imbroider'd Coat of Eyes and Ears,
Proclaims the Triumph, and theſe Lovers glory;
Then in a book of Steel Records the Story.
And now a Youth of more than God-like form,
Did th'inward minds of the dumb Throng Alarm;
All nak'd, each part betray'd unto the Eye,
Chaſtly, for neither Sex ow'd he or ſhe.
And this was Heav'nly Love; by his bright hand,
A Boy of worſe than earthly ſtuffe did ſtand;
His Bow broke, his Fires out, and his Wings clipt,
And the black Slave from all his falſe flames ſtript;
Whoſe Eyes were new reſtor'd, but to confeſſe
This days bright bliſſe, and his own wretchedneſſe;
Who ſwell'd with envy, burſting with diſdain,
Did cry to cry, and weep them out again.
And now what Heav'n muſt I invade, what Sphere
Rifle of all her Stars t'inthrone her there?
No *Phœbus*, by thy Boys fate we beware,
Th' unruly flames oth' firebrand, thy Carr;
Although ſhe there once plac'd, thou *Sun* ſhouldſt ſee
Thy day both Nobler governed and thee.
Drive on *Bóötes* thy cold heavy wayn,
Then greaſe thy VVheels with Amber in the Main,
And *Neptune*, thou to thy falſe *Thetis* gallop,
Appollo's ſet within thy Bed of Scallop:
VVhilſt *Amoret* on the reconciled VVinds
Mounted, is drawn by ſix Cæleſtial Minds;
She armed was with Innocence, and fire
That did not burn, for it was *Chaſt Deſire*;

VVhilſt

VVhilſt a new Light doth gild the ſtanders by;
Behold! it was a Day ſhot from her Eye;
Chafing perfumes oth' Eaſt did throng and ſweat,
But by her breath, they melting back were beat.
A Crown of Yet-nere-lighted ſtars ſhe wore,
In her ſoft hand a bleeding Heart ſhe bore,
And round her lay Millions of broken more;
Then a wing'd Crier thrice aloud did call,
Let Fame proclaim this one great Priſe for all.
By her a Lady that might be call'd fair,
And juſtly, but that *Amoret* was there,
VVas Pris'ner led; th' unvalewed Robe ſhe wore,
Made infinite Lay Lovers to adore,
VVho vainly tempt her Reſcue (madly bold)
Chained in ſixteen thouſand links of gold;
Chryſetta thus (Loaden with treaſures) Slave
Did ſtrow the paſs with Pearls, and her way pave.
But loe! the glorious Cauſe of all this high
True heav'nly ſtate, Brave *Philamore* draws nigh!
VVho not himſelf, more ſeems himſelf to be,
And with a ſacred Extaſie doth ſee;
Fixt and unmov'd on's *Pillars* he doth ſtay,
And Joy transforms him his own *Statua*;
Nor hath he pow'r to breath, or ſtrength to greet
The gentle Offers of his *Amoret*,
VVho now amaz'd at 's noble Breaſt doth knock,
And with a Kiſs his gen'rous heart unlock;
VVhilſt ſhe and the whole pomp doth enter there,
VVhence Her nor *Time* nor *Fate* ſhall ever tear.
But whether am I hurld! ho! Back! Awake
From thy glad Trance; to thine old Sorrow take!
Thus, after view of all the *Indies* ſtore,
The Slave returns unto his Chain and Oar;

Thus

Thus *Poets* who all Night in bleſt Heav'ns dwell,
Are call'd next morn to their true living *Hell*;
So I unthrifty, to my ſelf untrue,
Riſe cloath'd with real wants, 'cauſe wanting you,
And what ſubſtantial Riches I poſſeſſe,
I muſt to theſe unvalued Dreams confeſſe.
But all our Clowds ſhall be oreblown, when thee
In our Horizon, bright, once more we ſee;
VVhen thy dear preſence ſhall our Souls new dreſs,
And ſpring an univerſal cheerfulneſſe;
VVhen we ſhall be orewhelm'd in Joy, like they
That change their Night, for a vaſt half-years day.
Then ſhall the wretched Few, that do repine,
See; and recant their Blaſphemies in VVine;
Then ſhall they grieve that thought I've ſung to free
High and aloud of thy true worth and Thee,
And their fowl Hereſies and Lips ſubmit
To th' all-forgiving Breath of *Amoret*,
And me alone their angers Object call,
That from my height ſo miſerably did fall;
And crie out my Invention thin and poor,
VVho have ſaid nought, ſince I could ſay no more.

Advice to my beſt Brother. *Coll*: Francis Lovelace.

FRank, wil't live handſomely? truſt not too far
Thy ſelf to waving Seas, for what thy ſtar
Calculated by ſure event muſt be,
Look in the Glaſſy-epithite and ſee.

Yet

Yet ſettle here your reſt, and take your ſtate,
And in calm *Halcyon*'s neſt ev'n build your Fate;
Prethee lye down ſecurely, *Frank*, and keep
VVith as much no noyſe the inconſtant Deep
As its Inhabitants; nay ſtedfaſt ſtand,
As if diſcover'd were a New-found-land
Fit for Plantation here; dream, dream ſtill,
Lull'd in *Dione*'s cradle, dream, untill
Horrour awake your sense, and you now find
Your ſelf a bubled paſtime for the VVind,
And in looſe *Thetis* blankets torn and toſt;
Frank to undo thy ſelf why art at coſt?

Nor be too confident, fix'd on the ſhore,
For even that too borrows from the ſtore
Of her rich Neighbour, ſince now wiſeſt know,
(And this to *Galileo*'s judgement ow)
The palſie Earth it ſelf is every jot
As frail, inconſtant, waveing as that blot
VVe lay upon the Deep; That ſometimes lies
Chang'd, you would think, with's botoms properties,
But this eternal ſtrange *Ixions* wheel
Of giddy earth, ne'r whirling leaves to reel
Till all things are inverted, till they are
Turn'd to that Antick confus'd ſtate they were.

VVho loves the golden mean, doth ſafely want
A cobwebb'd Cot, and wrongs entail'd upon't;
He richly needs a Pallace for to breed
Vipers and Moths, that on their feeder feed;
The toy that we (too true) a Miſtreſs call,
VVhoſe Looking-glaſs and feather weighs up all;
And Cloaths which Larks would play with, in the Sun,
That mock him in the Night when's courſe is run.

To

To rear an edifice by Art ſo high
That envy ſhould not reach it with her eye,
Nay with a thought come neer it, would'ſt thou know
How ſuch a Structure ſhould be raised? build low.
The bluſt'ring winds inviſible rough ſtroak,
More often ſhakes the ſtubborn'ſt, prop'reſt Oak,
And in proud Turrets we behold withal,
'Tis the Imperial top declines to fall.
Nor does Heav'ns lightning ſtrike the humble Vales
But high aſpiring Mounts batters and ſcales.

A breaſt of proof defies all Shocks of Fate,
Fears in the beſt, hopes in the worſer ſtate;
Heaven forbid that, as of old, Time ever
Flouriſh'd in *Spring*, ſo contrary, now never:
That mighty breath which blew foul Winter hither,
Can eas'ly puffe it to a fairer weather.
VVhy doſt deſpair then, *Franck*? *Æolus* has
A *Zephyrus* as well as *Boreas*.

'Tis a falſe Sequel, Solœciſme, 'gainſt thoſe
Precepts by fortune giv'n us, to ſuppoſe
That 'cauſe it is now ill, 't will ere be ſo;
Apollo doth not always bend his Bow;
But oft uncrowned of his Beams divine,
VVith his ſoft harp awakes the ſleeping Nine.

In ſtricteſt things magnanimous appear,
Greater in hope, howere thy fate, then fear:
Draw all your Sails in quickly, though no ſtorm
Threaten your ruine with a ſad alarm;
For tell me how they differ, tell me pray,
A cloudy tempeſt, and a too fair day.

An

An Anniverſary

On the Hymeneals of my noble Kinſman Tho. Stanley Eſquire.

1.

THe day is curl'd about agen
To view the ſplendor ſhe was in;
When firſt with hallow'd hands
The holy man knit the myſterious bands;
When you two your contracted Souls did move,
Like *Cherubims* above,
And did make Love;
As your un-underſtanding iſſue now
In a glad ſigh, a ſmile, a tear, a Vow.

2.

Tell me, O ſelf-reviving Sun,
In thy Perigrination,
Haſt thou beheld a pair
Twiſt their ſoft beams like theſe in their chaſt air;
As from bright numberleſſe imbracing rayes
Are ſprung th' induſtrious dayes;
So when they gaze,
And change their fertile Eyes with the new morn,
A beauteous Offſpring is ſhot forth, not born.

3.

Be witneſs then, all-ſeeing Sun,
Old Spy, thou that thy race haſt run,
In full five thouſand Rings;
To thee were ever purer Offerings
Sent on the Wings of Faiths? and thou, oh Night!
Curtain of their delight,
By theſe made bright,
Have you not marked their Cœleſtial play,
And no more peek'd the gayeties of day?

4.

Come then pale Virgins, Roſes ſtrow,
Mingled with *Io*'s as you go;
The ſnowy Oxe is kill'd,
The Fane with pros'lite Lads and Laſſes fill'd,
You too may hope the ſame *ſeraphick* joy,
Old time cannot deſtroy,
Nor fulneſſe cloy,
When like theſe, you ſhall ſtamp by Sympathies,
Thouſands of new-born-loves with your chaſt eyes.

Paris's *ſecond Judgement,*

Upon the three Daughters of my Dear Brother Mr. R. Cæſar.

BEhold! three Siſter wonders, in whom met,
Diſtinct and chaſt, the Splendors counterfeit
Of *Juno*, *Venus*, and the warlike Maid,
Each in their three Divinities array'd!
The Majeſty and State of Heav'ns great Queen,
And when ſhe treats the gods, her noble Meen;
The ſweet victorious beauties, and deſires
O' th' Sea-born Princeſs, Empreſſe too of Fires;
The ſacred Arts, and glorious Lawrels, torn
From the fair brow o' th' Goddeſſe Father-born;
All theſe were quarter'd in each ſnowy coat,
With canton'd honours of their own to boot:
Paris by Fate new-wak'd from his dead Cell,
Is charg'd to give his doom impoſſible.
He views in each the brav'ry of all *Ide*;
Whilſt one, as once three, doth his Soul divide.
Then ſighs! ſo equally they're glorious all,
What pity the whole World is but one Ball.

Peinture.

A Panegyrick to the best Picture of Friendship Mr. Pet. Lilly.

IF *Pliny* Lord High Treasurer of all
Natures exchequer shuffled in this our ball;
Pincture, her richer Rival, did admire,
And cry'd she wrought with more almighty fire,
That judg'd the unnumbered issue of her Scrowl,
Infinite and various as her Mother Soul,
That contemplation into matter brought,
Body'd *Idæa's*, and could form a thought:
VVhy do I pause to couch the Cataract,
And the grosse pearls from our dull eyes abstract?
That pow'rful *Lilly*, now awakened, we
This new Creation may behold by thee.
 To thy victorious pencil, all that Eyes
And minds can reach, do bow; the Deities
Bold *Poets* first but feign'd, you do, and make,
And from your awe they our Devotion take.
Your beauteous Pallet first defin'd Loves Queen,
And made her in her heav'nly colours seen;
You strung the Bow of the Bandite her Son,
And tipp'd his Arrowes with Religion.
Neptune, as unknown as his Fish might dwell,
But that you seat him in his throne of Shell.
The thunderers Artillery, and brand
You fancied *Rome* in his fantastick hand.

And

And the pale frights, the pains and fears of Hell,
Firſt from your ſullen Melancholy fell.
Who cleft th' infernal Dog's loath'd head in three,
And ſpun out *Hydra's* fifty necks? by thee
As prepoſſeſs'd w' enjoy th' *Elizian* plain,
VVhich but before was flatter'd in our brain.
VVho ere yet view'd Airs child inviſible,
A hollow Voice, but in thy ſubtile skill?
Faint ſtamm'ring *Eccho*, you ſo draw, that we
The very repercuſſion do ſee.
Cheat *Hocus-pocus*-Nature an Eſſay
O' th' Spring affords us, *Præſto* and away;
You all the year do chain her, and her fruits,
Roots to their Beds, and flowers to their Roots.
Have not mine eyes feaſted i' th' frozen *Zone*,
Upon a freſh new-grown Collation
Of Apples, unknown ſweets, that ſeem'd to me
Hanging to tempt as on the fatal Tree;
So delicately limn'd I vow'd to try
My appetite impos'd upon my Eye.
You Sir alone, Fame and all-conqu'ring Rime,
Files the ſet teeth of all devouring time.
VVhen Beauty once thy vertuous paint hath on,
Age needs not call her to Vermilion;
Her beams nere ſhed or change like th' hair of day,
She ſcatters freſh her everlaſting Ray;
Nay, from her aſhes her fair Virgin fire
Aſcends, that doth new maſſacres conſpire,
Whilſt we wipe off the num'rous ſcore of years,
And do behold our Grandſires as our peers,
With the firſt Father of our Houſe, compare
We do the features of our new-born Heir;

For

For though each coppied a Son, they all
Meet in thy firſt and true Original.
  Sacred Luxurious! what Princeſſe not
But comes to you to have her ſelf begot?
As when firſt man was kneaded, from his ſide
Is born to's hand a ready made up Bride.
He husband to his iſſue then doth play,
And for more Wives remove the obſtructed way:
So by your Art you ſpring up in two moons
What could not elſe be form'd by fifteen Suns;
Thy Skill doth an'mate the prolifick flood,
And thy red Oyl aſſimilates to blood.
  Where then when all the world pays its reſpect,
Lies our tranſalpine barbarous Neglect?
When the chaſt hands of pow'rful *Titian*,
Had drawn the Scourges of our God and Man,
And now the top of th' Altar did aſcend,
To crown the heav'nly piece with a bright end;
Whilſt he who to ſeven Languages gave Law,
And always like the *Sun* his Subjects ſaw,
Did in his Robes Imperial and gold,
The baſis of the doubtful Ladder hold.
O *Charls*! A nobler monument then that,
Which thou thine own Executor wert at.
When to our huffling *Henry* there complain'd
A grieved Earl, that thought his honor ſtain'd;
Away (frown'd he) for your own ſafeties, haſt,
In one cheap hour ten Coronets I'l caſt:
But *Holbeen*'s noble and prodigious worth,
Onely the pangs of an whole Age brings forth.
Henry! a word ſo princely ſaving ſaid,
It might new raiſe the ruines thou haſt made.

O

O ſacred *Peincture*! that doſt fairly draw
What but in Miſts deep inward *Poets* ſaw;
'Twixt thee and an Intelligence no ods,
That art of privy Council to the Gods,
By thee unto our eyes they do prefer
A ſtamp of their abſtracted Character;
Thou that in frames eternity doſt bind,
And art a written and a body'd mind;
To thee is Ope the *Juncto* o' th' Abyſſe,
And its conſpiracy detected is;
Whileſt their Cabal thou to our ſenſe doſt ſhow,
And in thy ſquare paint'ſt what they threat below.
Now my beſt *Lilly* let's walk hand in hand,
And ſmile at this un-underſtanding land;
Let them their own dull counterfeits adore,
Their Rainbow-cloaths admire, and no more;
Within one ſhade of thine more ſubſtance is
Than all their varniſh'd Idol-Miſtreſſes:
Whilſt great *Vaſari* and *Vermander* ſhall
Interpret the deep myſtery of all,
And I unto our modern Picts ſhall ſhow,
What due renown to thy fair Art they owe,
In the delineated lives of thoſe,
By whom this everlaſting Lawrel grows:
Then if they will not gently apprehend,
Let one great blot give to their fame an end;
Whilſt no Poetick flower their Herſe doth dreſſe,
But periſh they and their Effigies.

To

To my Dear Friend Mr. E. R. *On his Poems Moral and Divine.*

CLeft, as the top of the inſpired Hill,
Struggles the Soul of my divided Quill,
Whilſt this foot doth the watry mount aſpire,
That *Sinai's* living and enlivening fire.
Behold my pow'rs ſtorm'd by a twiſted light
O' th' Sun, and his, firſt kindled his Sight,
And my left thoughts invoke the Prince of day,
My right to th' Spring of it and him do pray.
Say happy youth, crown'd with a heav'nly ray
Of the firſt Flame, and interwreathed bay,
Inform my Soul in Labour to begin,
Io's or *Anthems*, *Pæans* or a *Hymne.*
Shall I a Hecatombe on thy Tripod ſlay,
Or my devotions at thy Altar pay?
While which t' adore th' amaz'd World cannot tell,
The ſublime Urim or deep Oracle.
Heark how the moving chords temper our brain,
As when *Apollo* ſerenades the main,
Old *Ocean* ſmooths his ſullen furrow'd front,
And *Nereids* do glide ſoft meaſures on't;
Whilſt th'Air puts on its ſleekeſt ſmootheſt face,
And each doth turn the others Looking-glaſſe;
So by the ſinewy Lyre now ſtrook we ſee
Into ſoft calms all ſtorms of Poeſie,
And former thundering and lightning Lines,
And Verſe, now in its native luſtre ſhines.
How wert thou hid within thy ſelf! how ſhut!
Thy pretious Iliads lock'd up in a Nut!

Not

Not hearing of thee thou doſt break out ſtrong,
Invading forty thouſand men in Song;
And we ſecure in our thin empty heat,
Now find our ſelves at once ſurpris'd and beat;
Whilſt the moſt valiant of our Wits now ſue,
Fling down their arms, ask Quarter too of you.
So cabin'd up in its diſguis'd courſe ruſt,
And Scurf'd all ore with its unſeemly cruſt,
The Diamond, from 'midſt the humbler ſtones,
Sparkling, ſhoots forth the price of Nations.
Ye ſage unridlers of the Stars, pray tell,
By what name ſhall I ſtamp my miracle?
Thou ſtrange inverted *Æſon*, that leap'ſt ore,
From thy firſt Infancy into fourſcore,
That to thine own ſelf haſt the Midwife play'd,
And from thy brain ſpring'ſt forth the heav'nly maid!
Thou Staffe of him, bore him, that bore our ſins,
Which but ſet down, to bloom, and bear begins.
Thou Rod of *Aaron* with one motion hurl'd,
Bud'ſt a perfume of Flowers through the World.
Thou ſtrange calcined Seeds within a glaſs,
Each Species *Idæa* ſpring'ſt as 't was;
Bright Veſtal Flame, that kindled but ev'n now,
For ever doſt thy ſacred fires throw.
Thus the repeated Acts of *Neſtor*'s Age,
That now had three times ore out-liv'd the Stage:
And all thoſe beams contracted into one,
Alcides in his Cradle hath out done.
But all theſe flour'ſhing hiews with which I dy
Thy Virgin Paper, now are vain as I;
For 'bove the Poets Heav'n th' art taught to ſhine,
And move, as in thy proper Chriſtalline;

Whence

Whence that Mole-hill *Parnassus* thou dost view,
And us small *Ants* there dabling in its dew;
Whence thy *Seraphick* Soul such Hymns doth play,
As those to which first danced the first day;
Where with a *thorn* from the *world-ransoming wreath*
Thou stung, dost *Antiphons* and *Anthems* breath;
Where with an *Angels* quil dip'd i' th' *Lambs* blood,
Thou sing'st our *Pelicans* all-saving Flood,
And bath'st thy thoughts in everliving streams
Rench'd from Earth's tainted, fat, and heavy steams.
There move translated youth! inroll'd i' th' Quire,
That only doth with holy lays inspire;
To whom his burning Coach *Eliah* sent,
And th' royal Prophet-priest his Harp hath lent,
Which thou dost tune in consort, unto those
Clap Wings for ever at each hallow'd close;
Whilst we now weak and fainting in our praise,
Sick, Eccho ore thy *Halleuiahs*.

To my Noble Kinsman T. S. *Esq*; *On his Lyrick* POEMS *composed by Mr*. J. G.

I.

WHat means this stately Tablature,
The Ballance of thy streins?
Which seems, in stead of sifting pure,
T' extend and rack thy veins;
Thy *Odes* first their own Harmony did break,
For singing troth is but in tune to speak.

2. Nor

2.

Nor thus thy golden Feet and Wings,
May it be thought falſe Melody
T' aſcend to heav'n by ſilver ſtrings,
This is *Urania's* Heraldry:
Thy royal Poem now we may extol,
And truly *Luna* Blazon'd upon *Sol.*

3.

As when *Amphion* firſt did call
Each liſtning ſtone from's Den;
And with the Lute did form his Wall,
But with his words the men;
So in your twiſted Numbers now, you thus,
Not only ſtocks perſwade, but raviſh us.

4.

Thus do your Ayrs Eccho o're
The Notes and *Anthems* of the *Sphæres*,
And their whole Conſort back reſtore,
As if Earth too would bleſſe Heav'ns Ears:
But yet the Spoaks by which they ſcal'd ſo high,
Gamble hath wiſely laid of *Vt Re Mi.*

On

On the Best, last, and only remaining Comedy of Mr. Fletcher.

The Wild Goose Chase.

I'M un-ore-clowded too! free from the mist!
The *Blind* and late *Heavens-eyes* great *Occulist*,
Obscured with the *false fires* of His Sceme,
Not half those Souls are lightned by this Theme.
Unhappy Murmurers, that still repine,
(After th' *Eclipse* our Sun doth brighter shine)
Recant your false grief and your true joys know,
Your blisse is endlesse, as you fear'd your Woe!
What fort'nate *Flood* is this? what *Storm* of Wit?
Oh who would *live* and not *ore-whelm'd* in it?
No more a *fatal Deluge* shall be hurl'd,
This *inundation* hath *sav'd* the world.
Once more the mighty *Fletcher* doth arise
Roab'd in a vest, studded with Stars and Eyes
Of all his former Glories; His last worth
Imbroidered with what yet light ere brought forth.
See! in this glad farewel he doth appear
Stuck with the *Constellations* of his *Sphere*,
Hearing we Numm'd fear'd no Flagration,
Hath curled all his Fires in this one *One*;
Which (as they guard his hallowed chast Urn)
The dull aproaching Hereticks do burn.
Fletcher at his adieu carouses thus,
To the Luxurious Ingenious;

As

As *Cleopatra* did of old out-vie,
Th' un-numbred dishes of her *Anthony*,
When (he at th' empty board a wonderer)
Smiling she calls for Pearl and Vineger;
First pledges him in's *Breath*, then at one Draught
Swallows *Three Kingdomes* off *To his best Thought.*
Hear oh ye valiant Writers, and subscribe;
(His force set by) y' are conquer'd by this Bribe.
Though you *hold out your selves*, He doth commit
In this a sacred Treason on your wit:
Although in Poems desperately stout,
Give up; This Overture must *Buy you out.*
Thus with some prodigal Us'rer 't doth fare,
That keeps his gold still *Vayl'd*, his Steel-breast *bare*;
That doth exclude his Coffers all but's *Eye*,
And his eyes Idol the *wing'd Deity*:
That cannot lock his *Mines* with half the Art
As some *rich* Beauty doth his *wretched Heart*;
Wild at his real Poverty, and so wise
To win her, turns himself into a *prise*.
First startles her with th' *Emerald Mad-lover*
The *Ruby Arcas*, least she should recover
Her daz'led Thought a *Diamond* he throws,
Splendid in all the bright *Aspatia's* woes;
Then to sum up the Abstract of his store,
He flings a *rope* of *Pearl* of *forty* more.
Ah see! the *stagg'ring Virtue faints!* which he
Beholding, darts his *Wealths Epitome*;
And now, to consummate her wished fall,
Shews this one *Carbuncle* that *Darkens* all.

To Dr. F. B. *On his Book of* Cheſſe.

SIR, now unravell'd is the Golden Fleece:
Men that could only fool at Fox and Geeſe,
Are new made Polititians by thy Book,
And both can judge and conquer with a Look.
The hidden fate of Princes you unfold;
Court, Clergy, Commons, by your Law control'd;
Strange, Serious Wantoning, all that they
Bluſter'd, and clutter'd for, *you play.*

To the Genius of Mr. John Hall.

On his exact Tranſlation of Hierocles his Comment upon the golden Verſes of Pythagoras.

TIs not from cheap thanks thinly to repay
Th' Immortal Grove of thy fair order'd bay,
Thou planted'ſt round my humble Fane, that I
Stick on thy Hearſe this Sprig of *Elegie:*
Nor that your Soul ſo faſt was link'd in me,
That now I've both ſince 't has forſaken thee:
That thus I ſtand a Swiſſe before thy gate,
And dare for ſuch another time and fate.
Alas! our Faiths made different Eſſays,
Our *Minds* and *Merits* brake two ſeveral ways;
Juſtice commands, I wake thy learned Duſt
And truth, in whom all cauſes center muſt.

Behold!

Behold! when but a Youth thou fierce didſt whip
Upright the crooked Age, and gilt Vice ſtrip;
A Senator *prætextat*, that knew'ſt to ſway
The faſces, yet under the Ferula;
Rank'd with the Sage ere bloſſome did thy Chin,
Sleeked without, and Hair all ore within;
Who in the School could'ſt argue as in Schools,
Thy Leſſons were ev'n Academie rules.
So that fair *Cam* ſaw thee matriculate
At once a Tyro and a Graduate.
At nineteen what *Eſſayes* have we beheld!
That well might have the Book of *Dogma*'s ſwell'd;
Tough *Paradoxes*, ſuch as *Tully*'s, thou
Didſt heat thee with, when ſnowy was thy Brow,
When thy undown'd face mov'd the Nine to ſhake,
And of the Muſes did a Decad make;
What ſhall I ſay? by what Alluſion bold?
None but the Sun was ere ſo young and old.
Young reverend ſhade, aſcend a while! whilſt we
Now celebrate this Poſthume Victorie,
This Victory that doth contract in Death
Ev'n all the pow'rs and labours of thy breath;
Like the *Judean Hero*, in thy fall
Thou pull'ſt the houſe of Learning on us all.
And as that Soldier Conqueſt doubted not,
Who but one Splinter had of Caſtriot,
But would aſſault ev'n death ſo ſtrongly charmd,
And naked oppoſe rocks with this bone arm'd;
So we ſecure in this fair Relique ſtand,
The Slings and Darts ſhot by each profane Hand;
Theſe Soveraign leaves thou left'ſt us are become
Sear clothes againſt all Times Infection.

Sacred

Sacred *Hierocles*! whoſe heav'nly thought,
Firſt acted ore this Comment ere it wrought;
Thou haſt ſo ſpirited, elixir'd, we
Conceive there is a noble Alchymie,
That's turning of this Gold, to ſomething more
Pretious then Gold we never knew before.
Who now ſhall doubt the Metempſychoſis,
Of the great Author, that ſhall peruſe this?
Let others Dream thy ſhadow wandering ſtrays
In th' *Elizian Mazes*, hid with bays;
Or that ſnatcht up in th' upper Region
'Tis kindled there a Conſtellation;
I have inform'd me, and Declare with eaſe,
Thy Soul is fled into Hierocles.

On Sanazar's *being honoured with ſix hundred Duckets by the* Clariſſimi *of* Venice, *for compoſing an* Eligiack Hexaſtick of *The City.*

A SATYRE.

'TWas a blith Prince exchang'd five hundred Crowns
For a fair Turnip; Dig, Dig on, O Clowns!
But how this comes about, *Fates* can you tell,
This more then Maid of Meurs,† this miracle?
Let me not live, if I think not St. *Mark*
Has all the Oar, as well as Beaſts in's Ark;

No

No wonder 'tis he marries the rich Sea,
But to betroth him to nak'd Poeſie,
And with a bankrupt Muſe to merchandiſe,
His treaſures beams ſure have put out his eyes.
His Conqueſt at *Lepanto* I'l let paſs,
When the ſick Sea with *Turbants* Night-cap'd was;
And now at *Candie* his full Courage ſhown,
That wain'd to a wan line the half-half Moon;
This is a wreath, this is a Victorie,
Cæſar himſelf would have look'd pale to ſee,
And in the height of all his Triumphs, feel
Himſelf but chain'd to ſuch a mighty wheel.
  And now me thinks we ape *Auguſtus* ſtate,
So ugly we his high worth imitate,
Monkey his Godlike glories; ſo that we
Keep light and form, with ſuch deformitie,
As I have ſeen an arrogant Baboon
With a ſmall piece of Glaſſe Zany the Sun.
  Rome to her Bard, who did her battails ſing,
Indifferent gave to Poet and to King;
VVith the ſame Lawrells were his Temples fraught
VVho beſt had written, and who beſt had fought;
The Self ſame fame they equally did feel,
One's ſtyle ador'd as much as th' other's Steel.
A chain or faſces ſhe could then afford
The Sons of *Phœbus*, we an Axe, or Cord;
Sometimes a Coronet was her renown,
And ours the dear prerogative of a Crown.
In marble ſtatu'd walks great *Lucan* lay,
And now we walk our own pale *Statua*:
They the whole yeer with roſes crownd would dine,
And we in all *December* know no wine;

Diſciplin'd,

Diſciplin'd, dieted, ſure there hath bin,
Ods 'twixt a Poet and a Capuchin.
  Of Princes, Women, VVine, to ſing I ſee
Is no *Apocrypha*; for to riſe high
Commend this Olio of this Lord, 'tis fit,
Nay ten to one but you have part of it;
There is that juſtice left, ſince you maintain
His table, he ſhould counter-feed your brain.
Then write how well he in his Sack hath droll'd,
Straight there's a Bottle to your chamber roll'd.
Or with embroidered words praiſe his *French* Suit,
Month hence 'tis yours, with his Mans curſe to boot;
Or but applaud his boſs'd Legs, two to none,
But he moſt nobly doth give you one:
Or ſpin an Elegie on his falſe hair,
'Tis well he cries, but living hair is dear;
Yet ſay that out of order ther's one curl,
And all the hopes of your reward you furl.
  VVrite a deep epick Poem, and you may
As ſoon delight them as the *Opera*,
VVhere they *Diogenes* thought in his Tub,
Never ſo ſowre did look, ſo ſweet a club.
  You that do ſuck for thirſt your black quil's blood,
And chaw your labour'd papers for your food,
I will inform you how and what to praiſe,
Then skin y' in Satin as young *Lovelace* plaies.
Beware, as you would your fierce gueſts, your lice,
To ſtrip the cloath of Gold from cheriſh'd vice;
Rather ſtand off with awe and reverend fear,
Hang a poetick pendant in her Ear.
Court her as her Adorers do their glaſs,
Though that as much of a true Subſtance has,

VVhilſt

VVhilſt all the gall from your wild ink you drain,
The beauteous Sweets of Vertues Cheeks to ſtain;
And in your Livery let her be known,
As poor and tattered as in her own.
Nor write, nor ſpeak you more of ſacred writ,
But what ſhall force up your arreſted wit.
Be chaſt Religion, and her Prieſts your ſcorn,
VVhilſt the vain Fanes of Idiots you adorn.
It is a mortal errour you must know,
Of any to ſpeak good, if he be ſo.
Rayl till your edged breath flea your raw throat,
And burn all-marks on all of gen'rous note;
Each verſe be an inditement, be not free
Sanctity 't ſelf from thy Scurrility.
Libel your Father, and your Dam *Buffoon*,
The Nobleſt Matrons of the Iſle *Lampoon*,
VVhilſt *Aretine* and 's bodies you diſpute,
And in your ſheets your Siſter proſtitute.
Yet there belongs a Sweetneſſe, ſoftneſſe too,
VVhich you muſt pay, but firſt pray know to who.
There is a Creature, (if I may ſo call
That unto which they do all proſtrate fall)
Term'd Miſtreſs, when they'r angry, but pleas'd high,
It is a Princeſſe, Saint, Divinity.
To this they ſacrifice the whole days light,
Then lye with their Devotion all night;
For this you are to dive to the Abyſſe,
And rob for Pearl the Cloſet of ſome Fiſh.
Arabia and *Sabæa* you muſt ſtrip
Of all their Sweets, for to ſupply her Lip;
And ſteal new fire from Heav'n for to repair
Her unfledg'd Scalp with *Berenice*'s hair;

Then ſeat her in *Caſſiopeia*'s Chair,
As now you 're in your Coach. Save you bright Sir
(O ſpare your thanks) is not this finer far
Then walk un-hided, when that every Stone
Has knock'd acquaintance with your Anckle bone?
VVhen your wing'd papers, like the laſt dove, nere
Return'd to quit you of your hope or fear,
But left you to the mercy of your Hoſt,
And your days fare, a fortified Toaſt.
How many battels ſung in Epick ſtrain,
Would have procur'd your head *thatch* from the *rain*?
Not all the arms of *Thebes* and *Troy* would get
One knife but to anatomize your meat,
A funeral Elegy with a ſad boon
Might make you (*hei*) ſip wine like Maccaroon;
But if perchance there did a Riband come,
Not the Train-band ſo fierce with all its drum;
Yet with your torch you homeward would retire,
And heart'ly wiſh your bed your fun'ral Pyre.
With what a fury have I known you feed,
Upon a Contract, and the hopes 't might ſpeed;
Not the fair Bride, impatient of delay,
Doth wiſh like you the Beauties of that day;
Hotter than all the roſted Cooks you ſat
To dreſſe the fricace of your Alphabet,
Which ſometimes would be drawn dough Anagrame,
Sometimes Acroſtick parched in the Flame;
Then Poſies ſtewed with Sippets, motto's by,
Of minced Verſe a miſerable Pye.
How many knots ſlip'd ere you twiſt their name,
With th' old device, as both their Heart's the ſame:
Whilſt like to drills the Feast in your falſe jaw,
You would tranſmit at leaſure to your Maw;

Then

Then after all your fooling, fat, and wine,
Glutton'd at laſt, return at home to pine.
Tell me, O Sun, ſince firſt your beams did play
To Night, and did awake the ſleeping day;
Since firſt your ſteeds of Light their race did ſtart,
Did you ere bluſh as now? Oh thou that art
The common Father to the baſe Piſſmire,
As well as great *Alcides*, did the fire,
From thine owne Altar which the gods adore,
Kindle the Souls of Gnats and Waſps before?
Who would delight in his chaſt eyes to ſee,
Dormiſe to ſtrike at Lights of Poeſie?
Faction and Envy now is downright Rage;
Once a five knotted whip there was, the Stage,
The Beadle and the Executioner,
To whip ſmall Errors, and the great ones tear.
Now as er'e *Nimrod* the firſt King, he writes,
That's ſtrongeſt, th' ableſt deepeſt bites.
The Muſes weeping fly their Hill, to ſee
Their nobleſt Sons of peace in Mutinie.
Could there nought elſe this civil war compleat,
But Poets raging with Poetick heat,
Tearing themſelves and th'endleſſe *wreath*, as though
Immortal they, their wrath ſhould be ſo too;
And doubly fir'd *Apollo* burns to ſee
In ſilent *Helicon* a Naumachie.
Parnaſſus hears theſe as his firſt alarms,
Never till now *Minerva* was in arms.
O more then Conqu'ror of the *World*, great *Rome*!
Thy *Hero*'s did with gentleneſs or'e come
Thy Foes themſelves, but one another firſt,
Whilſt Envy ſtript, alone was left, and burſt.

The

The learn'd *Decemviri*, 'tis true did ſtrive,
But to add flames to keep their fame alive;
Whilſt the eternal Lawrel hung ith' Air;
Nor of theſe ten Sons was there found one Heir,
Like to the golden Tripod it did paſs,
From this to this, till 't came to him whoſe 't was:
Cæſar to *Gallus* trundled it, and he
To *Maro*, *Maro*, *Naſo*, unto thee;
Naſo to his *Tibullus* flung the wreath,
He to *Catullus*; thus did each bequeath,
This glorious Circle to another round,
At laſt the Temples of their God it bound.
  I might believe, at leaſt, that each might have
A quiet fame contented in his Grave,
Envy the living, not the dead, doth bite,
For after death all men receave their right. } *Ov. El.* 15.
If it be Sacriledge for to profane
Their Holy Aſhes, what is't then their Flame?
He does that wrong unweeting or in Ire,
As if one ſhould put out the Veſtal fire.
  Let Earths four quarters ſpeak, and thou *Sun* bear
Now witneſſe for thy Fellow-Traveller,
I was ally'd dear *Uncle* unto thee
In blood, but thou alas not unto me;
Your vertues, pow'rs, and mine differ'd at beſt,
As they whoſe Springs you ſaw, the Eaſt and Weſt:
Let me a while be twiſted in thy Shine,
And pay my due devotions at thy Shrine.
  Might learned *Waynman* riſe, who went with thee
In thy Heav'ns work beſide Divinity,
I ſhould ſit ſtill; or mighty *Falkland* ſtand,
To juſtifie with breath his pow'rful hand;

The

The glory that doth circle your pale Urn
Might hallow'd ſtill and undefiled burn;
But I forbear; Flames that are wildly thrown
At ſacred heads, curle back upon their own;
Sleep heav'nly *Sands*, whilſt what they do or write,
Is to give God himſelf and you your right.
There is not in my mind one ſullen Fate
Of old, but is concentred in our ſtate.
Vandall ore-runners, Goths in Literature,
Ploughmen that would *Parnaſſus* new manure;
Ringers of Verſe that All-in All-in chime,
And toll the changes upon every Rhime.
A Mercer now by th' yard does meaſure ore
An Ode which was but by the foot before;
Deals you an Ell of Epigram, and ſwears
It is the ſtrongeſt and the fineſt Wears.
No wonder if a Drawer Verſes Rack,
If 'tis not his 't may be the Spir't of Sack;
Whilſt the Fair Bar-maid ſtroaks the Muſes teat,
For milk to make the Poſſet up compleat.
Ariſe thou rev'rend ſhade, great *Johnſon* riſe!
Break through thy marble natural diſguiſe;
Behold a miſt of Inſects, whoſe meer Breath,
Will melt thy hallow'd leaden houſe of Death.
What was *Criſpinus* that you ſhould defie
The Age for him? He durſt not look ſo high
As your immortal Rod, He ſtill did ſtand
Honour'd, and held his forehead to thy brand.
Theſe Scorpions with which we have to do,
Are Fiends, not only ſmall but deadly too.
Well mightſt thou rive thy Quill up to the Back
And ſcrue thy Lyre's grave chords untill they crack.

For

For though once Hell reſented Muſick, theſe
Divels will not; but are in worſe diſeaſe.
How would thy maſc'line Spirit, Father *Ben*,
Sweat to behold baſely depoſed men,
Juſtled from the Prerog'tive of their Bed,
Whilſt *wives* are per'wig'd with their *husbands head.*
Each ſnatches the male quill from his faint hand
And muſt both nobler write and underſtand,
He to her fury the ſoft plume doth bow,
O Pen, nere truely juſtly ſlit till now!
Now as her ſelf a Poem ſhe doth dreſſe,
And curls a Line as ſhe would do a treſſe;
Powders a Sonnet as ſhe does her hair,
Then proſtitutes them both to publick Aire.
Nor is 't enough that they their faces blind
With a falſe dye, but they muſt paint their mind;
In meeter ſcold, and in ſcann'd order brawl,
Yet there's one *Sapho* left may ſave them all.
  But now let me recal my paſſion,
Oh (from a noble Father, nobler Son!)
You that alone are the *Clariſſimi*,
And the whole gen'rous ſtate of *Venice* be,
It ſhall not be recorded *Sanazar*
Shall boaſt inthron'd alone this new made ſtar;
You whoſe correcting Sweetneſſe hath forbad
Shame to the good, and glory to the bad,
Whoſe honour hath ev'n into vertue tam'd,
Theſe Swarms that now ſo angerly I nam'd.
Forgive what thus diſtemper'd I indite,
For it is hard a *Satyre* not to write.
Yet as a Virgin that heats all her blood,
At the firſt motion of bad underſtood,

Then

Then at meer thought of fair chaſtity,
Straight cools again the Tempeſts of her Sea;
So when to you I my devotions raiſe,
All wrath and ſtorms do end in calms and praiſe.

TRANSLATIONS.

TRANSLATIONES.

Sanazari *Hexasticon.*

Viderat Adriacis quondam Neptunus *in undis*
Stare Urbem, & toto ponere Jura mari:
Nunc mihi Tarpeias quantumvis Jupiter Arces
Objice & illa mihi mœnia Martis, ait,
Seu pelago Tibrim præfers, Urbem aspice utramque,
Illam homines dices, hanc posuisse Deos.

In Virgilium. Pentadii.

Pastor, Arator, Eques; pavi, colui, superavi;
Capras, Rus, Hostes; fronde, ligone, manu.

De Scævola.

Lictorem pro Rege necans nunc Mutius ultro
Sacrifico propriam concremat igne manum:
Miratur Porsenna virum, pœnamque relaxans
Maxima cum obsessis fœdera victor init,
Plus flammis patriæ confert quam fortibus armis,
Una domans bellum funere dextra suâ.

De Catone.

Invictus victis in partibus omnia Cæsar
Vincere qui potuit, te Cato *non potuit.*

Item.

Ictu non potuit primo Cato solvere vitam;
Defecit tanto vulnere victa manus:
Altius inseruit digitos, quà spiritus ingens
Exiret, magnum dextera fecit iter.
Opposuit fortuna moram, involvitque Catonis
Scires ut ferro plus valuisse manum.

Item.

TRANSLATIONS.

Sanazar's *Hexastick*.†

IN *Adriatick* waves when *Neptune* ſaw,
The City ſtand, and give the Seas a Law,
Now i'th Tarpeian tow'rs *Jove* rival me,
And *Mars* his Walls impregnable, ſaid he;
Let Seas to *Tyber* yield, view both their ods,
You'l grant that built by Men, but this by Gods.

In Engliſh.

A Swain, Hind, Knight; I fed, till'd, did command
Goats, Fields, my Foes; with leaves, a ſpade, my hand.

Engliſhed.

The hand by which no King but Serjeant dies,
Mutius in fire doth freely Sacrifice;
The Prince admires the *Hero*, quits his pains,
And *Victor* from the ſeige peace entertains;
Romes more oblig'd to Flames, than Arms or pow'r,
When one burnt hand ſhall the whole war devour.

Of *Cato*.

The World orecome, victorious *Cæſar*, he
That conquer'd all; great *Cato*, could not thee.

Another.

One ſtabbe could not fierce *Cato*'s Life unty;
Onely his hand of all that wound did dy;
Deeper his Fingers tear to make a way
Open, through which his mighty Soul might ſtray.
Fortune made this delay to let us know,
That *Cato*'s hand more then his Sword could do.

Another.

Item.

Jussa manus sacri pectus violare Catonis
Hæsit, & inceptum victa reliquit opus.
Ille ait infesto contra sua vulnera vultu,
Estné aliquid magnus quod Cato non potuit?

Item.

Dextera quid dubitas? durum est jugulare Catonem;
Sed modo liber erit, jam puto non dubitas:
Fas non est vivo quenquam servire Catone,
Nedum ipsum vincit nunc Cato si moritur.

Pentadii.

Non est, falleris, hæc beata non est
Quod vos creditis esse, vita non est,
Fulgentes manibus videre gemmas
Et Testudineo jacere lecto,
Aut pluma latus abdidisse molli,
Aut auro bibere, aut cubare cocco,
Regales dapibus gravare mensas,
Et quicquid Lybico secatur arvo,
Non unâ positum tenera cella:
Sed nullos trepidum timere casus,
Nec vano populi favore tangi,
Et stricto nihil æstuare ferro:
Hoc quisquis poterit, licebit illi
Fortunam moveat loco superbus.

Ad M. T. Ciceronem.
Catul. Ep. 50.

Disertissime Romuli nepotum
Quot sunt, quotque fuere Marce Tulli,
Quotque post alios erunt in annos,
Gratias tibi maximas Catullus
Agit pessimus omnium Poeta;
Tanto pessimus omnium Poeta,
Quanto tu optimus omnium Patronus.

Ad

Another.

The hand of ſacred *Cato* bad to tear
His breaſt, did ſtart, and the made wound forbear,
Then to the gaſh he ſaid with angry brow,
And is there ought great *Cato* cannot do?

Another.

What doubt'ſt thou hand? ſad *Cato* 'tis to kill;
But he'l be free, ſure hand thou doubt'ſt not ſtill;
Cato alive 'tis juſt all men be free,
Nor conquers he himſelf now if he die.

Engliſhed.

It is not, y' are deceav'd, it is not bliſſe
What you conceave a happy living is;
To have your hands with Rubies bright to glow,
Then on your Tortoiſe-bed your body throw,
And ſink your ſelf in Down, to drink in gold,
And have your looſer ſelf in purple roll'd;
With Royal fare to make the Tables groan,
Or elſe with what from *Lybick* fields is mown,
Nor in one vault hoard all your Magazine;
But at no Cowards fate t' have frighted bin,
Nor with the peoples breath to be ſwol'n great,
Nor at a drawn *Stiletto* baſely ſweat.
He that dares this, nothing to him's unfit,
But proud o' th' top of Fortunes wheel may ſit.

To Marcus T. Cicero.

In an Engliſh Pentaſtick.

Tully to thee *Rome*'s eloquent Sole Heir,
The beſt of all that are, ſhall be, and were:
I the worſt Poet ſend my beſt thanks and pray'r,
Ev'n by how much the worſt of Poets I,
By ſo much you the beſt of Patrones be.

To

Ad Juvencium. Cat. Ep. 49.

Mellitos oculos tuos Juvenci
Si quis me ſinat uſque baſiare,
Uſque ad millia baſiem trecenta;
Nec unquam videat ſatur futurus;
Non ſi denſior aridis ariſtis,
Sit noſtræ ſeges Oſculationis.

De Puero & Præcone. Catul.

Cum puero bello præconem qui videt eſſe,
Quid credat? niſi ſe vendere diſcupere.

Portii Licinii.

Si Phœbi Soror es mando tibi Delia cauſam,
Scilicet ut fratri quæ peto verba feras:
Marmore Sicanio ſtruxi tibi Delphice templum,
Et levibus calamis candida verba dedi.
Nunc ſi nos audis, atque es divinus Apollo,
Dic mihi qui nummos non habet unde petat.

Senecæ ex Cleanthe.

Duc me Parens celſique Dominator poli
Quocunque placuit, nulla parendi mora eſt
Adſum impiger, fac nolle, comitabor gemens,
Maluſque patiar facere, quod licuit bono,
Ducunt volentem Fata, nolentem trahunt.

Quinti Catuli.

Conſtiteram exorientem Auroram forte ſalutans
Cum ſubitò á lævâ Roſcius exoritur.
Pace mihi liceat, cœleſtes dicere veſtrâ
Mortalis Viſu pulchrior eſſe Deo.

Blanditur puero Satyrus vultuque manuque,
Nolenti ſimilis retrahit ora puer:
Quem non commoveat quamvis de marmore? fundit
Penè preces Satyrus; penè puer Lachrymas.

Floridi.

To Juvencius.

Juvencius, thy fair ſweet Eyes,
If to my fill that I may kiſſe,
Three hundred thouſand times I'de kiſſe,
Nor future age ſhould cloy this Bliſſe;
No not if thicker than ripe ears,
The harveſt of our kiſſes bears.

Catul.

With a fair boy a Cryer we behold.
What ſhould we think? but he would not be ſold.

Engliſhed.

If you are *Phœbus* Siſter *Delia*, pray
This my requeſt unto the Sun convay:
O Delphick God, I built thy marble Fane,
And ſung thy praiſes with a gentle Cane,
Now if thou art divine *Apollo*, tell,
Where he whoſe purſe is empty may go fill.

Engliſhed.

Parent and Prince of Heav'n O lead I pray,
Where ere you pleaſe; I follow and obey;
Active I go, ſighing if you gainſay,
And ſuffer bad what to the good was law,
Fates lead the willing, but unwilling draw.

Engliſhed.

As once I bad good morning to the day,
O' th' ſudden *Roſcius* breaks in a bright Ray:
Gods with your favour, I've preſum'd to ſee,
A mortal fairer then a Deitie.

With looks and hands a Satyre courts the boy,
Who draws back his unwilling Cheek as coy.
Although of Marble hewn, whom move not they?
The Boy Ev'n ſeems to weep, the Satyre pray.

Of

Floridi. de Ebrioſo.

Phœbus me in ſomnis vetuit potare Lyæum,
Pareo præceptis, tunc bibo cum vigilo.

De Aſino qui dentibus Æneidem conſumpſit.

Carminis Iliaci libros conſumpſit Aſellus,
Hoc Fatum Troiæ eſt, aut Equus aut Aſinus.

Auſo. lib. Epig.

Trinacrii quondam currentem in littoris ora
Ante canes leporem Cæruleus rapuit;
At lepus! in me omnis terræ pelagique rapina eſt
Forſitan & cœli, ſi canis aſtra tenet.

Auſo. lib. Epig.

Olla, polenta, tribon, baculus, ſcyphus, arcta ſupellex
Hæc fuerant Cynici, ſed putat hanc nimiam:
Namque cavis manibus cernens potare bubulcum,
Cur, ſcyphe, te, dixit, guſto ſupervacuum?

Auſo. lib. 1. Epig.

Theſauro invento qui limina mortis inibat,
Liquit ovans laqueum quo periturus erat,
At qui quod terræ abdiderat non repperit aurum,
Quem laqueum invenit nexuit & periit.

A la Chabot.

Object adorable et charmant,
Mes ſouſpirs & mes pleurs teſmoignent mon torment,
Mais mes reſpects m'empechent de parler;
Ah! que peine diſſimuler
Et que je ſouffre de martyre
D'aimer et de n'oſer le dire.

Theophile

Of a Drunkard.

Phœbus aſleep forbad me Wine to take,
I yield; and now am only drunk awake.

The Aſſe eating the Æneids.

A wretched Aſſe the *Æneids* did deſtroy,
A Horſe or Aſſe is ſtill the fate of *Troy*.

Engliſhed.

On the *Sicilian* ſtrand a Hare well wrought
Before the Hounds was by a Dog-fiſh caught;
Quoth ſhe; all rape of Sea and Earth's on me,
Perhaps of Heav'n, if there a Dog-ſtar be.

Engliſhed.

The *Cynicks* narrow houſhold ſtuffe of Crutch,
A ſtool and diſh, was lumber thought too much;
For whilſt a Hind drinks out on 's palms, o'th' ſtrand
He flings his diſh, cries, I've one in my hand.

Engliſhed.

A treaſure found one entring at death's gate,
Triumphing, leaves that cord was meant his fate,
But he the gold miſſing which he did hide,
The Halter which he found, he knit, ſo dy'd.

To the ſame Ayre in Engliſh, thus,

Object adorable of charms
My ſighs and tears may teſtifie my harms,
But my reſpect forbids me to reveal;
Ah what a pain 'tis to conceal,
And how I ſuffer worſe then Hell,
To love and not to dare to tell.

Theophile *being deny'd his addreſſes to King* James, *turned the Affront, to his own glory, in this Epigram.*†

Si Jaques le Roy du ſcavoir
Ne trouve bon de me voir
Voila la cauſe infallible,
Car ravy de mon eſcrit
Il creut que j'eſtois tout eſprit
Et par conſequent inviſible.

Auſonius.

Vane quid affectas faciem mihi ponere pictor
Ignotamque oculis ſollicitare manu?
Aeris & Venti ſum filia, mater inanis
Indicii; vocem quæ ſine mente gero.
Auribus in veſtris habito penetrabilis Echo;
Si mihi vis ſimilem pingere, pinge ſonum.

Auſon.

Toxica Zelotypo dedit uxor mæcha marito,
Nec ſatis ad mortem credidit eſſe datum;
Miſcuit argenti lethalia pondera vivi
Ut celeret certam vis geminata necem.
Ergo inter ſeſe dum noxia pocula certant
Ceſſit lethalis noxa ſalutiferae,
Protinus in vacuos alvi petiere receſſus,
Lubrica dejectis quæ via nota cibis.
Quàm pia cura Deûm! prodeſt crudelior uxor,
Sic cùm fata volunt, bina venena juvant.

Auſon.

Lineally Translated out of the FRENCH.

If *James* the King of wit
To ſee me thought not fit,
 Sure this the cauſe hath been,
That raviſh'd with my merit,
He thought I was all ſpirit,
 And ſo not to be ſeen.

In Engliſh.

Vain Painter why doſt ſtrive my face to draw,
With buſy hands a Goddeſſe eyes nere ſaw?
Daughter of Air and Wind; I do rejoyce
In empty ſhouts (without a mind) a Voice.
Within your ears ſhrill echo I rebound,
And if you'l paint me like, then paint a ſound.

In Engliſh.

Her jealous Husband an Adultreſſe gave
Cold poyſons, which to weak ſhe thought for's grave.
A fatal doſe of Quickſilver, then ſhe
Mingles to haſt his double deſtinie;
Now whilſt within themſelves they are at ſtrife,
The deadly potion yields to that of Life,
And ſtraight from th' hollow ſtomack both retreat,
To th' ſlipp'ry pipes known to digeſted meat.
Strange care o' th' Gods! the Murth'reſſe doth avail,
So when fates pleaſe ev'n double poyſons heal.

Auson. Epig.

Emptis quod libris tibi Bibliotheca referta est,
Doctum & Grammaticum te Philomuse putas?
Quinetiam Cytharas, chordas & barbita conde,
Mercator hodie, cras citharœdus eris.

Avieni v. c. ad amicos.

Rure morans, quid agam, respondi pauca rogatus,
Mane deum exoro, famulos post arvaque viso,
Partitusque meis justos indico labores.
Inde lego, Phœbumque cio, Musamque lacesso.
Tunc oleo corpus fingo, mollique palæstra
Stringo libens animo, gaudens ac fœnore liber
Prandeo, poto, cano, ludo, lavo, cæno, quiesco.

Ad Fabullum, Catul. lib. 1. *Ep.* 13.

Cænabis bene mi Fabulle apud me
Paucis, si tibi dii favent, diebus,
Si tecum attuleris bonam atque magnam
Cænam, non sine candida puella,
Et vino & sale & omnibus cachinnis.
Hæc si inquam attuleris Fabulle noster
Cænabis bene, nam tui Catulli
Plenus sacculus est aranearum.
Sed contra accipies meros amores,
Seu quod suavius elegantiusve est:
Nam unguentum dabo quod meæ puellæ
Donarunt Veneres Cupidinesque;
Quod tu cum olfacies, Deos rogabis
Totum te faciant Fabulle nasum.

Mart. lib. 1. *Epi.* 14.

Casta suo gladium cum traderet Arria Pæto,
Quem de visceribus traxerat ipsa suis:
Si qua fides, Vulnus, quod feci, non dolet, inquit:
Sed quod tu facies, hoc mihi, Pæte, dolet.

Mart.

In English.

Becauſe with bought books, Sir, your ſtudy's fraught
A learned Grammarian you would fain be thought,
Nay then buy Lutes and ſtrings, ſo you may play
The Merchant now, the Fidler the next day.

Engliſhed.

Ask'd in the Country, what I did, I ſaid
I view my men and meads, firſt having pray'd;
Then each of mine hath his juſt task outlay'd.
I read, *Apollo* court, I rouſe my Muſe.
Then I anoynt me, and ſtript willing looſe
My ſelf on a ſoft plat, from us'ry bleſt
I dine, drink, ſing, play, bath, I ſup, I reſt.

Engliſhed.

Fabullus I will treat you handſomely
Shortly, if the kind gods will favour thee.
If thou doſt bring with thee a del'cate meſſe,
An *Olio* or ſo, a pretty Laſs,
Brisk wine, ſharp tales, all ſorts of Drollery,
Theſe if thou bringſt (I ſay) along with thee
You ſhall feed highly friend, for know the ebbs
Of my lank purſe are full of Spiders webs,
But then again you ſhall recieve clear love
Or what more grateful or more ſweet may prove,
For with an ointment I will favour thee,
My *Venus's* and *Cupids* gave to me,
Of which once ſmelt, the gods thou wilt implore
Fabullus that they'd make thee noſe all ore.

Engliſhed.

When brave chaſt *Arria* to her *Pætus* gave
The Sword from her own breaſt did bleeding wave,
If there be faith, this wound ſmarts not ſaid ſhe,
But what you'l make, ah that will murder me.

In

Mart. Epi. 43. lib. 1.

Conjugis audîſſet fatum cum Portia Bruti,
Et ſubſtracta ſibi quæreret arma dolor:
Nondum ſcitis, ait, mortem non poſſe negari,
Credideram ſatis hoc vos docuiſſe patrem.
Dixit, & ardentes avido bibit ore favillas.
I nunc, & ferrum turba moleſta nega.

Mart. Ep. 15. lib. 6.

Dum Phaetontea formica vagatur in Umbra,
Implıcuit tenuem ſuccina gutta feram,
Dignum tantorum pretium tulit illa laborum:
Credibile eſt ipſam ſic voluiſſe mori.

Mar. lib. 4. Ep. 33.

Et latet & lucet Phaetontide condita gutta
Ut videatur apis Nectare clauſa ſuo:
Sic modo quæ fuerat vitâ contempta manente
Funeribus facta eſt jam precioſa ſuis.

Mart. lib. 8. Ep. 19.

Pauper videri Cinna vult, & eſt pauper.

Out of the Anthologie.

Ἔσβεσε τὸν λύχνον μῶρος ψύλλων ἀπὸ πολλῶν
Δακνόμενος, λέξας, οὐκ ἔτι με βλέπετε.

In Rufum, Catul. Ep. 57.

Noli admirari quare tibi fœmina nulla
Rufe velit tenerum ſuppoſuiſſe femur;
Non ullam raræ labefactes munere veſtis,
Aut pelluciduli deliciis lapidis.
Lædit te quædam mala fabula, quâ tibi fertur
Valle ſub alarum trux habitare caper.

Hunc

In English.

When *Portia* her dear Lord's ſad fate did hear,
And noble grief ſought arms were hid from her,
Know you not yet no hinderance of death is,
Cato I thought enough had taught you this,
So ſaid, her thirſty lips drink flaming coales,
Go now deny me ſteel officious fools.

Engliſhed.

Whilſt in an Amber-ſhade the Ant doth feaſt
A gummy drop enſnares the ſmall wild beaſt,
A full reward of all her toyls hath ſhe,
'Tis to be thought ſhe would her ſelf ſo die.

In Engliſh.

Both lurks and ſhines hid in an Amber-tear
The Bee in her own Nectar priſoner;
So ſhe who in her life time was contemn'd
Ev'n in her very funerals is gemm'd.

In Engliſh.

Cinna ſeems poor in ſhow,
And he is ſo.

In an Engliſh Diſtick.

A Fool much bit by fleas put out the light,
You ſhall not ſee me now (quoth he) good night.

To Rufus.

That no fair woman will, wonder not why,
Clap *(Rufus)* under thine her tender thigh;
Not a ſilk gown ſhall once melt one of them,
Nor the delights of a tranſparent gemme.
A ſcurvy ſtory kills thee, which doth tell
That in thine armpits a fierce goat doth dwell.

Him

Hunc metuunt omnes, neque mirum, nam mala valde est
Bestia, nec quicum bella puella cubet.
Quare aut crudelem nasorum interfice pestem,
Aut admirari desine cur fugiant.

Catul. Ep. 71.

De Inconstantia fœminei amoris.

Nulli se dicit mulier mea nubere velle
Quam mihi, non si Jupiter ipse petat:
Dicit, sed mulier cupido quod dicit amanti,
In vento & rapidâ scribere oportet aqua.

Ad Lesbiam, Cat. Ep. 73.

Dicebas quondam solum te nosse Catullum,
Lesbia, nec præ me velle tenere Jovem;
Dilexi tum te, non tantum ut vulgus amicam
Sed pater ut gnatos diligit & generos.
Nunc te cognovi, quare & impensius uror,
Multo mi tamen es vilior & levior.
Qui potis est inquis? quod amantem injuria talis
Cogat amare magis, sed bene velle minus.

De Amore suo. Cat. Ep. 86.

Odi & amo, quare id faciam fortasse requiris,
Nescio, sed fieri sentio & excrucior.

In Lesbiam Cat. Ep. 76.

Huc est mens deducta tuâ mea Lesbia culpâ
Atque ita se officio perdidit ipsa suo;
Ut jam nec bene velle queam tibi, si optima fias,
Nec desistere amare omnia si facias.

Ad

Him they all ſear full of an ugly ſtinch,
Nor 's 't fit he ſhould lye with a handſome wench;
Wherefore this Noſes curſed plague firſt cruſh,
Or ceaſe to wonder why they fly you thus.

Female Inconſtancy.

My Miſtreſſe ſayes ſhe'll marry none but me,
No not if *Jove* himſelf a Suitor be:
She ſayes ſo; but what women ſay to kind
Lovers, we write in rapid ſtreams and wind.

Engliſhed.

That me alone you lov'd, you once did ſay,
Nor ſhould I to the King of gods give way,
Then I lov'd thee not as a common dear,
But as a Father doth his children chear;
Now thee I know, more bitterly I ſmart,
Yet thou to me more light and cheaper art.
What pow'r is this? that ſuch a wrong ſhould preſs
Me to love more, yet wiſh thee well much leſſe.

Engliſhed.

I hate and love, wouldſt thou the reaſon know?
I know not, but I burn and feel it ſo.

Engliſhed.

By thy fault is my mind brought to that paſs,
That it it's Office quite forgotten has;
For be'eſt thou beſt, I cannot wiſh thee well,
And be'eſt thou worſt, yet muſt I love thee ſtill.

To

Ad Quintium Cat. Ep. 83.

Quinti si tibi vis oculos debere Catullum,
Aut aliud si quid carius est oculis;
Eripere ei noli multo quod carius illi
Est oculis, seu quid carius est oculis.

De Quintia & Lesbia. Ep. 87.

Quintia formosa est multis, mihi Candida, longa,
Recta est, hæc ego sic singula confiteor:
Tota illud formosa nego: nam multa venustas;
Nulla in tam magno est corpore mica salis.
Lesbia formosa est, quæ cum pulcherrima tota est,
Tum omnibus una omneis surripuit veneres.

De Suo in Lesbiam amore Ep. 88.

Nulla potest mulier tantum se dicere amatam
Vere, quantum a me Lesbia amata mea est.
Nulla fides ullo fuit unquam fœdere tanta,
Quanta in Amore suo ex parte reperta mea est.

Ad Sylonem Ep. 104.

Aut sodes mihi redde decem sestertia Sylo,
Deinde esto quamvis sævus, & indomitus,
Aut si te nummi delectant, desine quæso
Leno esse atque idem sævus, & indomitus.

To Quintius.

Quintius if you'll endear *Catullus* eyes,
Or what he dearer then his eyes doth prize,
Raviſh not what is dearer then his eyes,
Or what he dearer then his eyes doth prize.

Engliſhed.

Quintia is handſome, fair, tall, ſtraight, all theſe
Very particulars I grant with eaſe:
But ſhe all ore's not handſome; here's her fault,
In all that bulk, there's not one corne of ſalt,
Whilſt *Lesbia* fair and handſome too all ore
All graces and all wit from all hath bore.

Engliſhed.

No one can boaſt her ſelf ſo much belov'd,
Truely as *Lesbia* my affections prov'd;
No faith was ere with ſuch a firm knot bound
As in my love on my part I have found.

Engliſhed.

Sylo pray pay me my ten *Seſterces*,
Then rant and roar as much as you ſhall pleaſe,
Or if that mony takes you, pray give ore
To be a pimp, or elſe to rant and roar.

ELEGIES

SACRED

To the Memory of the

AUTHOR:

By ſeveral of his Friends.

Collected and Publiſhed

BY

D. P. L.

Nunquam ego te vitâ frater amabilior
Adſpiciam poſthac; at certè ſemper amabo.

Catullus.

London, Printed 1660.

ELEGIES.

To the Memory of my Worthy Friend, Coll. Richard Lovelace.

TO pay my Love to thee, and pay it ſo,
As Honeſt men ſhould what they juſtly owe;
Were to write better of thy Life then can
The aſſured'ſt Pen of the moſt worthy man:
Such was thy compoſition, ſuch thy mind
Improv'd to vertue, and from vice refin'd,
Thy Youth an abſtract of the Worlds beſt parts,
Inur'd to Arms and exercis'd in Arts;
Which with the Vigour of a man, became
Thine and thy Countries Piramids of Flame;
Two glorious Lights to guide our hopeful Youth,
Into the paths of Honour and of Truth.
These parts (ſo rarely met) made up in thee
What man ſhould in his full perfection be;
So ſweet a Temper into every ſence
And each affection breath'd an Influence
As ſmooth'd them to a Calme, which ſtill withſtood
The ruffling paſſions of untamed Blood,
Without a Wrinckle in thy face, to ſhow
Thy ſtable breſt could no diſturbance know.
In Fortune humble, conſtant in miſchance,
Expert in both, and both ſerv'd to advance

Thy

Thy Name by various Trialls of thy Spirit,
And give the Teſtimony of thy merit;
Valiant to envy of the braveſt men
And learned to an undiſputed Pen,
Good as the beſt in Both, and great, but Yet
No dangerous Courage *nor offenſive* Wit:
Theſe ever ſerv'd, the one for to defend,
The other Nobly to advance thy friend,
Under which title I have found my name
Fix'd in the living Chronicle of Fame,
To times ſucceeding; Yet I hence muſt go
Diſpleas'd, I cannot celebrate thee ſo;
But what reſpect, acknowledgement and love,
What theſe together, when improv'd improve;
Call it by any Name (ſo it expreſs
Ought like a Tribute to thy Worthyneſs,
And may my bounden gratitude become)
LOVELACE *I offer at thy Honour'd Tomb.*
And though thy Vertues many friends have bred
To love thee liveing, and lament thee Dead
In Characters far better couch'd then theſe,
Mine will not blott thy Fame nor theirs encreaſe,
'Twas by thine own great merits rais'd ſo high,
That Maugre time, and Fate, it ſhall not dye.

Sic flevit.

Charles Cotton.

Upon

Upon the *Posthume* and precious Poems of the nobly extracted Gentleman Mr. *R. L.*

THe Rose and other Fragrant Flowers smell best
When they are pluck'd and worn in Hand or Brest;
So this fair flow'r of Vertue, this rare bud
Of VVit, smells now as fresh as when He stood;
And in these Posthume-*Poems lets us know,*
He on the Banks of Helicon *did grow:*
The beauty of his Soul did Correspond
VVith his sweet out-side, nay, it went beyond;
LOVELACE, *the Minion of the Thespian Dames,*
Apollo'*s darling, born with Enthean flames,*
VVhich in his Numbers wave, and shine so clear
As Sparks refracted in rich gemmes appear;
Such flames that may inspire, and Atoms cast
To make new Poets, not like him in hast.

Jam. Howell.

AN ELEGIE,

Sacred to the Memory of my late Honoured Friend, Collonell *Richard Lovelace.*

PArdon (blest shade) that I thus crowd to be
'Mong those that sin unto thy memory;
And that I thine unvalu'd Reliques spread;
And am the first that pillages the dead:
Since who would be thy mourner as befits,
But an officious sacriledge commits.

How my tears ſtrive to do thee fairer right!
And from the Characters divide my ſight.
Untill it (dimmer) a new torrent ſwells,
And what obſcur'd it falls my ſpectacles.
Let the luxurious floods (impulſive) riſe
As they would not be wept, but weep the eyes,
The while earth melts, and we above it lye,
But the weak bubbles of Mortalitie;
Until our griefs are drawn up by the Sun,
And that (too) drop the exhalation.
How in thy duſt we humble now our pride,
And bring thee a whole people mortifi'd!
For, who expects not death, now thou art gone,
Shows his low folly, not Religion.
Can the Poetick heaven ſtill hold on
The golden dance when the first mover's gon?
And the ſnatch'd fires (while circularly hurl'd)
In their strong Rapture glimmer to the VVorld?
And not stupendiouſly rather riſe,
The tapers unto theſe Solemnities?
Can the Chords move in tune, when thou doſt dye
At once their univerſal Harmony?
But where Apollo's *harp (with murmur) laid*
Had to the ſtones a melody convey'd;
They by ſome pebble ſummon'd would reply
In loud reſults to every battery;
Thus do we come unto thy marble room,
To eccho from the muſick of thy tombe.
May we dare ſpeak thee dead, that wouldeſt be
In thy Remove only not ſuch as we?
No wonder the advance is from us hid,
Earth could not lift thee higher then it did!

And

And thou that did'st grow up so ever nigh,
Art but now gone to immortality:
So near to where thou art thou here didst dwell,
The change to thee is less perceptible.
Thy but unably-comprehending clay,
To what could not be circumscrib'd gave way.
And the more spacious tennant to return,
Crack'd (in the too restrain'd estate) its urn.
That is but left to a successive *trust,*
The Soul's first buried in his bodies dust.
Thou more thy self now thou art less confin'd
Art not concern'd in what is left behind;
While we sustain the losse that thou art gone
Un-essenc'd in the separation;
And he that weeps thy funerall, in one,
Is pious to the widdow'd Nation.
And under what (now) Covert must I sing
Secure as if beneath a Cherub's wing:
VVhen thou hast tane thy flight hence and art nigh
In place to some related Hierarchie,
VVhere a bright wreath of glories doth but set
Upon thy head an equal Coronet;
And thou above our humble converse gon,
Canst but be reach'd by contemplation.
Our Lutes (as thine was touch'd) were vocall by,
And thence receiv'd the soul by sympathy;
That did above the threds inspiring creep,
And with soft whispers broke the am'rous sleep:
VVhich now no more (mov'd with the sweet surprise)
Awake into delicious Rapsodies.
But with their silent Mistress do comply,
And fast in undisturbed slumbers lye.

How from thy firſt aſcent thou didſt diſperſe
A bluſhing warmth throughout the univerſe,
VVhile near the morns Lucaſta's *fires did glow,*
And to the earth a purer dawn did throw,
VVe ever ſaw thee in the Roll of fame
Advancing thy already deathleſs name;
And though it could but be above its fate,
Thou would'ſt however ſuper-errogate.
Now as in Venice, *when the wanton ſtate,*
Before a Spaniard *ſpread their crowded plate;*
He made it the ſage buſineſs of his eye,
To find the Root of the wild treaſury.
So learn't from that Exchequer, but the more
To rate his Maſters vegetable Ore:
Thus when the Greek and Latin Muſe we read
As the but cold inſcriptions of the dead;
VVe to advantage then admired thee
VVho did'ſt live on ſtill with thy Poeſie:
And in our proud enjoyments, never knew
The end of the unruly wealth that grew.
But now we have the laſt dear Ingots gain'd,
And the free vein (however rich) is drein'd;
Though what thou haſt bequeathed us, no ſpace
Of this worlds ſpan of time ſhall ere embrace:
But as who ſometime knew not to conclude
Upon the waters ſtrange viciſſitude;
Did to the Ocean himſelf commit,
That it might comprehend what could not it:
So we in our endevours muſt, out-done,
Be ſwallowed up within thy Helicon.
Thou now art layd up in thy precious cave,
And from the hollow ſpaces of thy grave,

VVe

VVe ſtill may mourn in tune, but muſt alone
Hereafter hope to quaver out a grone;
No more the chirping ſonnets with ſhrill notes
Muſt henceforth Volley from our treble throtes.
But each ſad accent must be humour'd well,
To the deep ſolemn Organ of thy Cell.
Why ſhould ſome rude hand carve thy ſacred ſtone,
And there inciſe a cheap inſcription;
When we can ſhed the tribute of our tears
So long, till the relenting marble wears?
Which ſhall such order in their cadence keep,
That they a native Epitaph ſhall weep;
Untill each Letter ſpelt diſtinctly lyes,
Cut by the myſtick droppings of our eyes.

El. Revett.

AN ELEGIE.

M*E thinks when Kings, Prophets, and Poets dye,*
We ſhould not bid men weep, nor ask them why,
But the great loſs ſhould by inſtinct impair
The Nations like a peſtilential ayr,
And in a moment men ſhould feel the Cramp
Of grief, like perſons poyſon'd with a damp;
All things in nature ſhould their death deplore,
And the Sun look leſs lovely than before,
The fixed Stars ſhould change their conſtant ſpaces,
And Comets caſt abroad their flagrant faces;
Yet ſtill we ſee Princes and Poets fall
Without their proper pomp of funerall,
Men look about as if they nere had known
The Poets Lawrell, or the Princes Crown;

Lovelace

Lovelace *hath long been dead, and we can be*
Oblig'd to no man for an Elegie.
Are you all turn'd to ſilence, or did he
Retain the only ſap of Poeſie,
That kept all branches living, muſt his fall
Set an eternal period upon all?
So when a Spring-tide doth begin to fly
From the green ſhoar, each neighbouring creek grows dry.
But why do I ſo pettiſhly detract
An age that is ſo perfect, ſo exact,
In all things excellent, it is a Fame,
Or glory to deceaſed Lovelace *Name;*
For he is weak in wit who doth deprave
Anothers worth to make his own ſeem brave;
And this was not his aim, nor is it mine,
I now concieve the ſcope of their deſigne,
Which is with one conſent to bring, and burn
Contributary Incence on his Urn,
Where each mans Love and Fancy ſhall be try'd,
As when great Johnſon *or brave* Shakſpear *dy'd.*
Wits muſt unite, for Ignorance we ſee,
Hath got a great train of Artillerie,
Yet neither ſhall, nor can it blaſt the Fame
And honour of deceaſed Lovelace *Name,*
Whoſe own Lucaſta *can ſupport his credit*
Amongſt all ſuch who knowingly have read it:
But who that Praiſe can by deſert diſcuſſe
Due to thoſe Poems that are Poſthumous;
And if the laſt conceptions are the beſt,
Thoſe by degrees do much tranſcend the reſt,
So full, ſo fluent, that they richly ſute
With Orpheus, *Lire or with* Anacreons *Lute,*

And

And he ſhall melt his wing that ſhall aſpire
To reach a Fancy or one accent higher.
Holland *and* France *have known his nobler parts,*
And found him excellent in Arms, and Arts.
To ſum up all, few Men of Fame but know
He was tam Marti, quam Mercurio.

To his noble friend Capt. *Dudley Lovelace*, upon his Edition of his Brother's Poems.

THy pious hand planting fraternal bayes,
Deſerving is of moſt egregious praiſe;
Since 'tis the organ doth to us convey,
From a deſcended Sun, ſo bright a Ray.
Clear Spirit, how much we are bound to thee,
For this ſo great a Liberalitie,
The truer worth of which by much exceeds
The Weſtern Wealth, which ſuch contention breeds.
Like the Infuſing-God, from the Well-head
Of Poeſie you have beſprinkled
Our brows with holy drops, the very laſt
Which from your Brother's happy Pen were caſt;
Yet as the laſt the beſt, ſuch matchleſſe skill
From his divine alembick did diſtill.
Your honour'd Brother in the Elyzian ſhade
Will joy to know himſelf a Laureat made
By your religious care, and that his Vrn,
Doth him on Earth immortal life return.
Your ſelf you have a good Phyſician ſhown,
To his much grieved friends, and to your own,
In giving this elixir'd Medecine,
For greateſt grief a ſoveraign anodine.

Sir

Sir, from your Brother y' have convey'd us bliss;
Now, since your Genius so concurs with his,
Let your own quill our next enjoyments frame,
All must be rich that's grac'd with Lovelace *name.*

Symon Ognell M. D. *Coningbrens.*

On the truly Honourable Coll. *Richard Lovelace*, occasioned by the Publication Of his Posthume-Poems.

ELEGIE.

GReat Son of *Mars*! *and of* Minerva *too!*
With what oblations must we come to woo
Thy sacred soul to look down from above,
And see how much thy memory we love,
Whose happy pen so pleased amorous Ears,
And lifting bright Lucasta *to the Sphears,*
Her in the Star-bespangled orb did set,
Above fair Ariadnes *Coronet,*
Leaving a pattern to succeeding Wits
By which to sing forth their Pythonick fits?
Shall we bring tears and sighs! no, no, then we
Should but bemone our selves for loosing thee,
Or else thy happiness seem to deny,
Or to repine at thy felicity:
Then whilst we chant out thine immortal praise,
Our offerings shall be onely Sprigs of Bays;
And if our tears will needs their brinks out-fly,
We'l weep them forth into an Elegy,

To

To tell the World *how deep Fates wounded wit,*
When Atropos *the lovely* Lovelace *hit;*
How th' active fire which cloath'd thy gen'rous mind,
Consum'd the water and the earth calcin'd,
Untill a stronger heat by death was given,
Which sublimated thy pure soul to heaven.
Thou knew'st right well to guide the warlike steed,
And yet could'st court the Muses with full speed,
And such success, that the inspiring nine
Have fill'd their Thespian *fountain so with brine,*
Henceforth we can expect no Lyrick lay,
But biting Satyres through the world must stray.
Bellona *joyns with fair* Erato *too,*
And with the Destinies do keep adoe,
Whom thus she queries; Could not you a while
Reprieve his life until another file
Of Poems such as these, had been drawn up?
The fates reply'd; that, Thou wert taken up
A Sacrifice unto the Deities;
Since things most perfect please their holy eyes,
And that no other Victim could be found,
With so much Learning and true Virtue crown'd.
Since it is so, in peace for ever rest;
'Tis very just that God should have the best.

Sym. Ognell M. D. *Coningbrens.*

On

On My Brother.

LOVELACE is dead! then let the World return
To its first Chaos, *Mufled in its Urn*;
The Stars and Elements together lye
Drench'd in perpetual obscurity;
And the whole Machine in confusion be,
As immethodick as an Anarchie;
May the Great Eye *of* Day *weep out his light,*
Pale Cynthia *leave the Regiment of Night,*
The Galaxia *all in Sables Dight,*
Send forth no corruscations to our Sight;
The Sister-graces *and the sacred* Nine
Statu'd with grief, attend upon his shrine.
Whose worth, whose loss, should we but truly rate
'Twould Puzzle our Arithmetick, to state
Th' accompt of vertu's so transcendent high,
Number and Value reach Infinity.
Did I pronounce him dead! no no, he lives,
And from his Aromatique Cell, he gives
Spice-breathed Fumes, whose Oderiferous scent
(In Zephire-gales *which never can be spent)*
Doth spread it self abroad, and much out-vies,
The Eastern Bird in her self-Sacrifice:
Or Father-Phœbus *who to th' World Derives*
Such various and such multiformed Lives,
Took notice that brave LOVELACE *did inspire,*
The Universe with his Promethean *Fire,*
And snatcht him hence before his Thred was spun,
Env'ing that here should be another Sun.

T. L.

On

On the Death of my Dear Brother.

EPITAPH.

TRead (Reader) gently, gently ore
The happy Duſt beneath this floor:
For, in this narrow Vault is ſet
An Alablaſter Cabinet,
Wherein both Arts and Arms were put,
Like Homers *Iliads in a Nut;*
Till Death with ſlow and eaſie pace,
Snatcht the bright Jewell from the Caſe.
And now, transform'd, he doth ariſe
A Conſtellation in the Skies,
Teaching the blinded World the way,
Through Night, to ſtartle into Day:
And ſhipwrackt ſhades, with ſteady hand
He ſteers unto th' Elizian Land.

Dudley Poſthumus-Lovelace.

FINIS.

[Lines

[Lines prefixed to John Davies' translation of Voiture's *Letters*, 1657.]

V*OITURE! whose gentle* Papers *so refin'd,*
As hee comes out, not Characters *but Mind;*
Whose LETTERS so abstract hee doth dispence,
That hee's not Writer, *but* Intelligence;
All Aire, Fire, Spirit; Reader be blest
To bee Calcin'd *thus nobly, and* Possest,
Whilst your first Thoughts *now breake as* Prim'tive Witt
And what you speak not Tasts on't, *but* is it.

R: Louelace.

NOTES

NOTES

1649

TITLE-PAGE. *Lucasta.* The entry on the Stationers' Registers under the 14th May, 1649, is:—

Master Harper — Entred . . . under the hands of S[r] NATH: BRENT and Master LATHAM warden (being licensed the 4th of Ffebr. 1647 [*i.e.* $1647/8$])

Poems called Lucasta or Epodes, Odes, Sonnetts, songs, by Rich: Lovelace, Esq[r]. . . . . vj[d]

(*A Transcript of the Registers*, 1913, vol. 1, p. 318.)

In 'A Catalogue of some Books Printed for, and sold by *Edw. Dod* at the *Gun* in *Ivy-Lane*', an advertisement leaf placed at the end of Whitefoote's *Deaths Alarum* [a funeral sermon on Joseph Hall] *London*, Printed by *W. Godbid*, for *Edward Dod*, at the *Gun* in *Ivy-lane*, *M. DC. LVI*, is an advertisement of 'Poems, Songs and Sonnets, written by *Richard Lovelace*, Esq. 8'. In his *Dictionary of the Booksellers and Printers*, Mr. Plomer states that Lovelace's *Poems* are included in a list of seventeen books advertised for sale by Dod and Nath: Ekins at the end of R. Bayfield's *Bulwarke of Truth*, published in 1657. From this it is clear that the sale of *Lucasta* was slow. Godbid, who printed *Deaths Alarum*, also printed *Lucasta. Posthume Poems*, and no doubt he obtained from Dod the plate of the Faithorne engraving which was included in both volumes of Lovelace's poems.

Thomas

Thomas Harper, printer in London, Little Britain, 1614–56, 'bought the printing business of George Wood and William Lee, which had previously belonged to Thomas Snodham, who in his turn succeeded Thomas East or Este' in 1634. In 1639 he was in partnership with Richard Hodgkinson. He printed Ruggle's *Ignoramus*, 1630, Weever's *Ancient Funeral Monuments*, 1631, Camden's *Annales*, 1635, Camden's *Remaines*, 1636, some music for John Playford, and, during the early years of the Rebellion, some pamphlets against the Parliament which brought him into trouble. He died March 22, 165$\frac{5}{6}$. See *A Dictionary of the Booksellers and Printers*, Plomer, 1907, p. 91.

Thomas Evvster or Euster is known from this volume to have been at the Gun in Ivy Lane in 1649. 'William Dugard also printed for him in the same year a little school manual entitled *The Plainest Directions for the true-writing of English.... By Richard Hodges... 1649*'. *Ibid.* p. 71.

PAGE 1. THE DEDICATION. I am indebted to Mr. G. Thorn-Drury, K.C., for the loan of his copy of Patherické Jenkyn, who has several imitations of Lovelace in *Amorea. The Lost Lover. Or The Idea of Love and Misfortune. Being Poems, Sonets, Songs, Odes, Pastoral, Elegies, Lyrick Poems, and Epigrams. Never before printed. Written by Patheric ke Jenkyn, Gent. London, Printed for William Leeke and are to be sold at the Sign of the Crown in Fleet street: between the two Temple Gates.* 1661. Compare with Lovelace's lines, *To Amorea; The Dedication*:

> To the fairest and divine,
> Next unto the Sacred Nine,
> To the Queen of love and beauty,
> I do offer up my duty;
> To the sweetest disposition,
> That e're Lover did petition,
> To the best and happ'est fortune,
> Ever man did yet importune,

To

To the Lady of all hearts,
That pretend to noble parts;
To the altar of her eyes,
I my self doe sacrifice;
To her ever winning glances,
Here I doe present my fancies;
And to her all commanding look,
I doe dedicate my book.

Anne Lovelace was the wife of John, second Lord Lovelace of Hurley. The daughter and eventual heiress of Thomas Wentworth, first Earl of Cleveland, she was born on July 20, 1623, according to her 'Nativity' which is preserved in the Bodleian. [MS. Ash. 243 (168b)]

Her marriage licence was granted by the Bishop of London in 1638. (Harleian Society, *Marriage Licences, 1611–1829*, vol. ii, p. 236.)

July 9. The Rt. Hon. John, Lord Lovelace, Baron of Hurley in co. Berks, Bachelor, 22, at his own disposal, & The Hon. Lady Anne Wentworth, dau. of the Rt. Hon. Thomas, Earl of Cleveland, Spinster, 15, & with her father's consent; alleged by Mr. William Witton, Clerk, Chaplain to sd. Earl of Cleveland; at St Bennet's, Paul's Wharf, Chelsea, Middx., or St. Giles in Fields.

l. 7. *Taper of the Thore.* The word 'thore' is an anglicized form of the mediaeval spelling 'thorus' of 'torus', a marriage bed. Compare:

May Heav'n show'r down its Manna on your Head,
And bless with an increase your *toral* Bed.

T(homas) S(teevens), *A Miscellany of Poems*, 1689, p. 33.

l. 13. *Carkanets.* Necklaces.

l. 17. *Whilst from the Pilgrim she wears.* Lovelace probably made 'pilgrim' a trisyllable.

l. 22. *Garnet-Dublet.* A Dublet is 'a counterfeit jewel of two pieces of crystal or glass cemented together with a layer

layer of colour between them or a thin slice of a gem cemented on a piece of glass or inferior stone'. (*N.E.D.*)

PAGE 2, l. 1. *oblieg'd.* The pronunciation of 'oblige' indicated by this spelling, which is common, survived until within living memory. Lovelace uses the spellings 'oblidg'd' and 'oblige' on p. 63, l. 8.

l. 10. *As if thy Child were illegitimate.* This would hardly have been tactful if Hunter's suggestion in *Chorus Vatum* as to the pedigree of Lucy Sacheverell were correct. See *Introduction*, pp. xlvii–xlix.

Francis Lovelace. As is mentioned in the *Introduction*, Colonel Francis Lovelace was in command at Carmarthen in 1644 until the town was taken by Langhorne. As the latter wrote on July 16, 1646, to the Speaker, 'They [a body of gentlemen already named] removed the King's forces out of the county, the better to enable them to raise their county's power, which, to the number of 1,500 men, were brought by them before the town of Carmarthen. There they all declared for the King and Parliament, and treated with the town, which received them, and unanimously made up one body and summoned the castle to surrender, which was commanded by Colonel Lovelace, and had good store of ammunition. The next day it surrendered to them, and passes were granted to Major-General Stradling, and the Governor with the gentry that entered the town to quiet the place, and the same day they delivered up the town and castle, with the ammunition and provisions, for King and Parliament. This action was a great step to the reduction of South Wales. (*Calendar of State Papers, Domestic Series*, 1645–7, p. 455.)

Further events in the life of Francis Lovelace may be traced from the *Calendar of State Papers*, but he must not be confused with his cousin the Recorder of Canterbury, who received Charles II on his landing in 1660 and presented him with an address 'together with a small Present of Gold (their Mite)', as his printed speech relates, or or with the second son of the first Lord Lovelace. The Recorder of Canterbury was concerned in the 'Christmas-Gamboll' of the 'high and mighty Mutineers of Canterbury' in 1648, and was arrested by the Parliamentary party after they had 'gathered together with their confederate friends . . . Chaplains and other instruments of war', an event to which he referred when in July, 1660, he petitioned for and obtained the office of Chief Steward of the Liberties of the late Monastery of St. Augustine for himself and his son Goldwell. He surrendered it in 1663, when it was given to Sir Anthony Aucher, and in 1664 a Mr. Lovelace, steward of the Chancery Court of the Cinque Ports, who may or may not have been the same man, died. Whether all the other references in the State Papers are to the same Francis Lovelace is not quite certain, but, as was suggested to me by Mr. Thorn-Drury, and has since been clearly proved by Captain G. Clarkson Shaw in *Notes and Queries* for January 1, 1921, the Governor of New York in 1671 was not the son of Lord Lovelace of Hurley, but the poet's brother. Captain Shaw quotes from an Ashmolean MS. entitled 'Interment of Mr. Wm. Lovelace, New York, 1671' (reprinted in *The American Historical Review*, vol. ix, 1904), which shows that present at the funeral were Thomas Lovelace, 'father of the deceased and his Lady in close Mourning', Colonel 'ffrancis Lovelace p'sent Govenor of New Yorke and uncle to the deceased in close mourning single', and 'Capt: Dudley Lovelace uncle also to the deceased in like Mourning single'. He goes on to show that the Minutes of the Executive Council of New York state that Thomas Lovelace, brother of the Governor, was at this time (1672) Alderman of New York City, having been so appointed October 31, 1671, and was a captain in the Foot Company of Staten Island on July 1, 1672. Captain Shaw gives further evidence, which need not be quoted here, to prove that the Governor of New York was the son of Sir William Lovelace of Woolwich.

The State Papers contain some references to Francis Lovelace previous to his appointment as Governor of New York. On May 1, 1650, a pass was given 'For Sir Hen. Moodie and Fras. Lovelace, with six servants, to Long Island, they subscribing the engagement.' On September 25, 1652, a pass was issued 'For Fras. Lovelace beyond seas'. It was possibly on one of these two occasions that Richard Lovelace wrote his lines 'Advice to my best Brother. Coll: Francis Lovelace'. On June 21, 1655, Mr. Manning writes to Thurloe from Cologne, 'Remember Cols. Fras. Lovelace and Edw. Villars, and Mr. John Denham', and on August 4, 1657, a pass was issued 'for Fras Lovelace and servant to Holland'. If these entries refer to the poet's brother, he must have returned to England in 1658–9, as the Thurloe Papers in the Bodleian [MS. Rawl. A 57 (191)] mention among the List of Prisoners in his Highness Tower of London under the custody of John Lord Barkstead, Louitenant of the Tower, one ffrauncis Louelace who on Nov. 6 was 'in close confinement for High Treason till he is delivered by due course of Law'. The State Papers record that he was committed on August 5, 1659, with Wm. Cooper, Mr. Denton, and Sir Bayham Throckmorton. (See also *Occurences from Forreigne Parts*, no. 17, 1659.) In 1661 Col. Francis Lovelace was Corporal in His Majesty's Life-Guard of Horse. (*Mercurius Publicus*, no. 11, March 1661, p. 174.) According to the State Papers, Fras. Loveless was deputy governor of Long Island in 1665, and in 1669 he is mentioned as Governor of New York. A Lieut.-Colonel and a Captain Francis Lovelace, possibly the same man, are included on June 13, 1667, in the 'minutes of commissions for officers in regiments of foot raised or to be raised, 1,000 in a regiment and 100 in each company', a list which also includes Dudley Lovelace. In 1672 Francis Lovelace was still Governor of New York, and on January 11, 1675, a warrant was issued to the Lieutenant of the Tower to receive Col. Lovelace, 'committed for not having defended the

the colony and fort of New York according to his commission and duty'. A Committee was appointed in February to examine him, but on April 26 a warrant was issued to Sir John Robinson, Lieutenant of the Tower, 'to release Col. Francis Lovelace, his prisoner, he giving security of 500*l.* to surrender when required, he having fallen dangerously ill of dropsy and being in great want of necessaries'. In 1678 he is mentioned as Governor-General of the Duke of York's territories in America, and in September 1689 the Duke of Schomberg, writing from Ireland about the bad discipline of his troops, mentions that a Lieut.-Colonel Lovelace behaved in such a manner that he had to arrest him.

One F. L. contributed some verses to Bosworth's *Chast and Lost Lovers*, 1651 (Saintsbury, *Caroline Poets*, vol. ii, pp. 528–9), and it may also be noticed that a Francis Lovelesse, Master of the Ordnance, was one of the prisoners at the surrender of Colchester, August 27, 1648. (John Wright's *Accounts*, September 2, 1648.)

PAGE 3, l. 3. *Pyraustam.* 'Pyrausta is a flie so called from πῦρ ignis; because it lives in the fire, and dieth without it. Plin. lib. ii. cap. 36.' (Swan, *Speculum Mundi*, 1635, p. 425.)

Thomas Hamersley matriculated at Peterhouse as a Pensioner in Lent Term, 1628–9, but did not take his degree. His father was Sir Hugh Hamersley, an alderman of London. On August 3, 1629, he was admitted to Gray's Inn and was knighted at Whitehall on August 8, 1641. (Venn's *Alumni Cantabrigienses*, Foster's *Register of Admissions to Gray's Inn*, 1889.)

Norreys Jephson matriculated as a Fellow Commoner at Emmanuel College, Cambridge, in Michaelmas Term, 1637. He did not take a degree. In the Scottish expedition he was an ensign in Jerom Brett's regiment, when Lovelace was an ensign under Goring. (Peacock's *Army Lists*, 1874.) In February 164$\frac{5}{6}$ he was in command of a regiment raised for service in Ireland. (*Calendar of of State Papers*, 1645–7, p. 354.) He and Lovelace both wrote verses printed before Beaumont and Fletcher's play *The Wild Goose Chase*, 1652.

PAGE 4, *John Jephson.* A Captain John Jephson on the Parliamentary side was taken prisoner in Basing Church when Colonel Gage relieved Basing House from Oxford on September 11, 1644. (*A Description of the Siege of Basing Castle*, 1644, p. 15.) William, Norreys (see above), and John were the three sons of Sir John Jephson of Mallow, co. Cork, and of Froyle, Hants, by his first wife Elizabeth, daughter of Sir Thomas Norreys.

PAGE 5, l. 9. *charmer.* Carew, whose poems were published in 1640.

l. 10. *Tyterus.* Waller.

l. 11. *Sacarissa.* 'Sacharissa (a name which the poet formed, "as he used to say pleasantly," from *sacharum*, sugar), or Lady Dorothy Sidney, was the eldest daughter of Robert, second Earl of Leicester, and Dorothy, daughter of Henry, ninth Earl of Northumberland. She was born at Sion House, and baptized October 5, 1617, at Isleworth.' She married Henry, Lord Spencer of Wormleighton—afterwards created Earl of Sunderland and killed at Newbury—on July 20, 1639, when the Sacharissa episode in Waller's life came to an end. (*Poems of Edmund Waller*, G. Thorn-Drury, pp. xxiii–xxx.)

l. 16. *interpale.* To interpale is to impale or circle with a garland.

l. 19. *bayes.* The use of 'bayes' as singular is common.

John Pinchbacke Col. Hazlitt suggested that this man was the same as 'old Jack Pinchbacke', mentioned by Sir Nicholas L'Estrange in his *Merry Passages and Jests* as a 'gamester and rufler, daubed with gold lace'. The following may refer to the same:

'Colonel Pinchbacke, an Englishman, and one of the colonels

colonels that colonel Blake gave passes to, to come from Scilly into Scotland kissed the King's hand; went as far as Glasgow with him towards England, but is come back hither, declaring much disaffection and dissatisfaction to the enemy's design, and says he will not join any more with them.' Mr Clarke to the Speaker. Stirling. August 19, 1651. (Cary, *Memorials of the Civil War*, ii. 328.)

In the list of Colonels killed on the King's side which is given in *Micro-Chronicon*, 1647, is the entry 'Col. *Pinchback* of Leic:shire, received his deaths-wound at Newbery,' but this can hardly be the author of the verses. No seventeenth-century Pinchbacke is mentioned in Nichols' *Leicestershire*.

PAGE 6. *Villiers Harington L. C.* 'Villiers Harrington aul. Clar.' has English verses before Gower's *Ovid's Festivalls*, 1640, and in *Voces Votivae*, 1640. He matriculated as a Pensioner at Clare Hall in Michaelmas Term, 1638, but does not appear to have taken a degree.

l. 21. *those chickens hatcht in furnaces.* Cf. '. . . . to see two sundry Ovens drawne, being full of young Chickens, which are not hatched by their mothers, but in the Furnace. . . . Surely this is an usuall thing, almost through all *Affricke*, which maketh that the Hennes with them are so innumerable every where.' (Lithgow's *Totall Discourse*, ed. 1640, pp. 380–1.)

PAGE 7. *W. Rudyerd.* The only son of Sir Benjamin Rudyerd, the politician and poet, to whom Ben Jonson addressed three Epigrams. William Rudyerd of Christ Church has some Latin verses in *Evcharistica Oxoniensia*, 1641.

l. 16. *Antiperistasis.* The 1649 reading *Antiparisthesis* is doubtless a misprint. Printers' mistakes in Greek words are common.

'Antiparistasis, A cohibition or restraint on euery side; whereby either colde or heat is made stronger in it selfe by by the restraining of the contrary: as the naturall heat of our bodies in Winter, through the coldnesse of the aire compassing it about: likewise the coldnesse of the middle region of the aire in Summer, by occasion of the heat on both sides causing thunder and haile, &c. (Holland, *Plutarch's Morals*, 1603, *An Explanation of Sundry Tearmes somewhat obscure*, Sig. Z z z z z.)

l. 24. *Knight o' th' Sun.* The original romance containing the Knight of the Sun is the Spanish *Espejo de Principes y Caballeros* (1562–89). It was written by Diego Ortuñez de Calahorra in 1562 and published at Saragossa; two other men continued it, Pedro de la Sierra (Alcalá de Henares and Saragossa, 1580) and Márcos Martinez (Alcalá, 1589). The original book, that published in 1562, was translated into English, under the title of *The Mirrour of Knighthood*: it was licensed August 4, 1578, and the first volume appeared in the following year. Nine parts were published in all between 1579 and 1601, making a complete translation. In 1617 the first volume appeared of a French translation by Rosset and Douet, entitled *L'admirable histoire du Chevalier du Soleil*: it finally ran into eight octavo volumes, 1620–6.

J. Needler, Hosp. Grayensis. John Needler, son and heir of John Needler of Horley, Surrey, Esq., was admitted to Gray's Inn on November 21, 1634. (Foster, *The Register of Admissions to Gray's Inn.*) He matriculated as a Pensioner at Christ's College, Cambridge, in Easter Term, 1632, and left the University without taking a degree.

PAGE 8, l. 22. *consistory.* A council of elders or presbyters.

PAGE 9, l. 1. *Some that you under sequestration are.* Compare Sedley, whose character of Eugenio may be meant as a portrait of Lovelace;

Fore. . . . his Father made a
Purchase of some Land, that lay next hedge
To mine, and gave a thousand pounds more
Than it was worth, only to buy it over my head:
Think

Think no more on him upon my blessing,
He is not the man he was; he had an Estate,
'Tis now sequester'd, he dare not show his
Head; and besides, I would not have a Son-in-
Law of his principles, for six times his fortune;
I shou'd be sorry to see any Child of mine
Solliciting her Husbands Composition at
A Committee.

The Mulberry-Garden, 1668, pp. 17–18, Act II. i.

ll. 3–4. See *Introduction* as to the presentation of the Kentish Petition in 1642.

Andr. Marvell. These verses seem to indicate that Marvell and Lovelace were friends before the latter and, for that matter, the former as well, went abroad in 1642 or 1643. From the point of view of Marvell's life, the lines are interesting as showing that he must have returned to England before 1649. 'The lines to Lovelace,' says Professor Sir Charles Firth in his article on Andrew Marvell in the *Dict. of Nat. Biog.*, 'together with the stanzas on the execution of the king in the "Horatian Ode", and the satire on the death of Thomas May, have been taken to prove that Marvell's early sympathies were with the royalist cause. They really show that he judged the civil war as a spectator rather than as a partisan, and felt that literature was above parties.'

PAGE 10. *John Hall* (1627–56) was born at Durham and went to Cambridge in February, 1646. In that year, at the age of nineteen, he published *Horae Vacivae, or Essays*—in which Howell found 'many choice and ripe Notions, which I hope proceed from a pregnancy, rather than precocity of spirit in you'—and a volume of *Poems*. Among his later works are a *Satyre against Presbytery*, 1648, *An Humble Motion to the Parliament of England concerning the Advancement of Learning and Reformation of the Universities*, 1649, which was written because he did not get the advancement at Cambridge in that year which he thought his due, and many political pamphlets on on the side of the Parliament. Lovelace contributed some verses to Hall's translation of Hierocles, in spite of their different political views.

PAGE 11, ll. 5–8. This story is told not of Apelles and Zeuxes, but of Apelles and Protogenes. See Pliny, *Hist. Nat.* xxxv. 36, § 11.

ll. 11–14. This story is told by Pliny of Zeuxis and Parrhasius, not Apelles.

l. 20. *who Poets once defended.* The *Defence of Poesie* by Sir Philip Sidney was written about 1583 and published in 1595 by William Ponsonby. Henry Olney's edition of the same year has the title *An Apologie for Poetrie.*

PAGE 12, l. 1. *Thy seraphique Sydneyan fire.* These were clearly alternative epithets: 'seraphique' was probably the original, 'Sydneyan' intended to replace it and echo 'As Sydneyes Prose' five lines before. On the other hand it is possible that Lenton intended to avoid the echo and that 'seraphique' was the revised epithet. In the circumstances both have been retained in the text, though one is superfluous.

Fra. Lenton. Little is known of Francis Lenton. He held the post, also held by Sir William Davenant, of 'Queenes Poet', under which title he is addressed by Sir Aston Cokain in his *Small Poems of Divers Sorts,* 1621, p. 163, in one of several stupid Epigrams and Anagrams:

> It is our grief, our mourning, and thy shame,
> That the Queenes Poet, and a man of name,
> Should drive *Apollo* from his breast with a
> Fine glass of six shillings, or a dish of Whey.

He published a few works between 1630 and 1640, of which the best known is *The Young Gallants Whirligigg,* 1629.

It may be noticed that, like Marvell and Hall, Francis Lenton was one of Lovelace's political opponents.

PAGE 13. *Thomas Rawlins* (1620?–1670) is better known as a medallist than as a poet. His initials are found

found on the coins produced at the Oxford Mint from 1644 to 1646, and during the same time he made many medals and badges for the Royalists. In 1648 he was formally appointed engraver to the Mint, and he appears to have fled to France in the same year. Returning in 1652, he earned a very precarious living till the Restoration, when he was reappointed chief engraver to the Mint. In 1657 he was imprisoned for debt and wrote to Evelyn for help. Evelyn describes him as 'Mr. Tho. Rawlins . . . an excellent artist, but debash'd fellow'.

Rawlins published *The Rebellion* in 1640, a play which gained considerable popularity. In 1677 was printed the comedy *Tom Essence, or the Modish Life*, and in the following year *Tunbridge Wells, or a Day's Courtship*, both of which have been attributed to him. He wrote some complimentary verses for *Messallina*, 1640, by Nathaniel Richards. 'A collection of poems called "Calantha" (subjoined to 'Good Friday, being Meditations on that Day', 1648, 8vo) is signed "T.R.", initials which Oldys identified with Thomas Rawlins.' See *Dict. of Nat. Biog.* He also has some verses before Tatham's *Mirrour of Fancies*, 1657.

Dudley Lovelace, Capt. Dudley Posthumus Lovelace, the poet's youngest brother, cannot have been born before 1627. According to Wood he returned from Holland with Richard and was imprisoned with him in 1648. (See *Introduction.*) After the poet's death he published his *Posthume Poems* in 1659, assisted, it would seem, as he was himself in Holland at that time, by Eldred Revett, two letters from whom to Dudley Lovelace are quoted in the *Introduction.* His name is printed in *A List of Officers Claiming to the Sixty Thousand Pounds, &c. Granted by His Sacred Majesty for the Relief of His Truly-Loyal and Indigent Party*, fo., 1663, 27. He is there described as a Captain of Horse under the command of George Chute. In the *Calendar of State*

Papers,

Papers, (Domestic Series,) June 13, 1667, his name is given as senior Lieutenant in Lieut.-Col. J. Ramsey's regiment. In 1672 he was in America. (See note to p. 2 above.)

According to *Archaeologia Cantiana* (vol. xx) he married a Maria Lovelace, and died about 1686. Mr. G. Thorn-Drury has kindly sent me the following lines from his copy of *Poems, by Eldred Revett* ... 1657. I have not been able to trace the book for which they were written. If it was ever printed it would almost certainly have contained some lines by Richard Lovelace, but, as no such verses were included by Dudley in his edition of *Lucasta. Posthume Poems*, it is probable that it never was published. It is possible, however, that Lovelace died early in 1657; that Revett's book was not published till the end of the year (see *Introduction*), and that Dudley's book was published between these two events, or even that it was published after Revett's *Poems*.

To Captain D. L. on his book
of Fortification, and
Geometrie.

As yet war not arriv'd at after hight
Was all but merely victory and flight,
And the tough souldier (garrison'd in limb)
Had no retreat of strength to shelter him;
But open lay to where you would assail,
Not to be reacht through trench, or single mail,
Until it grew an Art and Pallas wove,
Her reconciled garlands from one grove,
That now the *Heroe* to new task assign'd
Not more in body labour'd than in mind;
While strength and judgement fights, and wit replies
By counter-stratagem, to batteries,
And thus (friend) you commence, that well apply
To the tame practice, the deep theory,

Teaching

Teaching us how to measure and how far,
We move proportionably Regular,
How the fields drawn in mystick order lie
Spread with the lines of streight Geometrie:
As the neat Art would into trammel get,
And for the God of War make a new net.

p. 81.

It may be noted that Wood states that the poet furnished Dudley with moneys for his maintenance in Holland, to study tactics and fortification in that school of war. For some lines by Dudley Lovelace on Stanley's *Ayres and Dialogues* see note to p. 186.

PAGE 14, l. 5. *Grolla ferox.* Groll is a walled town in the province of Zutphen taken by the Prince of Orange for the States Confederate. Anno 1627. (Heylyn's *Cosmographie*, 1666, Bk. ii. 26.) Groll surrendered on August 26 after a month's siege and after the Comte de Borgh coming to its assistance had twice been repulsed. A full account of the siege is given in *Histoire Generale de la Gverre de Flandre*... par Gabriel Chappvys, ed. 1633, ii, pp. 665–87. The passage where he mentions the death of Sir William Lovelace is quoted in a note to the *Introduction*. See pp. xv–xvi.

l. 13. *Quicquid Roma vetus, vel quicquid Græcia jactat.* Compare

the comparison
Of all, that insolent Greece, or haughtie Rome
sent forth,

Ben Jonson, *Verses contributed to First Folio of Shakespeare*, 1623.

l. 14. *alma Calena.* 'Some there have bin that have attributed the foundation thereof [i.e. Oxford] to Olenus Calenus, a Romane, about 70 years after Christ, and therefore called Calena; but this being exploded by divers judicious authours, I shall not now endeavour to averre it.' (*Survey of Antiquities of Oxford*, by Anthony Wood, Oxf. Hist. Soc., 1889, vol. i, p. 42.)

'"Calena",

'"Calena", a pseudo-classical name for Oxford, current in the 16th century; probably originating in the belief that Oxford was the Roman Calleva, with the customary hesitancy between "u" (i.e. "v") and "n" in reading MSS.' (*Ibid.*, note on above passage.)

l. 17. *Dunkerka.* For the story of Lovelace's presence at the siege of Dunkirk see *Introduction.*

PAGE 15, l. 9. ἐσσῆν. A rare and late word meaning a 'king-bee'. The Greeks did not know it was a queen.

Jo. Harmarus. John Harmar (1594–1670) 'was a most excellent Philologist, and a tolerable Latine Poet' as well as 'an excellent Greecian of his time'. Educated at Winchester and Magdalen, he took orders and held various posts, 'Usher of the School joyning to his College', chief Master of the Free-school at St. Albans, under-Master of the College school at Westminster, King's Greek Professor at Oxford, and Rector of the Donative of Ewhurst in Hampshire. He lost his employments at the Restoration, and retired to Steventon in Hampshire, where he died. He wrote a number of school-books, orations, and Greek and Latin poems and translations, among the last being one or more of the plays of Margaret, Duchess of Newcastle, 'for which he was well rewarded'. (*Athenae Oxonienses*, 1691, ii, 347–9.) Herrick has some lines to him (*Hesperides*, 1648, p. 357), and Harmar was no doubt the J. H. C. W. M. who wrote the lines under Marshall's portrait of Herrick. He also contributed verses to Hannay's *The Nightingale* in 1622 and to Parkinson's *Theatrum Botanicum*, 1640. There is a Latin letter 'Scripsit I. H. C. W. M.' before *Pathomyotomia or a Dissection of the significative Muscles of the Affections of the Minde*, Jo(hn) B(ulwer), 1649. Harmar's portrait is in the Bodleian.

PAGE 17. *To Lucasta, Going beyond the Seas.* In this poem Lovelace gives expression to one development of the fashionable theory of 'Platonic Love' to which there are many references in seventeenth-century literature.

Mr.

Mr. Henry Lawes. Henry Lawes (1596–1662) was the younger and more famous of the two brothers. He composed the music for *Comus* in 1634, and is said to have taken the part of the 'Attendant Spirit' himself. He also wrote the music for Carew's masque *Coelum Britannicum.* Many of his printed songs are to be found in *Ayres and Dialogues*, 1653, 1655, and 1658; Playford's *Select Musicall Ayres and Dialogues*, 1652, 1653, and 1659, and in *The Treasury of Musick*, 1669. In 1626 he was appointed one of the Gentlemen of the Chapel Royal and Clerk of the Cheque to Charles the First. His setting of this song exists in the MS. belonging to the Rev. H. R. Cooper Smith, D.D.

PAGE 18. *Mr. John Laniere.* John Laniere (d. 1650) was the eldest son of Nicholas Laniere, who was musician to Queen Elizabeth in 1581, and cousin of the better known Nicholas Laniere. Like all his family John was a musician in the service of the Crown. (*D. N. B.*) His setting of this song does not appear to be in existence

ll. 16–17. *As you too shall adore;*
I could not love thee (Deare) so much,

Lovelace appears to aim at a definite effect in his change from the formal 'you' to the more familiar 'thee', but the singular and plural were sometimes used indifferently. Compare *Henry VIII*, Act III, ii, fo., 1623, ii, p. 222:

Sur. By my Soule,
Your long Coat (Priest) protects you,
Thou should'st feele
My Sword i'th' life blood of thee else.

Dr. Johnson himself was guilty of a manner of speech which Sir Arthur Quiller Couch took the liberty of silently correcting in the case of Lovelace in the *Oxford Book of English Verse*:—'After we had again talked of my setting out for Holland, he said, "I must see thee out of England; I will accompany you to Harwich"'.

Boswell, ed. G. Birkbeck Hill, i. 462.

l. 18. *Lov'd I not Honour more.* If Sedley intended the

the character of Eugenio in *The Mulberry Garden* as a portrait of Lovelace, he probably had this song in mind when he gave Eugenio the lines,

> Now thoū hast touch'd me in the tendrest part,
> Though Love possess, Honour must rule my heart;
>
> 1668, p. 35.

PAGE 19, l. 19. *Heav'nly Sydney.* Sir Philip Sidney's *Arcadia* was published in 1590.

PAGE 20. *Song. . . . To Amarantha, That she would dishevell her haire.* The first four stanzas of this poem, printed as two, were included in Cotgrave's *Wits Interpreter, The English Parnassus*, 1655. In the second edition of 1662, they were given the title of 'Amarantha *counselled*'. As suggested by Hazlitt, Cotgrave no doubt used Playford's *Ayres and Dialogues*, rather than *Lucasta*.

Set by Mr. Henry Lawes. This setting was printed in *Ayres and Dialogues, For One, Two, and Three Voyces. By Henry Lawes Servant to his late Ma:tie in his publick and private Musick. The First Booke. London, Printed by T. H. for John Playford*, . . . 1653. The MS. is in Dr. Cooper Smith's volume of Henry Lawes' songs.

PAGE 22, l. 24. *Fall too againe.* The spellings 'to' and 'too' were often used indifferently. Compare p. 174, l. 15 below and

> This Field-bed is to cold for me to sleepe,

Romeo and Juliet, II. i. So undated quarto and 1623 folio. Quartos of 1597 and 1599 read 'too cold'.

> I was to violent
>
> (Jonson, *The Foxe*, fo., 1616, p. 520.)

> I knew them all, ile too him,
>
> . . . .
>
> 3 *Goss.* And now I'le tell you Gossip, she 's too free.
> 4 *Goss.* To free?

Middleton, *A Chast Mayd in Cheape-side*, 1630, p. 34.

> *O. Fost.* What Idoll kneeles that heretique too.

W. Rowley, *A New Wonder, A Woman never vext*, 1632, p. 45.

. . . you

. . . you have a great many Bags, and a great many buildings to sir. Brewer, *The Country Girle*, 1647, Sig. E 3.

Eust. Then put it too most voyces.

Heywood, *The Foure Prentises of London*, ed. 1632, Sig. L 1.

PAGE 23. *Mr. Hudson.* The identity of this Hudson is uncertain. He was probably an amateur musician and friend of Lovelace, possibly the same as the Mr. George Hudson mentioned with Doctor Charles Colman, Captain Henry Cook, and Mr. Henry Lawes as having composed the music for a Masque by Davenant (ed. 1673, p. 359). Playford's *Court Ayres*, 1655, contains some music by him. The two brothers Robert and Thomas Hudson, musicians of the Chapel Royal to James VI, were probably dead before the earliest date that Lovelace could have composed this poem.

ll. 1–6. Compare Marston:

Her. All things under the Moone are subject to their mistris grace; horns, lend me your ring my *Don*, Ile put it on my finger, now tis on yours againe, why is the gold now ere the worse in lustre or fitnesse? (*The Fawne*, Act II, sc. i, ed. 1633, Sig. T 3.)

l. 2. *And Crowne mine with't awhile.*

Compare

. . . he won my hand,
To crowne his finger with that hoope of gold.
North-Ward Hoe, 1607, Sig. B 3 verso.

Dr. John Wilson. Dr. John Wilson (1595–1674) was considered the best lutenist in England, and was a great favourite with Charles I. As a boy he is supposed to have sung 'Sigh no more ladies' and 'Take oh take those lips away' in some of the early performances of *Much Ado*. The 1600 quarto of the play gives the stage direction 'Enter Balthaser with musicke'. In the folio of 1623 the direction is 'Enter Prince, Leonato, Claudio and Iacke Wilson'. This identification, however, is doubtful. Wilson's works are scattered through Playford's and Hilton's publications, and he himself published *Cheerful*

Ayres or Ballads in 1660, 'the first Essay . . . of printing Musick that ever was in Oxford'. In that year he was Professor of Music at the University He early acquired a considerable reputation and was employed to write the music for *The Maske of Flowers*, 1613, before he was twenty. Wood speaks of him as 'the greatest and most curious Judge of Musick that ever was', but he made his name by his skill as lutenist and singer. Herrick mentions him in some lines '*To M.* Henry Lawes, *the excellent Composer of his Lyricks*'. *Hesperides*, 1648, p. 326. I have not found the setting to this song.

PAGE 24, ll. 2–3. Aurora, pale with envy, despairs of matching the rose.

PAGE 26. *The Scrutinie.* This was one of the most popular of Lovelace's songs. It was included in Cotgrave's *Wits Interpreter*, 1655, the title of 'To his Mistress, who unjustly taxed him of leaving her off', being added in the second edition of 1662. A 'Reply' was written to it:

Reply

I sweare hadst thou not bin forsworne
  When Mine thou vow'dst to bee
Or had that night bin long, e're Morne
  It had bin impossible for mee
  for to haue seene thy Periurye.

One Howre to loue thee were too longe
  A too too tedious space
And I should much my beauty wronge
  to take delight in thy imbrace
  unless thou hadst a better face.

The Joyes w[ch] are in my Browne hayre
  Thou neuer yet hast found
And they are fooles both black & fayre
  That suffer thee to Plough their Ground
  Or their rich virgins Mines to sound.

Goe

Goe prethee loue the whole world round
Soe that thou wilt leaue mee
With any Spoyles if thou art Crown'd
Of meanest Beautyes it must bee
And they soon Sated too with thee.
Mr. Hen. Ventrice.

These lines follow a MS. transcript of Charles's setting of 'The Scrutinie', in the British Museum Additional MS. 29396, f. 38. Almost the whole of the MS. is in the hand of Edward Lawe, organist of the Chapel Royal (1661–82). (See *Catalogue of Manuscript Music*, by A. Hughes-Hughes, 1908, vol. ii, pp. 478–9.) There is a second MS. copy of 'The Scrutinie' in the British Museum (Additional MSS. 31813) which dates from the late 18th century. Henry Bold twice translated it into Latin (*Latine Songs*, 1685, pp. 25–7).

Set by Mr. Thomas Charles. The song was printed in Playford's *Select Musicall Ayres, and Dialogues, For one and two Voyces, to sing to the Theorbo, Lute, or Basse Violl . . . London, . . . 1652.* In the 'Table of the Ayres' it is simply called 'French Ayre', but in *Select Musicall Ayres and Dialogues, in Three Bookes . . . London, . . . 1653*, the music, as here, is attributed to 'Mr. Charles'. The volume of 1652 omits the last line of the poem. In *Select Ayres and Dialogues For One, Two, and Three Voyces; To the Theorbo-Lute or Basse-Viol . . . 1659*, the same setting to the song, there called *Loves Scrutiny*, is attributed to 'Mr. Henry Lawes'.

PAGE 27. *Princesse Löysa.* At the end of one of the two copies of *Lucasta* which he left to the Victoria and Albert Museum, Dyce noted that 'Princesse Löysa', daughter of the King of Bohemia (and grand-daughter of James I), was taught by her mother's favourite painter, Gerard Honthorst.

Lovelace probably met Princess Louise at The Hague. She was certainly acquainted with the Gorings.

l. 11. *Diety.* An obsolete but correct spelling. Compare p. 97, l. 12.

l. 18. *ith' coole oth' Sunne.* The forms 'ith'', 'oth'', 'toth'' are correct, but were beginning to drop out of use about the middle of the seventeenth century. They are not always used in Lovelace, and they seldom occur, for instance, in the publications of Humphrey Moseley.

l. 19. *her delight.* Narcissus. Cupid had betrayed Echo as Narcissus did not return her love. See Sandys' *Ovid*, 1626, bk. iii, pp. 54–5.

PAGE 28, l. 6. *then wafts his faire.* 'Waft. To beckon with the hand.' (Halliwell's *Dictionary*.)

l. 9. *Anaxerete.* Iphis hanged himself when disdained by Anaxerete.

l. 14. *Leucothoë* was buried alive by her father when he heard of her amour with Apollo. Sandys' *Ovid*, iv, pp. 70–1.

PAGE 29. *Princesse Katherine.* The lines were contributed by Lovelace at the age of twenty to *Musarum Oxoniensium Charisteria Pro Serenissima Regina Maria, Recens E Nixus Laboriosi discrimine receptâ. Oxoniæ. Typis Leonard. Lichfield Academiae Typographi* M.DC.XXXVIII, and are there signed 'Rich. Lovelace. Mag. Art. A. Glouc. fil. Guil. Lovelace Eq. Aur. Nat. Max.'

As Lovelace had taken his degree two years earlier he was probably not in Oxford in 1638, and this is borne out by the fact that the book was originally issued without his contribution, which is not found in all copies. It was inserted on a special sheet bb with other poems between sheets b and c in the second part of the book. That this sheet was an afterthought is proved not only by the signature, but also by the catchword 'Seduce' on b 4 verso. In the first part of the book, which contains Latin verses, there is a sheet DD after D which is also not found in all copies, being in all probability added at the same time as the other sheet. It would seem to show that Lovelace had obtained some reputation as a poet at the University if it was considered desirable to obtain a special contribution from him to an Oxford book of verse when he had been away for two years.

'On

'On Sunday [January 20] morning last Her Majesty was brought to bed with a daughter, who lived to be christened Princess Katherine and then died; this child is said to have gone nearer to the Queen than ever any yet did but she is indifferently well: . . .' (*Calendar of State Papers* (*Domestic Series*), 163 8/9, January 24.)

l. 24. *then the ground.* It is unnecessary to adopt the reading of *Charisteria* here and insert 'to', as Lovelace uses 'ayre' as a disyllable. The *North American Review*, July, 1864, points out a similar use of the word in *The Toad and Spyder*, p. 164, l. 32, and in the lines to Thomas Stanley, p. 187, l. 13.

PAGE 30, l. 4. *And showe's.* i.e. 'Show us'.

l. 18. The word 'Like' has dropped out in some copies (e.g. British Museum 238. b. 52), and is omitted both by Singer and the reprint in *Hutchinson's Popular Classics.*

PAGE 31. *Set by Mr. Henry Lawes.* Lawes' setting of this song is included in Dr. Cooper Smith's MS. I have not been able to find it in print.

PAGE 32. *A loose Saraband.* Compan gives the following account of the Saraband in his *Dictionnaire de Danse*, 1787, pp. 346–7:

'Sarabande. Espèce de Danse grave, qui paroît nous être venue d'Espagne. Elle se dansoit autrefois avec des Castagnettes. La *Sarabande*, à le bien prendre, n'est qu'un Menuet dont le mouvement est grave, lent & sérieux. M. des Yveteaux, mourant à Paris à l'âge de plus de 80 ans, fit jouer une *Sarabande*, afin, disoit-il, que son âme passât plus doucement. Elle a été ainsi nommée, selon quelques-uns, à cause d'une Comédienne appellée *Sarabanda*, qui la dansa la première en France. Selon d'autres, la *Sarabanda* est venue des *Sarasins*, aussi bien que la Chaconne. D'autres enfin, croyent que ce nom vient de *Saras* qui, en Espagnol, signifie *Bal*. On la danse ordinairement en Espagne au son de la guitarre. Elle a un mouvement qui est gai & amoreux.'

Compare p. 131, l. 21, and p. 139.

Set

Set by Mr. Henry Lawes. I have not been able to find the setting to this song. It is noticeable that Dr. Cooper Smith's MS. includes the three other songs which are said to have been put to music by Henry Lawes and a fourth as well, the poem *To Ellinda.* It is possible that this song was attributed to Lawes in mistake for the other.

PAGE 33, l. 1. *purchase.* In *A Notable Discouery of Coosnage*, 1591, Robert Greene gives a list of terms, 'being proper to none but to the professors thereof', used by the cony-catchers of his day. 'In Coni-catching law the money that is won' is called Purchase (ed. Grosart, vol. x, p. 38). The word in the sense of 'prize' or 'loot' is, however, common in the sixteenth and seventeenth centuries.

l. 13. *false beliefe.* Cf. Beaumont and Fletcher:

When ever you love, a false beliefe light on ye.

The Loyall Subject, 1647, IV. iii, Sig. Fff 2.

l. 15. *morning-Cushionet.* A pin-cushion.

l. 18. *rac'd.* Pricked.

PAGE 34, l. 7. *sleave-silke.* 'Silk thread capable of being separated into smaller filaments for use in embroidery.' *N. E. D.*

PAGE 37. *Set by Mr. Curtes.* In Wood's *Life and Times* (Oxford Historical Society), vol. i, p. 205, there is a reference to Curtes, with no Christian name, 'a Lutinist lately ejected from some choir or Cathedral church. After his Majesty's restoration, he became gent. or singing-man at Christ Church in Oxon.' He is one of the people who took part in the weekly meetings of musicians, referred to by Wood on the previous page (p. 204) as taking place in a house 'opposite to that place whereon the Theatre was built'. No further record of him seems to exist.

l. 10. *And Musick of her face.* Cf. Byron:

. . . the Music breathing from her face,

Bride of Abydos, l. 180.

and his note defending the expression.

PAGE 38. *Mr. Charles Cotton.* Charles Cotton, the poet, for whose marriage Lovelace wrote *The Triumphs of Philamore and Amoret.* See p. 169 and note.

l. 13. *Drunke ev'ry night with a Delicious teare.* 'The Stellions after a sort be of the nature of Chamælions living only upon dew and spiders. Grashoppers also live much after the same manner . . . they have a certaine sharpe pointed thing in their breast . . . and with it they sucke and licke in the dew.' (Holland's *Pliny*, i. 325.)

PAGE 39, ll. 7–8. If, as has been suggested by Professor H. J. C. Grierson, Lovelace intended these lines to mean that the grasshopper makes men and himself merry and Melancholy flows away, he chose a very obscure way of saying it. The equally possible interpretation is more likely to be right; the lines are grammatical and make sense if 'streames' is a noun and if in reading them a slight pause is made between the words 'merry' and 'men'. We then understand that the grasshopper makes men, himself, and 'Melancholy streames' (perhaps those in which Cotton fished) merry. The capital letter to 'Melancholy' is no objection to this interpretation; in the third line of the poem we find a 'Delicious teare', and both examples are ordinary instances of the use of the emphasis capital.

PAGE 40, ll. 9–12. This stanza is involved. The meaning would seem to be that 'just as Hesperus shines clearer as the day draws to a close, so will our tapers whip Night from the lighted casements of the room where we amuse ourselves, and, by stripping her black mantle from the dark Hagge, put everlasting day in the place of Night'. It might be objected that the evening star is the harbinger of night and consequently not the best comparison for tapers which drive out night and turn the darkness into day, but Lovelace was thinking of the star which becomes brightest as the darkness comes on. It is just possible that he wrote 'Night *and* clear Hesper', meaning that Night and even the clear light of the evening star will be driven out by a brightness which rivals the daylight.

PAGE 41. *Set by Mr. John Gamble.* The date of Gamble's birth is not known, but he died 'advanced in years' in 1687. After being apprenticed to Beyland, one of Charles the First's violinists, he played at a London theatre. (*D. N. B.*) In 1656 he published *Ayres and Dialogues (To be Sung to the Theorbo-Lute or Base-Violl) by John Gamble . . . London, Printed by William Godbid, for the Author, 1656.* There was a second edition of this book *Printed by W. Godbid for Humphry Mosley at the Princes-Arms In St Paul's Church-yard, 1657.* The poems in this volume, to which Lovelace contributed some verses, are by Stanley. (See p. 186.) It brought Gamble considerable fame and Wood was 'proud to entertain' him in July, 1658. In 1659 he published *Ayres and Dialogues For One, Two, and Three Voyces; To be sung either to the Theorbo-Lute or Basse-Viol. Composed by John Gamble. . . . The Second Book. London, Printed by W. Godbid for Nathaniel Ekin at the Gun in S^t. Pauls Church-yard. 1659.*

On the Restoration Gamble was admitted to the King's Household and is said to have played the violin in the King's band. (*D. N. B.*)

This setting is printed in the second book of *Ayres and Dialogues*, 1659. This volume corrects the misprint in *Lucasta* which gives ll. 5–6 to *Chorus*.

PAGE 42, after l. 18. *Chorus*, i. e. 'Chorus again, Vaine dreames', &c.

PAGE 43, ll. 7–8. Lovelace occasionally uses a bare assonance for a rime. For a more extraordinary example compare p. 90, ll. 1–2.

To Ellinda. That lately I have not written. Cf. p. 80, ll. 11–12.

PAGE 44. *William Lawes.* I have not been able to find the setting to this or either of the next two songs.

William Lawes was the elder of the two brothers and was one of the Musicians in Ordinary to Charles I. He joined the Royalist army on the outbreak of the Civil War, 'was made a commissary by Lord Gerrard, to exempt

him

him from danger, but his active spirit disdaining that security, he was killed by a stray shot during the siege of Chester 1645'. (Grove's *Dictionary*.) Many poets wrote elegies on him. Herrick has one *Upon M. William Lawes the rare Musitian*; Thomas Jordan in *The Muses Melody in a Consort of Poetrie* has *An Epitaph on Mr. Will. Lawes Batchelor in Musick, who was mortally shot at the siege of Westchester*; Tatham in *Ostella* has some lines *On the Report of Master William Lawes his Death*; Robert Heath has an elegy on him in *Clarastella*.

l. 14. *incessantly*. Immediately.

ll. 19–20. An allusion to the belief that shooting stars became jellies on falling to the earth. Compare p. 137, ll. 32–3.

PAGE 45. *Lucasta Weeping*. This poem was not included in the Table of the Contents of *Lucasta*.

PAGE 46. *The Vintage to the Dungeon*. This song may have been composed at the same time as *To Althea. From Prison*. It cannot have been written during the poet's second confinement, as William Lawes was killed in 1645.

PAGE 47. *Elizabeth Filmer*. Sir Edward Filmer (d. 1629) 'had issue by his wife [Elizabeth, daughter of Richard Argall and his wife Mary] . . . who died on Aug. 9, 1638, nine sons and nine daughters', one of whom was named Elizabeth. (Hasted, *History of Kent*, 1782, vol. ii, p. 418.)

PAGE 48, ll. 21–2. The meaning is 'I do not ask liberty from my prison but of thee, Lucasta, whose prisoner I have long been, in order that leaving thee for awhile I may be able to turn my fancy to anything else'.

PAGE 50, l. 13. *The Publick Faith*. Money was borrowed on the Publick Faith, a common object of satire. Cf. Cleveland's lines with that title, 1659, p. 89, and *Hudibras*, ii. 2, ll. 191–6.

PAGE 51. *Lucasta's Fanne*. According to Stowe fans were introduced into England through France from Italy about 1572. In the sixteenth and seventeenth centuries they were made of feathers.

l. 15.

l. 15. *guttur-neck.* Throat.

l. 16. *feedst.* 'Thou feedst.' A similar carelessness in construction is often to be met with in Lovelace.

PAGE 52, l. 2. *edifice.* The fan to which the ostrich's feathers have been transferred.

ll. 5–6. The ostrich's feathers in the fan have been dyed all the colours of the rainbow.

l. 9. *Somtime they wing her side.* Robert Heath in *Clarastella*, 1650, has a poem and an epigram on a lady 'wearing a Looking-glass at her girdle'.

ll. 15–16. The construction is 'In which when she saw her fresh aspect and then saw her Foe retired (participle) to the West', she said, 'Deare Engine ...'

PAGE 56, ll. 2–3. *Blest with an unstained flood*
Flowing both through soule and blood;

If Hunter's conjecture in *Chorus Vatum* as to the parentage of Lucy Sacheverell were correct, these lines would show a striking lack of tact and of accuracy on the part of Lovelace. See *Introduction*, pp. xlvii–ix.

PAGE 57. *To my Worthy Friend Mr. Peter Lilly: on that excellent Picture of his Majesty, and the Duke of Yorke, drawne by him at Hampton-Court.* This picture is in the possession of the Duke of Northumberland at Syon House. It was painted during the time that Charles I was at Hampton Court and his children at Syon House in the charge of the tenth Earl of Northumberland.

There is a copy of the head of the King from this picture in the Ashmolean Gallery at Oxford. Lely received £30 for the picture, and his receipt is still in the possession of the Duke of Northumberland.

Born at Soest in the same year as Lovelace, Lely came to England in 1641 in the train of William of Orange. He obtained considerable distinction under Charles I, but reached the height of his fame after the Restoration, when he painted his famous Beauties of the Court of Charles the Second. Pepys speaks of him as 'a mighty proud man' and 'full of state'. See note to p. 180.

Walpole

Walpole says of this picture:—'The king has none of the melancholy grace which Vandyck alone, of all his painters, always gave him. It has a sterner countenance, and expressive of the tempests he has experienced.' (*Anecdotes of Painting in England. Works*, 1798, vol. iii, p. 292.)

PAGE 58, l. 12. *None but my Lilly ever drew a Minde.* Compare:

> The Author musing here survay,
> How He may THEOPHIL portray:
> Where Others Art surpast you find,
> They draw the Body, He the Mind.

Lines beneath the engraving which follows the title-page in Benlowe's *Theophila*, 1652.

l. 13. *Thou snowy Farme with thy five Tenements!* It would seem that white gloves were commonly worn by ladies. Compare Ben Jonson's song quoted below. Thomas Heywood speaks of 'such a hand hid in a gloue of snow' (*The Foure Prentises of London*, ed. 1632, Sig. H 3 verso), and James Howell more than once writes for a supply of white kid-skin gloves to serve as presents to women. (*Familiar Letters*, 1645, i, p. 24, and ii, p. 40.)

PAGE 59, ll. 1–2. Cf. Jonson's song in *Cynthia's Reuells*, fo., 1616, p. 228:

> *Thou more then most sweet gloue,*
> *Vnto my more sweet loue,*
> *Suffer me to store with kisses*
> *This emptie lodging, that now misses*
> *The pure rosie hand, that ware thee,*
> *Whiter then the kid, that bare thee.*
> *Thou art soft, but that was softer;*
> CVPIDS *selfe hath kist it ofter,*
> *Then e're he did his mothers doues,*
> *Supposing her the Queene of* loues,
> *That was thy Mistresse,*
> *Best of gloues.*

l. 4. *Minikin.* The treble string of a lute or viol. Cf.

Rossa.

Rossa. By this Gold, I had rather haue a servant with a short nose, and a thinne hayre, then haue such a high stretcht minikin voyce. (*Antonio and Mellida*, First part, Act v, ed. 1633, Sig. E 2.)

Fel. Fut, what trebble minikin squeakes there, ha?
Ibid. Act III, Sig. C 7 verso.

To Fletcher reviv'd. These lines were contributed to the first folio of Beaumont and Fletcher, *Comedies and Tragedies*, 1647. Among other contributors were Denham, Waller, Howell, L'Estrange, Stanley, Corbet, Cartwright, Ben Jonson, Herrick, Brome, and Shirley. Lovelace's lines with others were not reprinted in the folio of 1679. For the marginal notes in the folio giving the names of the various plays to which Lovelace refers, see 'Textual Notes'.

PAGE 61, l. 14. *the austere Skarlet had approv'd.* The long and bitter quarrel between the Puritans and the stage ended in a temporary triumph for the former when all playing was forbidden by the ordinance of September 2, 1642. The 'austere Skarlet' is probably a reference to the doctors of the Westminster Assembly.

Strange Scarlet Doctors these, they'l passe in Story
For sinners halfe refin'd in Purgatory;
Or parboyl'd Lobsters, where there joyntly rules
The fading Sables and the coming Gules.
Cleveland, 'The Mixt Assembly' (1647, p. 29).

It is possible that Lovelace meant the judges who wore scarlet gowns. Compare Vittoria Corombona's exclamation in answer to her judge:

O poore charity!
Thou art seldome found in scarlet.
Webster, *The White Divel*, 1612, Sig. E 3.

Do the Lords bow, and the regarded scarlets,
Kiss their Gumd-gols, and cry, we are your servants?
Beaumont and Fletcher, *Philaster*, fo., 1679, p. 38.

'Even the Bench,' says Lovelace, 'so stern in judging immorality, would have approved plays like yours if the reformation

reformation of dramatic manners commenced by you had not died with you.' But there is more point in the fantastic suggestion that the 'austere'—an epithet more appropriate to the Puritans than to the Bench—Westminster divines would have swallowed 'loose thoughts' if they had generally been so well expressed as Fletcher expressed them.

l. 24. *the best piece Hermes to Love e're read.* Lovelace may have had in mind Correggio's *Mercury teaching Cupid to read*, now in the National Gallery and formerly in the collection of Charles I.

PAGE 62. *The Lady A. L.* Possibly Anne, Lady Lovelace.

PAGE 64, l. 19. *Naught.* Evil.

l. 21. *Bayes.* See note to p. 5, l. 19.

PAGE 65. *A Prologue to the Scholars. A Comœdy presented at the White-Fryers.* Lovelace's play was acted at Salisbury Court. The Whitefriars, where the Children of the King's Revels played, was closed in 1621, and 'after its re-edification for the adult players' known as Salisbury Court. (See *The Elizabethan Playhouse and other Studies by W. J. Lawrence*, First Series, pp. 16 and 26.) Lovelace keeps the older name, which enables him to make his quibble, '*Faire* still to th' *Blacke*, *Blacke* still to the *White-Fryers*.'

PAGE 66, l. 24. *2 hour's time.* Compare 'the two houres traffique of our Stage' (*Romeo and Juliet*) and Prologue to *Henry VIII.* An almost contemporary Cambridge play is said to have occupied three hours. (*The Prologve and Epilogve to a Comedie, Presented, at the Entertainment of the Prince His Highnesse, by the Schollers of Trinity Colledge in Cambridge, in March last, 1641. By Francis Cole. London: Printed for James Calvin, 1642.*) and there are other references to three-hour performances.

PAGE 67, ll. 1–2. Mr. W. J. Lawrence quotes these lines (Second Series, p. 100) as testifying 'that a progressive spirit actuated the builders of the last of the private theatres, for they indicate that in Salisbury Court, which dated from 1629,

1629, playgoers were provided with more than one entrance to the auditorium proper'.

ll. 7–8. *in which the Throne*
To their amazement should descend alone,

Cf. Jonson's Prologue to *Every Man in his Humour*:

> Nor creaking throne comes downe, the boyes to please;
> Nor nimble squibbe is seene, to make afear'd
> The gentlewomen;

and

'I will have all these descend from the top of my roof, in a Throne, as you see *Cupid* or *Mercury* in a Play'. (Shackerley Marmion, *The Antiquary*, 16, Sig. H 3.)

In a note on the former passage in his edition of *Every Man* Mr. Percy Simpson quotes similar references from Lodge and Greene, *A Looking Glasse, for London and England*, 1598, and Greene's *Alphonsus*, 1599.

ll. 9–10.
The rosin-lightning flash, and Monster spire
Squibs,

Mr. Lawrence quotes from *A Warning for Faire Women* (1599), a 'sarcastic reference . . . to the stage-lightning of the period':

> Then of a filthy whining ghost
> Lapt in some foul sheet or a leather pilch,
> Comes screaming like a pig half stick'd and cries
> Vindicta! revenge, revenge.
> With that a little rosin flasheth forth
> Like smoke out of a tabacco pipe or a boy's squib . . . .

and adds a reference to this passage. (*Op. cit.*, Second Series, p. 19.)

l. 18. *not their Crimes.* Cf. Jonson, Prologue to *Every Man in his Humour*, fo., 1616, p. 5:

> But deedes, and language, such as man doe vse:
> And persons, such as *Comoedie* would chuse,
> When she would shew an Image of the times,
> And sport with humane follies, not with crimes.

PAGE 68.

PAGE 68. *Clitophon and Lucippe translated.* These lines were contributed to Anthony Hodges's translation of *The Loves of Clitophon and Levcippe. A most elegant History, written in Greeke by Achilles Tatius: And now Englished. . . . Oxford, Printed by William Turner for Iohn Allam.* 1638. Lovelace's lines are printed in larger type than those of other contributors. There are so many variations between the two versions that the earlier is here given in full:

To the Ladies.

FAire ones, breathe: a while lay by
Blessed *Sidney's Arcady*:
Here 's a Story that will make
You not repent *Him* to forsake;
And with your dissolving looke
Vntie the Contents of this Booke;
To which nought (except your sight)
Can give a worthie Epithite.
Tis an abstract of all Volumes,
A Pillaster of all Columnes
Fancie e're rear'd to wit, to be
Little *Love's* Epitome,
And compactedly expresse
All Lovers Happy Wretchednesse.

Brave *Pamela's* majestie,
And her sweet Sisters modestie
Are fixt in each of you, you are
Alone, what these together were:
Divinest, that are really
What *Cariclea 's* feign'd to be;
That are every One, the Nine;
And on Earth *Astræ's* shine;
Be our *Leucippe*, and remaine
In *Her*, all these o're againe.

Wonder!

Wonder! Noble *Clitophon*
Me thinkes lookes somewhat colder on
His beauteous Mistresse, and she too
Smiles not as she us'd to doe.
See! the Individuall Payre
Are at oddes, and parted are;
Quarrell, emulate, and stand
At strife, who first shall kisse your hand.

A new warre e'rewhile arose
'Twixt the *Greekes* and *Latines*, whose
Temples should be bound with Glory
In best languaging this Story:
You that with one lovely smile,
A Ten-yeares Warre can reconcile;
Peacefull *Hellens*, awfull, see
The jarring languages agree;
And here all Armes laid by, they doe
Meet in *English* to court you.

Rich: Lovelace, Ma: Ar: A: Glou: Eq: Aur: Fil: Nat: Max.

Wood mentions Anthony Hodges, Chaplain of New College, as refusing the degree of Bachelor of Divinity in 1646 (*Athenae Oxonienses*, 1691, ii. 738), and in his Autobiography has an account of him under the year 1649.

Wood mentions two 'impressions' of *The Loves* in 1638, one apparently without the commendatory verses.

Hodges wrote some Latin verses for *Musarum Oxoniensium Charisteria*, 1638. Achilles Tatius, about whom little is known, probably wrote *Clitophon and Leucippe* towards the end of the third century A. D. He was one of the most popular of the Greek novelists. Hodges does seem to have known the earlier translation by William Burton which was published in 1597.

PAGE 69, l. 6. *Cariclea.* The heroine of Heliodorus' romance of *Theagenes and Chariclea.*

l. 8. *Astrea.* The pastoral romance *L'Astrée* was written

written by Honoré d'Urfé, Marquis de Valromey (1567–1625). The first part was published in Paris in 1610, the second being added in 1612, and the third and fourth in 1618. The book was left unfinished, but was completed by d'Urfé's secretary Barro from his papers. Other continuations were also written. There were numerous editions of the Romance; '*Astrea* finding so good entertainement in her owne countrey, as hauing passed the Presse in the 3. principall Cities of France, namely, Paris, Roan, and Lyons, is now encouraged to crosse the seas, and to try what welcome she shall meete with here in England', says John Pyper in the Dedication to his *The History of Astrea. The First Part. In Twelue Bookes: Newly Translated out of French* ... 1620. A complete translation, by 'A Person of Quality', was printed in three volumes, folio, 1657–8. Leonard Willan's *Astræa, or True Love's Myrrour. A Pastoral* 1651, is based on d'Urfé's romance.

l. 19. *A new Dispute. Clitophon and Leucippe* was not printed till 1544, when a Latin translation of the last four books by Annibale della Croce appeared at Lyons, the whole book by the same translator being printed at Basle in 1554. The Greek text first appeared at Heidelberg in 1601, with Longus and Parthenius in the same volume. (See *Achilles Tatius*, S. Gaselee, 1917.) Another edition with the Greek and Latin text was printed at Heidelberg in 1606, and another with notes by Dionysius Petavius in Part I of his *Uranologion*, Paris, 1630.

PAGE 70. *To my truely valiant, learned Friend,*... These lines were prefixed to *Pallas Armata. The Gentlemans Armorie; Wherein the right and genuine use of the Rapier and of the Sword, as well against the right handed as against the left handed man is displayed: And now set forth and first published for the common good by the Author.... Printed at London by I D for Iohn Williams, at the signe of the Crane in S. Pauls Church-yard. 1639.*

They are signed 'Rich Lovelace, *A Glouces: Oxon.*'

The Preface to the book is signed G. A., possibly George Ashwell

Ashwell of Wadham, who contributed Latin verses to Oxford collections of poems such as *Musarum Oxoniensium Charisteria*, 1638, *Flos Britannicus*, 1638, and *Horti Cardini Rosa Altera*, 1640; or Gideon Ashwell of King's, who has verses in Συνῳδία, *Sive Musarum Cantabrigiensium Concentus et Congratulatio*, 1637.

l. 8. *And Conquer by the Booke?* Cf.

Del. He hath read all the late seruice,
As the City Chronicle relates it,
And keepe two Painters going, onely to expresse
Battailes in modell.
Sil. Then hel; fight by the book.

The Tragedy of the Dutchesse of Malfy, 1623, Sig. G 4 verso.

l. 9. *Take then this Mathematick shield.* Cf.

'What, a Dog, a Rat, a Mouse, a Cat to scratch a man to death: a Braggart, a Rogue, a Villaine, that fights by the booke of Arithmeticke, . . .' (*Romeo and Juliet*, III. i.)

PAGE 71. *Amyntor.* Hazlitt suggested that Amyntor here and in the dialogue *Amyntor from beyond the Sea to Alexis* might be identified with Endymion Porter, and that Arigo was 'unquestionably no other than Henry Jermyn'. It is possible that both these poems were addressed to Porter, but this cannot be argued on the assumption that Arigo is Henry Jermyn, who is associated with Endymion Porter as 'Arigo' by Davenant. Arigo and Gratiana in this poem are the 'Blooming Boy, and blossoming Mayd' who fly in 'Cleare as the skye from whence they came', and must represent Porter's children Thomas and Mary or, more probably, James and Lettice, according to the date on which the lines were written. Henry Jermyn was not aged five in 1648.

Although there does not seem to be any record that Porter himself possessed pictures attributed to Titian, Raphael, and Giorgione, he may have done so as he was frequently abroad on missions to buy pictures for the king, and though these were sometimes a cloak for secret diplomacy he certainly had a great deal to do with the formation of Charles I's collection

collection, and was the friend and patron of Vandyck, Rubens, and other of the famous painters of the day.

Lovelace must have been acquainted with Porter at the Court, where the latter held the post of Gentleman of the Bedchamber, having been with the king since the days of his visit to Madrid in 1623. He might also have met Porter during the expeditions to the north when he himself was in George Goring's regiment. Goring was related by marriage to the Porters, his sister having married George Porter, Endymion's eldest son. Chloris would be Olivia, Endymion's wife, who was the daughter of Lord Boteler.

In 1646 or 1647 Endymion Porter fled to France, where he was joined by his wife in April 1647, and he spent the next two years there and in the Low Countries, returning to England in the winter of 1648–9 and dying the following August. This would date the *Dialogue*, in which Amyntor invites Alexis across the sea to the 'watry land', in 1648. See p. 101.

PAGE 73, l. 9. *the Indians richest prize.* Probably tobacco.

ll. 29–30. *he wrote but five,*
Yet spake eighteene,

He wrote himself but five (i.e. was only five years old), though from his way of speaking it might have been thought that he was eighteen.

Compare: . . . I writ my selfe
(And truly) lover ere I could write man,
Heywood, *A Challenge for Beavtie*, 1636, Sig. B 3 verso.

PAGE 74. *Against the Love of Great Ones.* W. C. Hazlitt occasionally cites a transcript of a few of Lovelace's poems which he found in a copy of Crashaw's *Poems*, 1648. The MS. seems to be of no importance, but it gives the correct reading 'bands' for 'bonds' in l. 3. of these verses.

PAGE 76, l. 8. *But we (defend us!) are divine.* Cf.

What 's great and faire? wee would be term'd divine.
Such as would give us our full character,
Must search for Epithites, and studie phrase.

Heywood, *A Challenge for Beavtie*, 1636, Sig. A 4 verso.

l. 16. *Booreinn.* A peasant woman, a female boor. (*N. E. D.*)

l. 21. *Play at Baloon.* Cf.

Sir Petro. . . . wee had a match at *Baloone* too, with my Lord *Whachum*, for foure crownes.

Gir. At *Baboone? Iesu!* you and I will play at *Baboone* in the countrey? Knight.

Sir Pet. O sweet Lady: tis a strong play with the arme.

Gir. With arme, or legge, or any other member, if it bee a court-sport. *Eastward Hoe*, 1605, Sig. B 1.

Coryate describes how he saw the game at Venice. (*Crudities*, 1611, p. 246.)

l. 27. *a dying Lives.* Compare p. 93. 'Now fie upon that everlasting Life, I Dye!'

PAGE 77. *Mrs. Bowes Barne.* Probably an unmarried cousin of Lovelace's mother—she and Lucasta are called 'equal Virgins'—a younger sister of the Carola Harsnett mentioned below. *Westminster Abbey Registers* (Harleian Society), 1876, p. 188, has the following entry in the list of Burials:

'1676 May [17] Carola wife of Major Harsnett (Cloisters).'

Note. 'Eldest dau. of Robert Barne of Great Grimsby, co. Lincoln, Esq. (second son of Sir William Barne, of Woolwich, Kent, Kt., by Anne, dau. of Edwin Sandys, Archbishop of York), by Elizabeth, dau. of Thomas Twysden, of Wye, co. Kent, Esq., and born about 1623.'

PAGE 78. *To Althea, From Prison.* This song has always been the best known of all Lovelace's poems. It was imitated by his contemporaries, Percy published a version of it in his *Reliques*, it was included in some anthologies of the second half of the 18th century at a time when the author was very little known, and in 1839 Robert Bell, in his *Lives of the Most Eminent Literary and Scientific Men of Great Britain*, stated that 'there is scarcely any single production of the seventeenth century which enjoys such extensive popularity'.

The

The poem was written, according to Wood, during the poet's confinement in the Gatehouse in 1642, but it was not published till seven years later, when it appeared in *Lucasta*. Although there are practically no seventeenth-century MSS. of Lovelace's other poems, there are no less than six of *To Althea*. One is that used by Percy, four others are in the British Museum, and one in the Bodleian. The following version has press-mark E. G. 2725 Farnb. fo. 10 (MS. A). The collection of poems in which it occurs was written about 1650, probably rather before than after that date, as none of the poems refers to Charles I as dead. It was, therefore, probably written before the song was printed.

A coppy of verses of captaine Lovelace his making when he was in prison.

When Loue with unconfined wings
Houers about my grates
And my divine Althea brings
Spic'd whispers to my gates,
When I intangled in her haire
Am fettered in her eye
The birds that wanton in the aire
Know noe such libertie.

When flowing cups run swiftly round
Like to the posting Thames
Our carelesse heads with chapplets crown'd
Our harts with loyall flames.
When thirsty griefe in wine wee steepe
When healths and draughts are free
Fishes that tipple in the deepe
Know noe such liberty.

When, like committed linnets, I
With shriller throat shall sing
The sweetnesse, virtue, Majesty
And mildnesse of my King

When

When I shall voice abroad how good
He is, how great should bee
Th' inlarged winds that curles the flood
Know no such liberty.

Stone walls doe not a prison make,
Nor iron grates a cage
A spotlesse mind, and innocence
Calls this an Hermitage
If I have freedome in my loue
And in my soule am free
Angells alone that soare aboue
Enjoy such liberty.

Dr. Bliss in his edition of Wood's *Athenae* printed a second MS. version of *To Althea*, 'to all appearance contemporary with the Author'. This MS., which formed Lot 192 at the sale of his books on August 21, 1858, is in the British Museum to-day, Add. MS. 22603. fo. 16 (MS. B.).

His beinge in Prison.

When Loue wth unconfinèd winges
  Houer'd within my gates;
And my diuine Allthea bringes
  To whisper at my grates.
When I lye tangled in her hayre
  And fettered in her eye
The Birds y[t] wanton in the ayr
  Know not such libertie.

2.

When flowing Cupps runne swiftly round
  With noe allayinge theames,
Our carelesse heads with Roses bound,
  Our heartes with loyall flames.
When thirsty griefes in wine wee steepe
  When healths and draughts are free,
Fishes y[t] tipple in the deepe
  Know no such Libertie.

3.

3.

When like comitted Linnets, I
With shriller notes shall singe,
The sweetnes, mercy, maiestie
And glories of my kinge;
When I shall voyce aloud, how good
He is, and great should be
Enlarged winds that curle ye flood
Know not such Libertie.

4.

Stone walls doe not a Prison make
Nor Iron barres a Cage,
A spotlesse mind, and Innocent
Calls that an Hermitage.
If I haue freedome in my loue
And in my soule am free
Angells alone that are aboue
Enjoy such Libertie.

In this MS. there follows an *Answer* in the same hand, the author of which is unknown:

The Answer

When Cynthia's wrapt within my armes
With warblinge notes doth singe,
New victories still wayte upon
The Progresse of our Kinge;
If I'me confin'd unto the same
May not her Eccho be,
Byrds that are cloyster'd in a Cage,
Know no such slauerie.

2.

When that my Genius doth inuite
And prompt me to a Lust,
To tell the world, how great he was,
How good he is and iust

If

If y^{t} my tounge may speake; my hearte
Be forc't to disagree
Men y^{t} are fetter'd in a Chayne
Know noe such slauerie.

3.

When wine shall crowne ye larger bowles
And each man quaffe his share
On bended knees to whom they list
And gracious Charles not there;
If I want freedome to beginne
Healthe to his M^{tie};
Camells y^{t} kneele to beare thyre weight
Know no such slauery.

4.

Proud buildinges not a Pallace make,
To yield a large Content.
A mind controlled in its will
Calls y^{t} Imprisonment.
If y^{t} I cannot w^{t} I will
But must will w^{t} I see
Vessells acquainted to the oare
Know no such slauerie.

A third version (MS. C.), attributed to Col. John Lovelace, is to be found in Bishop Percy's MS., which he collated with the text printed in *Lucasta*, 1649, and printed in his *Reliques of Ancient English Poetry*, 1765, vol. ii, pp. 325–6. The text of the MS. is taken from Hales and Furnivall's edition, 1868, vol. ii, pp. 19–20.

When Loue with unconfinèd.

When Love w*i*th vnconfined wings
hovers w*i*thin my gates,
& my divine Althea brings
to whisp*er* at my grates,

when

when I lye tangled in her heere
  & fettered w*i*th her eye,
the burds *tha*t wanton in the ayre
  enioyes[1] such Lybertye.

When, Lynett like confined, I
  w*i*th shriller note shall sing
the mercy, goodnesse, maiestye
  & glory of my kinge,
when I shall voice aloud how good
  he is, how great shold bee,
the enlarged winds *tha*t curles the floods
  enioyes such Lybertye.

When flowing cupps run swiftly round
  w*i*th woe-allaying theames,
our carelesse heads w*i*th roses crowned,
  our harts w*i*th Loyall flames,
when thirsty soules in wine wee steepe,
  when cupps and bowles goe free,
ffishes *that* typle in the deepe
  enioyes such Lybertye.

Stone walls doe not a prison make,
  nor Iron barrs a cage,
the spotlesse soule an[d] Inocent
  Calls this an hermitage.
if I haue freedome in my loue,
  & in my soule am free,
angells alone *tha*t sores aboue
  enioyes such Lybertye!
ffins.

There is also in the Bodleian (MS. Rawlinsonian D 1267 [2]) another version of the last stanza. There is no indication of the date when the lines were written, but they are

[1] This final s and several others have been marked through by a later hand. [Note by Furnivall.]

in

in a seventeenth-century hand and the volume in which they occur was owned by Tho. Hearne in September 1709 (MS. D.).

Stone walls doe not a prison make, nor iron barrs a cage
The spotlesse soule & innocent calls that an hermitage
He y[t] hath freedome in his wishe, & in his soule is free
Angells alone y[t] serve aboue know no such liberty

Among the Harleian MSS. there are two versions of *To Althea*. The following has press-mark 2127. f. 20 (MS. E.):

When Love, with unconfined Winge
Hovers about my Gates
And my divine Althea singe
And whispers at my Grates
When I lie tangled in her haire
And fettered in her Eye
The Birds that wanton in the aire
Know noe such Libertie.

When flowing Cupps runne sweetly round
With noe allaying theames
Our careles heads with roses cround
Our Loyall hearts with fflames
Whil'st thirstie Griefe in wine we steepe
And Healthes in Bowles runne free
ffishes that tipple in the deepe
Knowe noe such Libertie.

When Lynnetts like, Committed we
With shriller noate doe sing,
The glory, might, and maiestye
And goodnes of our King.
When wee shall vote aloud how good
He is; how great should bee:
Inlarged Windes that curles the floud
Know noe such Libertie.

Stone

Stone Walls can not a prison make
Nor Iron Barrs a Cage
A spotles minde, and Innocent
Calls that an hermitage.
Whil'st we have freedome in our Love
And in our Soules are free
Angells alone that soare above
Inioy such Libertie.

The volume in which the above version is written is described in the Catalogue of Harleian MSS. as 'A thin Book in folio . . . by the third Randle Holme entituled "Songs & Sonnetts", . . . written by different Hands, besides which here are Epitaphs, Lampoons, Libells &c in Prose, as well as in Verse; particularly some against the Welsh and Scots; some for King Charles the first, the Bishops &c, and others against them. . . .'

This Randle Holme lived from 1627 to 1699. The same catalogue describes Harl. MS. 6918, fo. 94[b], which has another version of *To Althea*, as a quarto containing a large collection of English poems, and it appears to have been written in the early part of the seventeenth century. It was once in Lord Somers' Library (MS. F.).

The verses are headed 'Captaine Loueles made this poem in his duresse at the Gatehouse'. With the following exceptions the version is the same as that given in Add. MSS. 22603: l. 2 hovers, l. 6 with her Ey, l. 7 the Gods, l. 8 knowe noe, l. 10 Thames, l. 18 shriller Throate, l. 22 how great, l. 24 knowe noe, l. 31 that dwell. There are also a few differences in spelling, punctuation, and capitals. The last stanza, in a different hand, is written in eight lines instead of in four as are the others. The word *Gods* in l. 7 is underlined in pencil and *Birds* written in the margin in a different hand and probably at a later date.

Most of the variations between the MSS. and the printed song are of little or no importance. The poem was circulated

lated in manuscript or by word of mouth for seven years before it was printed, and this would be quite sufficient to account for small differences. In the last stanza, however, a correction has obviously been made. The MSS. all read 'the spotlesse minde (*or* soule) and innocent',[1] while *Lucasta* reads 'Minds innocent and quiet'. There can be no doubt that we have here a deliberate correction, made when Lovelace 'framed his poems for the press'.

There is one other reading which challenges attention. That is *Gods* in l. 7 of the first stanza. All the MSS. but one read *Birds*; the one MS. and the printed version read *Gods*, which must be accepted as the correct reading and as that which was finally approved by the poet. Were it not for the Harleian MS., it would seem certain that the very obvious *Birds* was what Lovelace had at first written. As it is, it appears more probable that early transcribers were as ready to alter this word to satisfy their notion of what is correct, as modern editors and anthologists have been to follow their example. Even in the Harleian MS. which gives the correct reading some one has added the inevitable 'Birds'. This reading was printed as early as 1659, and again in 1660 by Dr. John Wilson in his *Cheerful Ayres and Ballads*.

Dr. Bliss wrote a note on the top of his MS. and he published another to the same effect in his edition of the *Athenae*: 'It is worthy of remark that in some copies this is read "The *Gods*" &c., and that Dr. Percy, bishop of Dromore, took the credit of the alteration to "*Birds*", as his own. It is needless to add, that the present MS. was written long before Dr. Percy was born. See Ellis's *Specimens*, iii. 277.' Percy, to whom credit is due for re-introducing this song to public favour, for it seems to have been very nearly forgotten in the first half of the eighteenth century, has been much abused for the text of *To Althea* which he printed. Hazlitt, who printed

[1] Compare 'Innocent and spotlesse hearts', Felltham, *Resolves*, ed. 1628, p. 231.

'birds'

'birds' without any hesitation, regarding the text of *Lucasta* as labouring under 'extraordinary corruptions', attacks him for 'very unnecessarily' altering 'like committed linnets' to 'linnet-like confined'; adding 'It is fortunate for the lovers of early English literature that Bp. Percy had comparatively little to do with it. Emendation of a text is well enough; but the wholesale and arbitrary slaughter of it is quite another matter.' Mr. Seccombe also, in his article on Lovelace in the *Dictionary of National Biography*, accused Percy of making 'several conjectural emendations which have since been universally condemned'. Percy made no 'conjectural emendations', but only, as he said he had done, collated the version of the song as given in *Lucasta* with his own MS., and, where he preferred it, adopted the reading of the latter.

To Althea enjoyed some contemporary popularity and was imitated more than once, by Jenkyn and Stanley for instance.

There is another poem, *The Liberty of the Imprisoned Royalist*, 'Beat on proud Billows, Boreas blow', which has been attributed to Lovelace. The attribution is due to the fact that the ideas dealt with in the two poems are in part the same. There is no sort of evidence or probability that Lovelace wrote it. There can be little doubt that the traditional attribution of the poem to Sir Roger L'Estrange is correct, and it is definitely stated to be his in the pamphlet *A Hymn to Confinement . . . To which is added, a POEM on the same Subject by the Famous Sir Roger L'Estrange, when in Newgate, in the Days of Oliver's Usurpation . . . London; Printed in the Year 1705. And Sold by the Booksellers* (*Price Six Pence*). The question of the authorship of this poem is dealt with by Mr. G. Thorn-Drury, K.C., in *Notes and Queries*, 1904. Mr. Thorn-Drury also gives a list of places other than the quarto where the verses are to be found. His conclusion that the first quarto, which was published without a title-page, belongs to 1647 is supported by the fact that two copies in the Worcester

College

College Library are bound among pamphlets of that year. Two other poems were included in this pamphlet.

Set by Dr. John Wilson. This setting was printed in the Third Part 'being *Songs* or *Ballads* for *Three Voyces*' of *Select Ayres and Dialogues For One, Two, and Three Voyces; To the Theorbo-Lute or Basse-Viol,* . . . *W. Godbid for J. Playford*: . . . 1659. Songs by Charles Colman, Henry and William Lawes, Nicholas Laneare, William Webb and 'other Excellent Masters of Musick' were included in this volume, which was an enlarged edition of *Select Musicall Ayres and Dialogues*, 1653. The sheets of it were reissued with a new title-page in 1669 as Book I of *The Treasury of Musick: Containing Ayres and Dialogues To Sing to the Theorbo-Lute or Basse-Viol*, 1669.

Wilson's setting was reprinted in 1660 in *Cheerful Ayres or Ballads First composed for one single Voice and since set for three Voices by John Wilson Dr. in Musick Professor of the same in the University of Oxford. Oxford. Printed by W. Hall, for Ric. Davis. Anno Dom. M DC LX.* See note to p. 23.

In the collection of Ballads 'chiefly belonging to the period of the Restoration', which formed Lot 433 in Messrs. Sotheby's sale catalogue of the first portion of the Huth Collection, 1911, one (Vol. ii, No. 53) reads: '"The Pensive Prisoner's Apology." Tune of "Love with unconfined wings": or, "No, no, no, no, not yet," *printed for F. Coles, T. Vere, J. Wright and J. Clarke.* 12 stanzas, with 4 cuts. In two parts.'†

ll. 13–14. Compare *Coriolanus*, II. i:

'I am knowne to be a humorous *Patritian*, and one that loues a cup of hot Wine, with not a drop of allaying Tiber in't. . . .'

and R. Baron, *Pocula Castalia*, 1650, p. 70:

> Now were our Heads with Rosebuds crown'd
> And flowing cups ran swiftly round,
> Wee all did drink like Fishes;

PAGE 79, l. 17. *Coran's.* Currants.

l. 19.

l. 19. *For Elles of Beere, Flutes of Canary.* An ell was strictly forty-five inches. *N. E. D.* states that several correspondents have written to say that they have seen on old public-houses notices advertising beer to be sold by the yard.

Flutes were 'tall slender wine glasses used especially for sparkling wines'. (*N. E. D.*)

l. 20. *pasties-mary.* An obsolete spelling of marrow.

l. 21. *Peason.* Peason is an absolete form of the word pease.

l. 22. *Widdow-Venson-pye.* The 'Venson-pye' is 'widdow' because some one has had a cut at it already. When it is finished Ellinda's brother will be able to begin on another which no one has touched. Compare:

'*A Widdow.* Is like a cold Pye thrust downe to the lower end of the Table, that has had too many fingers in't. . . .' (Wye Saltonstall, *Picturae Loquentes*, 1631, Sig. B 11 verso).

PAGE 80, l. 2. *With Knuckles far as any deepe in.* Compare: 'neither let thy *Fingers* be knuckle deep in the *Sauce*, for that is *loathsom*, and savours of *Slovenry*.' (*Counsellor Manners his last Legacy to his Son*, ed. 1698, p. 10.)

Forks were unknown in England before the beginning of the seventeenth century, and the credit of introducing them into the country may be claimed by Thomas Coryate, who relates in a well-known passage how he found them used in Italy. (*Crudities*, 1611, pp. 90–1.)

l. 4. *Loyne right-worshipfull.* The sirloin of beef is said to have been knighted by James I at Hoghton Towers, Lancashire. Compare Mr. Supple . . . 'the Sight of the Roast-beef struck him dumb, permitting him only to say Grace, and to declare he must pay his Respect to the Baronet: For so he called the Sirloin.' (*Tom Jones*, 1749, iv, ch. x; vol. ii, p. 67.)

ll. 11–12. Compare p. 43. *To Ellinda, that lately I have not written.*

l. 16. *Will take out Hans from pretty Kelder.* For other instances of a common expression compare D'Urfey:

Defend

Defend the Vertues of your Elders,
That get on Strumpets *Hans en Kelders;*
Collin's Walk through London and Westminster,
1690, p. 177.

or Cleveland (ed. 1647, p. 12):

That name hath tipt his hornes: see on his knees
A health to Hans-en-Kelder *Hercules.*

PAGE 81, l. 3. *That Amadis, Sir Guy and Todaz*
With his fleet Neigher . . .

Three of the most renowned heroes of Romance. For Sir Amadis de Gaul see *Don Quixote*, bk. 1, chap. 6.

The early English metrical romance of Sir Guy of Warwick is printed by the Early English Text Society. The story spread everywhere in songs and ballads and manuscripts. Sir John Paston had a copy of the story in his library. Lydgate gave a version of it. The first printed edition of the story is the *History of Guy Earl of Warwick*, printed by Richard Pynson in the last decade of the fifteenth century. It went on spreading in every variety of form, from full-blown romance to chapbook, into the eighteenth century.

For Sir Topaz compare Holland:

'. . . he summons the Squire of his body *Soto*, . . . to read the Chronicle History of Saint *George*, . . . or the hard Quest of Sir *Topaz* after the Queen of *Clues* to *Barwick*, or of Sir Guy and the fierce Boar of *Boston*; . . .' (*Wit and Fancy in a Maze*, 1656, p. 2.)

ll. 5–6.

But now to close all I must switch-hard,
Servant ever;
Lovelace Richard.

Compare Bold's *Poems*, 1664, p. 150:

And *Drink* your *Health*, however fare I,
Till then, and ever;
Your
Bold Harry.

and

But

But none like him who will be ever
Sir, your true servant, *Richard Leavor.*
Songs and Poems of Love and Drollery, T. W., 1654, p. 49.

To Generall Goring. This poem is addressed to the younger Goring (1608–57), in whose regiment Lovelace served as an ensign during the Scottish expedition, having no doubt previously made his aquaintance at Court, where Goring was a leader among the most brilliant and extravagant of the younger generation.

After the second expedition he took a part in the alleged army-plot, on suspicion of being concerned in which Suckling fled the kingdom, making 'that odious proposition' of 'bringing up the army presently to London, which would so awe the Parliament that they would do anything the King commanded'. He then betrayed the plot to the Parliament almost at the same time as he was undertaking 'with a crew of officers and good fellows, who, he said, were at his disposal, to rescue the Earl of Strafford from the Tower, and so enable him to make an escape into foreign parts'.

He was examined before Parliament, and for his services in betraying the plot, given public thanks, 'for preserving the kingdom and the liberties of Parliament'.

He was sent back to Portsmouth, of which he had been made Governor early in 1639, on his return from the Low Countries, where he had been in the Dutch service, and remained there till September, 1642, when Portsmouth was captured by the Parliament shortly after Goring had declared for the King. He returned to Holland to recruit for the King among the English regiments in that country, and it is probable that Lovelace went in his train. Goring returned in the same year to take a prominent part in the Civil War, retiring to France in November, 1645, and obtaining the command of the English regiments in the Spanish service two years later.

Lovelace may have met Goring again, as he was present at the siege of Dunkirk in September–October, 1646, return-

 ing

ing to England shortly afterwards. Goring remained abroad till his death in 1657.

l. 7. *at the Foes rate.* Upon the terms of the enemy. The first of the two 'Bishop's Wars' was brought to a conclusion by the Pacification at Berwick in June, 1639.

l. 12. *see't goe round.* Compare Heywood, *The Royall King, and The Loyall Subject*, 1637, Sig. D I verso:

King. Lords this Health:
See it goe round, 'twas to our victory.

and the last lines of the fourteen stanzas of Patrick Carey's song 'Come (fayth) since I'me parting', e. g. 'Then lett his health goe round'; 'Besure her health goe round'; 'But see that itt goe round'; 'Itt must, itt must goe round'; 'Each health still goeing round'. (*Trivial Poems and Triolets*, ed. Sir Walter Scott, 1820, pp. 11–13.)

PAGE 82, l. 6. *To Lettice.* Goring married 'his lovely bride', Lettice, the third daughter of Richard Boyle, Earl of Cork, on July 25, 1629, that is ten years before these lines were written.

Sir Thomas Wortley. 'Wortley, (Sir) Thomas, of Yorks, militis fil. Trinity Coll., matric. 26 Oct., 1621, aged 18, B.A. 7 July, 1623; (3 s. Sir Richard) knighted 24 July, 1629; brother of Francis'. (*Alumni Oxonienses*, by Joseph Foster, 1891, vol. iv, p. 1682.)

He has verses before the Earl of Monmouth's translation of Malvezzi's *Romulus and Tarquin*, 1637.

Sir Francis Wortley, the author of *Characters and Elegies*, 1646, Thomas' elder brother, was a well-known Royalist poet.

One line has dropped out of the first stanza of Wortley's 'sonnet'.

PAGE 84. *Set by Mr. William Lawes.* I have not been able to find this setting.

PAGE 85. *the Curtaine of Lucasta's Picture.* In the sixteenth and seventeenth centuries it was usual to cover pictures with a curtain to keep the dust from them. Compare *Twelfth Night*, I. iv.

PAGE 86. *my Brothers untimely Death.* William Lovelace,

lace,

lace, the third son, was killed at Carmarthen, probably in 1644, when under the command of his brother Francis, to whom this poem is addressed. See *Introduction* and note to p. 2.

PAGE 87. *Mrs. Cassandra Cotton.* The sister of the elder Charles Cotton, and the aunt of the poet.

PAGE 88, l. 10. The line should perhaps read:

'Or Herald, though by no one understood'

PAGE 90, l. 16. *Bitterns do Carol through a Reed.* Compare Sir Thomas Browne, 'Of the noyse of a Bitterne by putting the bill in a Reed'. 'That a Bittor maketh a mugient noyse, or as we terme it Bumping by putting its bill into a reed as most beleeve, or as Bellonius and Aldrovand conceive, by putting the same in water or mud, and after a while retaining the ayre by suddenly excluding it againe, is not so easily made out. For my own part though after diligent enquiry, I could never behold them in this motion; . . .' (*Pseudodoxia Epidemica*, 1646, iii. 25, p. 173.)

PAGE 91, l. 1. *Consort.* Any body of musicians or singers was known as a 'consort'.

l. 17. *Love-bang.* One who loves 'bangs', and so one who is fond of noise, noisy.

ll. 18–19. *for freage of Mate*
With edge of steele the square wood shapes.

The meaning is that Kate is making a skewer to hold the meat when she scrapes or minces it, 'freage' being another way of spelling 'fridge', and 'mate' a recognized form of 'meat'.

l. 20. *Dido.* Compare Beaumont and Fletcher:

Petill. In love, indeed in love, most lamentably loving, to the tune of Queen *Dido.*

Benduca, I. ii, fo., 1647, iv, p. 51;

and

Fra. These are your eyes;
Where were they *Clora*, when you fell in love
With the old foot-man, for singing of Queen *Dido*?

The Captain, III. iii, fo., 1647, ii, p. 58.

 In

In Thomas Deloney's *Strange Histories*, 1602, 'The Dutchesse of *Suffolkes* Calamitie' has 'the tune of Queene Dido' given as an alternative for the music printed. (*Deloney*, ed. F. O. Mann, 1911, p. 389.) Percy printed a version of the old ballad in his *Reliques*, 1765, vol. iii, pp. 192–7, collated with two different printed copies, both in black letter in the Pepys collection. He gives the ballad the title of 'The Wandering Prince of Troy'. There is another ballad, 'Aeneas and Dido', in the Percy Folio which was reprinted by D'Urfey in *Pills to Purge Melancholy*, 1719–20, vi, pp. 192–3, though the tune given by D'Urfey is different from that in '*The Ayres that were sung and played at Brougham Castle* . . . 1618'. (See Hales and Furnivall's reprint, vol. iii, p. 260.)

PAGE 92, ll. 7–8.

Like the thin throat of PHILOMEL,
And the smart Lute who should excell.

The story told in Strada's *Prolusiones* of

The sweetest and most ravishing contention
That art or nature ever were at strife in,

has been used by Ford in *The Lovers Melancholy*, Act I, sc. i, Crashaw in *Musick's Duel*, Francis Wortley, Strode, Ambrose Phillips, and others. Herrick refers to it in 'Oberons *Feast*':

The broke-heart of a Nightingale
Ore-come in musicke; *Hesperides*, 1648, p. 137.

l. 11. *Yet can I Musick too.* Cf. l. 30. *N.E.D.* quotes no instance of 'music' as a verb earlier than the eighteenth century (1788).

PAGE 93, l. 11. *With counter-wrought and Travers Eyes.* The sense is difficult owing to Lovelace's imperfect mastery of his technical terms. He means that he will attack his mistress with his eyes both directly and by zigzags, as though attacking a town. 'Peals' is used in the sense of 'volleys'. As both 'counter-wrought' and 'Travers' are adjectives which must be taken with 'Eyes', the hyphen between the last two words has been deleted in the text.

l. 16.

l. 16. *pray't.* *Lucasta* reads 'pray'd', a reading which Hazlitt thought unintelligible and absurd and altered to 'pread' = pillage. This makes nonsense of the two previous lines; the simpler alteration adopted in the text is intelligible and more probably correct.

PAGE 96, l. 1. *brave Tamyris.* Presumably Tomyris, Queen of the Massagetae, the story of whom Herodotus tells (Bk. I, 505–14).

l. 3. *Finding she could not looke, she strook him dead.* Compare:

Qu. . . .
Whose Majesty can look a subject dead.
Clo. How? look me dead? I do not fear his frowns.
Hemings, *The Fatal Contract*, 1653, Sig. D 3.

La Bella Bona Roba. These lines were printed without a title in *Lucasta*, 1649. The preceding poem, 'Tell me, ye subtill Judges', was headed *La Bella Bona Roba. To my Lady H. Ode*, the title 'Bona Roba' being quite inappropriate to the lines which follow. It was possibly intended at first to print the poems in reverse order, but, however that may be, there can be little doubt that the *Ode* was given the titles of both and that the second, to which the title is quite appropriate, should be *La Bella Bona Roba*, the word being a common expression for a harlot.

l. 5. *Marmoset.* Compare:

Stult. . . . I am so: am I not sweet *Monkie*?
Monk. Thou art my deare Baboon.
Stult. Very pretty names in faith: I prethee let's enterchange them still betwixt us: or Marmoset, or Apes face. *The Knave in Graine*, 1640, Sig. I 3.

l. 15. *After his 'Say, nought but his Keepers Fees.* 'First where he appointeth the Deares foote to bee cut off, and to bee presented to the King or chiefe, our order is, that the Prince or chiefe (if so please them) do alight and take assaye of the Deare with a sharp knife, the which is done in this maner. The deare being layd upon his backe, ye Prince, chiefe, or such as they shall appoint, comes

comes to it. And ye chiefe huntsman (kneeling, if it be to a Prince) doth hold the Deare by the forefoote, whiles the Prince or chief, cut a slit drawn alõgst the brysket of the deare, somewhat lower than the brysket towards the belly. This is done to see the goodnesse of the flesh, & howe thicke it is.' (Turbervile, *The Noble Arte of Venerie or Hunting*, ed. 1611, pp. 132–4.)

The 'Keepers Fees' are explained in *Philaster*, IV. ii, and in the following passage from the character of 'A Keeper' in Wye Saltonstall's *Picturae Loquentes*, 1631, Sig. F. 4: 'Hee wishes all Noble men were Nimrods, mighty hunters; for besides their liberality, the bounty of beasts gives him the shoulder and the Humbles for his fee.'

l. 18. *Rascall Deare.* Compare:

Dol. You muddy rascal, is that all the comfort you give me?

Fal. You make fat rascals, Mrs. *Dol.*

2 Henry IV, Act II, sc. viii;

on which Dr. Johnson comments: '*Falstaff* alludes to a phrase of the forest; *lean* deer are called *rascal* deer. He tells her she calls him wrong, being *fat* he cannot be a *rascal*.'

PAGE 99. *To Ellinda.* This song was set to music by Henry Lawes. See note to p. 32.

PAGE 100, l. 2. *Vizard of a feavor.* In the guise of fever.

PAGE 101. *Amyntor from beyond the Sea to Alexis.* See note to p. 71. Whether these lines were addressed to Porter in 1648 or not, it is clear that they were written long after 1642. (See VIII.) The suggestion that Lovelace should revisit the Low Countries, 'Your watry Land', and bring with him 'Lucasta that bright Northerne star' provides further evidence, if any is needed, that there is no truth in Wood's story of Lucasta's marriage.

PAGE 103, l. 16. *In silver Chaines and silken Clue.* Compare p. 142, ll. 15–16 and note. The 'Clue' is the thread of silk held by the person carrying the hawk.

PAGE 104,

PAGE 104, l. 1. *The swelling Admirall of the dread Cold Deepe.*

Possibly John, second Baron Lovelace of Hurley, to whose wife this poem is addressed, was at one time a sailor or connected with the sea. His father certainly was, but it would seem unlikely, though not impossible, that the reference is to him. Anne Lovelace was eleven years old at the time of his death.

l. 11. *Her Captive (Foole) outgazes him.* It is useless to seek shelter in the chariot of the sun, as even the lady's captive falcon, 'Eagle-ey'd of Eagle kind', can outgaze the sun.

l. 20. *Nobler is the Shee.* The 'Nobler is the Shee' in 'Falcon's Monarchy' because the tercel is the smaller bird.

PAGE 107. *Aramantha.* It would seem at first sight as though this was a misprint for 'Amarantha', but, as the spelling is repeated six times in the course of the poem, on the title-page, and again in the Table of the Contents, it is probably correct.

Aramantha. A Pastorall. Wood says that a 'musical Composition of two parts was set to part' of this pastoral by Henry Lawes. It does not seem to be in existence today. Hazlitt stated with an air of authority that this was a mistake, and seems to suggest that Wood confused *Aramantha* with *To Amarantha, That she would dishevell her haire.* This is hardly convincing, as the latter poem was not set for two voices, and Wood certainly speaks as though he knew the setting.

PAGE 108, l. 2. *Mercury.* Mercury water was a special wash for the skin.

l. 31. *Heliotropian.* The name Heliotrope was given to the Sunflower, Marigold, or any other flower which follows the sun. They were also known as Solsequium or Turnesol from the same habit.

PAGE 109, l. 6. *poore Girle.* The violet.

l. 7. *The July-flow'r.* The Clove pink (*Dianthus caryophyllus*), Chaucer's 'cowe-gilowfre', Drayton's 'Cloves of of Paradise', was prized second only to the rose in the sixteenth and seventeenth centuries.

PAGE 110, l. 31. *writheld.* Wrinkled.

l. 34. *Her breath.* i. e. Lucasta's breath.

PAGE 113, l. 33. *But as she heard* Lucasta. Thus far she has passed under the name of Aramantha.

l. 34. *Posses her round.* It was pointed out in the *North American Review* for July, 1864, that 'posses' is another form of the word push, nearer the French 'pousser', from the Latin 'pulsare'.

PAGE 116, l. 13. *stripping.* Moving or passing swiftly.

l. 23. *Alexis.* Although such names were common property and in general use, it is possible that the combination of Aramantha and Alexis was suggested to Lovelace by *L'Amaranthe de Gombavld. Pastorale.* 1631.

PAGE 117, ll. 3–4, &c.

How chac'd by Hydraphil, and tract,
The num'rous foe to Philanact.

These lines seem to contain a direct reference to the Civil Wars. Philanact must stand for 'Cavalier', and 'Hydraphil'—the lover of the many-headed beast, the multitude, the 'num'rous foe' to the Cavalier—for the 'Puritan' or 'Parliamentarian'. The 'Bards Decrees, and Druids rite' are Law, supposed to be given by the bards, and Religion, their championship of which was constantly and confidently asserted by both parties. The meaning of 'Caelia', a few lines below, is more obscure. Possibly she is the 'Heavenly', the Anglican Church. Spenser uses the word in the same sense:

Dame *Caelia* men did her call, as thought
From heauen to come,

F. Q. I. x. iv. 1.

NOTES

NOTES

1659–1660

TITLE-PAGE. *Lucasta. Posthume Poems of Richard Lovelace Esq.* The book is entered on the Stationers' Registers under November 14, 1659.

[Page 157.]

Clement Derby	Entred . . . under the hand of Master THRALE warden a booke called *Lucasta Posthume Poems*, by Richard Lovelace, Esqr. . . . vj[d]

A Transcript of the Registers, 1913, vol. ii, p. 241.

It was not published till the following year, when it was issued with the *Elegies Sacred to the Memory of the Author: 1660.*

In the Bodleian Library and the Library of Trinity College, Cambridge, are preserved presentation copies from the editor which contain some MS. corrections of misprints in his handwriting. The former bears an inscription, 'For the Worthiest of Freindes Mrs. Elizabeth Hales From the Vnworthiest of Seruantes Dudley Posthumus-Louelace', the lady's name being inserted in a different handwriting, no doubt her own.

The Trinity College copy has the inscription, 'For the Worthy of all Honour HENRY NEWTON Esq. From the unworthiest of Seruants Dudley Posth. Louelace'. Newton presented this copy to Trinity.

The Britwell Court copy, bought by Messrs. Quaritch in 1924, has the inscription, 'For the worthiest of Freinds S[r] EDMVND BOWYER From y[e] unworthiest of his servants Dudley Posthumus-

Posthumus-Louelace'. Hunter quotes this note in *Chorus Vatum*, and states that the copy had been in the possession of Mr. George Hibbert. This copy also has corrections of misprints by the editor, as have the copies in the possession of Mr. John Drinkwater and Mr. H. T. Butler.

These Honours . . .

Ad Faustinum.

Ede tuos tandem populo, Faustine, libellos,
Et cultum docto pectore profer opus:
Quod nec Cecropiae damnent Pandionis arces,
Nec sileant nostri, praetereántque senes.
Ante fores stantem dubitas admittere famam,
Téque piget curae praemia ferre tuae?
Post te victurae, per te quoque viuere chartae
Incipiant: cineri gloria sera venit.

The epigram is numbered 25 in some editions but 26 in others, such as that printed at Venice in 1521 or the folio edition printed at Paris in 1617.

William Godbid, printer in London; Over against the Anchor Inn in Little Britain, 1656–77. He printed Gamble's *Ayres and Dialogues*, 1657 and 1659, Henry Lawes's *Ayres and Dialogues*, 1658, and *Treasury of Music*, 1669, and Hilton's *Catch that Catch can*, 1658, 1667, and 1669. He also printed Sir Aston Cokain's *Plays and Poems*, 1658. 'In the survey of the press made in July, 1668, he was returned as having three presses, five workmen, and two apprentices.' (Plomer, *A Dictionary of the Booksellers and Printers*, 1907, p. 83.)

Clement Darby is only known from the imprint to this volume. His address has not been found. *Ibid.*, p. 61.

PAGE 121. *John Lovelace* was the eldest son of John, second Baron Lovelace of Hurley, and of his wife Anne, to whom *Lucasta*, 1649, was dedicated. His grandfather Sir Richard Lovelace was elevated to the peerage in 1627. He

He played an important part in bringing over the Prince of Orange in 1688. From 1680 onwards he was notorious as a violent and somewhat disreputable Whig. He died in 1693 after wasting his estates in gambling and betting.

'*May* 11. [1712]. The late lord Lovelace was a man of good natural parts, but of very ill and very loose principles. Dr. Brabourn principal of New Inn Hall, says, that tho' he knew and was acquainted with him 12 years or more, yet he never knew him sober but twelve hours, and that he used to drink every morning a quart of brandy, or something equivalent to it, to his own share.' (*Reliquiae Hearnianae*, ed. Bliss, 1857, i, p. 251.) There is a portrait of him in his old college, Wadham, and another at Dulwich. At the time this Dedication was written he was 20 or 21.

PAGE 122, ll. 7–8. An allusion to a picture so painted that it showed an angel or devil according to the angle from which it was approached. Compare Cleveland's *The Rebell Scot*:

> As in a picture, where the squinting paint
> Shewes Fiend on this side, and on that side Saint.
>
> ed. 1647, p. 37.

PAGE 124. *N'entendez vous pas ce language.* I have not been able to find this song. The line is probably from the chorus or refrain of some popular contemporary poem.

PAGE 125, l. 7. 'But (when you were) deaf.'

PAGE 126. *Night.* A line has dropped out of the second stanza, between lines 2 and 3.

PAGE 128, l. 21. Compare p. 96, l. 3. In = into.

PAGE 130, l. 11. *Jessamine.* Compare Jordan's 'A Defence for women' (*Wit in a Wildernesse Of Promiscuous Poesie.* Sig. † 3):

> And though he want bread (a sad story to utter)
> His hair hath a breakfast of Gesemin butter.

PAGE 131, l. 9. Compare Baron's *Upon a Black patch on Eliza's cheek*:

At

At distance, like a *Cloud* it showes
I' th' Skie when Morn doth first disclose,
Or like a *Fly* upon a *Rose*.

Pocula Castalia, 1650, p. 87.

PAGE 132, l. 1. *Sent'nel Stars.* Campbell's line 'And the sentinel stars set their watch in the sky' (*Soldier's Dream*) is probably a reminiscence of Lovelace, and it was possibly to Campbell that Keats owed

. . . The legend cheers
Yon centinel stars.

Endymion, Bk. II. 841–2.

l. 16. *I' th' Autumn of a Summers day.* Compare I. M.'s poem 'In the non-age of a Winter's day' (Lawes's *Second Book of Ayres, and Dialogues*, 1655).

l. 19. *this Almond blanch'd.* The word is used of whitening almonds by skinning them. Compare:

. . . to blanch your bread from chippings base,
And in a moment, as thou would'st an Almond,

The Elder Brother, II. iii. 1637, Sig. D 3.

PAGE 133, l. 22. *Blains of Inde.* Sores or blisters. The word survives in chilblains.

PAGE 134, l. 13. *thou great good Husband.*

Hard. O y'are a great good husband.

Brome, *The New Academy, Or, the New Exchange*, 1658, p. 100.

l. 22. *So Cato sometimes the nak'd Florals saw.* Cato did not see the 'nak'd Florals'. Valerius Maximus says that the respect in which he was held was so great that the people forbore to demand 'ut Mimae nudarentur' till he, rather than prevent a popular custom, left the theatre.

PAGE 135, l. 2. *fields of Fueillemort.* Of a faded colour. Compare: '. . . yester day I wore fuille-mote; greedeline; and Isabella; fuille-mote is withered, greedeline is absent, and Isabella is beauty: . . . your fuille-mote is a withered leafe; . . .' (Duke of Newcastle, *The Country Captaine*, 1649, p. 28.)

l. 15.

l. 15. *Madam, Margaret Pie.* Compare Chapman and Shirley:

> *Fre.* I do ly
> At the signe of *Dona Margaretta de Pia*
> In the Strand.
> *Gud.* At the Magget a Pie in the Strand sir.
> *The Ball*, 1639, Sig. A 4 verso.

ll. 15–16. The commas after *Madam* and *Meagre* are here equivalent to a dash. Compare:

> Svb. (*read* Svr.) What call you her, brother?
> Jonson, *The Alchemist*, II. iii (Folio, 1616, p. 629).
> P. Simpson, *Shakespearian Punctuation*, 1911, p. 31.

PAGE 136, l. 31. *Cubbs of India.* Compare Stephens: 'And aboue all, most admirable is natures ingenuity, that forraine creature, called by the name of *Su*; touching which (being persecuted) shuts vp her Cubbes in a depending scrip. and so protects them from the Huntsman.' (*Satyrical Essayes*, 1615, p. 90.) Topsel, however (1607, p. 660), makes the Su carry its young on its back. The name given it by the Pantagones, inhabitants of a region in the south of the new-found world called Gigantes, 'signifieth water': The Semivulpa or Apish Fox of the 'Country of *Payran*' carries its young in a 'skinne like a bagge or scrip' (*ibid.*, p. 19).

PAGE 137, l. 11. *As Warlike Scythians travayl'd.* See Herodotus iv. 1–142. In iv. 45 he refers to the Scythians as '*φερέοικοι*', an epithet which Hesiod uses of the snail, 'Αλλ' ὁπότ' ἂν φερέοικος ἀπὸ χθονὸς ἂμ φυτὰ βαίνῃ (l. 569).

l. 33. *Like a shot Star.* See note to p. 44, ll. 19–20.

PAGE 138, l. 1. *The Centaur, Syren.* Eldred Revett has lines on *The Centaur* and *The Syren.* (*Poems*, 1657, pp. 1 and 70.)

l. 3. *mixed Sphynx.* 'Mixed' because the Sphynx was supposed to have the head of a man or woman, the body of a lion, and the wings of a bird.

l. 4. *the renown'd Hermaphrodite.* The story of Salmacis and Hermaphroditus is told by Ovid in the *Metamorphoses.*

Metamorphoses. Cleveland wrote two poems, *Upon an Hermaphrodite* and *The Authors Hermaphrodite, made after M. Randolphs death, yet inserted into his Poems*, both printed in 1647. They were included with *Salmacis & Hermaphroditus: or The Hermaphrodite* in *Poems: by Francis Beaumont, Gent. 1653.* Sherburne's *Salmacis* was printed in 1651.

ll. 13–14.

That like the fam'd Ship of Trevere,
Did on the Shore himself Lavere.

Trevere is probably Vere on the island of Walcheren, north of Flushing. According to Howell the town had an important trade with Scotland during the seventeenth century.

'Other Towns are passably rich, and stor'd with shipping, but not one very poore, which proceeds from the wholsome policy they use, to assign every Town som firm Staple commodity, . . . to *Trevere* (the Prince of *Orenge* his Town) the *Scots* trade, . . .' (*Familiar Letters*, 1645, ii, pp. 30–1.)

It is possible, but not likely, that the reference is to Treves—Augusta Treviorum, 'Trevirs' as Coryate spells it—and that this 'fam'd Ship' was among the wonders preserved there. Trevere, however, was probably the name under which Lovelace knew Vere and he may have been there. The spelling is not unusual. A ship of Treveer is mentioned in the *Calendar of State Papers* (Domestic Series) under the date August 16, 1655. The ship to which Lovelace refers, however, sailed on land, 'lavere' meaning to tack. So Suckling writes in *The Goblins* (1646, p. 39):

With as much ease as a Skippar,
Would laver against the wind.

Land boats were not unknown in Holland. 'The force of wind in the motion of sails may be applied also to the driving of a Chariot, by which a man may sail on the land as well as by a ship on the water. . . : That such

Chariots

Chariots are commonly used in the Champion plains of *China*, is frequently affirmed by divers credible Authors. [Compare *Paradise Lost*, iii. 438–90.] *Boterus* mentions that they have been tried also in *Spaine*, though with what success he doth not specifie. But above al other experimẽts to this purpose, that sailing Chariot at Sceveling in Holland, is more eminently remarkable. It was made by the direction of *Stephinus*, & is celebrated by many Authors.' (*Mathematicall Magick.* By I. W.[ilkins], 1648, pp. 154–5.)

Wilkins, who gives an illustration of this land boat, says it was so swift 'that in some few howers space it would convey 6 or 10 persons, 20 or 30 German miles.'

Simon Stevinus, the inventor (1548–1620), was Quartermaster-General to Maurice of Orange. Of all his inventions this interested his contemporaries most, and later Uncle Toby, who of course possessed Stevinus' book on Fortifications, knew all about it: 'Because, continued my uncle Toby, the celebrated sailing chariot, which belonged to Prince Maurice, and was of such wonderful contrivance and velocity, as to carry half a dozen people thirty *German* miles, in I dont know how few minutes, —was invented by *Stevinus*, that great mathematician and engineer.' James Howell also saw this boat at The Hague, and on April 10, 1633, sent an account of it to Sir John Smith. Another account of this sailing coach, which 'would fly upon the shore, as a ship upon the Sea', is given by Wanley in his *Wonders of the Little World*, 1678, p. 223.

It does not anywhere appear that this land boat sailed at Trevere, and Lovelace speaks of the boat as tacking 'himself'. If this is to be taken literally, the identification with the sailing chariot of Stevinus is wrong. Lovelace may have mistaken the place, however, and the fact that Trevere was 'the Prince of Orange's Town' and that the boat belonged to him might conceivably account for this discrepancy. The difficulty of the ship sailing itself

itself remains and, for the purposes of Lovelace's comparison, the ship, like the snail, should be 'Pilot both and Barque'.

Perhaps the reference is to one of those models under sail which, mounted on wheels, were drawn in the naval and nautical pageants of which the Dutch were so fond in the seventeenth century. It may, again, have been a ship of fireworks like that 'cunning peece . . . framed in forme like to the Arke of Noye, being 24 yardes high, and eight yardes broad', which Webbe made for the Turks in 1583 (*His Trauailes*, 1590, Sig. c 4), or the three ships devised by John Tindale, Gunner, of which John Taylor, the Water Poet, gives an account. (*Workes*, 1630, iii, p. 120.)

But in spite of the difficulty of accepting the identification in the face of Lovelace's wording, if the great contemporary reputation of Stevinus' invention is considered, and Lovelace cannot but have heard of it, it still seems most probable that he had the land boat in mind when he wrote these lines.

l. 17. *Double man.* The snail, when sick, himself takes the duties of the two men who were necessary to carry a Sedan chair and lifts his own.

l. 19. 'Luyck & Liege, Leodium & Leodicum, urbs Germaniae.' (Baudrand, *Geographia*, 1681, vol. ii, p. 581.)

'The Bishoprick of *Liege*, or *Luyck*, is a Part of the Circle of *Westphalia*.' (*The Great Historical, Geographical & Poetical Dictionary*, 1694.)

l. 20. *Huyck.* Modern *huke.* 'A huke is a womans gown or habit (Huke, pulla, toga, pallium Belgicis feminis usitatum. *Skin.*) Skelton mentions it in his *Elinour Rumming*:

"Her *huke* of Lyncole grene."

"All women in generall," says Moryson, speaking of the Netherlands, "when they goe out of the house, put on a hoyke or vaile, which covers their heads, and hangs downe vpon their backs to the legges, &c." (*Itinerary*, 1617, part 3, p. 169.)' *Robin Hood*: Ritson, ed. 1823, pp. cxvii–cxviii.

The first quotation is from Skinner's *Etymologicon*

Linguae

Linguae Anglicanae, 1671. Compare also: 'The women have great covertures over their heads, coming from their shoulders, as the Hoyks in *Flanders*.' (*A . . . Relation Of what passed for many Years Between Dr. John Dee . . . and Some Spirits*, 1659, p. 155.)

PAGE 139. *Courante Monsieur.* 'Courante. Sorte de Danse ainsi nommée à cause des allées & des venues dont elle est remplie plus qu'aucune autre; . . . cette danse est très grave, & inspire un air de noblesse.' (Campan, *Dictionnaire de Danse*, 1787, p. 109.) There were various dances of this name; Marsenne, in *Harmonie Universelle*, mentions one 'à la reyne'. This, no doubt, was in honour of 'Monsieur'. 'La Courante', says Marsenne, 'est la plus frequente de toutes les danses pratiquées en France, & se dance seulement par deux personnes à la fois, . . .' Compare: 'He may marry a Knights daughter, a creature out of fashion, that has not one commendable quality, more than to make a corner pye and a sallad, no manner of courtship, but two or three dances, as old as *Monsieur*, and can play a few Lessons on the Virginalls that she learnt of her Grandam: . . .' (Shackerley Marmion, *A Fine Companion*, 1633, IV. i, Sig. G 2.) This play itself gave a name to a dance, a 'Round for eight'. See Playford's *The Dancing Master*, ed. 1652, p. 26.

l. 8. *meant me.* Compare Middleton's *The Changeling*, 1653, Sig. B 2: 'This was the man was meant me', or Herbert's 'The Church-Porch':

who aimeth at the sky,
Shoots higher much, than he that means a tree.
The Temple, ed. 1678, p. 12.

PAGE 140, l. 1. *crowned Venice.* Venetian glass was highly prized in the sixteenth and seventeenth centuries. Compare Holinshed's *Chronicles*, 1586, i, pp. 166–7.

PAGE 141. *The Falcon.* Turbervile, in his *Book of Falconrie*, gives seven kinds of falcons: the Falcon gentle—Chaucer's 'The gentyl faucon, that with his feet distreyneth, The kingis hond'—which, 'for her nobleness and hardy courage, & withal the francknes of her mettell', he places in chief; the Haggart Falcon, the Barberie or Tartaret Falcon, the Gerfalcon, the Sacre, the Laner, and the Tunician.

PAGE 142, l. 16. *Vervails* or varvels were the rings round the hawks' feet on which the owner's name was usually inscribed. In *Occurrences from Foreign Parts*, 1659/60, no. 52, p. 564, there is an advertisement for a lost goshawk, 'it is written in the Verviles the name of *William* Lord *Peters* of *Thorndon*, . . .'

PAGE 143, l. 9. *The Heron.* 'A flight at the hearon . . . the most noblest and stately flight that is, and pleasant to behold.' (Turbervile, *Book of Falconrie*, ed. 1611, p. 160.)

l. 11. *hut.* Hide.

l. 14. *The Dogs.* 'How necessary a thing a Spaniell is to Falconrie, & for those that use that pastime, keeping hawks for their pleasure and recreation, I deem no man doubteth as wel to spring and retriue fowle being flowen to the marke, as also diuers other wayes to assist and ayde Falcons and Goshawkes.' (*The Booke of Falconrie*, ed. 1611, pp. 362–3.) Compare also Heywood's *A Woman killed with Kindness*, I. i and iii. The 'spaniell', or, as it was generally called, the land-spaniel, was a setter.

l. 15. *And now he takes the open air.* 'When your Hawke will kill a traine lustily, and boldly, then may you goe into the field to finde a wilde Hearon at siege, and when you haue found her, win in as nie to her as you can, and goe with your Hawke under the wind, where hauing first loosed her hoode in a readinesse, as soone as the Hearon leaueth the siege, off with her hoode, and let her flee: and if she climb to the Hearon, and beat her so that shee bring her down, runne in apace to rescue her, thrusting the Hearon's bill into the ground, and breaking her wings and legges (as is aforesaide) feede her and reward

reward her upon your hawking gloue, in manner before declared.' (Turbervile, *op. cit.*, p. 164.)

PAGE 144, ll. 21–2. Compare: 'The Custom of the Hearn when she sees the Hawk, stooping at her, and no way of escape, is to turn her Long Bill upwards, upon which the Hawk not being able to stop, runs itself through, and so both often drop down dead together.' (Wesley, *Maggots*, 1685, p. 10.)

A heron will not often kill a falcon in the air in this way, but there is a danger of his doing so when on the ground. Compare Turbervile's instructions quoted above and his description of the hawk's training: 'You must get a liue Hearon, upon the upper part of whose bill or truncke you must conuey the ioynt of a reede or Cane, so as she may not hurt the hawke therewith.'

l. 27. *her own Bells.* The bells fastened to the rings round the falcon's feet. 'As the Oxe hath his bow sir, the horse his curb, and the Falcon her bels, so man hath his desires, . . .' (*As You Like It*, III. iii.)

PAGE 145, ll. 7–11. *Hobby*, *Musket*, *Lanner*, *Goshawk*. The Hobby was 'a Hawke of the lure, and not of the fist : . . . They will lie upon their wings reasonablie wel, following men and Spaniels, fleeing upon them many times, to the end that when any Partridge or Quaile is sprung, they may the better stoupe from their wings, and so seaze on the fowle, which sundry times they doe.' These small hawks were also 'used of such as go with nets', when the larks and other small birds seeing them 'dare in no wise commit themselues to their wings, but do lie as close and flat on the ground as they possible may do, & so are taken in the nets, which with us in England is called *Daring*, a sport of all other most proper to the Hobbie'. See note below to p. 175, l. 31.

The Musket was a small sparrow-hawk which was taken out hooded and flown at partridges and larks. 'All these kind of hawks have their male birds and cocks, as the sparrow-hawk his musket.'

'The Laner is a Hawke common in all Countries, specially in France', and was noted for its power of maintaining long flights. 'With this Hawke may you flye the riuer, as well with the Laner as the Laneret, for they are both good, and likewise may you use them to other kinds of flights, and specially to the field to kill the Partridge, the Fesant, the Hare, the Choffe, the Dawe, and all such sort of lesser fowle.'

The Goshawk was a large, powerful hawk, which, 'manned and cunning', was flown at wild geese, cranes, duck, hares, and rabbits.

The 'tercel' or 'tiercel' was the male of the goshawk.

l. 12. '*new bows'd*'. The word 'bows'd', as used in the terms of falconry, signified to drink.

PAGE 146, l. 3. *direct Hebrew.* The idea that Hebrew was the original language was supported by Genesis xi. 1: 'And the whole earth was of one language, and of one speech.'

PAGE 148, l. 17. *Dishevell'd Queens. Lucasta. Posthume Poems* reads 'Queen'. The *s* has been added by Dudley Lovelace in the copies now in the Bodleian and the Library of Trinity College, Cambridge.

PAGE 149, ll. 1–2.

> *But since to Ladies 't hath a Custome been*
> *Linnen to send.*

Compare: '. . . if you want clouts, al I'le promise, is to rip vp an old shirt or two;' (Ford, *Love's Sacrifice*, 1633, Sig. G 1;)

> Gentlemen and Lady's, I am sent to you,
> Not to beg cast by sheets, a shirt or two,
> Or clouts for th' teeming women, . . .

Epilogue to *The London Chaunticleres*, 1659; and Middleton, *The Witch*, II. i. 121–2.

l. 9. *mine one Monument.* 'One' was a recognized spelling of 'own'. Compare Jonson's change of 'his owne shirt' to 'his one shirt' in *Euery Man in his Humour*,

III.

III. vi. 52 (ed. P. Simpson, 1919, pp. xvii and 66), where a quibble is possibly intended.

PAGE 150, l. 14. *the Princes Arms in Light.* Strutt, in his *Sports and Pastimes* (ed. 1845, pp. 373–5), was not aware of any reference to an illuminated device so early as this. Such a thing seems to have been unknown to John Bate, whose description of 'Fire-works for Tryumph and Recreation' was published in 1634.

l. 18. Cassiope,

that starred Etiop queen that strove
To set her beauty's praise above
The Sea Nymphs,

was the wife of Cepheus, king of the Ethiopians, and the mother of Andromeda. Lovelace refers to her after her translation into the constellation Cassiopœia.

PAGE 151, l. 3. *Castara* was published anonymously in 1634 in two parts, with the characters of and poems to a Mistress and a Wife. The second edition, with the addition of eight elegies to 'my best friend and Kinsman, George Talbot, Esquire', was published in the following year. The full edition appeared in 1640, the character of *A Holy Man* and some sacred poems which constitute the third part being added. Castara was Lucy Herbert, younger daughter of William Herbert, first Lord Powys, whom Habington married in 1630.

l. 4. *Saccarisa.* See note to p. 5, l. 11.

l. 12. 'Aurum fulminans (= Fulminate of gold), an explosive precipitate obtained by adding ammonia to a solution of auric chloride.' *N.E.D.* Compare Garth's *The Dispensary*, 1699, p. 41:

Some *Aurum Fulminans* the Fabrick shook.

ll. 19–20.

When a fat mist we view, we coughing run;
But that once Meteor drawn, all cry, undone.

Lovelace's meaning is that we take little notice of anything near the ground like a mist; we merely cough and get out of it as soon as possible. But should the mist be drawn

drawn up into the air and become a meteor, every one regards it as a portent and cries out that he is undone. Compare: '. . . whereof there needs no other proofe but the Meteors, which being bred of nothing else but of the vapors and exhalations sucked vp by the Sun out of the earth, the sea, and waters, yet are the same smoakie vapors turned and transformed into raines, snowes, deawes, hoare frosts, and such like waterie Meteors, as by the contrary the rainie clouds are often transformed and euaporated in blustering windes.' (King James, 'A counterblaste to Tobacco', *Workes*, 1616, p. 217.)

l. 21. *How bright the fair Paulina did appear,*
When hid in Jewels she did seem a Star.

The wife of Gaius. For her life see *Prosop. Imp. Rom.* 1897, II, p. 297. Pliny gives the following account of her extravagance: 'Lolliam Paulinam, quae fuit Caii principis matrona, ne serio quidem, aut solemni caerimoniarum aliquo apparatu, sed mediocrium etiam sponsalium coena, vidi smaragdis margaritisque opertam, alterno textu fulgentibus, toto capite, crinibus, spira, auribus, collo, monilibus, digitisque: quae summa quadringenties H. S. colligebat: ipsa confestim parata mancupationem tabulis probare.' (*Historia Naturalis*, ix. 58.)

PAGE 152, l. 22. *falsify.* A feint.

PAGE 153, l. 1. *quarrel.* For the use of the word in the transitive compare King:

If any quarrel your attempt or style,
Poems, 1657, p. 123.

PAGE 154, l. 19. *Tarquin.* Charles II was frequently so called, e. g. in all the early numbers of *Mercurius Politicus*, 1650:

'She [the Queen of Sweden] hath been lately sick, but now recovered; and our *Cavaliers* would make us believe, it was for the love of yong *Tarquin*; . . .' (no. 1, p. 12).

'They say, *Yong Tarquin* is Landed among his *gude People*, . . .' (no. 4, p. 49).

'One

'One *Rout* or *Retreat* makes *Tarquin* not worth a Pamphlet; . . .' (no. 6, p. 81).

PAGE 155, l. 3. See note to p. 44, l. 19.

l. 5. In February, 1648/9, after the execution of the King, the Royal Arms were ordered to be taken down throughout the land.

l. 7. The House of Lords was abolished in 1649, so the Commons was the only house left.

l. 10. *their Spent-gorge.* The phrase would seem to be a quibble on the 'full-gorge' of feeding hawks and may mean 'their cut-throats have emptied themselves', and metaphorically that the knights have been destroyed. It is certainly obscure, but there may be an allusion to 'Pride's Purge' in November, 1648.

PAGE 156, ll. 7–8. See below, note on p. 158, ll. 23–4.

l. 16. *his poyson feed.* 'All Spyders are venemous, but yet some more, and some lesse.' (Topsell, *The Historie of Serpents*, 1608, p. 246.) Compare note to p. 164, l. 10.

ll. 29–30. *As the Rhinoceros doth dy*
Under his Castle-Enemy.

Compare Sylvester's *Du Bartas, His Deuine Weekes and Workes Translated*: The Sixt Daie of the First Week, ed. 1611, p. 145:

But, his huge strength, nor subtle wit, can not
Defend him from the sly *Rhinocerot*: &c.

Topsell gives the same account: 'Elephants are enimies to wilde Bulles, and the Rhinocerots, . . . They fight in the woods for no other cause, but for the meat they liue vpon, . . .'

l. 31. *the Cranes trunk Throat.* For the use of 'trunk' in the sense of 'tube' compare Ben Jonson:

. . . I haue told 'hem in a voice,
Thorough the trunke, like one of your *familiars.*
The Alchemist, fo. 1616, p. 617.

PAGE 157, l. 13. *A Snowball-heart.* There is an allusion to the contemporary method of cooling wine by snow.

PAGE 158,

PAGE 158, ll. 23–4. *the Sun's son*... Phaethon, nearly setting the earth on fire when his father's horses became unmanageable, was killed by Zeus with a flash of lightning and fell into the river Eridanus.

PAGE 159, l. 1. *Auricular.* 'The little finger, as the one most easily inserted in the ear: cf. Fr. *doigt auriculaire.*' *N. E. D.*

Female Glory. These lines are probably based on an Italian sonnet or one by a French follower of Petrarch. Although in his verses addressed to Lely, Lovelace refers to Vasari, of whom there was no English translation in the seventeenth century, it is not certain that he knew Italian, but this was not an unusual accomplishment for a gentleman. I have not been able to find the original.

PAGE 160, l. 7. *Laura.* The use of this name both here and in the last line of the preceding poem suggests the bare possibility that Laura was Lucasta's Christian name.

PAGE 161. *A Mock Charon. Dialogue.* The original of the dialogues with Charon, of which several were written in the seventeenth century, would appear to be French. Compare the *Sonnet* by Olivier de Magny (? d. 1560):

Magny

Hola, Charon, Charon, Nautonnier infernal!

Charon

Qui est cet importun qui si pressé m'appelle.

Oxford Book of French Verse, 1908, p. 106.

Compare also the song in the fourth Act of *The Mad Lover*:

Orph. Charon o Charon
Thou wafter of the soules to blisse or bane
Cha. *Who calls the Fery man of Hell?*

1647, p. 15.

Various Dialogues with Charon were set to music by Henry and William Lawes. Two are printed in the Second Book of John Playford's *Select Musicall Ayres, and Dialogues*, 1652, '*Charon*, O *Charon* draw thy Boat', a song 'Occasioned by the death of the yong Lord Hastings',

Hastings', the words of which are by Herrick and were first printed in *Lachrymae Musarum*, 1649 (see *Herrick*, ed. F. W. Moorman, 1915, p. 416), and 'Charon O gentle Charon', a Dialogue with Philomel, which is also by Herrick. (*Hesperides*, 1648, pp. 292–3). The former was set to music by Henry Lawes and was reprinted in the second part of *The Treasury of Musick*, 1669: the latter was reprinted in 1653, in *Select Ayres and Dialogues*, 1659, which was reissued in 1669 as Part I of *The Treasury of Musick*, and again in 1667 in John Playford's *Catch that Catch can: or The Musical Companion*. The setting was composed by William Lawes. William Lawes also wrote the music for *A Dialogue. Charon and Amintor*, 'Charon, O Charon! Hear a wretch opprest', which is printed in Part II of *The Treasury of Musick*, 1669, and Henry Hall that for *A Dialogue betwixt Oliver Cromwell and Charon*, 'Hast *Charon*, hast', which is printed in the Second Book of *The Theater of Music*, 1685. Another Dialogue between Cromwell and Charon was printed in the political play *Hells Higher Court of Justice*, 1661:

Charon O gentle Charon
O come come bring thy boat to land,

A similar dialogue between Venus and Vulcan, 'Vulcan, Vulcan, O Vulcan, my Love!' was printed by John Playford in 1653. It is reprinted in *Select Ayres and Dialogues*, 1659. There is a dialogue between Phillis and Charon in Matthew Stevenson's *Occasions off-spring*, 1654, p. 45:

Ph. A Boat, a Boat Charon, come set me over.
Ch. Who calls hells fatall ferriman?

Matthew Coppinger's 'Dido *and* Charon' is a similar dialogue:

Did. A Boat, a Boat. *Ch.* Who calls? *Did. Charon*, 'tis I,
Poems, 1682, p. 89.

Compare also Flatman's 'Orpheus *and* Euridice' (*Poems*, ed. 1682, p. 96) and the 'Dialogue between Pluto and Oliver' (*Rump Songs*, 1662, p. 339). In William Hemminge's

Hemminge's 'Elegy on Randolph's Finger' (ed. G. C. Moore Smith, 1923, p. 16), which was written about 1632, the Water Poet makes an Oration to Charon, to which the latter replies, beginning:

Charron Oh Charron, thou from whom we knowe
the Arte of Nauigation, how to row.

Cha. W. Perhaps the W. stands for Philip, fourth Baron Wharton (1613–96), a man described by Clarendon as very fast to the Parliamentary party.

PAGE 162. *The Toad and Spyder.* 'A Toad is of a most cold temperament, and bad constitution of nature, and it useth one certaine herb wherewithal it preserveth the sight, and also resisteth the poyson of Spyders, whereof I have heard this credible History related, from the mouth of a true honourable man, and one of the most charitable Peers of *England*, namely, the good Earl of *Bedford*, and I was requested to set it down for truth, for it may be justified by many now alive that saw the same. It fortuned as the said Earl travailed in *Bedfordshire*, neer unto a Market-town called *Owbourn*, some of his company espyed a Toad fighting with a Spyder, under a hedge in a bottom, by the high-way-side, whereat they stood still, until the Earl their Lord and Master came also to behold the same; and there he saw how the Spyder still kept her standing, and the Toad divers times went back from the Spyder, and did eat a piece of an herb, which to his judgement was like a Plantain. At the last, the Earl having seen the Toad do it so often, and still return to the combate against the Spyder, he commanded one of his men to go, and with his dagger to cut off that herb, which he performed and brought it away. Presently after the Toad returned to seek it, and not finding it according to her expectation, swelled and broke in pieces: for having received poyson from the Spyder in the combate, nature taught her the vertue of that herb, to expel and drive it out, but wanting the herb, the poyson did instantly work and destroy her. And this (as I am informed) was often-

times

times related by the Earl of *Bedford* himself upon sundry occasions, and therefore I am the bolder to insert it into this story.' (Topsell, *History of Serpents*, ed. 1658, p. 729.)

l. 17. *Defies his foe with a fell Spet.* Compare: '. . . we would haue spet at him as a toade, . . .' (Nash, *Pierce Penilesse*, ed. McKerrow, vol. i, p. 205.)

'Spet' is a correct form both for spelling and pronunciation.

l. 21. *Arachne.* See Ovid, *Metamorphoses*, vi. 1–145, and Virgil, *Georgics*, iv. 246.

l. 23. *thine own Mother.* Athena leapt fully armed from the head of Zeus.

l. 24. *thy Brother.* This is wrong. Artemis, not Pallas, was the sister of Apollo.

PAGE 163, l. 7. *Charact.* The carack or càract was a development of the Italian galleon, which was in turn developed from the old round trading ship, the 'vaisseau rond'. A merchant vessel, armed like all merchant ships of the time, rather than a war-ship, the carack attained to a very considerable size in the sixteenth and seventeenth centuries, as may be seen from the long and detailed account in Hakluyt of the Portuguese carack, the *Madre de Dios*, captured by Sir Walter Raleigh's men in 1592. She was 1600 tons burthen, had a draught of 26 feet after being lightened and 31 feet when laden, and had between 600 and 700 souls aboard. *Las Cinque Llagas*, captured the following year, was said by some to have been even larger. (*The Principal Navigations*, ed. J. MacLehose, 1904, vol. vii, p. 116 seq.)

PAGE 164, l. 10. *Her poyson, on his poyson, feeds.* Compare Nash as to the poisonous nature of both toads and spiders and their sucking poison from plants. '*Spyders*, . . . sucke out theyr mallice from very good hearbes.' (*Pasquill and Marforius*, ed. McKerrow, vol. i, p. 93.) 'A toade swels with thicke troubled poison.' (*The Unfortunate Traveller*, vol. ii, p. 266.) '. . . those floures and hearbs, . . . were subiect to the infection of euery

Spider

Spider and venimous Canker, and not a loathsome Toade (how detestable soeuer) but reposde himselfe vnder theyr shadow, and lay sucking at their rootes continually.' (*Pierce Penilesse*, vol. i, p. 225.)

PAGE 165, l. 15. *pickear.* To scout or reconnoitre. Compare Fanshaw's *The Lusiad*, 1655 (i. 86):

But the keen MOORS (pickeering on the Strand ...)

PAGE 166, l. 20. *Periphrasis.* A larger edition or amplification of himself. Cf. Cleveland's 'The Hecatomb to his Mistresse' (*Poems*, 1651, p. 7):

She, she it is, she that contains all blisse,
And make the vvorld but her Periphrasis.

PAGE 167, l. 10. *with each fires.* With each other's fires.

l. 11. *Lar.* Cf. Herrick's 'Larr', *Hesperides*, 1648, p. 148, &c.

l. 12. *Dispatch'd.* 'Dispath'd' 1659. Dudley Lovelace added the *c* in the copy which is now in the Library of Trinity College, Cambridge. He did not make the correction in the Bodleian copy.

l. 20. *First burst himself.* Compare: '... though they swell at him with enuie like a nest of foule Toades, till their bodies splyt, and poure out theyr bowels vppon the earth.' (Nash, *Pasquill and Marforius*, ed. McKerrow, vol. i, p. 103.)

PAGE 169. *The Triumphs of Philamore and Amoret.* This poem was written for the occasion of the marriage of Charles Cotton the poet to his cousin Isabella, daughter of Sir Thomas Hutchinson, of Owthorpe, Notts., in the summer of 1656. The lady died in 1670, and Cotton married again before 1674. He sold the house at Beresford in Staffordshire to Joseph Woodhouse of Wollescote, Derby, in 1681. He was born there in 1630 and died in 1687. As a poet—his collected works were published in 1689—Cotton was admired by both Wordsworth and Coleridge. He is also well known as the friend of Izaak Walton, and author of the second part of *The Compleat Angler*. George Savile, Marquis of Halifax, said of Cotton's translation

translation of Montaigne, which was dedicated to him, that, 'it is the book in the world I am best entertained with'. Cotton has some lines on Lovelace's death. See p. 223.

l. 10. *Canton.* A term used in heraldry for a separate space, smaller than a quarter, on a shield. To canton is to divide off such a space.

It seems certain from these lines that Charles Cotton rendered Lovelace some important service at this time. If the lines may be taken literally, he obtained the poet's release from prison, and this service was possibly the origin of the story of Wyld's carrying money to Lovelace from Cotton which is told by Aubrey and Wood.

l. 11. *Spahy's.* Possibly the hero of a romance.

PAGE 170, l. 4. *anoynts out both his Eyes.* Compare: 'And it is forbidden to all Christians upon paine of death, to come neere Mecha within five miles: . . . after the sight whereof, many of their old men (which thinke never to come thither againe) use to pull out both their eyes, after they have seene so holy a sight.' (*Purchas His Pilgrimes*, ed. MacLehose, 1905, vol. viii, pp. 287–8.)

l. 23. *back-flung.* Hazlitt and the edition in *Hutchinson's Popular Classics* read 'black-flung', so some copies of *Lucasta. Posthume Poems* may have that reading. The Bodleian, the Museum, and other copies I have seen are correct. For the story of Deucalion and Pyrrha see Sandys' *Ovid's Metamorphosis Englished*, 1626, p. 11.

PAGE 171, l. 7. *The twice-born God.* '. . . Dithyrambus seems to have been, in the first instance, the name, not of the hymn, but of the god to whom the hymn is sung; and, through a tangle of curious etymological speculations as to the precise derivation of this name, one thing seems clearly visible, that it commemorates, namely, the double birth of the vine-god; that he is born once and again; his birth, first of fire, and afterwards of dew; the two dangers that beset him; his victory over two enemies, the capricious, excessive heats and colds of spring. He is πυριγενής, then, fire-born, the son of lightning; . . . And his second

second birth is of the dew.' (Walter Pater, 'A Study of Dionysus' in *Greek Studies*, ed. 1911, pp. 25–6.)

l. 19. *Piacle.* A crime.

PAGE 172, l. 3–4. *Herald Fame . . . In an imbroider'd Coat of Eyes and Ears.* As pictured by Virgil, *Aeneid*, IV.

PAGE 174, l. 15. *to free.* See note, p. 22, l. 24.

Coll: Francis Lovelace. See note to p. 2.

l. 23. *handsomely.* 'Unhandsomely' 1659. The word is corrected in various copies by Dudley Lovelace.

l. 26. *Glassy-epithite.* Lovelace seems to have had the first stanza of Horace's Ode (IV. ii) in mind:

Pindarum quisquis studet aemulari,
Iule, ceratis ope Daedalea
Nititur pennis vitreo daturus
Nomina ponto.

PAGE 175, l. 25. The rest of the poem is based on Horace, Book II, Ode x.

l. 31. *Cloaths which Larks would play with.* The allusion is to the falconer's device of 'daring' a lark with a piece of scarlet cloth. To 'dare' was a term used for bewildering and dazzling the bird with a mirror or piece of colour, or terrifying it into immobility with a merlin or other small hawk, so that in the one case it would approach within gunshot and in the other remain on the ground till it could be taken with a net. Compare *Henry VIII*, III. ii. 276–9:

If we liue thus tamely,
To be thus Iaded by a piece of Scarlet,
Farewell Nobilitie: let his Grace go forward,
And dare vs with his Cap, like Larkes.

See also note to p. 145, ll. 7–11 above.

PAGE 176, ll. 11–12.

Sperat infestis, metuit secundis
Alteram sortem bene praeparatum
Pectus.

Horace, II. x.

PAGE 177. *Thomas Stanley* (1625–78), poet, translator, and

and scholar, was a distant cousin of Lovelace. He was famous in his own day as the editor of Aeschylus and as the author of the *History of Philosophy*; Winstanley speaks of him as 'the glory and admiration of his time'. In 1647 he printed privately a volume of *Poems and Translations*, which was reprinted in 1649 and reissued with additions in 1650. His translations from Anacreon, Bion, Moschus, and others were reprinted in 1651, as was his volume of *Poems*. Selections from this volume, which contains more than one echo from Lovelace, were set to music by John Gamble in 1656, and Lovelace wrote some lines for the book (p. 186). As a young man he married Dorothy, daughter and co-heiress of Sir James Enyon, Bart., of Flore or Flower in Northamptonshire, the anniversary of which event Lovelace here records.

l. 6. 'Cherubim' as a plural would seem to have been unknown to both Stanley and Lovelace (compare p. 73, l. 20). Mr. Grierson, in his edition of Donne, shows how that poet, like Shakespeare, uses 'Cherubin' as a singular (1912, ii, p. 195).

PAGE 178, l. 5. The correction of the misprint 'of Night' to 'oh Night' is one of those made by Dudley Lovelace in various copies.

The correction of 'Faith' to 'Faiths' was made by him in the copy now at Trinity College, Cambridge.

PAGE 179. *Mr. R. Caesar*, son of Sir Julius Caesar, the Master of the Rolls, married Lovelace's sister Johanna. The copy of *Lucasta*, 1649, which belonged to his wife and has 'Johana Caesar her book 1649' written over the *Dedication*, is still in existence.

l. 12. *canton'd*. See p. 169, l. 10.

PAGE 180, l. 17 et seq. The half-dozen mythological pictures by Lely which Lovelace here describes are not easy to trace. Very few pictures of this nature by Lely are known, and they probably were some of the painter's earliest work before he came to England; afterwards he was almost exclusively a portrait painter. The picture of 'Love's

'Love's Queen', however, may be the 'naked Venus asleep' at Windsor mentioned by Walpole:

'Few of his historic pieces are known; at Windsor is a Magdalen, and a naked Venus asleep; the duke of Devonshire has one, the story of Jupiter and Europa; Lord Pomfret had that of Cimon and Iphigenia, and at Burleigh is Susanna with the two Elders. In Streater's sale was a Holy Family, a sketch in black and white, which sold for five pounds; and Vertue mentions and commends another, a Bacchanal of four or five naked boys, sitting on a tub, the wine running out; with his mark, P. L. Lens made a mezzotinto from a Judgement of Paris by him; another was of Susanna and the Elders. His designs are not more common; they are in Indian ink, heightened with white. He sometimes painted in crayons, and well; I have his own head by himself: Mr. Methuen has Sir Peter's and his family in oil. They represent a concert in a landscape. A few heads are known by him in water-colours, boldly and strongly painted: they generally have his cypher to them.' (*Anecdotes of Painting in England*, by Horace Walpole, ed. 1862, pp. 31–2.)

There is a drawing of a *Satyr and Nymph* in the British Museum, no 15, under Lely, in the *Catalogue of Drawings by British Artists and Artists of Foreign Origin working in Great Britain*, L. Binyon, vol. iii, p. 54.

Mr. C. H. Collins Baker has informed me that a small picture of a woman seated and a gallant on his knees before her was at Christie's a few years ago, and Mr. C. F. Bell tells me that in 1911 Mr. C. Fairfax Murray presented Lely's *Nymphs at a Fountain* (no. 555) to the Dulwich Gallery.

PAGE 181, l. 11. *Hocus-pocus*. 'Nature', says Lovelace, 'gives us but an illusion of Spring, it is here one moment and gone the next: the painter fixes his Spring on the canvas for ever.' A juggler was known as 'Hocus-pocus'. The derivation of the name is uncertain: '... the fact that *hokuspokusfiliokus* is still used in Norway and Sweden suggests that there may be something in the old theory of

a

a blasphemous perversion of the sacramental blessing, *hoc est corpus (filii)*.' (*An Etymological Dictionary of Modern English*, E. Weekley, 1921.)

l. 25. The 'hair of day' is, of course, a reference to the beams of the rising sun, which later, as the sun grows older, 'shed or change' their colour.

PAGE 182, ll. 15–22. A somewhat similar anecdote to this of Charles V holding the bottom of the ladder while Titian put his last touches to a picture of 'the Scourges of our God and Man', possibly the *Mocking of Christ* in the Louvre to-day, or the picture on the same subject at Munich, is given in a note to Vasari's *Lives of Seventy of the most eminent Painters, Sculptors and Architects* in the edition by E. H. and E. W. Blashfield and A. A. Hopkins, vol. iv, p. 289. The story runs 'that once when Titian who had climbed upon a table that he might see a picture hung high upon the wall, found the picture still too far off, the emperor made several of his gentlemen help him to raise the table upon their shoulders'.

ll. 23–4. Charles V abdicated at Brussels on October 25, 1555, before retiring to Yuste.

ll. 25–30. Lovelace no doubt learnt Dutch during his stay in Holland, and in all probability got this anecdote from Carel Van Mander, whom he mentions below. (*Le Livre des Peintres de Carel van Mander*, Traduction, Notes et Commentaires par Henri Hymans, 1884–5, vol. i, pp. 216–17.)

PAGE 183, l. 13 et seq. Lovelace, who was given the Freedom of the Painters, clearly had a genuine love for and some understanding of painting, an art which he was able to study with advantage in the Low Countries. What is said in these lines of the indifference of the ordinary Englishman to painting, though he liked to admire his own portrait, is borne out by the general lack of interest in continental pictures shown by the writers of seventeenth-century guide-books, e. g. Howell's *Instructions for Forreine Travell*, 1642, pp. 108–9.

l. 19. *Vasari and Vermander.* Giorgio Vasari (1512–74) first published his *Delle Vite De' Più Eccellenti Pittori, Scultori et Architettori* in 1550, and dedicated it to Cosimo de' Medici. The book was afterwards enlarged.

Karel van Mander published in quarto at Haarlem in 1604 *Het Schilder-Boeck waer in voor eerst de leerlustighe Jueght den Grondt der Edel Vry Schilderconst in verscheyden veelen wort voorghedragen.*

The complete second edition appeared in 1618. M. Henri Hymans speaks of the book as 'la plus précieuse des sources pour servir à l'étude de l'École néerlandaise', and he says of the author, 'Peintre et poète très célèbre de son temps, van Mander serait probablement ignoré du nôtre sans le *Livre des Peintres*'.

PAGE 184. *To my Dear Friend Mr. E. R. On his Poems Moral and Divine.* These lines are addressed to Eldred Revett and were included in *Poems, by Eldred Revett . . . 1657.* In this book the lines *To my dear Friend* | Mr. ELDRED REVETT, | On his Poems | *Moral, and Divine*, begin at the top of A 6 verso and are continued on A 7 (both sides). They are followed by lines signed B. H. and Will. Revett. For all information relative to this book, and for collating these lines as well as the elegy on Lovelace by Revett, I am indebted to Mr. G. Thorn-Drury, K.C.

From the two letters written by Revett and quoted in the *Introduction*, letters with which he seems to have been pleased as he copied them out into a commonplace book, though they did not show him as master of a lucid prose style, it will be seen that Revett acted as a kind of literary agent to Lovelace. I have been able to find out very little about him. He matriculated at Cambridge as a Pensioner at Clare Hall on December 15, 1650. Mr. J. R. Wardale has kindly informed me that the only entry relative to him at Clare is that 'Eldred Rivet' was admitted June 29, 1650. He took no degree. In some verses which he contributed to Gilbert Swinhoe's *The Tragedy of*

The

The unhappy Fair Irene, 1658, Revett refers to the author as 'his much honoured Kinsman'. He also wrote verses before Beaumont and Fletcher's *The Wild Goose Chase*, 1652, *The Royall Game of Chesse-Play*, 1656, Gamble's *Ayres and Dialogues*, 1656, and Hall's *Hierocles upon the Golden Verses of Pythagoras*, 1657.

In addition to the commonplace book mentioned above, which has on the title 'Definitions and Characters. Eldred Reuett', the University Library at Cambridge possesses two other similar MSS. bound together. One bears the inscription 'Eld: Revetti Clarensis liber', and the other, which contains a number of songs and verses, 'Eld Revett Clarensis'. Both these belonged subsequently to Thomas Fvelyn and bear his signature. (D. D. S. 60–1.) See also note to p. 229.

l. 7. *left* . . . *Lucasta. Posthume Poems* reads 'lost'. Dudley Lovelace corrected the word to 'left' in the copies now in the Bodleian and the Library of Trinity College, Cambridge. Revett prints the word correctly.

PAGE 185, ll. 1–2.

Not hearing of thee thou dost break out strong,
Invading forty thousand men in Song.

This is copied from what Waller said of Denham:

'At last, viz. 1640, his play of *The Sophy* came out, which did take extremely: Mr. Edmund Waller sayd then of him, that he *broke-out like the Irish Rebellion* †—*threescore thousand strong*, before any body was aware.'

† His play came out at that time.

Dupl. with 'when nobody suspected it'. (Aubrey, *Brief Lives*, ed. A. Clark, Clarendon Press, 1898, i, p. 217.)

l. 11. *sage. Lucasta* reads 'safe'. In the Britwell Court copy the word has been corrected by Dudley Lovelace.

l. 13. *Aeson.* See Ovid's *Metamorphoses*, vii. 251–93.

l. 16. See note to p. 162, l. 23.

ll. 17–20. The first reference is to the legend of the

 suitors

suitors for the hand of the Virgin Mary, Joseph being shown as the chosen candidate by the fact that his staff budded. Raphael illustrates the incident in his picture of the *Marriage of the Virgin* in the Brera at Milan, where an unsuccessful suitor is depicted breaking his rods.

For the rod of Aaron see Numbers, chap. xvii.

PAGE 186, l. 10. *Rench'd.* Rinsed.

To my Noble Kinsman T. S. Esq; On his Lyrick Poems composed by Mr. J. G. These lines, signed 'Richard Lovelace', were prefixed to Gamble's first book of *Ayres and Dialogues*, 1656. (See note to p. 41.) Others who contributed to the Stanley-Gamble folio were Brome, Tatham, Eldred Revett, and Lovelace's youngest brother Dudley, who wrote the following verses:

To my much honored Cozen
Mr. *Stanley*, Upon his Poems set
by Mr. *John Gamble.*

I.

Enough, Enough, of Orbs and Spheres,
Reach me a Trumpet or a Drum,
To *sound* sharp *Synnets* in your Ears,
And *Beat* a Deep *Encomium.*

II.

I know not th' *Eight Intelligence*;
Those that do understand it, Pray
Let them step thither, and from thence
Speak what they all do Sing or Say:

III.

Nor what your *Diapasons* are,
Your *Sympathies* and *Symphonies*;
To me they seem as distant farre
As whence they take their Infant rise.

IV.

IV.

But I've a grateful Heart can ring
 A *peale* of *Ordnance* to your praise,
And *Volleys* of *small Plaudits* bring
 To Clowd or Crown about your Baies.

V.

Though Lawrel is thought Thunder-free;
 That Storms and Lightning Disallows,
Yet *Caesar* thorough Fire and Sea
 Snatcht her to twist his Conquering Brows.

VI.

And now me thinks like him you stand
 I' th' head of all the Poets Hoast,
Whilest with your Words you do Command,
 They silent do their Duty Boast.

VII.

Which done, the Army Ecchoes o're
 Like *Gamble Ios* One and all,
And in their various Notes implore
 Long live our noble Generall.

Dudley Posthumus *Lovelace.*

PAGE 187, l. 18. *Vt Re Mi.* The first three signs of the Gamut.

PAGE 188. *The Wild Goose Chase.* These lines were printed in larger type than the others and given the place of honour among the verses prefixed to *The Wild-Goose Chase. A Comedie. As it hath been Acted with singular Applause at the Black-Friers: Being the Noble, Last, and Onely Remaines of those Incomparable Drammatists, Francis Beaumont, and John Fletcher, Gent. Retriv'd for the publick delight of all the Ingenious; . . . By a Person of Honour . . . London, Printed for Humpherey Moseley, and are to be sold at the Princes Armes in St. Paules Church-yard.* 1652.

l. 2.

l. 2. *The Blind and late Heavens-eyes great Occulist.* The blind 'Occulist' of the Eye of Heaven who with his false 'scheme' did not mislead half the number of people that Fletcher enlightened with his newly found comedy, was probably Galileo. Galileo elaborately described the *faculae* (Lovelace's *false fires*) of the sun and in the last years of his life was blind. The man who claimed to have found spots and 'faculae' in the sun might well be called the 'Occulist' of Heaven's eye.

PAGE 189, l. 2. *Th' un-numbred dishes of her Anthony.* The story of the Order made between Antony and Cleopatra, which they called 'Amimetobion (as much as to say, No life comparable and matchable with it) one feasting each other by turnes, and in cost, exceeding all measure and reason', is told in North's translation of Plutarch's *Lives.*

ll. 3–6. Pliny tells this story in *Historia Naturalis*, ix. 119 seq. Wanley gives a rendering of it in *The Wonders of the Little World*, 1678, p. 389.

l. 26. *a rope of Pearl of forty more.* Including the plays which Lovelace has just mentioned the 1647 folio of Beaumont and Fletcher contained thirty-four plays and one masque, that is everything which had not been printed before with the exception of the *The Wild Goose Chase.*

PAGE 190. *To Dr. F. B. On his Book of Chesse.* These lines, signed R. Lovelace, and headed 'To his honoured Friend on his Game of Chesse-play', were one of three sets of verses prefixed to *The Royall Game of Chesse-Play. Sometimes The Recreation of the late King, with many of the Nobility. Illustrated With almost an hundred Gambetts. Being The study of Biochimo the famous Italian. London, Printed for Henry Herringman, and are to be sold at his shop at the sign of the Anchor, in the lower walk of the New Exchange, 1656.*

In a copy of the book recently in the possession of Messrs. P. J. and A. E. Dobell a row of printer's ornaments takes the place of the heading and the verses are unsigned.

Dr.

Dr. F. B. may be Francis Beale who signs the 'Epistle Dedicatory', in which he speaks of himself as publishing the book, or Dr. Budden to whom the third, anonymous, set of commendatory verses is addressed. These anonymous verses were reprinted in *Musarum Deliciae*, ed. 1656, p. 41.

l. 2. *Fox and Geese.* A game played with seventeen pieces called geese and a larger piece which represents the fox. The player with the geese tries to enclose the fox so that he cannot move, his opponent to take so many pieces that he cannot be blocked. See Strutt's *Sports and Pastimes*, ed. 1845, pp. 318–19.

To the Genius of Mr. John Hall. These lines head the commendatory verses after the 'Account of the Author' in *Hierocles upon the Golden Verses of Pythagoras; Teaching a vertuous and worthy Life. Englished by J. Hall, Esquire. Opus Posthumum.... London, Printed by John Streater for Francis Eaglesfield at the Signe of the Marigold in Saint Pauls Church-yard. 1657.*

Hierocles was a Neo-Platonic writer, born at the beginning of the fifth century, probably at Alexandria. This commentary on the *Golden Verses* of Pythagoras is the only complete work by him in existence. It was first printed at Padua in 1474 by Aurispa in a Latin translation. The Greek text was published at Paris in 1538 by J. Curterius.

In his *Commentary* Hierocles supports the theory of souls and pre-existence.

For Hall see note to p. 10.

l. 11. *humble Fane.* Hall wrote some verses for *Lucasta*, 1649.

PAGE 191, l. 2. *gilt Vice strip.* A reference to Hall's *Humble Motion*, 1649.

l. 3. Lovelace probably scanned the line 'A Sen'tor praetextàt, that knew'st to sway', the accent copying the Latin *praetextātus.* In Hall's *Hierocles* the reading is 'that couldst sway', but this was published two years earlier and

and a second revised version giving a syllable too much is unlikely. Shortenings like 'sen'tor' are common in Lovelace.

l. 11. *At nineteen.* Hall published *Horae Vacivae* at the age of nineteen in 1646.

l. 26. *Who but one Splinter had of Castriot.* 'At which time the Turkes hauing gotten the towne of *Lissa*, did with a vehement and earnest desire search out the bodie of *Scanderbeg*: and hauing found it, they drew it foorth of the supulture, and (it may be some diuine dispensation working that motion in them) they tooke a singular pleasure and contentment to see it, to reuerence it, and in a manner to adore it being now dead and dissolued, which being a liue they so greatly redoubted and stood in feare of, that the onely brute and sound of his name did make them to flie away confounded and astonished. They ranne thither from all partes, flocking together in troupes and companies with so greedie and vehement a desire and longing to see his bones, that happie was he which might come to touch them, or but to haue a sight of them onely: but much more glad and ioyfull was he that could get or cary away any peece of his bodie were it neuer so litle: and those that had any part thereof, caused the same most religiously to be set and curiously enchased, some in siluer, some in golde, bearing it about them vpon some part of their bodies as a thing most holy, diuine and fatall: and they did with singular reuerence and deuotion obserue and keepe it very carefully: being fully perswaded, that all such as did beare those reliques about them, should enioy the like fortune, felicitie and priuiledge during their liues which *Scanderbeg* (by the gift and grace of God) onely and alone within the memorie of man, had vsed and enioyed all his life time.' (*The Historie of George Castriot, Svrnamed Scanderbeg, King of Albanie. Containing his famous actes, his noble deedes of Armes, and memorable victories against the Turkes, for the Faith of Christ . . . By Iaqves de Lavardin Lord of Plessis Bovrrot, a Nobleman of France. Newly*

Newly translated out of French into English by Z. *I. Gentleman* . . . . 1596, p. 496.)

An earlier account of Castriot appeared in 1562, 'translated oute of Italian into Englishe by John Shute'. See also Lithgow's *Totall Discourse*, ed. 1640, p. 57, and the Epistle before *The Medal*, 1682.

Scanderbeg (1403–69) was the last king of Albania.

PAGE 192. *On Sanazar's being honoured.* 'I heard in Venice that a certaine Italian Poet called *Iacobus Sannazarius* had a hundred crownes bestowed vpon him by the Senate of Venice for each of these verses following. I would to God my Poeticall friend Mr. *Beniamin Iohnson* were so well rewarded for his Poems here in England, seeing he hath made many as good verses (in my opinion) as these of *Sannazarius.*' (Coryate, *Crudities*, 1611, p. 159.)

For a translation by Lovelace of the lines which Coryate quotes see p. 203 and note.

l. 15. *a blith Prince.* Louis XI of France. Hazlitt refers to the story in *Tales, and quicke answeres* where 'kynge Lowes of Fraunce, the xi of that name', gives to 'one Conon a homely husbande man', to whose house he had often 'resorted from huntynge' and there eaten 'radysshes rotes', 'a thousande crownes of golde' for a radish after he had been 'restored home, and had the gouernance of France in his hande'.

Possibly the extravagance of Louis by which he tried to distract attention from the sickness which was growing on him towards the end of his reign gave rise to such stories. Cf. *Histoire de Louys XI. Roy de France*, 1610, p. 444; *Les Memoires de Messire Philippe de Comines*, ed. 1649, pp. 252–3, &c.

l. 18. *Maid of Meurs.* Among the Shirburn Ballads (ed. A. Clark, 1907, pp. 54–9) is printed one *Of a maide nowe dwelling at the towne of* meurs *in* dutchland, *that hath not taken any foode this 16 yeares, and is not yet neither hungry nor thirsty; the which maide hath lately beene presented to to the lady* elizabeth, *the king's daughter of* england. *This song was made by the maide her selfe, and now translated into* english.

A contemporary print of the 'Mayd that liued at Muers in Clueland without Food. ætat. 40. The Pourtrayture of Eua Fliegen the Miraculous', with her flowers, is reproduced as frontispiece to the book. The lines below the portrait state that she prayed she might never eat any more 'Cause my stepmother grutched me my food'.

Compare:

> *Aur.* What would you have me doe?
> D'you think I'me the Dutch Virgin that could live
> By the sent of Flowers?
>
> *The City Match*, 1658, ii. 4, p. 1.

'Fabricius ("Obs. Chirurg." cent. v., obs. xxxi. *Opp.*,' p. 413 *sqq.* Francof., 1646) has an account of her, with the letters of various correspondents, extending over several folio columns. Her name was Eve Fleigen or Fligen, of Meurs, and she is described as "Morsiana puella". When he published the early edition of his *Observations*, he thought it a case of "prodigiosa inedia" (p. 413). But before the above edition [appeared] he was undeceived, as her deception had been detected; yet he refused to correct what he had said, as he was not ashamed to have been taken in with several most eminent men (pp. 421–3). Before her detection her history had been published in London, in a translation from the Dutch. (Hakewell, *Apology*, p. 440, Ox., 1635).' *Notes and Queries*, 6th ser., v, p. 103.

PAGE 193, l. 5. *Lepanto*. The battle of Lepanto was fought on October 7, 1572.

l. 7. *Candie*. If Lovelace wrote these lines as late as 1656 or 1657, the siege of Candia to which he refers was not more than half over. In 1645 the Turks suddenly attacked Crete, and the defence of their island by the Venetians lasted for twenty-four years. The siege of Candia lasted twenty-two. Although the island was surrendered on September 6, 1669, twenty years later it was again

again in the hands of the Venetians, being recaptured by Francesco Morosoni, Il Peloponesiaco, in 1689.

l. 29. *In marble statu'd walks great Lucan lay.* Lucan was the nephew of Seneca and grandson of the rhetorician whose gardens were supposed to be more magnificent than those of Nero.

PAGE 194, l. 2. *Capuchin.* A friar of the Order of St. Francis of the new rule of 1528. They were called 'Capuchin' from their 'capuche', which was adopted in 1525 and confirmed to them three years later by Pope Clement VII.

l. 5. *Olio.* A hotchpotch.

l. 12. *his Mans curse.* The original and all subsequent editions omit 'curse'. The word was inserted by Dudley Lovelace in five copies which I have seen.

l. 26. *Then skin y' in Satin as young Lovelace plaies.* In *The Scornful Lady* (fo., 1679, p. 69) Young Loveless, sometimes printed 'Lovelace' in the quartos, says:

> Why, now thou art able to discharge thine office, and cast up a reckoning of some weight; I will be knighted, and for my state will bear it, 'tis sixteen hundred boyes: off with your husks, I'le skin you all in Sattin.
>
> *Capt.* O sweet *Loveless*!
>
> *Savil.* All in Sattin? O sweet *Loveless*!

Compare also: '. . . he is naked, and where to skinne himselfe agen, if I know, or can devise . . .' *Wit without Money*, 1639, Sig. F 2 verso.

PAGE 195, l. 12. *all marks.* Compare: '. . . a Name, so ful of authority, antiquity, and all great marke, is . . . become the lowest scorne of the age: . . .' Ben Jonson, Dedication to *The Foxe*, fo., 1616, p. 445.

l. 17. *Aretine.* Pietro Aretino, the 'scourge of princes', the 'divine' as he called himself, dramatist, satirist, and poet, was born at Arezzo in 1492 and died in Venice in 1556. From the end of the sixteenth century onwards he had a considerable reputation in England, based partly on his position as the champion of men of letters,

letters, and partly on the notoriety which he had obtained as a writer of licentious verse and as a satirist with whom emperors and kings were anxious to keep on good terms. As a young man he was banished to Perugia because of some lines he had written against papal indulgences, but later he went to Rome, where he stayed for seven years under Leo X and Clement VII. In 1524 he was expelled from the city because of a set of sonnets, the *Sonetti Lussuriosi*, which he made on some drawings by Giulio Romano. In 1526 he went to Venice, the interval having been spent in the service of Giovanni dei Medici, and at Venice he stayed for the greater part of the rest of his life, though he paid a visit to Rome after the election of Julius III, in the hope that he might be made a cardinal, to qualify for which position he had written some devotional works. His portrait by Titian, a 'terrible marvel', as he himself called it, is in the Pitti.

l. 32. *Berenice's hair.* Berenice dedicated her hair in the temple of Arsinoë at Zephyrum for the safe return of her husband Ptolemy from an expedition against Syria. On his return the hair was missing. The mathematician Conon suggested that it had been taken up to heaven and turned into a constellation, an idea which was used by Callimachus in a poem now lost. Catullus, however, translated it. See his poem no. 66.

PAGE 196, l. 15. *Maccaroon.* Compare Donne's 4th Satyre:

> Like a bigge wife, at sight of loathed meat,
> Readie to travaile: So I sigh, and sweat
> To heare this Makeron talke in vaine: . . .
>
> ed. 1633, pp. 340–1;

and R. B.'s elegy on Donne:

> 'Tis true, they quitted him, to their poore power,
> They humm'd against him; And with face most sowre
> Call'd him a strong lin'd man, a Macaroon,
> And no way fit to speake to clouted shoone,
>
> *Ibid.*, p. 401.

l. 32.

l. 32. *drills.* Monkeys or baboons as in 'mandrill'.

PAGE 197, l. 7. *Pissmire.* The ant.

PAGE 198, ll. 15–16.

Envy the living, not the dead, doth bite,
For after death all men receave their right.

Quoted verbatim from Ben Jonson's retouching of Marlowe's rendering of Ovid. See *Poetaster*, I. i, fo., 1616, p. 279.

Marlowe's lines are:

The liuing, not the dead can enuie bite,
For after death all men receiue their right.
ed. Tucker Brooke, pp. 580, 582.

l. 23 et seq. *Sandys, Waynman,* and *Falkland.* George Sandys (1578–1644), the youngest son of Edwin Sandys, Archbishop of York, was Lovelace's great-uncle. As a young man he travelled through France to Italy and on to Turkey, Egypt, and Palestine. As a record of his travels he wrote the prose *Relation of a Journey Begun A.D. 1610*, which was published in 1615 and dedicated to Prince Charles. Six years later he sailed for America as Treasurer of the Virginia Company and, after settling there, he was three times appointed a member of the Virginia Council by the Crown. He returned to England in 1631 and became a gentleman of the Privy Chamber to Charles I. It was probably at this time that he made the acquaintance of Falkland, who held the same position at Court. His translation of the *Metamorphoses* was begun before his journey to Virginia and the first five books were probably published in 1621, Drayton urging him to continue the work. The other ten books were translated at sea and in America and the whole published in England in 1626.

Sandys became very intimate with both Sir Francis Wenman, who married his niece and at whose house near Witney he used to stay, and with Lucius Cary, second Viscount Falkland (1610–43), who, highly rated as a poet himself by his contemporaries, gathered about him at his house

house at Great Tew men of letters and of learning. As a boy Lovelace may have visited him there from Oxford.

Had these two been living, it would have been unnecessary according to Lovelace to defend Sandys against posthumous attacks, and Falkland certainly held a high opinion of Sandys. He contributed long commendatory poems, as is noted by Lovelace, to Sandys' *Paraphrase upon the Psalmes and upon the Hymnes dispersed throughout the Old and New Testaments*, 1636, which was reprinted with Lawes' music in *A Paraphrase upon the Divine Poems*, 1638, and other verses to the *Paraphrase upon the Psalmes of David*, in which he praises all Sandys' work. He furnished the only contribution to *Christs Passion. A Tragedie.* 1640.

'Sir *Francis Wenman* would not look upon himself under any other Character, than that of a Country Gentleman; though no Man of his Quality in *England* was more esteemed in Court. He was of a noble Extraction, and of an ancient Family in *Oxfordshire*, where He was possessed of a competent Estate; but his Reputation of Wisdom, and Integrity, gave him an Interest and Credit in that Country, much above his Fortune; and no Man had more Esteem in it, or Power over it. He was a Neighbour to the Lord *Falkland*, and in so entire Friendship and Confidence with him, that He had great Authority in the Society of all his Friends, and Acquaintance. He was a Man of a great Sharpness of Understanding, and of a piercing Judgment; no Man better understood the Affections and Temper of the Kingdom, or indeed the Nature of the Nation, or discerned further the Consequence of Counsels, and with what Success They were like to be attended. He was a very good *Latin* Scholar, but his Ratiocination was above his Learning; and the Sharpness of his Wit incomparable: He was equal to the greatest Trust and Employment, if He had been ambitious of it, or solicitous for it; but his Want of Health produced a Kind of Laziness of Mind, which disinclined him to Business,

Business, and He died a little before the general Troubles of the Kingdom, which He foresaw with wonderful Concern, and when many wise Men were weary of living so long.' (*The Life of Edward Earl of Clarendon*, 1759, pp. 23–4.)

Lovelace may refer, however, to the poet Thomas Wenman (1596–1665), second Viscount Wenman, of Thame Park, Oxfordshire, who is placed close to Sandys in Suckling's *A Sessions of the Poets.* Thomas Wenman has some verses before the second book of Browne's *Britannia's Pastorals*, 1616, and *The Legend of Mary, Queen of Scots and other Ancient Poems*, printed by John Fry of Bristol in 1810, is attributed to him. There is a MS. of *The Legend* in the Bodleian (Rawl. B. 161).

PAGE 199, ll. 11–12.

Ringers of Verse that All-in All-in chime,
And toll the changes upon every Rhime.

Compare: 'Thus they kill a man over and over, as *Hopkins* and *Sternhold* murder the Psalmes, with another to the same; one chimes all in, and then the other strikes up, as the Saints-Bell.' (Cleveland, *The Character of a London Diurnall*, 1647, p. 3.)

'All-in' is a technical term in bell-ringing for the final strokes or peal before the service begins.

Wee now are going
To Church, in way of matrimony, some on us:
Tha' rung all in a' ready.

Jonson, *A Tale of a Tub*, II. ii, 1640, p. 70 [i.e. 80]; which is as much to say that they are late already and must hurry. So the 'Ringers of Verse' of whom Lovelace writes advertise the necessity of every one hurrying up to read them.

l. 13. *Mercer.* Mr. Thorn-Drury suggests that the reference is to Lieut.-Col. William Mercer (1605?–75), the author of *Angliae Speculum*, . . . 1646, *An Elegie in Memorie and at the interring of the bodie of the most famous and truly noble Knight, Sir Henry Mervyn*, . . . 1646, *An Elegie*

Elegie upon the Death of the Right Honble., most Noble, worthily Renownend, and truly valiant Lord, Robert, Earle of Essex and Ewe, . . . 1646, and other works. See *D. N. B.* Mervyn was Mercer's father-in-law, and through Essex, to whom *Angliae Speculum* was dedicated, he had obtained a commission as captain of horse in the Parliamentary army. 'The majority of his verses are mere doggerel, and display an inordinate self-conceit' (*D.N.B.*), which compensates in some measure for the extreme rarity of his books.

l. 25. *Crispinus.* The name under which Jonson attacked Marston in *The Poetaster*, 1601.

ll. 27–8 and 31.

He still did stand
Honour'd, and held his forehead to thy brand.
. . . .
Well mightst thou rive thy Quill up to the Back.

A reminiscence of Ben Jonson's own 'Apologeticall Dialogue' appended to the folio text of *The Poetaster.* The lines in both cases are spoken by the author:

Or, liuing, I could stampe
Their foreheads with those deepe, and publike brands
That the whole company of *Barber-Surgeons*
Should not take off, with all their art, and playsters.
. . . .
O, this would make a learn'd, and liberall soule,
To riue his stayned quill, vp to the back,
And damne his long-watch'd labours to the fire;
fo., 1616, pp. 352–3.

PAGE 200, ll. 3–18. The various ladies whom Lovelace attacks cannot be identified with certainty. He refers particularly to married women and may have had in mind Margaret Cavendish, Duchess of Newcastle—the 'mad, conceited, ridiculous woman' as Pepys called her, Charles Lamb's 'princely woman, the thrice noble Margaret Newcastle'—and possibly Mrs. Anne Bradstreet, Lady Howe, and Anne Collins. The Duchess of Newcastle's *Poems and*

Fancies

Fancies and *Philosophical Fancies* were published in 1653, but the bulk of her work was not printed till after Lovelace's death. Anne Bradstreet's *The Tenth Muse, lately sprung up in America* was published in London in 1650. Anne King, who married in turn John Dutton and Sir Richard Howe, wrote but did not publish any verse. Henry King has a poem 'To my Sister Anne King, who chid me in verse for being angry'. (*Poems*, 1657, p. 83.) James Howell wrote some lines 'For the admitting of Mrs. *Ann King* to be the Tenth Muse', and said, 'they are a choice race of Brothers, and it seems the same Genius diffuseth itself also among the Sisters'. In another letter he says that he thought to bequeath 'my Poetry, such as it is, to Mistress *A. K.*, who I know is a great minion of the Muses'. (*Familiar Letters*, ed. Jacobs, pp. 406 and 422.) Anne Collins' *Divine Songs and Meditations* was printed in 1653. (Brydges' *Restituta*, 1815, vol. iii, p. 123.) The majority of 'celebrated scribbling women' did not come into prominence till after the Restoration, but in his 'Il Insonio Insonnadado', published with the *Albino and Bellama* in 1638, Nathaniel Whiting seems to refer to a poetess:

> Up comes the Marget with a mincing pace,
> A city-stride, court-garb, and smirking face,
>
> *Caroline Poets*, ed. Saintsbury, vol. iii, p. 543.

Nicholas Oldisworth, in a MS. volume of poems belonging to Messrs. P. J. and A. E. Dobell, also addresses some lines 'To the worshipfull, M[ris] Strange of Summerford, a Poëtesse' who was his cousin.†

The 'one *Sapho* left may save them all' is, perhaps, Katherine Philips, the 'Matchless Orinda' who, though she had printed nothing by the time of Lovelace's death except some commendatory verses which were included among the large collection prefixed to Cartwright's *Poems* in 1651—her collected poems were published in 1667, a pirated edition having appeared three years earlier—was already well known as a poetess. In the same year as

Cartwright's poems were printed, Vaughan addressed some lines to her, praising her 'rich numbers' in *Olor Iscanus*. Mrs. Philips has some verses to him 'On his Poems'. It is not impossible, however, that the Society which was formed by Katherine Philips, and the friendship with the female members of it which she particularly celebrates in her poems, were the real objects of Lovelace's satire. It has been suggested above that Lucasta may have been a member of the family of Lucas. If this was so it is worth noting that the Duchess of Newcastle was 'Daughter to *Thomas Lucas* of St. *Johns* near *Colchester*, in *Essex*, Esquire', and Lovelace may, in consequence, have intended to pay a compliment to a relation of Lucasta.

l. 28. *angerly*. Compare:

Hee . . . angerly calculates his cost, . . .

Hall, *Characters of Vertves and Vices*, 1608, p. 169;

How sweet she smil'd, and angerly she frown'd.

Chalkhill, *Thealma and Clearchus*, 1683, p. 75;

And all its curtains of Aurorian clouds
Flush'd angerly:

Keats, *Hyperion*, i. 182.

l. 30. Juvenal's 'Difficile est saturam non scribere' (*Satires*, i. 30).

PAGE 202. *Translationes.* The printers of *Lucasta*, 1659, frequently got muddled over the catchwords in the *Translations* which occupy pp. 86–107. In five cases the catchword is given for the next page instead of the next page but one, which would continue the original texts or the translations as the case may be, and in three others the word is wrongly spelt or given wrong.

PAGE 203. *Sanazar's Hexastick.* Robert Baron wrote an Antithesis, *to the conclusion of* Sannazarius *his Epigram on the City of* Venice. (*Pocula Castalia*, 1650, p. 122.)

There is another translation given in *Wits Recreations*, Hotten's reprint, n.d., pp. 64–5. Howell translated the same epigram, *Familiar Letters*, 1645, p. 68: '*Sanzanarus*', he remarks, 'had given him by Saint *Mark* a hundred

Zecchins,

Zecchins, for evry one of these Verses, which amounts to about 300 pounds. It would be long before the Citie of *London* would do the like: ...'

He has a different version prefixed to his *Survay of the Signorie of Venice*, 1651.

PAGE 206. *De Puero & Præcone.* This epigram would be 107 according to the numbering followed by Lovelace.

ll. 20–7. These two epigrams were given as one in *Lucasta.* They are clearly different, and only the first is printed in *Diversorum Veterum Poetarum in Priapum Lusus*, &c., 1517, as by Quintus Catulus (p. 79 verso). I have not found the second, which is probably not by Catulus.

PAGES 208–12. *Epigrams from Ausonius.* These epigrams have been collated with three editions of Ausonius, that of Scaliger printed at Lyons in 1574–5 in two vols. (the Epigrams coming in the volume of 1575), an edition printed at Amsterdam in 1629, and the *Corpus* printed at Lyons in 1603. The references in the Textual Notes are to Scaliger's edition of 1575. The epigrams are numbers 14, 52, 21, 11, 10, and 43.

PAGE 210. *Theophile.* Théophile Viaud or De Viau (1591–1626) was banished in 1619 by Louis XIII because of various satires which he had written. Coming to London and being unable to obtain an audience of James I, he wrote this epigram. I do not find it in the 1622 edition, the second, of his works, or in the edition of 1629, the only two of over twenty seventeenth-century editions I have seen. It is not in the 1660 edition of *Le Parnasse Satyrique*, but his connexion with this book is doubtful. It is printed, however, on p. 126 of vol. iii of *Recueil des plus belles pieces Des Poëtes François*, 1692. Swinburne described Théophile, who was highly praised by Gautier, as 'a born Huguenot, nominal Papist, and natural Pagan; ... the supreme libertine and perfect poet of his time'. He compared Théophile with Crashaw, 'a Christianized Théophile, ... a far smaller figure, a much weaker and

 perverser

perverser man; . . .' (*Théophile*, ed. Gosse, 1915, pp. 11 and 21.)

ll. 10–11. Lovelace has here omitted two lines which in the 1575 edition of Ausonius read:

> Extremos pereunte modos à fine reducens,
> Ludificata sequor verba aliena meis.

ll. 16–17. Lovelace here omits two lines:

> Diuidat haec si quis: faciunt discreta venenum.
> Antidotum sumet, qui sociata bibet.

PAGE 211, l. 14. *to.* See note to p. 22, l. 24.

PAGE 212. *Avieni.* In Wernsdorf's edition of Avienus, 1848, p. 133, there are two further lines to this epigram:

> Dum parvus lychnus modicum consumit olivi;
> Haec dat nocturnis nox lucubrata Camoenis.

l. 13. The spelling 'dii' is found in seventeenth-century editions of Catulus. It is, of course, a monosyllable.

PAGE 214. *Martial. Epigrams*, Bk. 6. 15 *and* Bk. 4. 33. Old editions of Martial differ considerably in the numbering of the epigrams. The numbers adopted by Lovelace follow the folio edition printed at Paris in 1617 and the *Corpvs Omnivm Vetrvm Poetarvm Latinorvm*, Lyons, 1603, except that he gives the number 33 to the epigram from the fourth book which these editions number 32, but this may be a slip. The text also agrees with the folio, though where that, in common with other editions, reads 'nunc preciosa', *Lucasta* reads 'jam'. Lovelace may have written down the epigrams from memory; it is curious that he should have transposed the last two lines of these two epigrams, giving to that from Book 6 the lines belonging to the epigram in Book 4 and vice versa. It is hardly likely to be a printer's error, as, even if he did confuse the Latin lines, the printer would not have altered the English version as well. It is also unlikely that any edition of Martial gives the readings printed in *Lucasta*, as the epigrams come from different books, and editions of

1595,

1595, 1602, 1603, 1615, 1617, 1619, and 1621 all print the same version.

PAGE 216. *De Amore suo.* This epigram is printed in *Lucasta* as the last two lines of epigram 73, without break or separate title. It is, of course, a different epigram which, according to the numbering followed by Lovelace, should be 86. The title here printed is that given in editions of Catullus of the first half of the seventeenth century.

PAGE 224, ll. 9–10. *I have found my name*
Fix'd in the living Chronicle of Fame.

Lovelace addressed *The Triumphs of Philamore and Amoret* to the 'Best of Friends, *Charles Cotton* Esquire'. See p. 169.

Charles Cotton. These lines were reprinted in *Poems on several Occasions. Written by Charles Cotton, Esq; London*, . . . 1689, p. 481.

PAGE 225. *Jam. Howell.* These lines were reprinted on p. 126 of *Poems on several Choice and Various Subjects. Occasionally Composed By An Eminent Author. Collected and Published By Sergeant-Major P. F. London: Printed by Ja: Cottrel; and are to be sold by S. Speed, at the Rain-bow in Fleetstreet, near the inner Temple-gate.* 1663. P. F stands for Payne Fisher, who dedicated the volume to Henry King. This book is found with two other title-pages, both dated 1664: *Mr. Howel's Poems Upon divers Emergent Occasions. London: Printed by James Cottrel*, 1664, and *Poems Upon divers Emergent Occasions: By James Hovvell Esquire. London: Printed by Ja: Cotterel; and are to be sold in Exchange-alley neer Lombard-street, 1664.*

There are some differences between the two versions, the last two lines being changed to:

Such sparks that with their Atoms may inspire
The Reader with a pure *Poetik* fire.

PAGE 228, l. 10. *a Spaniard.* Compare: '. . . And evry one knowes the tale of *Pacheco* the Spanish Ambassador, who coming out of curiosity to see this Tresury [i.e. St. Mark's], fell a groping whether it had any bottom, and being

being asked why? he answerd, *In this among other things my great Masters Tresures differs from yours, that* his *hath no bottom as yours I find hath*, alluding thereby to the Mines of *Mexico* and *Potosi*.' (Howell, *A Survay of the Signorie of Venice*, 1651, p. 38.)

l. 28. *That it might comprehend what could not it.* 'But howsoever he taught, or whatsoever he thought, this we find, that nothing troubled him more. For (as *Cœlius Rhodiginus* writeth) when he had studied long about it, and at the last being weary, he died through the tediousnesse of such an intricate doubt. Some say he drowned himself in *Negropont*, or *Euripus*, because he could find no reason why it had so various a fluxion and refluxion, ebbing and flowing seven times a day at the least; adding, before that his untimely and disastrous precipitation, these words, 'Επειδὴ 'Αριστοτέλης ὀυχ (*sic*) εἶλε τὸν Ἔυριπον, Ἔυριπος ἐχετω τὸν Αριστοτέλη. *Quandoquidem Aristoteles non cepit Euripũ, Euripus capiat Aristotelem;* That is, *Although Aristotle hath not taken Euripus, yet Euripus shall take Aristotle*: meaning that that should end him, whose cause could not be comprehended by him.' (John Swan, *Speculum Mundi*, 1644, pp. 203–4.)

PAGE 229. *El. Revett.* See note to p. 184, and *Introduction.*

An Elegie. These lines were written by Samuel Holland and were separately published on a single folio leaf, headed 'The Death Of My | Much Honoured Friend, | Colonel *Richard Lovelace.* | An Elegie'. They are signed 'Samuel Holland', and a deep black line of mourning is printed on both sides of the verses.

Next to the copy in the University Library, Cambridge (Sel. 3. 162[12]), are bound verses by Holland 'On the Death of Mr. *Marmaduke Scot.* An Elegie', printed in the same style. The broadside is undated, but knowledge of the date of its publication would help little in determining the date of Lovelace's death as it was clearly written some time after the event—'Lovelace hath long been dead'—and probably

probably especially for Dudley Lovelace's collection of *Elegies*. It may be noted, however, that the expression 'hath long been dead' is more appropriate to 1657 than to 1658.

PAGE 231, l. 6. *tam Marti, quam Mercurio.* This motto was used by George Gascoigne and Sir Walter Raleigh.

PAGE 233, l. 6. *pure soul.* The correction of 'poor' to 'pure' is one of those made by Dudley Lovelace in some of his presentation copies.

Symon Ognell. Mr. V. G. Plarr, Librarian to the Royal College of Surgeons, informs me that there is no record of Ognell in the books or lists of the Royal College. His medical degree must have been taken at the University of Königsberg, which was founded by Duke Albert of Brandenburg in 1544.

PAGE 234, l. 20. The change from *Zephre* to *Zephire* is one of those made by Dudley Lovelace in the Bodleian copy.

PAGE 236. These lines were contributed to J. D.'s translation of Voiture's *Letters of Affaires Love and Courtship*, 1657. (See *Introduction* under Text of the Poems.) J. D. was John Davies of Kidwelly (1627–93), who after travelling in France returned to England about 1652 and employed himself in translating for the booksellers. (See *D. N. B.*) He was a friend of John Hall and prefixed an account of the translator and his works to *Hierocles upon the Golden Verse of Pythagoras*, 1657.

Lovelace's verses take the place of some French lines which appeared under the same portrait when it was prefixed to a French edition. In that of 1657 these lines read:

Tel fut le Celebre Voiture,
l'Amour de tous les beaux Espris:
Mais bien mieux qu'en cette peinture,
Tu le verras dans ses escris. D. P.

ADDITIONAL

ADDITIONAL NOTES

It is interesting to know that Walter Pater considered writing an 'Imaginary Portrait' of Lovelace. Mrs. Daniel suggested to him that he should contribute it to the little volume containing Wood's account of Lovelace which was printed by Dr. C. H. O. Daniel, late Provost of Worcester College, on his private press in 1896 and presented by him to the members of the Lovelace Club on the occasion of their 200th meeting. 'I should think it an honour to contribute, as you propose, to what I know will be so exquisite a volume, and for so excellent a purpose.' Unfortunately he was unable to do it in the time available.

PAGE xxiv, l. 7. Compare also

> I Marvel *Dick*, That having been
> So long abroad,

Merry Drollery ed. 1875, p. 54.

PAGE xliii, note 2. It was also printed in *New Ayres and Dialogues*, 1678, p. 132.

PAGE xlix, ll. 21–6. More conclusive evidence is furnished by the fact that Lovelace's signature as witness occurs on a document—a letter from Barth: Hall to Sir John Lenthall authorizing him to discharge Arthur Knight from prison—dated Nov. 4, 1646. The document is preserved at Charterhouse.

PAGE 255, note on p. 18, ll. 16–17. In fairness to Dr. Johnson it should be added that his precept was better than his practice. In the *Life of Roscommon* he wrote: 'In the verses on the Lap-dog, the pronouns *thou* and *you* are offensively confounded.'

PAGE 286, ll. 21–8, note on p. 78 'Set by Dr. John Wilson'. There is a copy of the ballad 'The Pensive Prisoners Apology' in the Pepys collection at Magdalene College, Cambridge. It furnishes evidence of the popularity not only of Wilson's setting but of Lovelace's poem. Another famous Cavalier song which was published with additions as a ballad, in this case without cuts, to be sung to its own tune was Montrose's 'My dear and only love'.

PAGE xxii

The Penitive Prisoners Apology.

Directed to his Fellow Prisoners wheresoever, exhorting & advising them to be obedient in their places, and patiently to endure their several imprisonments, and to keep their vows, thereby the way to their liberty.

Tune of, [illegible]

[illegible]

[illegible]

The Penſive Priſoners Apology.

Directed to his Fellow-Priſoners whereſoever, wherein he adviſeth them to be ſtedfaſt in faith and hope, and patiently to indure their careful impriſonment, and to keep their Vows, ſhewing the way to true liberty.

Tune of, *Love with unconfined wings*, Or, *No, no, no, no, not yet.*

Love with unconfined Wings,
hovers about my gates,
And my divine Althema begins,
to whiſper at my grates,
When I lye tangled in her hair,
being fettered in her eye,
The birds that wanton in the air,
knows no ſuch Liberty.

When like contented Linits I,
with ſilver notes will ſing,
The very meekneſs of the heart,
and glory of the thing:
When I ſhall noiſe abroad and ſpread
how good their vertues be,
Fiſhes that tipple in the deep,
knows no ſuch liberty.

My lodging is on the cold boards,
my cloaths are thin and bare,
Falſe-hearted friends with flatering (words,
doth ſeek me to inſnare:
They counſel me to change my mind,
and ſo my words deny:
And I thereby ſhall ſurely find,
a perfect Liberty.

Faith, Hope, & Patience is my guide,
my Conſcience pure and clear,
So that the Lord be on my ſide,
what Foe need I to fear:
I neither fear the ſtroak of Death,
nor tyrants villany:
So ſoon as Chriſt receives my breath,
I gain true Liberty.

A faithful vow I once did make,
which now I will maintain:
Whilſt I have tongue and breath to (ſpeak
and life in me remain:
Rather then from Religion turn,
in fiery flames to fry,
And if my Corps to aſhes burn,
my ſoul gains Liberty.

Patience makes plaiſters for my ſores
love lives without controul,
They lock my body within the doors,
but cannot lock my ſoul:
My Muſes too and fro doth run,
above and beneath the ſky:
The greateſt Potentate under the (Sun,
oft wants ſuch Liberty.

The second Part, to the same tune.

OUr Keepers cruelty is great,
to one and to us all,
He bids us eat our flesh for meat,
or stones that's in the wall:
Yet though I am in prison cast,
my sences mount on high,
The wind that bloweth where it list,
knows no such liberty.

Tis neither pardon from the Pope
nor prayers made to Saints,
That can inlarge my further scope,
nor shorten my complaints:
Tis Christ above, the Lord of love,
which for mankind did dye,
None but he can pardon me,
nor work my liberty.

There's many men hath Treasure (store,
yet are so worldly bent,
Having too much they scrape for more
yet never are content,
Whilst I that am the poor'st of all
from worldly care am free, (thrall,
Which makes me think they live in
and I at liberty.

the man that bears a wavering mind
is subject to much woe,
He that to anger is inclin'd,
must sorrow undergo.
But he that hath a patient heart,
though he a prisoner be,
Exceeds both nature, skill, and art,
in point of liberty.

You pensive prisoners every one
with hearts loyal and true.
This lines of mine to work upon,
I dedicate to you.
Let faith and patience be your guide,
and you in time shall see,
The powers of heaven will so provide
you shall have liberty.

Stone walls cannot a prison make,
nor Iron barrs a Cage,
A spotless soul being innocent,
calls that his hermitage
So I am blameless in my choice,
and from all troubles free,
Angels alone that are above,
enjoys such liberty.

Printed for *F. Coles*, *T. Vere*, *J. Wright*; and *J. Clarke*.

PAGE xxii, note 1. Mr. R. L. seems to have been Richard Loe as indicated in the B.M. copy of Jordan.

PAGE xxvii, l. 3. Boteler's share in the presentation of the petition, 'after his return from Celebrating St. *George* his Feast with his Majesty (being then his Gentleman Pensioner)', is noted in David Lloyd's *Memoires of . . . Excellent Personages*, 1668, p. 688, though this says Lovelace was in Newgate.

PAGE xli. Glapthorne christened his daughter 'Loualis' according to the Baptismal Registers of St. Bride's, Fleet Street, quoted by Mr. H. J. Walter in *The Times Literary Supplement*, Sept. 19, 1936.

PAGE li. There is an interesting, if inconclusive, account of the arrest of Lovelace in 1648 in *The Oxinden and Peyton Letters, 1642–1670*, ed. Dorothy Gardiner, 1937, p. 145. Writing on Oct. 26, 1648 to Henry Oxinden, whom Lovelace would have known in Kent, the lawyer James Thompson says: 'News to you I believe it may bee that Colonell Lovelace is sent to Peterhouse. The reason and manner of it, (as I am told) thus. Search was made for Franke Lovelace in his lodging, who not being found instantly, the Colonell that was imployed imagined hee might bee concealed (I thinke) in his brother's Cabinet, and commanded the violation of that, where a discovery was made of divers Delinquent Jewells. Them they forthwith seized on as Prisoners. Dicke, incensed at so great a loss, takes upon him stiffly to argue property, a note which it must be supposed they could not digest when it was in order to disgorging a prize and therefore instantly packed him to Peterhouse, upon pretence of answering some matters contained in papers of his; but his Treasure was ordered to a more private prison. When the day of redemption for either will dawne, we are yet to expect.'

This letter does not mention Dudley Lovelace, but makes it reasonably clear that the Captain Lovelace who, according to the entry in *The Calendar of State Papers*, was committed to Peterhouse on June 9, 1648, was Dudley. If it had been

been Richard—his rank might have been wrongly given—the fact would hardly have been news on Oct. 26. Even as it is, Thompson was a little late with his information, if we eliminate the unlikely possibility that Lovelace was involved in a second 'business' during the first three weeks of October. Perhaps Thompson hints as much in his opening words. As Moore was sent for by the Committee on Oct. 3 and Oct. 17 it seems likely that he was the Colonel who searched for Francis Lovelace and found the delinquent jewels, the appropriation of which led Richard to speak stiffly in defence of the rights of property. But, unless Thompson means that they were not his own, the affair of the jewels would hardly by itself have led to Lovelace being imprisoned for six months, though the loss may have had some effect on his later fortunes.

The authorities were probably suspicious of Lovelace. Though he seems to have taken no part in the Civil War, his views were known; one of his brothers had been killed on the Royalist side, another was in prison, and search was being made for a third, who may or may not have been the Fran. Lovelesse, Master of the Ordnance, who was taken prisoner at the surrender of Colchester on Aug. 27 or 28 (*A Letter From his Excellency the Lord Fairfax ... Concerning the surrender of Colchester*, 1648, p. 6). In the circumstances it was probably easy to find matter in Lovelace's papers which could be held to require an answer.

PAGE lii, ll. 10–11. The author of the lines in *Musarum Deliciae*, 1655 (2nd ed. 1656, p. 69),

Nay, said Sir *Richard Lovelace* to end the difference,
It were fit with the Lords to have a conference,

may refer to the poet.

PAGES lxv–lxvi. *Lovelace's reputation.* 'Love Conquer'd' (p. 31) was included in the *Poetical Register*, 1801. Three poems by Lovelace are printed in *Lyre of Love*, 1806, and there are four quotations in Hazlitt's *Select Poets*, 1825, among the songs at the end of the book. Lovelace is not included

included in the 'Critical List of Authors'. John Ferriar writes in 'The Bibliomania':

> 'Tis thus ev'n Shirley boasts a golden line,
> And Lovelace strikes, by fits, a note divine.
>
> *Illustrations of Sterne: with other Essays and Verses*, ed. 1812, vol. ii, p. 204.

In *Melmoth the Wanderer*, 1820, vol. i, p. 117, Charles Maturin describes a loyalist tailor 'who had run mad with drink and loyalty on the burning of the Rump', singing 'fragments of the ill-fated Colonel Lovelace's songs' with scraps from Cowley and specimens from Mrs. Behn's plays.

In a chapter on 'Neglected Poets' in *The Bachelor's Wife*, 1824, pp. 147–55, John Galt's characters discuss and give some quotations from Lovelace and Carew. 'Tommy Moore himself has given us nothing more melodious than some of his songs' and 'although song-writing, particularly of the amatory strain, was, without question, the forte of Lovelace, many of his other poems possess a high degree of beauty. His address to the grasshopper is singularly elegant. . . .' Galt quotes from this and from 'The Rose'. 'I am . . . a little disposed to wonder how compositions of so much merit should have fallen so entirely into oblivion, as to be known only to a few bookworms' He also reprints 'Tell me not, sweet, I am unkind', the last stanza of which was misquoted by Scott in the following year as a heading to one of the chapters in *The Talisman* and attributed to 'Montrose's *Lines*' (*Tales of the Crusaders*, 1825, vol. iv, p. 246).

PAGE 10. *John Hall.* In the course of an attack on Hall someone, possibly Sir George Wharton, wrote: 'Art thou a fit *Associate* for such *Ingenious* and candid *soules* as Col. *Lovelace*, *captaine Sherburne*, Mr. *Shirley*, or Mr. *Stanley*? They shall kick thee out of their *acquaintance* and tel thee thou art no *legitimate* Son of the *Muses*, but a *Traytor* to *Ingenuity*, a meere *excrementitious scabb* of *Learning*. . .' (*Mercurius Elencticus*, No. 27, May 24–31, 1648, p. 206).

Another

Another Royalist with whom Hall exchanged the compliment of verses was Sir Thomas Urquhart, a prisoner in London after the battle of Worcester. Writing as J. de la Salle in 1653 he commends the honoured, noble translator of Rabelais, and in the same year Urquhart contributed verses to de la Salle's *Paradoxes*. This is an honour the remarkable knight of Cromartie extended to no one else. With the possible exception of Alexander Ross, there is no contemporary man of letters, Scottish or English, with whom he seems to have been on friendly terms. His intended role was that of 'a Mecaenas, a patron, a promover of learning, a favorer of the Muses, and protector of scholars'.

PAGE 26. *The Scrutinie*. 'Mr. Lovelaces Song with the Answer' was printed in *Oxford Drollery*, 1671, pp. 99–100. The anonymous answer is printed in italic.

Her answer.

1. I Needs must say thou art forsworn
   Since mine thou vowd'st to be,
True oaths do bind both night and morn,
   And when last night you vow'd to me
   I ghess'd it possibility.

2. It may be call'd love much not long
   Contains but twelve hours space:
You did my beauty all the wrong,
   And rob'd me of my just embrace
   When you look'd on another's face.

3. You say all joys in my brown hair
   In others may be found,
And that you'l court the black and fair,
   But prove a mineralist unsound
   By searching in unplow'd up ground.

4. And when that you have lov'd your round,
   I'le prove no constant she,
With spoils of meaner beauties crown'd
   If laden you return to me
   It must be with infirmity.

'The

'The Scrutinie' was reprinted in *The Loyal Garland*, 5th ed., 1686 (Percy Society Reprint, 1850, p. 44); as Song 278 in *The New Academy of Compliments*, 1713, p. 274; and in *The Hive*, vol. ii, 1724, p. 133.

PAGE 31. *Love Conquer'd.* See *Poetical Register*, 1801, p. 224.

PAGE 32. *Set by Mr. Henry Lawes.* This setting has been reproduced in *Publications of the Modern Language Association of America*, vol. liv, Sept. 1939, by Miss Willa McClung Evans from a contemporary manuscript belonging to the Drexel Collection of the New York City Public Library.

PAGE 44. *William Lawes.* William Lawes's setting is reproduced in *P.M.L.A.* vol. lx, June 1945, by Miss Evans from John Gamble's manuscript collection of songs in the New York City Public Library. From a comparison of the text of this manuscript with that of the poem as printed in *Lucasta*, Miss Evans argues that Lovelace 'clearly recognized the difference between a lyric intended to be sung and one intended to be read, and that he exercised great care in altering his lines'. The chief variants are:

Stanza i, ll. 3–4. I lou'd thee, lou'd thee bestt
Lady twas not in jestt;
l. 8. you *for* thee
Stanza ii, l. 5. your starrs bereftt

Alternatives for the last two lines. The second is the same as that in *Lucasta*; the first runs:

this chang'd, then maddame I am bound noe more
then swearinge to a saintt, yt proues a whore

PAGE 58, l. 12. 'It hath been thought a vast Commendation of a Painter, to say his Figures *seem to breathe*; but surely, it is a much greater and nobler Applause, *that they appear to think*.' H. Fielding. Preface to *Joseph Andrews*.

PAGE 66, l. 24. The separately printed Prologue mentioned in the note is to Cowley's *The Guardian*.

PAGE 78. There is another manuscript of 'To Althea' in

in the library of the Duke of Portland at Welbeck Abbey with peculiar but unimportant variations. Mr. Norman Ault recorded Bodley MS. Ashm. 36–7 in his *Seventeenth Century Lyrics* and stated that the poem is included in three editions of *A New Help to Discourse*, 1669–80–84.

Wilson's setting of 'To Althea' was printed in 1659. Some setting was known in 1656 when the tune of 'The languishing Lover' in *The Academy of Pleasure*, p. 2, was given as 'When Love with unconfined wings' The same or another setting was known nine years earlier, two years before *Lucasta* was published. *The Gossips Feast or, Morrall Tales... By a well known moderne Author. London*, ... 1647, a pamphlet received by Thomason on Aug. 23, is possibly by a ballad writer. It is partly in verse and refers to Martin Parker and his 'sweet Ballad, *When the King injoyes his own again*'. Gammer Gowty Legs 'began to sing, *Sir Iohn Louelesse his Althea.*

What madnesse was it did possesse,
Your minds you faithlesse crew.
That you to farr durst to transgresse,
From what Gods word doth shew.' ...

This can only be a reference to the *tune* of Lovelace's 'Althea' and seems to be the earliest mention of the poem in print, though Tatham's reference must have been written in or before 1645 (see pp. xliv–xlv).

PAGE 78 (p. 286, ll. 21–8 of Notes). There are two editions of the ballad version of this song, that in the Pepys Collection which is reproduced in this volume, and another among the Roxburghe Ballads which is without a printer's or publisher's name. There are few differences between the two. In his edition of the latter (*Roxburghe Ballads*, iii, p. 178) W. Chappell says that 'My lodging is on the cold boards'; introduced in the third stanza, 'is a parody upon [Davenant's] "My lodging it is on the cold ground", sung by Nell Gwyn in [James] Howard's play *All mistaken*'. So far as the ballad is concerned the parody is limited to the one line. In *All Mistaken* the allusion was to the

fatness

fatness of Moll Davis, who sang Davenant's song in *The Rivals*:

> But that which Troubles me most is
> The Fatness of my Dear.

PAGE 79, l. 1. *committed Linnets* Cf.:

> Men may confine the *Bodie*, but the *Minde*
> (Like Natures Miracles, the Winde
> And Dreams) do's, though secured, a free enjoyment find. . . .
> *Linnets* their Cage to be a Grove, Bars Boughs esteem.
> Edward Benlowes, *Theophila*, 1652, p. 244.

PAGE 84. *A Guiltlesse Lady imprisoned.* In the *Modern Language Review*, July 1926, Professor Mario Praz points out that Lovelace was evidently well read in contemporary literature, as were most of the poets of his age, and indicates the French and Italian sources which inspired poems such as this and 'The faire Begger' (p. 98) which is ultimately to be traced to Achillini's *Bellissima Mendica.*

PAGE 96, l. 15. *Keepers Fees.* There is a second meaning here of horns Cf.:

> How ere you iuggle, if you doe agree,
> You must be pleas'd to weare the keepers fee.
> John Day, *Law-Trickes*, 1608 (Malone Society Reprint), ll. 438-9.

PAGE 98. *The faire Begger.* In an article in *Revue de Litérature Comparée*, Jan.–March 1925, M. Pierre Legouis has shown that the origin of the poems on 'La belle gueuse' is Italian and that these poems derive from Claude Achillini (1574–1640) and François Tristan l'Hermitte (1601–1655) whose own 'Belle gueuse' is imitated from Achillini. Lovelace was probably inspired by Achillini 'mais l'absence du *concetto* final interdit de l'affirmer. Tristan a pu servir d'intermédiaire, puisque ses *Vers héroïques* paraissent un an avant *Lucasta.*'

PAGE 132, l. 1. *Sent'nel Stars.* Perhaps Campbell is more likely to have had Charles Churchill than Lovelace in mind.

Like

Like Centinels i' th' starry way,
Who wait for the return of day
Almost burnt out, and seem to keep
Their watch, like Soldiers, in their sleep, . . .

'The Ghost.' *Poems*, ed. 1763, p. 309.

But the comparison is not uncommon. Habington calls the stars 'bright cent'nels of the skies' (*Castara*, 1640, p. 48), and Baron 'winking Centinels of Night' (*Pocula Castalia*, 1650, p. 49).

PAGE 144, ll. 21–2. For a description of the heron killing the falcon as described by Lovelace see William Somerville's *Field-Sports*, 1742.

PAGE 154. *A Mock-Song*. In the *Philological Quarterly*, Oct. 1945, Miss Willa McClung Evans reproduced a musical setting of these lines by John Cave from Gamble's collection of manuscript songs in the New York Public Library. There are some textual variants between what Miss Evans believes to be 'an authentic early version of the poem' and the verses as printed in *Lucasta*, 1659. The most important are ll. 4–5

now thatt earthly kings
are butt ayery things;

l. 7 now Clark tarquin the Childe; (possibly the last word refers rather to position than age, as in ballads).

ll. 5–8 of stanza 2.

are tumbled downe
and the bodies all butt a belley
in puer sankteffi'ed wine
our grose spiritts reffine
and drowne all brine

and the addition of the word 'Choris' before the last four lines in each stanza.

PAGE 192, l. 18. *Maid of Meurs*. For some other references to the Maid of Germany see the editor's letter to *T.L.S.*, July 1948.

PAGE 200, ll. 3–18. *Eliza's Babes, or the Virgins offering Being Divine Poems and Meditations. Written by a Lady, &c.*

&c. is advertised in no. 132 of *A Perfect Diurnall*, June 1652.

PAGE 203. *Sanazar's Hexastick.* For an earlier translation by John Gordon, Dean of Salisbury (1544–1619) see *Hist. MSS. Comm.* vi, p. 684. See also Cokayne's *Small Poems*, 1658, p. 185.

PAGE 210. *Theophile.* The epigram was earlier given to Marc de Maillet and was printed in his *Les Epigrammes*, Paris, 1620. It appeared anonymously in *Les Muses sérieuses*, 1673, and was first attributed to Théophile in the 1692 *Recueil* mentioned in the note.

TEXTUAL NOTES

PAGE 1. 13 Carkanets *1649* 15 by. *1649*

PAGE 2. 10 illgitimate. *1649*

PAGE 3. 2 cartior *1649* 4 centingenti *1649* 9 ἐυλικρ νὴς, *1649*

PAGE 4. 3 coo'd *1649*

PAGE 5. 25 straines *1649*

PAGE 6. ΕΞΑΣΤΙΚΟΝ. *1649* 1 ἀμείβεν *1649* 2 πάν των *1649* 3 Ωδὴν *1649* 4 Ον *1649* 5 Ωδην μὲν (?) ὤγαθε, *1649* 6 Ως ἥε *1649* 12 flat, *1649* 23 write *1649*

PAGE 7. 16 Antiparisthesis. *1649*

PAGE 8. 2 Muse *1649*

PAGE 9. 8 lov'd best, (?) defended best. *1649* 10 hand. *1649* 14 been. *1649* 24 refin'd *1649*

PAGE 11. 8 In Zeuxeses *1649* 15 best *1649* 17 Poetry? *1649*

PAGE 12. 6 learned, though *1649* 7 reherse *1649*

PAGE 13. 8 to 'th shrine, *1649*

PAGE 14. 2 honoratas *1649* 6 Pacta globis. *1649*

PAGE 15. 5 φύλον αὐτιφυλῶ .ἀγάκλυτον *1649* 7 Ος τύτθαις *1645* 8 ἕκαστον *1649* 9 ποκινῶν *1649* 10 Εν *1649* 4 ἐστι *1649*

PAGE 18. 3 it' h' skies *1649* (*both versions*)

PAGE 19. 5 delight, (?) *1649*

PAGE 20. The first four stanzas of this poem were set to music in Playford's *Ayres and Dialogues*, *1653*, and reprinted in Cotgrave's *Wits Interpreter*, *1655* 8 fair *1655* 9 Forbear to brade *1653 and 1655*. hair, *1653* hair; *1655* 10 eye *1655* 11 hov'ring *1653* flye; *1653* 13 ravisher *1655* wind, *1653 and 1655* 14 ha's *1653* has *1655* the East *1655* 15 this spicy Nest. *1653* ore his spicy nest. *1655*

PAGE 21. 1 Eve'ry *B* (*2*) confest *so 1655* confest; *1649*

1649 confest, *1653* 2 best, *1653* at least *1655* at the least *Cotgrave 1662* 3 clew *1653 and 1655* thread *1653* 4 ravelled; *1653* 5 Doe not winde *1655* 6 Night, *1653* night *1655* 7 ray, *so 1653 and 1655* ray; *1649*

PAGE 22. 2 *The reprinted Sheet B reads* possesse

PAGE 23. 2 awhile *1649*

PAGE 25. 10 ev'n *1649* 15 arts; *1649*

PAGE 26. 7 shouldst thou *Select Musicall Ayres, and Dialogues, 1652*, and Cotgrave's *Wits Interpreter, 1655* *Possibly Lovelace wrote* foresworn? *and the question mark was taken to the next line by mistake* 8 be, *1652* 10 It was *1652 and 1655* 11 This *1652 and 1655* impossibilitie, *1655* 12 long? *1655* 13 months space: *1655* space, *1652* 14 I should *1652 and 1655* 15 rob me *1652* imbrace, *1652* embrace, *1655* 16 Should *Select Musicall Ayres, 1653, and Cotgrave, 1655*

PAGE 27. 1 Not that all Joyes *1652 and 1655* haire *1653* hair *1655* 2 In others *1655* found: *1652* 3 I will *1652 and 1655* the black, *1652 and 1655* the faire, *1652* the fair, *1655* 4 Miners that sound *1652* (corrected to 'Mineralists' in *1653*) 5 treasures in unplowed ground. *1652* treasures in unhidden ground. *1655* 6 Then when I have lov'd *1652* Then if when *1653 and 1655* thee round *1652 and 1655* (in Bodleian copy of *1653* 'thee' has been altered to 'them') 7 prove, *1652 and 1655* she, *1652* she: *1655* *Possibly* Thou prove the pleasant'st she; 8 In spoyle of *1652* In spoil of *1655* 10 Even *1655* The whole line is omitted in *1652* 23 Toye cri'd she? *1649*

PAGE 28. 10 *Possibly* on all: 13 Phæbus *1649*

PAGE 29. 9 can haply *Musarum Oxoniensium Charisteria, 1638* 12 Tune Life *1638* 13 Spheares *1638* 14 Inke, teares; *1638* 15 Here, here *1638* 17 Greatnesse wombe, *1638* 18 Cradle *1638* 19 warble; *1638* 20 Sheet? *1638* 21 Weepe or shoute solemnity *1638* 22 Christned and Buried Thee? *1638*

23 sound, *so 1638* sound. *1649* 24 then to the Ground? *1638*

PAGE 30. 1 this? *1638* 4 shew a setting *1638* 5 Martyrdome, *1638* 6 Religion? *1638* 8 Blood! *1638* 10 doores, *1638* 12 Ornament: *1638* 13 hastend death! *1638* 14 deifi'd! *1638* 15 has *1638* 16 condemn'd *1638* 21 pompe, *so 1638* pompe *1649* 26 Birth-right preheminence! *1638* 29 uneven, *1638* 30 Earth *1638*

PAGE 31. 2 looks, *1638* 4 fixt, Canonize: *1638* 5 Throne *1638* 6 Coronation; *1638* 9 Feasts: *1638* 10 up, Cries: *1638* 11 joy *1638* 12 before: *1638*

PAGE 32. 1 Art *1649*

PAGE 35. 2 Cruels't *1649*

PAGE 38. *The Grasse-hopper. Title* COTTGN *1649*

PAGE 39. 13 Ice, *1649*

PAGE 40. 7 beginne *1649*

PAGE 41. 5–7, 'If then . . . to thine', are given to *Chorus* in *1649* Correction as above made in Gamble's second book of *Ayres and Dialogues, 1659* 5 stay, *1659* 6 bosome, and my Soule to thine: *1649*

PAGE 42. 5 nee're *1649* 16 sphere: *1649*

PAGE 43. 16 brought, *1649* 18 spell; *1649*

PAGE 44. 19 of which their Spheres bereft *1649*

PAGE 45. 7 Flame *1649*

PAGE 46. 7 manckell *1649*

PAGE 49. 8 she will *1649*

PAGE 52. 16 West. *1649* 17 day *1649*

PAGE 53. 4 Invisible *1649*

PAGE 54. 9 bowers *1649*

PAGE 55. 2 this; *1649*

PAGE 56. 16 Virginsstrow *1649*

PAGE 57. 4 line *1649* 19 and didst *possibly* thou didst

PAGE 58. 7 same *1649*

PAGE 59. *To* Fletcher *reviv'd.* These lines were first printed

printed in the first folio edition of Beaumont and Fletcher, 1647 19 runne; *1647* 21 this, live: *1647*

PAGE 60. 3 brave *Aëtius so 1647* Where the brave Ætius *1649* In the play *Valentinian* the name is printed 'Æcius' 7 Valentinian *Marginal Note in 1647* 10 The Mad Lover. *Idem* 15–16 Tragi-comedies. *Idem* 15 ah, *1647* 17–18 Arcas. Bellario. *Marginal Note 1647* 23–p. 61, l. 2 Comedies. The Spanish Curate. The Humorous Lieutenant. The Tamer Tam'd. The little French Lawyer. *Idem*

PAGE 61. 4 it. *1647* 5 The custom of the Countrey. *Marginal Note 1647* 13 lov'd; *1647* 14 Lines; approv'd, *1647* 18 inliv'ning fire, *1647* 20 fall. *1647* 27 recite: *1647*

PAGE 63. 3 Ah's, *1649* 6 Friends grieve *1649* 24 Skies *1649* 29 Dearth *1649*

PAGE 64. 27 done *1649*

PAGE 65. 16 Wits, *1649*

PAGE 66. 11 Pow'rs; *1649* 17 on *1649* 22 at: *1649*

PAGE 67. 26 t'h'ave *1649*

PAGE 68. 1 few *1649* Clitophon *and* Lucippe *translated.* These lines were contributed to Hodges' translation of *The Loves of Clitophon and Levcippe, 1638.* See Notes, where earlier version is quoted in full

PAGE 69. 4 were: *so 1638* were, *1649* 8 shine; *so 1638* shine, *1649*

PAGE 70. These verses were contributed to *Pallas Armata. The Gentlemans Armorie 1639* To the Reader; *1639* 1 Hearke Reader, would'st be learn'd ith' Warres? *1639* 2 Captaine *1639* 3 Bookes *1639* Scarres? *1639* 4 And weare of both the Crowne? *1639* 5 one *1639* 6 could *1639* 7 Schollar *1639* Garrison? *1639* 13 agen *1639* 15 Penne *1639*

PAGE 72. 5 *Phænix 1649*

PAGE 73. 8 T'is *1649* 11 Thyme *1649*

PAGE 74.

PAGE 74. 5 blood *1649* 25 bonds *1649*

PAGE 75. 10 brow, *1649* 13 Lightning, *1649* 24 dombe. *1649*

PAGE 76. 8 divine *1649* 14 allayd almost *1649* 15 appeare: *1649* 18 Father, *1649* 27 dying, *1649*

PAGE 77. 9 Apostacy *1649*

PAGE 78. *To Althea.* See Notes

PAGE 80. 22 i'd *1649*

PAGE 81. 18 Round *1649*

PAGE 82. 8 Ocean *1649* 11 shine *1649* *Title* Wortley's, *1649* A line has dropped out in the first verse

PAGE 83. 13 Dart, (?) *1649*

PAGE 85. 11 bonds *1649* 15 Soul's, *1649*

PAGE 87. 2 Saint *1649* 20 more *1649*

PAGE 88. 3 Daere *Uncorrected copies 1649* 10 *See Notes* 16 tombe *1649* 28 lament *1649*

PAGE 89. 3 see *1649* 15 het eyes *1649*

PAGE 91. 26 PHÆBUS *1649*

PAGE 92. 1 ULISSES *1649*

PAGE 93. 7 Conquests *1649* 11 Travers-Eyes *1649* 16 pray'd *1649*

PAGE 94. 2 Rouud; *1649*

PAGE 95. Title *La Bella Bona Roba. To my Lady* H. Ode. *1649* 16 chrusht *Uncorrected copies 1649*

PAGE 96. 1 dread *1649* *Title* No title in *1649*

PAGE 97. *Title* au plus *1649* ci *1649*

PAGE 99. 6 Ill *1649* 13 well *1649*

PAGE 100. 6 inured *1649*

PAGE 101. 8 it' h' *1649*

PAGE 102. 13 why *1649*

PAGE 105. 3 Wombe. *1649* 5 Heovenly *Uncorrected copies 1649* 9 colme *Uncorrected copies* VI *1649*

PAGE 106. 4 Trumpets doe *some copies 1649* Eate *1649* 17 below *1649*

PAGE 107. 5 Carnation mantled *1649*

PAGE 108. 3 this *1649* 6 spells, *1649* 12 loook *Uncorrected*

Uncorrected copies 1649 24 weeds, *1649* 32 Sun; (?) *1649* 33 And her *Uncorrected copies 1649* 34 loayall *Idem*

PAGE 109. 1 sight. *Uncorrected copies 1649* 20 *Tast*, *1649* 32 To stop *Uncorrected copies 1649*

PAGE 111. 8 *hollowed 1649* 18 look *1649* 30 blest. *Uncorrected copies 1649*

PAGE 112. 12 cracking squirrels *some copies 1649* 13 The softy *Uncorrected copies 1649*

PAGE 113. 31 *Lucasta*, nam'd *1649* 33 *Lucasta*, smiles *1649*

PAGE 114. 2 tempting *Uncorrected copies 1649* 15 *Some copies read* my breaths *this was altered in others to* thy breaths 21 of bth *Uncorrected copies 1649*

PAGE 115. 3 *Possibly* and the *skies*, 29 *Lucasta*, *Aramantha* said! *1649*

PAGE 116. 12 th' Rage *Uncorrected copies 1649* Drumme *1649* 14 He sends *Uncorrected copies 1649* 15 exposing *Idem* 22 wound *1649*

PAGE 117. 3 tract *1649* 30 Roses. *1649*

PAGE 118. 1 content *1649*

PAGE 123. 10 fiue *some copies 1659* 18 yout self *1659*

PAGE 125. Cho. *is printed against* 10 *in 1659*

PAGE 126. 13 sctued *1659*

PAGE 128. 9 to deceive, *1659* 20 Bore; *1659* 21 Herse, *1659*

PAGE 130. 11 there. *1659* 17 Stars. *1659* 20 Skreen. *1659*

PAGE 134. 15 Cart *1659*

PAGE 135. 4 sport, *1659* 14 Law: *1659* 19 untrify *1659*

PAGE 136. 22 State: *1659*

PAGE 138. 9 winne; *1659* 19 i' th *1659* 24 Virtue, *1659*

PAGE 139. 14 yet closer *1659*

PAGE 141. 10 Gyant, *1659* 12 plyant. *1659*

PAGE 142. 12 Whcn *1659* 14 thouwert *1659*

PAGE 143.

PAGE 143. 3 varions *1659*
PAGE 145. 1 Victory! unhap'ly wonne, *1659* 4 Ait *1659*
PAGE 146. *Stanza 3 numbered 1 in 1659*
PAGE 147. 9 Clasp *Singer and Hazlitt* (*? some copies 1659*) Clap *1659* 21 above, *1659* 23 off their *1659*
PAGE 148. *Title* withchild *1659* 17 Queen *1659 See Notes* 22 Down *1659*
PAGE 149. 1 fince *1659* 6 me *1659* 7 spun: *1659*
PAGE 151. 14 raised, (?) *1659*
PAGE 152. 7 fafe *1659* 9 faith, *1659*
PAGE 153. 12 is uow *1659*
PAGE 154. 1. *omitted in 1659*
PAGE 155. 23 Toyl; *1659*
PAGE 156. 2 Ray, *1659* 11 Air. *1659*
PAGE 157. 7 is said *1659* *Judging from spacing the letter t has dropped out* 17 'Tis, this, *1659*
PAGE 159. 5 breath, *1659*.
PAGE 160. 9 dcad *1659* 15 Air. *1659*
PAGE 161. 7 Cavaleer *1659* 10 disagtee *1659* 11 unnumbred *so Hazlitt* numbred *1659*
PAGE 162. 2 canot *1659* 13 Load, *1659*
PAGE 163. 3 Pallus assents! *1659* 8 Sea *1659* 10 Alms house *1659* 14 het self spins: *1659*
PAGE 164. 2 the Brain; (?) *1659* 8 full. *1659* 21 Scars; *1659*
PAGE 165. 3 blent *1659* 24 Air, *1659* 30 'vantage *1659*
PAGE 166. 2 house, *1659*
PAGE 167. 12 Dispath'd *1659* *See Notes* 32 Rayes, *1659*
PAGE 169. 1 birth *1659*
PAGE 170. 6 It is *1659*
PAGE 171. 32 swets *1659*
PAGE 172. 29 Amôret *1659* 30 Mounted, and *1659* Minds, *1659*
PAGE 173. 5 wote *1659* 12 led, *1659*

PAGE 174.

PAGE 174. 23 unhandsomely? *1659 See Notes*

PAGE 175. 10 VVind; *1659* 11 tost, *1659* 19 Deep, *1659* 20 properties *1659* 26 npont; *1659* 28 feed. *1659*

PAGE 176. 17 *Franck*, *1659* 21 cause *1659*

PAGE 177. 11 Perigrination! *1659*

PAGE 178. 5 Faith, *1659* thou of Night *1659 See Notes* 9 day. *1659*

PAGE 180. 10 abstract, *1659* 11 *Lilly 1659* 21 nnknown *1659*

PAGE 181. 12 th' Spring *1659* 30 Grandsire *1659*

PAGE 182. 9 noons *1659* 20 saw; *1659* 24 at; *1659* 27 hast *1659*

PAGE 183. 22 owe; *1659*

PAGE 184. These lines were included in *Poems, by Eldred Revett . . . London . . . 1657 To my dear Friend* | *M*r ELDRED REVETT, | On his Poems | *Moral and Divine 1657* 1 Cleft (as the top of the inspired hill;) *1657* 2 soul quill: *1657* 3 aspire *1657* 4 en-liv'ning *1657* fire. *1657* fire, *1659* 5 Behold! power's *1657* 6 his first kindled his sight. *1657* 7 left *1657 and corrected in Bodleian and T. C. C. copies of 1659* lost *1659* Day, *1657* 8 spring *1657* 9 youth *1657* 10 flame, inter-wreathed *1657* 11 soul labour *1657* 12 Anthems, Paans, or a Hymne, *1657* Pœans *1659* 13 tripod *1657* 14 thine Altar pay: *1657* 15 the maz'd world *1657* tell *1657 and 1659* 17 brain! *1657* 20 Nereides *1657* 21 Whil'st th' Aire *1657* 22 Looking-glass. *1657* 23 thy sinewie (we see) *1657* 24 Poesie: *1657* 25 thund'ring lines *1657* 26 Verse native lustre *1657* 27 were't self? shut *1657* 28 *Iliads* l ckt up in a nut? *1657*

PAGE 185. 1 (Not hearing from thee) strong *1657* 2 (fourty thousand men) song *1657* 3 (secure in our thin, empty, heat) *1657* 4 beat; *1657* beat, *1659* 5 While wits *1657* 6 Armes, quarter *1657* 7 cabbin'd disguis'd, course, *1657* 8 scurf'd *1657* crust. *1657 and 1659*

1659 9 Diamond (from midst the humbler stones) *1657* 10 (Sparkling) Nation's *1657* 11 sage *1657* safe *1659* tell *1657* 12 Miracle? *1657* 13 leapst *1657* 14 infancie, foursore; *1657* 15 ha'st mid-wife plaid! *1657* 16 maid! *1657* maid *1659* 17 staff of him; *1657* 18 That (but set down) begins! *1657* down *1659* 19 that with one hurl'd *1657* 20 world? *1657* 21 seeds *1657* 22 species *Idea* 'twas! *1657* 23 vestal flame, but now *1657* 24 the sacred fiers throw! *1657* 25 re-iter'd acts age *1657* 26 (That stage, *1657* 27 one) *1657* 28 cradle *1657* 29 hues die, *1657* 30 paper now, I, *1657* 31 heaven *1657* 32 move Chrystalline: *1657*

PAGE 186. 1 mole-hil *Parnassus*, *1657* 2 Ants dew, *1657* 3 Seraphick soul hymnes play *1657* 4 those, *1657* day; *1657* day, *1659* 5 thorn worlds ransoming wreath *1657* 6 (stung) Antiphons, Anthems breath, *1657* 7 Angels quill, dipt lambs *1657* 8 sin'gst Pellicans *1657* 9 ever-living streams. *1657* 10 Rinc't fat heavie *1657* 11 youth! *1657* youth *1659* enrol'd quire *1657* 12 holy layes inspire, *1657* wholy *1659* 13 *Elias* *1657* 14 the Royal Prophet-Priest *1657* 15 concert *1657* 16 wings hallowed *1657* close; (?) *1659* 17 While *1657* 18 (Sicke) *1657* *Title* These lines were contributed to *Ayres and Dialogues* . . . by John Gamble . . . *1656* 21 seems *1656* pure *1656* 22 veins: *1656*

PAGE 187. 1 Wings *1656* 2 Harmonie *1656* 4 Heraldrie; *1656* 6 truely, *1656* Blazon'd *1659* 8 Den, *1656* 9 the Wall, *1656* 10 Words, *1656* 11 So in their *twisted Numbers* now you thus *1656* 13 Ayres *1656* 17 High *1656*

PAGE 188. *Title* These verses were prefixed to *The Wild-Goose Chase*, Beaumont and Fletcher, *1652* 1 Clear from *1652* 2 Oculist *1652* 3 Sceme *1652* 5 Murmurers repine *1652* 8 Endles *1652* 19 Fearing we *1659* Flagration *1652* 20 ONE, *1652* 23 thus *1652* 24 Ingenious. *1652 and 1659*

PAGE 189.

PAGE 189. 1 out-vie *1652* 2 un-numbred *1652* unn-umbred *1659* Anthonie *1652* 3 When (he *1652* When he (at *1659* 4 Smiling she *1652* Smilings he *1659* 7 Writers subscribe! *1659* 8 Bribe; *1652* 10 on *1652* in *1659* Witt; *1652* 13 fare *1652 and 1659* 14 keepers, bare, *1659* 15 exclude *1652* exceed *1659* Eye *1652* 16 Deitie; *1652* 18 heart: *1652* 21 Emerald-Mad *1652* 22 Rubie-Arcas; *1652* 23 throwes *1652* 25 store *1652* 28 Epitomie, *1652* 29 now Fall *1652*

PAGE 190. *Title* These lines were contributed to *The Royall Game of Chesse-Play*, .. *1656* To his honoured Friend on his Game of Chesse-play. *1656* 1 Fleece, *1656* 2 Geese *1656* 3 Politians by the *1656* 4 And can both judge *1656* 5 fates unfold, *1656* 6 laws controll'd. *1656* 7 wantoning! *1656* 8 Bluster'd and clutter'd wisely for, *1656* Contributed to *Hierocles upon the Golden Verses of Pythagoras*; . . . J. Hall, . . *1657* *Title* exact *1657* exxct *1659* Hierocles's Comment on *1657* 10 well-order'd *1657* 12 Elegie; *1657* 13 thy Soul *1657* 14 Thee; *1657* 16 dare, another, Fate; *1657* 17 Alas, *1657* 18 sev'rall wayes, *1657* 19 dust, *1657*

PAGE 191. 1 Behold, *1657* 2 age *1657* 3 *Pretextat* *1657* that couldst sway *1657* 4 Ferula. *1657* 5 Sage, chin, *1657* chin *1659* 6 within *1657* 8 Academick Rules: *1657* 9 matriculate, *1657* 10 *Graduate* *1657* 11 beheld, *1657* 12 swell'd: *1657* 14 Brow. *1659* 15 undown'd *1657* nndown'd *1659* 17 say? bold? *1657* say, bold, *1659* 18 ere was *1657* 19 Shade! *1657* 20 thy Posthume Victorie; *1657* 21 death, *1657* 22 breath. *1657* 23 fall, *1657* 26 That but *1657* 28 his *Bone* arm'd: *1657* 29 Relick, stand *1657* 30 darts and slings *1657* hand: *1657* Hand, *1659* 31 us, *1657*

PAGE 192. 1 *Hierocles*, thought *1657* 2 wrote, *1657* 4 nobler *1657* 5 *Gold* to somewhat *1657* 6 Gold, *1657*

1657 7 Metempochosis *1657* 8 Author *1657* 11 Region, *1657*

PAGE 193. 31 dine *1659*

PAGE 194. 4 *Apochrypha*, *1659* 12 curse *omitted in 1659 See Notes*

PAGE 195. 1 vild *Reading suggested in North American Review*, *1864*. 13 free, *1659* 23 high *1659*

PAGE 196. 11 your *head thatch 1659* 18 rerire *1659*

PAGE 197. 23 th endlesse *1659*

PAGE 198. 10 Catullus *1659* 15 living *1659*

PAGE 199. 11 that All-in chime, *1659* 25 shonld *1659* 26 him, he *1659*

PAGE 200. 3 Farher *1659* 14 Aire *1659* 32 understood. (?) *1659*

PAGE 201. 1 *Perhaps Lovelace wrote* the meer thought

PAGE 202. 1 Venetam Neptunus *Sannazarii*, . . .*Opera*, *1727*, *p. 201* *Title* Pentadii *1659* 12 obscessis fædera *1659* 22 Scires, *1659*

PAGE 203. Translations *1659*

PAGE 204. 14 & cubare *Opera et Fragmenta Veterum Poetarum Latinorum*, 1713, ii, p. 1574 25 aliis erunt in annis *Sixteenth and seventeenth editions of Catullus* 27 Poeta, *1659* 28 Poeta ; *1659*

PAGE 205. 10 is; (?) *1659* 17 Magazine, *1659* 26 I *1659*

PAGE 206. 4 Nec unquam inde ero *or* saturum inde cor futurum est *old editions* 18 bono *1659* 20 Aurorem *1659* 24–7 Printed as part of foregoing epigram in *1659 See Note*. 26 fnndit *1659*

PAGE 207. 8 but that he would be sold ! *Hazlitt*

PAGE 208. 1 Phæbus *1659* 5 Trinacrii quondam *Ausonius*, *ed. Scaliger*, *1575* Trinarii quodam *1659* 6 lәporem *1659* Auso *1659* 9 Pera, polenta, *1575* Polla, potenta, *1659* 10 Cynici : *1575* Cinici, *1659* 12 snpervacuum ? *1659* 13 Thesanro *1659* 19 m'empeche *1659*

PAGE 209.

PAGE 209. 1 a sleep *1659* 7 me *1659* 18 harms *1659*

PAGE 210. 2 trouue *1659* N'a pas trouvé *Recueil des plus belles pieces Des Poëtes François, 1692* 3 voicy *1692* 4 C'est que ravy *1692* 8 solicitare manu *1659* sollicitare deam *1575* 9 Aëris et linguae *1575* 12 Et si vis *1575* sonum *1575* sonos *1659* 14 datum. *1575* 16 Cogeret ut celerem *1575* 18 salutiferae. *1575* saltuiferi *1659* 19 Protinus & vacuos *1575*

PAGE 211. 8 saw; *1659* 14 grave *1659* 21 avail *1659*

PAGE 212. 3 Hoc genere & chordas, & plectra, & barbita cõde. *1575* 5 respondeo *Rufi Festi Avieni Carmina*, Wernsdorf, 1848, p. 133 6 Luce Deos oro, *1848* 9 fingo, (?) *1659* 10 gaudens ac *1848* gaudensque ac *1659* *See Note* 13 si tibi dii *Editions of Catullus* dii tibi *1659* 17 Venuste noster *Catullus* 21 quid suavius *Catullus* 23 Cnpidinesque; *1659* 27 viscerbus *1659*

PAGE 213. 8 Muse *1659* 26 Pœtus *1659*

PAGE 214. 14 *Old editions read* nunc preciosa 16 πόλλων *1659* 17 βλέπετε *1659* 20 Si illam *old editions* 21 pelluciduli *old editions* pellucidulis *1659*

PAGE 215. 19 why *1659* 22 gemme *1659*

PAGE 216. 1 mirum *1659* 5 nubere malle *old editions* *De Amore suo.* No heading in *1659* where these two lines are given as the final couplet to the preceding epigram 21 fias *1659* 22 fácias *1659* The accent is probably the dropped comma from the previous line misunderstood by the printer

PAGE 217. 5 bnt *1659* 17–18 These lines have no separate heading in *Lucasta*

PAGE 218. 1 Catnllum, *1659* 7 Totum illud *old editions* 13 fædere *1659* 18 indomitus *1659*

PAGE 219. 7 fault *1659* 15 Sest erces *1659* 17 takes you *Hazlitt* takes, pray *1659* ore; *1659*

PAGE 223. *Title* These lines were reprinted in *Poems on several Occasions* by Charles Cotton, *1689* 1 so, *1689* so; *1660*

1660 2 owe, *1689* 6 to *Vertue*, *1689* from *1660* refin'd. *1689* refin'd *1660* 7 Youth, *1689* 8 Arms, *1689* in Arts; *1689* to Arts; *1660* 9 Man *1689* 10 Thine, *1689* Flame; *1689* Fame *1660* 11 Youth *1689* 12 paths *1689* path's *1660* *Honor*, *1689* 13 thee, *1689* 15 sence, *1689* 16 influence, *1689* 20 a disturbance *1689* 21 *Mischance*, *1689* mischance *1660* 22 of both *1689*

PAGE 224. 1 Name, *1689* 3 Men, *1689* 5 and great; but yet *1689* Yet. *1660* 6 dangerons *1660* *Courage*; *1689* 7 serv'd, defend, *1689* ser'vd defend *1660* 8 Friend: *1689* 12 Displeas'd so. *1689* 13 respect, acknowledgment, *1689* respect *1660* 14 these together, when improv'd, improve; *1689* these, together improve *1660* 16 worthiness, *1689* Worthyness, (?) *1660* 17 become,) *1689* 20 Dead, *1689* 21 these, *1689* these *1660* 22 Fame; increase; *1689* 24 That, *1689*

PAGE 225. *Title* These lines were reprinted in *Poems on several Choice and Various Subjects . . . 1663* *See Notes* *Upon the Posthume-Poems of Mr. Lovelace. 1663* 1 with other *1663* 2 pluck'd, Brest; *1663* 4 stood, *1663* 5 know *1663* 6 That he upon grow, *1663* 8 With his fair outside, if not go beyond. *1663* 9 Lovelace *1663* 10 Darling *1663* 11 cleer, *1663* 12 from rich appeer *1663* 13–14 Such sparks that with their Atoms may inspire The Reader with a pure Poetik fire. *1663*. Printed in *Poems, by Eldred Revett . . . London . . . 1657* *See Notes* AN ELEGIE, | *Sacred to the Memory of my late* | *honoured Friend, Collonel* | Richard Lovelace. *1657* 16 Among those, sin *1657* 17 thine *1657* think *1660* 20 officious *1657* officicus *1660*

PAGE 226. 3 it dimmer *1657* *Errata* 5 flouds *1657* 8 Mortality: *1657* 11 all our pride? *1657*

PAGE 227. 8 two *1657 and 1660* 10 in the *1657* 26 soules *1657*

PAGE 228. 5 never *1657* *corrected to* ever *in Errata*

12

12 treasury. *1660* 20 grew. *1657* grew: *1660* 21 bave *1660* gain'd. *1657* 24 erə *1660* 25 sometimes *1657 and 1660* 31 ow *1660*

PAGE 229. 8 inscription. *1657* 9 tears. *1657* 10 long weares: *1657* 11 keep. *1660* 19 Cramp *1660*

PAGE 230. 6 all *1660* 8 dry *1660* 25 credit *1660* 26 it, *1660*

PAGE 231. 18 haypy *1660*

PAGE 233. 6 pure *See Notes* poor *1660*

PAGE 234. 2 Chaos; (?) *1660* 20 Zephire *See Note* Zephre. *1660*

PAGE 236. 8 it *1657*

PR
3542
L2

21454

Date Due

APR 27 '72			
APR 1 0 1980			
MAY 7 '81			

The Library

COLLEGE of MARIN

Kentfield, California

COM